MICHIGAN LEGAL STUDIES

SURVEY OF METROPOLITAN COURTS FINAL REPORT

SURVEY OF METROPOLITAN COURTS
FINAL REPORT

BY MAXINE BOORD VIRTUE

Prepared for
The University of Michigan Law School
and
The Section of Judicial Administration
of the American Bar Association

ANN ARBOR
THE UNIVERSITY OF MICHIGAN PRESS

PUBLISHED UNDER THE AUSPICES OF THE UNIVERSITY OF MICHIGAN LAW SCHOOL (WHICH, HOWEVER, ASSUMES NO RESPONSIBILITY FOR THE VIEWS EXPRESSED) WITH THE AID OF FUNDS DERIVED FROM GIFTS TO THE UNIVERSITY OF MICHIGAN BY WILLIAM W. COOK.

Library of Congress Catalog Card No. 62-9960
Published in the United States of America by
The University of Michigan Press and simultaneously
in Toronto, Canada, by Ambassador Books Limited
Printed and bound by CPI Group (UK) Ltd, Croydon, CR0 4YY

Paperback ISBN: 978-0-472-75199-0

Report of the Committee on Metropolitan Trial Courts, Section of Judicial Administration

THE Committee now reports completion of its Survey of Metropolitan Courts, commenced in 1947 when Judge Alfred P. Murrah, then chairman, appointed the undersigned as chairman of a Committee on Judicial Administration in Metropolitan Trial Courts. This committee requested The University of Michigan Law School to make a professional study of the special problems of metropolitan trial courts. The faculty designated the late Edson R. Sunderland to supervise the work, and employed Maxine Boord Virtue to conduct the survey. In 1952, after two years of field and library work, the pilot study, *Survey of Metropolitan Courts: Detroit Area,* was published jointly by the Section and The University of Michigan Law School.

Since 1952, other metropolitan court studies have been carried on by this Committee and by others working in the field. In 1956, a companion study, *Survey of Metropolitan Courts: Los Angeles Area,* prepared by Professor James G. Holbrook, was published by the University of Southern California.

In 1956, at the request of the Committee, and with the approval of the Section Council, the faculty of The University of Michigan Law School approved a final study designed to summarize the results of recent studies of the operations of metropolitan trial courts carried on or participated in by committee personnel, and to state general conclusions.

Following this approval, the law school appointed Maxine Boord Virtue, who has been secretary of the Committee throughout its existence, as research fellow, to prepare the report, and requested Professor Lewis M. Simes, now retired, and Professor Charles W. Joiner to act as faculty sponsors and supervisors. At the request of the undersigned, Attorney General Paul L. Adams of Michigan approved a part-time leave of absence for Mrs. Virtue from her duties as Assistant Attorney General, in order to facilitate the work of preparing the report.

In 1959, it was decided to circulate questionnaires to section, committee, and other professional personnel in order to enrich and round out the material in the final report. This was done with the cooperation of Mr. Justice Tom Clark and Mr. Ben MacKinnon of the Section staff. Questionnaires were accepted for inclusion until April 1, 1960.

The manuscript has now been completed, and is recommended to the Council by your Committee.

Its publication will complete the work of the Committee on Metropolitan Trial Courts.

Respectfully submitted,

IRA W. JAYNE
Chairman
Committee on Metropolitan
Trial Courts

FOREWORD

Ed. Note: *This study was completed and approved in basic form in 1960. The late Honorable Ira W. Jayne was the inspirational leader of the metropolitan court study. His was the driving force and vision that set it in motion, kept it going fifteen years, and brought it to final statement in this volume. All connected with the study had hoped that he would live to hold the published book in his hand. Only a few hours before his death, on Sunday, January 22, 1961, Judge Jayne put the finishing touches on the following foreword. Although the editing and printing of the volume have taken some time beyond his active contact with the work, his foreword is included in recognition of his leadership in the project.*

THIS volume is a companion to *Survey of Metropolitan Courts: Detroit Area,* and, like the Detroit study, has been prepared for The University of Michigan Law School at the request of the Section of Judicial Administration of the American Bar Association by Maxine Boord Virtue. In the foreword to the first study, published in 1950, the undersigned pointed out that the American Bar Association initiated these studies of metropolitan court problems because of the realization of the section Council and its Committee on Metropolitan Trial Courts that the conduct of judicial business in a big city is different from that in a one-judge court in a small community. The former has little in common with the latter but the law, and even that may differ in application.

This realization was first translated into action when the Honorable Alfred P. Murrah, then chairman of the Section of Judicial Administration, in 1947 reactivated the dormant Subcommittee on Metropolitan Trial Courts, and appointed the undersigned chairman. The Committee requested The University of Michigan Law School to make a professional study of the special problems of metropolitan trial courts. The faculty, through its research committee, then under Professor Lewis M. Simes, designated the late Professor Edson R. Sunderland to supervise the work and employed Mrs. Virtue to conduct the survey. A practicing attorney, she is equipped with experience in general practice as well as unusual acquaintance with social work, and has had a background of scholarly writing in various fields.

Detroit was selected for the first study. Its findings so clearly pointed to the need for further work in the field that the Committee on Metropolitan Trial Courts of the Section of the Judicial Administration has been kept in being. Numerous local studies, described in detail in the text, have been made or supervised by the Committee. The Los Angeles study, *Survey of Metropolitan Courts: Los Angeles Area,* prepared by Professor James G. Holbrook of the University of Southern California, was undertaken in response to the request of the Committee, though as published in its final form it was not presented as a unit in this series. In addition, the work of the Committee has resulted directly or indirectly in countless introspective analyses of their court structures by judicial and bar association groups in many of the most rapidly growing metropolitan areas. One of the most interesting of the unpublished studies made by committee personnel is Mrs. Virtue's field study in London, England, where she spent a reconnaissance period to obtain all possible comparative data in order to achieve maximum objectivity in formulating conclusions. She has also conducted various other studies, referred to in the text.

In order to round out the series and state conclusions, The University of Michigan Law School has sympathetically maintained its sponsorship. Thanks are hereby rendered to Dean Allan F. Smith, the former Research Chairman and present Dean of the Law School, to Professor Lewis M. Simes, who acted as faculty sponsor and supervisor of the study until his retirement, and to Professor Charles W. Joiner, faculty cosponsor and supervisor of the study since 1958. Their interest and participation in the problems through the years from 1947 to the present have made possible this concluding volume.

As we lay down the study, we conclude that one of the basic problems confronting those who administer justice in the vast congestions of Metropolis is that of applying business administration principles to the conduct of court business in such a way as to make the law as useful as possible to all individuals. Although the law is the law everywhere, these studies show that without efficient and alert administration of courts, even-handed justice may be beyond the reach of many.

As a judge now retired from thirty-seven years of experience, many of them as presiding judge of an eighteen-judge court in a large metropolitan area, the undersigned offers a few observations.

Metropolitan areas are communities which have outgrown city and county boundaries. In order to be effective, the judicial system serving a metropolitan community should reach the entire area.

Judges of all the various courts throughout the metropolitan area, courts existing on many levels which have grown up to meet immediate needs and hence constitute a hodgepodge of scattered tribunals rather than an orderly metropolitan-wide structure, should be brought together in one judicial organization, with each judge having rank and pay equal to that of all other judges in the metropolitan area, regardless of the size or nature of the cases with which each judge deals. There is really no such thing as a "superior" court. Human rights are the proper concern of justice, and in achieving them the courts must not emphasize the size of the amount of money disputed or the seriousness of the charge made. This metropolitan-wide organization of judges should be under a permanent presiding judge, selected by his colleagues for his aptitude for administrative detail, and for his possession of a considerable amount of patience. As our departed leader and brother Vanderbilt so wisely remarked, judicial reform is "no sport for the short-winded."

The entrenched judiciary, conditioned as they are to *stare decisis,* must guard against permitting their respect for traditional structures to offer a stumbling block to needed administrative changes.

That these and other changes are being made, to the credit of the bench and bar, will be apparent from the text of the study, though the rate of progress be slow and at times uncertain. For example, the trend towards the use of the specialist judge assigned as part of a flexible general court rather than the throwing up of a myriad of rigid specialist courts seems to be a strong and commendable change in the direction of progress.

We offer no panaceas, nor have we searched out all relevant information. We have, however, probed deep enough into the remote corridors of metropolitan justice to present this series of studies to document the existence of a special metropolitan court problem and to suggest the direction of development towards proper court systems for metropolitan areas.

The rest is for the bench and bar of each metropolitan locality, and for laymen interested in better government, to work out. To them, we offer this book.

Ira W. Jayne
Chairman
Committee on Metropolitan Trial Courts
Section of Judicial Administration
American Bar Association

Resolution of the Section of Judicial Administration of the American Bar Association, Adopted in August 1960 and February 1961

RESOLVED that the Council of the Section of Judicial Administration of the American Bar Association authorizes The University of Michigan to publish the volume entitled "Metropolitan Court Survey: Final Report," prepared at the instance of the Section by Maxine Boord Virtue, provided that as published the volume shall contain the statement that the author's interpretation of the materials discussed therein and her recommendations and conclusions reflect merely the personal views of the author and do not represent the views or action of the American Bar Association or of the Section of Judicial Administration or its Council.

That the Council expresses its gratitude to Mrs. Maxine Boord Virtue for the excellence and thoroughness of this outstanding contribution to the field of judicial administration, to Judge Ira W. Jayne for his foresight and leadership in the conception, planning, execution, and publication of the survey, and to The University of Michigan Law School for financing and sponsoring it and providing the necessary personnel.

Acknowledgments

The author extends thanks on behalf of the University of Michigan School of Law, the late Judge Ira W. Jayne, and herself to the many judges, lawyers, and laymen who worked on this project. Special thanks are due to committeemen and others who answered questionnaires; to Mr. Ben MacKinnon, formerly of the staff of the Section of Judicial Administration, for his work on the questionnaires and otherwise; and to Mr. Justice Tom C. Clark of the United States Supreme Court, who prepared and sent out a covering letter to recipients of questionnaires.

A statement of acknowledgments would be incomplete without recognition of the debt we all owe to the members of the judiciary. Calamandrei expressed it thus:

> There are times in the career of every lawyer when, forgetting the niceties of the codes, the arts of oratory, the technique of debating, unconscious of his robes or those of the judges, he turns to the judges, looking into their eyes as into the eyes of an equal, and speaks to them in the simple words a man uses to convince his fellow man of the truth. In these moments justice is reborn and he who pronounces the word feels a suppliant tremor in his voice like that in the prayers of the faithful.
>
> These moments of humble and solemn sincerity repay the lawyer for all his labor.*

May these moments never diminish.

Maxine Boord Virtue

Ann Arbor
April 1962

* Eulogy of Judges 6 (Adams & Phillips transl. 1942).

Contents

List of Tables

PART I

THE METROPOLITAN COMMUNITY

CHAPTER I

Introduction

SECTION 1. HISTORY OF PROJECT

IN 1947, the Section of Judicial Administration of the American Bar Association addressed its attention to an inquiry as to the existence and nature of special problems of metropolitan courts and possible methods for solving them. This inquiry is part of the Section's continuing survey of courts to improve the standards of judicial administration.

The first step in the metropolitan court study was taken when the University of Michigan Law School agreed to furnish a two-year study of the organization and operation of the trial court system of the Detroit metropolitan area. This was published in 1950 as *Survey of Metropolitan Courts: Detroit Area.* In that study, an attempt was made (in Chapter I) to state certain hypotheses then entertained as to the kinds of problems, quantitative and qualitative, which are common to and characteristic of courts in metropolitan areas,[1] namely:

1. Jurisdictional defects arising out of the special relationships between the metropolitan area and its population (e.g., insufficiently extensive, overlapping, duplicating, nonexistent jurisdiction).

2. Organizational problems accompanying the heavy caseloads of metropolitan courts (e.g., recruitment and supervision of personnel in multi-judge courts, devising machinery for handling docket and assignment of cases, control of funds and records, extent of departmentalization). In this group of organizational problems the problem of court con-

[1] VIRTUE, SURVEY OF METROPOLITAN COURTS: DETROIT AREA 3-30 (1950) [hereinafter cited as DETROIT STUDY].

gestion, logjam, or, as it was called in the Detroit study, "machinery for handling assignment and docket," has received considerable attention in the decade since the Detroit study was made.

3. Reflection of special behavior patterns of metropolitan population in caseloads containing, as compared to non-metropolitan courts, disproportionately large numbers of criminal, domestic relations, mental, and other "personal problem" cases. Such cases are not satisfactorily disposed of through the adversary process at the end of a single "day in court." Some of them, for example, juvenile cases, may remain in active court contact for years, while others, such as divorce cases, may make numerous intermittent appearances in the caseload over a long period of time. In this area are many sensitive and provocative problems, e.g., the optimum extent of specialization of judicial and other court services in special types of cases; the legitimate use of non-legal professionals such as probation officers, marriage counselors, and child welfare workers as part of the court facility serving special types of cases; and the relaxing of safeguards essential to due process in order to achieve expert, prompt, and convenient disposition of certain types of cases. If these problems are indeed peculiarly acute in metropolitan areas, then it is appropriate to analyze metropolitan courts realistically, in terms of the work they are called upon to perform in *their* communities, rather than in terms applicable elsewhere.

Having stated the above hypotheses, the Detroit study then turned to an exhaustive factual examination of the organization and operation of the trial court system of the Detroit area, in order to provide the first study to which others of similar scope, purpose, and method would be added, so as finally to provide an accumulation of data from which the special problems of metropolitan courts could be demonstrated to exist, and from which concrete recommendations could be made. By this means it was proposed to avoid projecting a "Detroit" problem as a "metropolitan court" problem, and to proceed step by step towards eventual generalization based on adequate empirical data.

As it happened, the series of studies planned for other metropolitan areas, one which was to provide fully comparable data to support such workmanlike conclusions, did not develop. Studies were designed and approved for New York, Philadelphia, Kansas City, London, and Los Angeles. The present writer conducted reconnaissance studies in New York, Chicago, and San Francisco, and spent a month observing the courts of London. The only complete study matching Detroit was Professor James C. Holbrook's study of the courts of Los Angeles, which was completed and published in 1957. The Haynes Foundation, which financed the Los Angeles study, required as a condition of its participation that the study focus on immediate improvement of the Los Angeles trial court system, by including concrete recommendations for that particular community. This requirement conditioned the primary focus of the project so that, although the study contains an abundance of material relevant to the basic metropolitan court question, it does not contain further critical evaluation or analysis of the nature of "the metropolitan court problem" as such.

Local bar associations and foundations have been more concerned with the immediate welfare of local courts than with the pursuit of a long-range research problem having as its nucleus a group of difficult definitional and qualitative value problems, and having only problematical relationship to the making of local changes for the betterment of each local court system. There has been rapid development of research in judicial administration in the decade since the Detroit study, but it has gone in the direction of examining court statistics, individual court operations, and specific problems (such as logjam) needing immediate remedial attention, rather than in the direction of inquiring into the basic identity and function of the metropolitan trial court as an attribute and facility of the metropolitan community.

Section 2. Objective of Present Report

Adhering to the view that the original question is important, unanswered, and essential to a proper development of standards of judicial administration, the Section arranged for the University of Michigan Law School to supervise and for the author of the Detroit study to prepare a final report for the metropolitan court survey, which will make use of such material as comes to hand from all available sources in an attempt to identify, characterize, and classify the special problems of metropolitan courts. The report will also include a discussion of the methods being brought to bear on those problems, their advantages and disadvantages, and their effectiveness. The report will deal with the concept of the metropolitan trial court as an attribute of the state court system, and, finally, with the question whether the special problems of metropolitan courts yield fully or in part to the same measures which improve the state court system as a whole, if those measures are multiplied to allow for the larger size of the metropolitan court.

This report, so prepared upon such data, will not be the scientific demonstration based upon adequate comparable materials which was originally planned and hoped for. Indeed, such a study will have some of the defects that the first study sought to avoid when the question was originally posed.

Nevertheless, it will provide for the bench and bar a presentation of the writer's conclusions about the problems of metropolitan courts as such, rounding out more than twelve years of study of that question by the Section's committee on metropolitan trial courts. It will at least challenge the assumption that the metropolitan court is the same as any other court, with a larger workload and uniformed elevator operators. This challenge should be of assistance to the profession in its task of improving the judicial process.

That the metropolitan court is a unique entity with problems peculiar to itself was perceived by Dean Roscoe Pound in 1930. With an eloquence and insight not since brought to bear on the subject, he pointed out that if you transfer the trial of Huck Finn's father from the small Missouri community where everyone knows his neighbor to the heart of a great metropolis, and if you see to it that the same number of man-hours are brought to bear on the trial, the end result will not be the equal of the disposition described by Mark Twain.[2] Something will be missing.

That "something" is the subject of this study.

[2] POUND, CRIMINAL JUSTICE IN AMERICA 190 (1930).

Chapter II

Nature and Characteristics of Metropolitan Community as Affecting Problems of Its Courts

Section 1. Definition of a Metropolitan Community

a. In General

WHAT is a metropolitan community?

Literally, the word means "mother city," or "principal" or "central city"—a densely settled nucleus of human population serving as the magnet for some form of activity.[1] In this century, the growth in size and influence of these "magnet" cities has received the attention of scholars in various fields dealing with the dynamics of population.

As Hawley points out:[2]

> In industrialized nations . . . peak densities occur at points of maximum accessibility with respect to interregional exchange. It is at those points that huge metropolitan cities appear. The thirty-seven cities in the world with populations of one million or more contain over eighty million people, or about 4 per cent of all population and a minute proportion of the total amount of land.[3]
>
> . . . the modern city is the consummate example of the territorial unit. The role of the city, its *raison d'être,* is to function as a service center. Cities arise with the separation of certain activities from primary production and their concentration at points where they may be most satisfactorily conducted from the standpoint of the largest number of persons. The city's population is always, therefore, a dependent group.[4]

A metropolitan community, then, in the sense in which sociologists use the term, is a large and densely populated

[1] Shorter Oxford English Dictionary; Webster's New International Dictionary (2d ed.).
[2] Hawley, Human Ecology: A Theory of Community Structure 98 (1950).
[3] Citing "W. S. Thompson, *Population Problems,* New York, 1942, 312."
[4] Hawley, *op. cit. supra,* at 216.

area, boiling with movement, which dominates a surrounding area, strongly exerting its influence on financial, industrial, trading, and other activities, so as to attract large numbers of people in constant movement to and from the central city to avail themselves of its services. Thus, the metropolitan community is culturally dominant, to the extent that and in the fields to which its drawing power extends, at the same time that it is dependent in the sense that its population does not grow and produce the goods it consumes.

b. United States Bureau of the Census

In 1910, the Bureau of the Census took cognizance of the rapidly emerging dominance of population groups surrounding certain large cities. At that time, the Bureau singled out 62 metropolitan areas and 23 major metropolitan areas.[5] In 1930, continuing its effort to delimit the "real city" from the political city, the Bureau established metropolitan districts for cities of 50,000 or more, provided the population in an adjoining territory of at least 150 per square mile in density was sufficient to make a total population of 100,000.[6]

In 1960, the United States Bureau of the Census replaced its former definition of "metropolitan district" by that of the "Standard Metropolitan Statistical Area." As stated in 1959, the general concept of a metropolitan area "is one of an integrated economic and social unit with a recognized large population nucleus."

To serve the statistical purposes for which metropolitan areas are defined, its parts must themselves be areas for which statistics are usually or often collected. Thus, each standard metropolitan statistical area will then include the county of such a central city and adjacent counties that are found to be metropolitan in character and economi-

[5] As reported in PICKARD, METROPOLITANIZATION OF THE UNITED STATES 16-17, (Urban Land Institute Research Monograph No. 2, 1959).

[6] As reported by MCKENZIE, THE METROPOLITAN COMMUNITY 39-40 (1933), citing U. S. CENSUS, 1930, METROPOLITAN DISTRICTS 5-6.

cally and socially integrated with the county of the central city. In New England the requirement with regard to a central city still holds but the units comprising the area are the towns rather than counties. A standard metropolitan statistical area may contain more than one city of 50,000 population. The largest city is considered the nucleus and usually gives the name to the area. The name may include other cities in the area if such cities have populations of 250,000, or have at least one-third the population of the largest city and a minimum population of 25,000. Standard metropolitan statistical areas may cross State lines.[7]

The criteria used by various agencies have been integrated to make it possible for all to base their work upon the same territory. These criteria have been revised and reissued in March 1958, following review and minor revision by the Federal Committee on Standard Metropolitan Statistical Areas, for use in connection with the 1960 censuses.[8]

In commenting on the criteria of metropolitan character, the Office of Statistical Standards reports that these relate primarily to the attributes of the county as a place of work or home for a concentration of nonagricultural workers. Criteria of integration relate primarily to the extent of economic and social communication between the outlying counties and central county.[9]

In 1950 the United States Bureau of the Census listed 168 standard metropolitan areas. This chapter was first

[7] U. S. BUREAU OF THE BUDGET, OFFICE OF STATISTICAL STANDARDS, STANDARD METROPOLITAN STATISTICAL AREAS 1 (1959). This definition marks a change from the 1950 "Standard Metropolitan Area." See HAWLEY, THE CHANGING SHAPE OF METROPOLITAN AMERICA: DECONCENTRATION SINCE 1920 at 5 *et seq.* (1956) [hereinafter cited as CHANGING SHAPE]. At that time, a "Standard Metropolitan Area" was defined as containing at least one city of 50,000 or more, and each city of that size was included in one standard metropolitan area. When two cities of 50,000 or more were within 20 miles of each other, they were ordinarily included in the same standard metropolitan area. Each standard metropolitan area comprised the county containing the city and any other contiguous counties deemed to be closely economically integrated with the city.

[8] U. S. BUREAU OF THE BUDGET, STANDARD METROPOLITAN AREAS 1 (1958).

[9] *Id.* at 2-3. For definitions as of 1957, see U. S. BUREAU OF THE CENSUS, STATISTICAL ABSTRACT OF THE UNITED STATES: 1957. For more detailed explanation, see HAWLEY, CHANGING SHAPE 5.

drafted on the basis of published data for these areas. Since that time, preliminary reports on the advance findings of the 1960 census have become available and indicate a new basis for definition, as shown above, together with a total of 189 metropolitan areas as of July 1960.

The nuclear frame of reference of this study was the series of population centers recognized as metropolitan communities by the Bureau of the Census for the 1950 census. These areas, with rate of growth for each between 1940 and 1950, and showing such information as was available in July 1960, on changes from 1950 to 1960, are shown in Table I.

But Metropolitan areas are more than collected population statistics. Thus, Luther Gulick is quoted as saying:

> The North American metropolitan complex is a large aggregation of human beings packed together in a geographic area of considerable size, in an economic and social pattern of private enterprise and great fluidity, enjoying a large measure of local representative self-government, at present in a complex pattern of largely unrelated jurisdictions which do not coincide with the patterns of work and life.
>
> . . . I propose we consider as "metropolitan problems" only those problems which arise from a large congested population, living and working interdependently in a considerable territory, rushing to and fro, with governments which do not coincide with the pattern of life.[10]

Thomas Reed Powell, in a review of Victor Jones' classic study *Metropolitan Government,* considers that Jones "apparently takes lying down the Census Bureau's definition of a metropolitan area," which Powell deems "no more than a statistical tour de force" leading to "practical absurdities."[11]

Actually, the Bureau of the Census itself has used its def-

[10] "Answers Wanted," in GOVERNMENT AFFAIRS FOUNDATION, PROCEEDINGS, NATIONAL CONFERENCE ON METROPOLITAN PROBLEMS., April 29-May 2, 1956, at 37-38, quoted at 25-26, PUBLIC ADMINISTRATION SERVICE, THE GOVERNMENT OF METROPOLITAN SACRAMENTO (1957).

[11] "Home Rule for Whom?" PUB. ADMIN. REV. II 171-75 (1942), cited at xi, RUTHERFORD, ADMINISTRATIVE PROBLEMS IN A METROPOLITAN AREA: THE NATIONAL CAPITAL REGION (1952).

TABLE I

Standard Metropolitan Areas, as defined by the United States Bureau of the Census, with 1950 population of each area, and rate of growth expressed in per cent of increase from 1940 to 1950. From *Statistical Abstract of the United States,* 1957, No. 10, p. 14. Information supplemented as of July, 1960, by table issued on June 21, 1960, as reported by *New York Times,* June 21, 1960, and by "Standard Metropolitan Statistical Areas," issued by Executive Office of the President, Bureau of the Budget, 1959. 1960 population supplied by "Standard Metropolitan Statistical Areas," Executive Office of the President, 1961.

Standard Metropolitan Area Continental United States	Population Apr. 1950	1940-1950 % increase	1960 population 215 areas	1950-1960 % increase (where available)
Total 1950, 172 areas	85,130,847	22.1		
Abilene (Texas) (new area, August, 1960)			120,377	
Akron (Ohio) area	410,032	20.8	513,569	
Albany (Ga.) (new area, August, 1960)			75,680	
Albany-Schenectady-Troy (N. Y.)	514,490	10.5	657,503	10.1
Albuquerque (N. M.)	145,673	109.9	262,199	
Allentown-Bethlehem-Easton (Pa.)	437,824	10.4	492,168	12.1
Altoona (Pa.)	139,514	−0.6	137,270	−2.5
Amarillo (Tex.)	87,140	41.8	149,493	
Ann Arbor (Mich.) (new area, May, 1959)			172,440	
Anderson (Indiana) (new area, 1958) (deleted, Nov., 1960)				
Asheville (N. C.)	124,403	14.4	130,074	
Atlanta (Ga.)	671,797	29.7	1,017,188	39.5
Atlantic City (N. J.)	132,399	6.7	160,880	18.7
Augusta (Ga.)	162,013	22.9	216,639	
Austin (Tex.)	160,980	45.0	212,136	
Bakersfield (Calif.) (new area, Dec., 1958)			291,984	
Baltimore (Md.)	1,337,373	23.5	1,727,023	21.4
Baton Rouge (La.)	158,236	79.0	230,058	
Bay City (Mich.)	88,461	18.0	107,042	
Beaumont-Port Arthur (Tex.)	195,083	34.2	306,016	
Billings (Mont.) (new area, August, 1960)			79,016	
Binghamton (N. Y.)	184,698	11.4	212,661	14.4
Birmingham (Ala.)	558,928	21.5	634,864	
Boston (Mass.)	2,369,986	8.8	2,589,301	6.3
Bridgeport (Conn.)	258,137	21.4	334,576	21.9
Brockton (Mass.)	129,428	8.5	149,458	
Brownsville-Harlingen-San Benite (Tex.) (new area, Aug., 1960)			151,098	
Buffalo (N. Y.)	1,089,230	13.6	1,306,957	19.8
Canton (Ohio)	283,194	20.6	340,345	
Cedar Rapids (Iowa)	104,274	17.0	136,899	
Champaign-Urbana (Ill.) (new area, Dec., 1958)			132,436	
Charleston (S. C.)	164,856	36.1	216,382	
Charleston (W. Va.)	322,072	16.6	252,925	

TABLE I (*Continued*)

Standard Metropolitan Area Continental United States	Population Apr. 1950	1940-1950 % increase	1960 population 215 areas	1950-1960 % increase (where available)
Charlotte (N. C.)	197,052	29.8	272,111	
Chattanooga (Tenn.)	246,453	16.5	283,169	
Chicago (Ill.)	5,495,364	13.9	6,220,913	18.8
Cincinnati (Ohio)	904,402	14.9	1,071,624	17.1
Cleveland (Ohio)	1,465,511	15.6	1,796,595	21.5
Colorado Springs (Colo.) (new area, Aug., 1960)			143,742	
Columbia (S. C.)	145,565	36.0	260,828	
Columbus (Ga.)	170,541	34.9	217,985	
Columbus (Ohio)	503,410	29.5	682,962	
Corpus Christi (Tex.)	165,471	78.6	221,573	
Dallas (Tex.)	614,799	54.3	1,083,601	
Davenport (Iowa)-Rock Island-Moline (Ill.)	234,256	18.3	270,058	
Dayton (Ohio)	457,333	38.0	694,623	
Decatur (Ill.)	98,853	16.7	118,257	
Denver (Colo.)	563,832	38.3	929,383	
Des Moines (Iowa)	226,010	15.4	266,315	
Detroit (Mich.)	3,016,197	26.9	3,762,360	24.7
Dubuque (Iowa)	71,337	11.9	80,048	
Duluth (Minn.)-Superior (Wis.)	252,777	−0.5	276,596	
Durham (N. C.)	101,639	26.7	111,995	
El Paso (Tex.)	194,968	48.8	314,070	
Erie (Pa.)	219,388	21.3	250,682	
Eugene (Oregon) (new area, Aug., 1960)			162,890	
Evansville (Ind.)	160,422	22.7	199,313	
Fall River (Mass.)	137,298	1.6	138,156	
Fargo-Moorhead (N. Dak.-Minn.) (new area, Aug., 1960)			106,027	
Fitchburg-Leominster (Mass.) (new area, June, 1959)			82,486	
Flint (Mich.)	270,963	18.9	374,313	
Fort Lauderdale-Hollywood (Fla.) (new area, Aug., 1960)			333,946	
Fort Smith (Ark.)	64,202	2.2	66,685	
Fort Wayne (Ind.)	183,722	18.5	232,196	
Fort Worth (Tex.)	361,253	60.2	573,215	
Fresno (Calif.)	276,515	54.9	365,945	
Gadsden (Ala.)	93,892	29.4	96,980	
Galveston (Tex.) (Texas City, Tex., added Aug., 1960)	113,066	39.3	140,364	
Gary-Hammond-E. Chi (new area, June, 1959)			573,548	
Grand Rapids (Mich.)	288,292	17.0	363,187	
Great Falls (Mont.) (new area, Aug., 1960)			73,418	
Green Bay (Wis.)	98,314	18.3	125,082	
Greensboro-High Point (N. C.)	191,057	24.1	246,520	
Greensville (S. C.)	168,152	23.1	209,776	
Hamilton-Middletown (Ohio)	147,203	22.4	199,076	

TABLE I (*Continued*)

Standard Metropolitan Area Continental United States	Population Apr. 1950	1940-1950 % increase	1960 population 215 areas	1950-1960 % increase (where available)
Hampton-Newport News-Warwick (Va.) (see Newport)	143,227	69.5		not listed 1960, see Newport
Harrisburg (Pa.)	292,241	15.9	345,071	10.7
Hartford (Conn.)	358,081	21.1	525,207	28.4
Houston (Tex.)	806,701	52.5	1,243,158	52.7
Huntington (W. Va.)-Ashland (Ky.)	245,795	8.9	254,780	
Huntsville (Ala.) (new area, Aug., 1960)			117,348	
Indianapolis (Ind.)	551,777	19.7	697,567	
Jackson (Mich.)	107,925	15.9	131,994	
Jackson (Miss.)	142,164	32.5	187,045	
Jacksonville (Fla.)	304,029	44.7	455,411	
Jersey City (N. J.) (new area, June, 1959)			610,734	−7.0
Johnstown (Pa.)	291,354	−2.4	280,733	−4.0
Kalamazoo (Mich.)	126,707	26.6	169,712	
Kansas City (Mo.)	814,357	18.6	1,039,493	26.7
Kenosha (Wis.)	75,238	18.5	100,615	
Knoxville (Tenn.)	337,105	37.0	368,080	
Lake Charles (La.) (new area, Aug., 1960)			134,475	
Lancaster (Pa.)	234,717	10.5	278,359	16.3
Lansing (Mich.)	172,941	32.4	298,949	
Laredo (Tex.)	56,141	22.3	64,791	
Las Vegas (Nev.) (new area, Aug., 1960)			127,026	
Lawrence-Haverhill (Mass.)	125,935	0.9	187,601	Haverhill added since '50
Lawton (Okla.) (new area, Aug., 1960)			90,803	
Lewiston-Auburn (Maine) (new area, Dec., 1958)			70,295	
Lexington (Ky.)	100,746	27.7	131,906	
Lima (Ohio)	88,183	20.3	103,691	
Lincoln (Nebr.)	119,742	19.0	155,272	
Little Rock-North L. R. (Ark.)	196,685	26.0	242,980	
Lorain-Elyria (Ohio)	148,162	31.8	217,500	
Los Angeles-Long Beach (Calif.)	4,367,911	49.8	6,742,696	53.2
Louisville (Ky.)	576,900	27.8	725,139	
Lowell (Mass.)	133,928	2.2	157,982	
Lubbock (Tex.)	101,048	95.1	156,271	
Lynchburg (Va.) (new area, May, 1959)			110,701	
Macon (Ga.)	135,043	42.0	180,403	
Madison (Wis.)	169,357	29.6	222,095	
Manchester (N. H.)	88,370	7.9	95,512	
Memphis (Tenn.)	482,393	34.7	627,019	
Meridan (Conn.) (new area, Sept., 1960)			51,850	
Miami (Fla.)	495,084	84.9	935,047	
Midland (Tex.) (new area, Aug., 1960)			67,717	

TABLE I (*Continued*)

Standard Metropolitan Area Continental United States	Population Apr. 1950	1940-1950 % increase	1960 population 215 areas	1950-1960 % increase (where available)
Milwaukee (Wis.)	871,047	13.6	1,194,290	24.0
Minneapolis-St. Paul (Minn.)	1,116,509	18.7	1,482,030	28.3
Mobile (Ala.)	231,105	62.8	314,301	
Monroe (La.) (new area, Aug., 1960)			101,663	
Montgomery (Ala.)	138,965	21.5	169,210	
Muncie (Ind.)	90,252	20.4	110,938	
Muskegon-Muskegon Heights (Mich.) (new area, Dec., 1958)			149,943	
Nashville (Tenn.)	321,758	25.1	399,743	
New Bedford (Mass.)	137,469	2.3	143,176	
New Britain-Bristol (Conn.) (*Bristol deleted June, 1959)	146,983	16.0	129,397	23.2*
New Haven (Conn.)	264,622	9.9	311,681	14.4
New London-Groton-Norwich (Conn.) (new area, Nov., 1960)			156,913	
New Oleans (La.)	685,405	24.1	868,480	
New York-Northeastern N. J.	12,911,994	10.7		

Note: Eight New Jersey counties were deleted June, 1959, leaving New York City as the area reported in 1959. In its issue of June 21, 1960, the *New York Times* reports: "The New York City area is four metropolitan areas by statistical definition. The central cities of the four areas are New York, Newark, Jersey City, and Paterson, Clifton and Passaic, N. J. They were reported as one area ten years ago, but have been divided on the basis of a government analysis of who works and lives where around these cities." The New York City area includes Nassau, Rockland, Suffolk, Westchester County.

The % increase 1950-1960 reported by the Census Bureau, and the population reported for the New York City area, is reported below:

			10,694,633	10.4
Newark, N. J. (new area, June, 1959)			1,689,420	17.6
Newport News-Hampton (Va.) (former title of Hampton, etc., changed. Warwick consolidated July, 1958. See Hampton)			224,503	
Norfolk-Portsmouth (Va.)	446,200	72.3	578,507	
Norwalk (Conn.) (new area, Sept., 1960)			96,756	
Odessa (Tex.) (new area, Aug., 1960)			90,995	
Ogden (Utah)	83,319	46.9	110,744	
Oklahoma City (Okla.)	325,352	33.3	511,833	
Omaha (Nebr.-Ia.)	366,395	12.7	457,873	
Orlando (Fla.)	114,950	64.0	318,487	
Paterson-Clifton-Passaic (N. J.) (new area, June, 1959)			1,186,873	34.7
Pensacola (Fla.) (new area, 1958)			203,376	
Peoria (Ill.)	250,512	18.3	288,833	
Philadelphia (Pa.)	3,671,048	14.7	4,342,897	11.2
Phoenix (Ariz.)	331,770	78.2	663,550	
Pittsburgh (Pa.)	2,213,236	6.3	2,405,435	8.2

TABLE I (*Continued*)

Standard Metropolitan Area Continental United States	Population Apr. 1950	1940-1950 % increase	1960 population 215 areas	1950-1960 % increase (where available)
Pittsfield (Mass.)	66,567	9.1	73,839	
Portland (Maine)	119,942	12.6	120,655	
Portland (Ore.-Wash.)	704,829	40.6	821,897	
Providence (R. I.) Pawtucket, R. I., added Aug, 1960)	737,203	8.9	816,148	
Pueblo (Colo.)	90,188	31.0	118,707	
Provo-Orem (Utah) (new area, Aug., 1960)			106,991	
Racine (Wis.)	109,585	16.5	141,781	
Raleigh (N. C.)	136,450	24.6	169,002	
Reading (Pa.)	255,740	5.7	275,414	6.3
Reno (Nev.) (new area, Aug., 1960)			84,743	
Richmond (Va.)	328,050	24.7	408,494	
Roanoke (Va.)	133,407	18.9	158,803	
Rochester (N. Y.)	487,632	11.3	586,387	19.5
Rockford (Ill.)	152,385	25.8	209,765	
Sacramento (Calif.)	277,140	62.7	502,778	
Saginaw (Mich.)	153,515	17.7	190,752	
St. Joseph (Mo.)	96,826	2.9	90,581	
St. Louis (Mo.-Ill.)	1,681,281	17.4	2,060,103	
Salt Lake City (Utah)	274,895	29.9	383,035	
San Angelo (Tex.)	58,929	49.9	64,630	
San Antonio (Tex.)	500,460	48.0	687,151	
San Bernadino-Riverside-Ontario (Calif.)	451,688	69.4	809,782	
San Diego (Calif.)	556,808	92.4	1,033,011	
San Francisco-Oakland (Calif.)	2,240,767	53.3	2,783,359	
San Jose (Calif.)	290,547	66.1	642,315	
Santa Barbara (Calif) (new area, Nov., 1956)			168,962	
Savannah (Ga.)	151,481	28.4	188,299	
Scranton (Pa.)	257,396	−14.6	234,531	
Seattle (Wash.)	732,992	45.2	1,107,213	
Shreveport (La.)	216,686	18.2	281,481	
Sioux City (Iowa)	103,917	0.3	107,849	
Sioux Falls (S. D.)	70,910	22.9	86,575	
South Bend (Ind.)	205,058	26.7	238,614	
Spokane (Wash.)	221,561	34.6	278,333	
Springfield (Ill.)	131,484	11.5	146,539	
Springfield (Mo.) area	104,823	15.8	126,276	
Springfield (Ohio)	111,661	16.7	131,440	
Springfield-Holyoke (Mass.) (Chicopee added Aug., 1960)	407,255	11.7	478,592	
Stamford-Norwalk (Conn.) (Norwalk deleted June, 1959)	196,023	22.3	178,409	
Steubenville-Weirton (Ohio-W. Va.) (new area, 1959) (Previously part of Wheeling, etc., Standard Metropolitan Area)			167,756	
Stockton (Calif.)	200,750	49.6	249,989	
Syracuse (N. Y.)	341,719	15.8	563,781	

TABLE I (*Continued*)

Standard Metropolitan Area Continental United States	Population Apr. 1950	1940-1950 % increase	1960 population 215 areas	1950-1960 % increase (where available)
Tacoma (Wash.)	275,876	51.5	321,590	
Tampa-St. Petersburg (Fla.)	409,143	50.4	772,453	
Terre Haute (Ind.)	105,160	5.5	108,458	
Texarkana (Tex.-Ark.) (new area, Aug., 1960)			91,657	
Toledo (Ohio)	395,551	14.9	456,931	
Topeka (Kan.)	105,418	15.5	141,286	
Trenton (N. J.)	229,781	16.5	266,392	
Tucson (Ariz.)	141,216	93.9	265,660	
Tulsa (Okla.)	251,686	30.2	418,974	
Tuscaloosa (Ala.) (new area, Aug., 1960)			109,047	
Tyler (Tex.) (new area, Aug., 1960)			86,350	
Utica-Rome (N. Y.)	284,262	8.0	330,771	
Waco (Tex.)	130,194	27.8	150,091	
Washington (D. C.) (Md.-Va added to description by 1959)	1,464,089	51.3	2,001,897	
Waterbury (Conn.)	154,656	11.4	181,638	
Waterloo (Iowa)	100,448	25.6	122,482	
West Palm Beach (Fla.) (new area, May, 1956)			228,106	
Wheeling (W. Va.)-Steubenville (Ohio) (see Steubenville, *supra*)	354,092	−2.8	190,342	
Wichita (Kan.)	222,290	55.1	343,231	
Wichita Falls (Tex.)	98,493	33.8	129,638	
Wilkes-Barre–Hazleton (Pa.)	392,241	−11.2	346,972	
Wilmington (Del.-N. J.)	268,387	21.0	366,197	
Winston-Salem (N. C.)	146,135	15.5	189,428	
Worcester (Mass.)	528,498	11.6	323,306	
York (Pa.)			238,336	
Youngstown-Warren (Ohio)			509,006	
Hawaii (Honolulu area)	353,020	36.7	500,409	
Puerto Rico:				
Mayaguez	87,307	14.1	84,576	
Ponce	126,810	20.6	146,480	
San Juan area	321,752	37.2	589,163	

The following "Standard Consolidated Areas" are also listed in 1961:

New York-Northeastern New Jersey: 14,759,429

New York, N. Y. (Newark, N. J., Jersey City, N. J., Paterson-Clifton-Passaic, N. J., standard statistical metropolitan areas, plus Middlesex and Somerset counties, N. J.)

Chicago, Ill.-Northwestern Indiana: Chicago, Ill. and Gary-Hammond-East Chicago, Ind., Standard Metropolitan Statistical Areas. 6,794,461

inition only as a "broad working concept."[12] Thus, in a recent study, the Council of State Governments points out that the 1950 definition was then the latest in a series employed by the Bureau, which has altered and eliminated various factors originally included and has experimented from time to time with various criteria of commercial, social, and economic activity now abandoned for lack of uniform data.[13]

Though the Bureau has consistently adhered to the basic concept of a central city of a specific minimum population, which exerts an attraction upon permanent and transient population in a variety of specialized ways, it is recognized that the trend of the population to cluster about such central cities has not reached its peak.[14] Accordingly, in an attempt to "encompass the full range of metropolitan influence," the Bureau of the Census recently brought into use the concept of "Extended Metropolitan Area,"[15] which is now being replaced, for greater statistical efficiency and coverage, by the concept "Standard Consolidated Areas."[16]

Thus, it is plain that the Census Bureau itself is constantly in the process of experimenting with its definition of "metropolitan area."

c. Total Community

This study will not restrict its definition of "metropolitan community" to the statistical device now or formerly used by the Bureau of the Census, but will seek to look beyond it to the phenomena of human behavior which the Bureau of

[12] COUNCIL OF STATE GOVERNMENTS, THE STATES AND THE METROPOLITAN PROBLEM 5 (1956).

[13] *Id.* at 4.

[14] *Id.* at 7. See also Bridge, *Metropolitan Areas: A Developing Field of Public Policy,* 19 OHIO ST. L. J. 80 (1958); Tunnard, *America's Super-Cities,* HARPER'S MAGAZINE (Aug. 59); WEBER, THE CITY (Martindale & Neuwirth transl., Free Press of Glencoe, 1958), especially Martindale's "Prefatory Remarks: The Theory of the City," containing an unusually readable summary of the various recent sociological hypotheses.

[15] HAWLEY, CHANGING SHAPE 6.

[16] U. S. BUREAU OF THE BUDGET, STANDARD METROPOLITAN STATISTICAL AREAS 1959, 2, 12. See also Table I *supra.*

the Census is attempting to consider and describe in inventing the various statistical devices used by it.

Beyond the statistics is the geographic area; within the geographic area occur the vast groupings of human beings described by the term "metropolitan community." The totality of their associations to the area and the dynamics of the forces that draw and hold them there and condition their behavior within the area are all part of the concept "metropolitan community" for the present purpose. "We are coming to think," says McKenzie,

> "of the city not only as an agglomeration of people but as a way of living, with an influence extending far beyond its own borders."[17]

Lewis Mumford, whose *Culture of Cities* is an imaginative and far-reaching exploration of the implications of metropolitanism upon various aspects of the outer and inner life of mankind, at one point calls metropolises "man-heaps, machine-warrens, not organs of human association."[18]

Culturally and socially, the behavior of the people within the metropolitan area is more strongly related to the mother-city than to any other legal entity within the area. To its department stores, the women throughout the area look for guidance in dress and home furnishings. Family celebrations of great occasions take place in restaurants in the mother-city; serious courting may be expressed by invitation to theaters or concerts in the metropolis. Whether or not John Doe gets the Ford dealership in a certain satellite city on the outskirts of the metropolitan area is decided on the fifteenth floor of an office building in the metropolis; so are the employment policies that will send thousands of migratory workers in or out of the metropolitan region in the next hiring season.

The editorial slant and bias of the metropolitan dailies is far more important in developing climate of opinion throughout the metropolitan community than is the subur-

[17] McKenzie, Metropolitan Community 434 (1933).
[18] Mumford, The Culture of Cities 146 (1938).

ban local. From the material delivered by the newscasters and commentators in the mother-city the people throughout the metropolitan community take their information and develop their attitudes; from the entertainment offered by television channels in the metropolis those in surrounding areas must choose, or turn off their sets.[19] Colored children in the outlying communities are immediately affected by the response of the metropolitan communications media to whatever current example of discrimination is in the headlines today.

The metropolitan community, then, to this study, is not a statistical device stopping short at a county line; it is a way of life nourished by and founded upon the mores of the mother-city. Though this may be less quantitatively exact than complete reliance upon the statistical definition, this writer submits that it is also more realistic and meaningful. There is room in it to include the sound of the bells that called Dick Whittington to return again to London, the march of feet along all the roads that led to Rome, Carl Sandburg's "Hog butcher for the World," Whitman's "Manahatta." So conceived, the concept includes the cities of the great art museums, operas, and universities.[20] It also includes Skid Row, the back alleys of Harlem, the ghettos, Chinatown. It includes the professional gangster, the professional murderer, the red light district, the headquarters of

[19] Many of the factors mentioned here, it can be argued, are ultimately developed in a few super-metropolises which in turn influence the regional metropolises. Some believe that future development of metropolitanism will take this pattern. See, for example, Tunnard, *Supra* note 14, at 59-65, especially 63 *et seq.* See also THE EXPLODING METROPOLIS, a series of articles compiled by the editors of Fortune. "This is a book by people who like cities."—Introduction, p. 1. The series explores methods of preserving the advantages of cities.

[20] Thus, Martindale, in "Prefatory Remarks: The Theory of the City," in WEBER, THE CITY 10-11, remarks that the city is known by every poet to be a living thing, a system of life which goes beyond humankind to penetrate "the structure of biological evolution. . . ." He alludes to the insect-denizens of Metropolis: the silverfish, carpet beetle, bedbug, and cockroach, likening them to the proletariat and the bureaucrat as typical natives of the scene. From the feathered world he draws such examples as the sparrow, starling, and pigeon, "dodging traffic with the same sang froid as the rest of the

the dope peddling ring. All of these are specialized functions of and are unique to the metropolitan milieu.

Suppose that Huck Finn's father had dwelt in a metropolis. What statistics and case histories the family service agencies, the marriage counselors, the mayor's committee on rehabilitating the alcoholic, the petty criminal court, the rent court, the installment purchase court, the school's visiting teacher, the juvenile court, the child guidance clinics, and the boys' training school could show of him and his family!

If Huck's father had been found drunk on a Detroit street, he would have been "golden-ruled"—that is, kept in jail overnight to sleep it off and released without charge the next morning. In the year 1957, Detroit police report that 4,938 persons including 536 women were "golden-ruled." The very use of the phrase demonstrates the special metropolitan attitude towards the drunk.

Upon repeated occurrences of similar nature, Huck's father would have received the specialized attention of a Recorder's Court probation officer, especially trained for and working exclusively with alcoholics. He might have been referred to Receiving Hospital for medical evaluation and would almost certainly have been given a battery of tests by the Psychopathic Clinic at Recorder's Court.

There might still have been a homicide. But, if Huck's father had lived in a metropolis, the community's approach

---

urbanites, disputing in the squares and holding council in the eaves—winning a livelihood from the by-products of commerce." Vividly describing the city in dawn and starlight, Martindale calls the city a "strident assertion of mankind against time itself."

Continuing in this poetic vein, Martindale refers to the city as "a statement in applied mathematics" and as a human petition expressed in statistics of infant mortality and disease as well as a protest set forth in "percentages of criminality, juvenile delinquency, prostitution, recidivism, mental illness, and senility."

From political parties and bosses through chambers of commerce and credit unions, including newspapers and factories, schools and welfare agencies, museums and zoos, slums and red-light districts, main streets and sanitation plants, the living dynamics of the city as a multiple form of life is provocatively described by Martindale.

and attitude towards him, and towards the murder, would have been entirely different. Its financial investment would have been greater, its involvement in number of man-hours deeper. Would its meaningful human knowledge have been, perhaps, less?

Section 2. Extent of Metropolitanization of Population

In 1900, 40 per cent of the population was classified as urban. In 1950, the 168 metropolitan areas recognized by the Bureau of the Census contained 56 per cent of the nation's population, or about 86 million people. Preliminary reports from the 1960 census available at this writing show that of the 189 metropolitan areas recognized as of this date, all but nine gained population between the 1950 and 1960 censuses, six of these nine being in the depressed coal mining regions of Pennsylvania and West Virginia. The population of the 189 areas as a whole increased by 24.3 per cent from 1950 to 1960, as compared to an over-all growth of the nation's population of 18.5 per cent, or 28,000,000.[21]

Between 1940 and 1950, there was an increase of 22.1 per cent in the population of metropolitan areas in the United States. Reference to Table I will disclose the rate of growth within particular metropolitan areas within the decade 1940 to 1950, and, where available, between 1950 and 1960. For example, Atlanta increased population throughout its metropolitan area 29.7 per cent from 1940 to 1950, and increased another 39.5 per cent from 1950 to 1960; Chicago, 13.9 per cent, 1940-1950, 18.8 per cent, 1950-1960; Detroit, 26.9 per cent, 1940-1950, 24.7 per cent, 1950-1960; Los Angeles, 49.8 per cent, 1940-1950, 53.2 per cent, 1950-1960.[22]

Analyzing the tremendous changes in the population pat-

[21] Hawley, Changing Shape at 1 *et seq.* New York Times, June 21, 1960, reporting a table released that day by the Bureau of the Census.

[22] Table I, *supra.*

tern in the United States within the last five decades, Hawley contrasts the nineteenth-century city, so compact that its radial scope seldom exceeded ten miles, with the expanded metropolitan community embracing the cities, villages, and other local governmental units within a radius of thirty-five miles from the mother-city. He emphasizes the fact that the latter now dominates the urban settlement pattern in the United States.

The same authority finds the growth of metropolitan population to be one of the most conspicuous features of our population movement in the first half of this century. He notes that in every decade since separate metropolitan statistics have been kept, the part of our population classified as metropolitan has "maintained a higher growth rate than has any other part of the nation's population. . . ." This rate he reports to have exceeded the rate of total population growth by 50 per cent or more in almost every decade and to have exceeded the growth rate of population residing outside metropolitan areas by 100 to 300 per cent. "Thus, in contrast to the 40 per cent of the total population that was classified as urban in 1900, the 168 metropolitan areas in 1950 contained 56 per cent of the nations's population, or about 86 million people."[23]

The general impact of growth continuing in the period between April 1950 and April 1959 is set forth in Table II. During that time the total population increased 16.1 per cent; within metropolitan districts, the rate of growth was 19.1 per cent as compared to a rate of growth of only 12.1 per cent outside the metropolitan areas.

These trends continued between 1950 and 1960. Such preliminary data as is available at this writing shows, as noted above,[24] that the nation's population rose 18.5 per cent between 1950, while in the same interval the population of the

[23] HAWLEY, CHANGING SHAPE 1.
[24] *Supra* p. 22.

TABLE II

Civilian Population, by Metropolitan and Urban-Rural Residence, 1950 and 1959

In thousands. Covers 168 areas listed in "Standard Metropolitan Area Definitions" issued by the Executive Office of the President, Bureau of the Budget, on October 17, 1950. For definition of standard metropolitan area, see headnote, Table 10; for definition of urban and rural, farm and nonfarm, see text, p. 2. A central city is any city over 25,000 within a standard metropolitan statistical area, with a maximum of 3 per area.

Residence	April 1950	April 1959	% increase, 1950 to 1959
Total	149,634	173,708	16.1
Standard metropolitan statistical areas	83,000*	99,924	19.2
Central cities	49,138	49,901	1.5
Outside central cities	34,663	50,023	44.3
Urban	23,704	29,711	25.3
Rural nonfarm	8,158	17,713	117.1
Rural farm	2,801	2,599	−7.2

* Differs from figure shown in Table I since the latter covers 173 areas.

SOURCE: U.S. DEP'T OF COMMERCE, BUREAU OF THE CENSUS, U.S. STATISTICAL ABSTRACT 1960, Table 11, p. 15.

189 metropolitan areas now recognized rose by 24.3 per cent. All but nine of the areas gained population between 1950 and 1960; within the area, one-third of the central cities lost population. In twenty-one areas the suburban section lost population while the central city and the over-all area gained.

There are 225 central cities in the 189 metropolitan areas described by today's report. . . . The combined population of the 225 cities increased by 8.2% between censuses; their suburbs by 47.2%, and the 189 areas as a whole by 24.3%.[25]

In New York, the area as now defined experienced an increase of 2.9 per cent in the city, of 73.4 per cent outside the city. The entire Kansas City metropolitan area grew 26.7 per cent between 1950 and 1960, of which 0.3 was in the city, 56.3 per cent outside the city. The Los Angeles area

[25] New York Times, June 21, 1960.

shows a total growth rate during the last decade of 53.2 per cent: 24.2 per cent in the city, 82.5 per cent outside. In the Milwaukee area, the growth between 1950 and 1960 is 25.0 per cent: 15.3 per cent inside the city, 41.5 per cent outside. In the Minneapolis area, total growth was 28.3 per cent: in the city, 7.8 per cent, outside city, 114.7 per cent. In the San Diego area, total growth was 80.2 per cent: city, 63.7 per cent, suburbs, 105.1 per cent. In the Trenton area, total growth was 15.7 per cent: city −10.9 per cent, suburbs, 49.1 per cent. In the Washington, D. C. area, there was a total of 34.5 per cent growth throughout the area from 1950 to 1960, of which −6.9 per cent was in the city, and 84.6 per cent in the suburban portion of the metropolitan area outside the core city.[26]

The population of the United States, then, is thickening and clotting like some gigantic omelette, and this trend appears certain to continue. By 1950, more than half the people in the United States had their abodes in metropolitan areas. Thus, the inquiry into the special problems of metropolitan courts relates to the tribunals serving the majority of our countrymen.

Add to this fact that the magnetizing influence of the metropolitan area daily brings many transient and occasional visitors to the mother-city. Translated into court probelms, this means that courts in metropolitan areas handle not only the majority of litigation brought by inhabitants of metropolitan areas, but also litigation affecting the many more who, being in the metropolitan area to obtain the specialized services it affords, come in one way or another within the orbit of some court within the metropolitan district.

Yet again, consider that the courts in metropolitan districts have an indirect yet powerful influence over other courts by reason of the strong influence of the metropolitan district over the behavior of other areas. The structures and

[26] *Ibid.*

methods of metropolitan courts influence and set standards for and are imitated by courts elsewhere.

For all of these reasons, the study of metropolitan courts as such is one which concerns a considerable majority of our population.

Section 3. Number and Distribution of Governmental Units

Exaggerated proliferation of overlapping governmental units is a characteristic factor of a metropolitan area, an inevitable attribute of growth of the geographic community beyond the original legal boundaries of the mother-city. It occurs along with congestion and mobility of population, breeding complex governmental problems. This, in turn, results in improvised and haphazard creation of special governmental units to meet the needs as they occur.

In the 1957 census of governments, it was reported that the 174 standard metropolitan areas in territorial United States in January 1957 were served by a total of 15,658 local governments.[27] The Council of State Governments, in a study published in 1956, reported that the number of local governments averaged 96 in each metropolitan area, and that the rapid increase of these overlapping units had become much more complex within the last decade. Fourteen per cent of all local governments in the United States were, in this study, reported to be located in metropolitan areas.[28]

> For each 1,000 square miles in metropolitan areas there are slightly more than seventy-five local governments—more than double the number for 1,000 square miles of nonmetropolitan territory.
>
> . . . the more populous . . . are the most complex governmentally. For example, the three largest contain the most governmental units and are interstate. The New York metropolitan area has 1,071 governmental units, the Chicago area 960, and the area centering on Philadelphia 702.[29]

[27] U. S. Bureau of the Census, 1957 Census of Governments 1.

[28] Council of State Governments, The States and the Metropolitan Problem 15 (1956).

[29] *Ibid.*

In a study of Metropolitan Sacramento in 1957, the Public Administration Service reported that Sacramento is a leader, in its population class, in that element of metropolitanism called "fractionated government."

> This dubious honor arises from the liberal use of special districts in both urban and rural areas. The latest count (February 1957) of an ever-fluctuating list shows Sacramento County to have 208 units of local government: the county, 5 municipalities, 45 school districts, and 157 special districts.[30]

This is compared with Atlanta, with 14 overlapping governmental units, and with Houston, Texas, which in 1956 considered fractionization to be one of its most serious problems, yet had only 87 tax-levying units of government in an area having over a million population.

As is pointed out in the Sacramento study,[31] the existence of such a political complex gives rise to considerable confusion as to who is paying for what portions of governmental services in the area.[32] This confusion, like other aspects of governmental multiplicity, is reflected in litigation.

In Miami, Florida, political complexity within the metropolitan district has recently been the subject of comment by the Public Administration Service.[33]

> Virtually all modern metropolitan regions are characterized by varying degrees of political complexity. It arises in part from the filling up of areas between previously organized and once quite separate municipal units. It arises from the ancient pattern of city-county jurisdictional relationships. It also comes about when new residents rush into a new subdivision, resist incorporation into existing municipal units, and finally in desperation incorporate themselves as a small political island in a growing metropolitan community that soon surges all around them. . . . An even more complex governmental structure

[30] PUBLIC ADMINISTRATION SERVICE, THE GOVERNMENT OF METROPOLITAN SACRAMENTO 32 (1957).

[31] *Id.* 33.

[32] Compare DETROIT STUDY 246 *et seq.*

[33] PUBLIC ADMINISTRATION SERVICE, THE GOVERNMENT OF METROPOLITAN MIAMI 27-28 (1954).

arises when a patchwork of special-service authorities and districts is imposed upon a metropolitan area.

Political complexity certainly characterizes the Miami metropolitan area, for within Dade County . . . are twenty-six separate municipalities, of which twenty-four are situated immediately within the Greater Miami urbanized region. . . .

Thirty metropolitan areas are intercounty and entirely within one state, and nineteen of these involve two counties. Six metropolitan areas consists of three countries each. Three (Denver, Minneapolis-St. Paul, Pittsburgh) include four counties each. Boston includes five counties, and San Francisco-Oakland six.[34] The territory of twenty-four metropolitan areas is interstate. Several, including those whose central cities are Buffalo, Detroit, and El Paso, are in fact international.[35]

An example of the way these phenomena relate to the special problems of metropolitan courts may be noted in current efforts reported by New York newspapers to develop a tri-state legal tribunal capable of dealing with litigation arising out of waterfront labor problems, in somewhat the same way as the Port of New York Authority was developed by tri-state agreement to handle administrative problems.

It is suggested, then, that considerable litigation reaches metropolitan courts by reason of intergovernmental disputes between individual overlapping units within the metropolitan district. Mr. Justice Traynor, commenting on this in a recent article, says of it that:

The familiar problems of family law, inheritance and succession take on strange countenance; they lack the simple innocence they would have in a self-contained state; they are riddled with the conflicts that armies of newcomers bring into the state with their belongings. . . .[36]

[34] COUNCIL OF STATE GOVERNMENTS, THE STATES AND THE METROPOLITAN PROBLEM 12.

[35] *Ibid.*

[36] Traynor, *The Work of State Appellate Courts*, 24 U. OF CHI. L. REV. 211, 213 (1957).

Furthermore, and more directly in point for this study, many of these overlapping units have the legal power to develop independent judicial tribunals, with competing or conflicting jurisdiction and without integration to the needs of the metropolitan area as such. Thus, in 1932, an observer of the judicial system found 556 autonomous courts in the Chicago metropolitan region, and 205 in Cook County alone. This writer found 145 judicial tribunals in the Detroit Metropolitan District as defined in 1940, in a study conducted in 1948-1950.[37]

SECTION 4. DISTRIBUTION OF POPULATION

a. Centrifugal Drift, Scatter

In the pilot study of Detroit, the tendency of stable family groups to move outside the city limits of the mother-city was noted, and its implications in terms of court problems discussed.[38] This current of movement is usually referred to as "centrifugal drift" by population students.

This tendency has accelerated in the decade since the Detroit study.

> High growth rates have shifted from the centers to the outlying parts of metropolitan areas . . . the proportion of metropolitan population occupying satellite area has increased steadily from 23 per cent, in the 44 districts reported in 1910, to 42 per cent in the 168 areas of 1950.[39]

This means not only that former city dwellers are moving in increasingly large numbers out into the suburbs but also that the rate of growth in the metropolitan districts, though

[37] DETROIT STUDY Table 1 at 6. And see HOLBROOK, A SURVEY OF METROPOLITAN TRIAL COURTS, LOS ANGELES AREA (1956) [hereinafter cited as LOS ANGELES STUDY] at 8 (political units in Los Angeles County) and at 9 *et seq.* (totality of courts in Los Angeles County). The Holbrook survey, a companion of the Detroit study and this present study, was restricted to Los Angeles County alone, and does not include the rest of the Los Angeles Metropolitan District as defined by the Census Bureau.

[38] DETROIT STUDY, and authorities therein cited.

[39] HAWLEY, CHANGING SHAPE 2.

it continues to rise, is concentrated mostly at the periphery of each district. Newcomers to the metropolitan area settle in the suburbs too, alongside those escaping from the inner zones of the mother-city. This can be seen in Table II,[40] showing the total growth rate between April 1950 and March 1956 to be 14.8 per cent. Of that rate, only 4.7 per cent occurred within the central cities, while the rate within the metropolitan districts but outside the central cities was 29.3 per cent. Hawley says that the scope of metropolitan influence as measured both by ratios of metropolitan growth rates to total United States rates, and also by the ratios of zonal rates to central city rates, was progressively extended during this period. He estimates that approximately 25 to 30 miles were added to the radius of metropolitan influence. The same author notes that redistribution of population, which moved toward concentration from 1900 to 1920, moved toward dispersion from 1920 to 1950. From this observation and from growth rates in central cities and in distance zones, he concludes that metropolitan development in the first half of the twentieth century involved, first, a rapid growth of centers at the expense of satellite areas, and, later, a centrifugal movement to satellite areas, to the detriment of growth in central cities. He comments: "It is probable that the maturation of centers is a requisite to the expansion of settlement in satellite areas."[41]

Thus, to the problem of a multiplicity of overlying and overlapping governmental units within a given metropolitan area is now added the problem of scatter—vast deconcentration toward the periphery of the metropolitan area into satellite settlements, occurring along with and as the major thrust of a continued vigorous over-all rate of growth of metropolitan areas as a whole.

The design for a trial court system with effective juris-

[40] *Supra* p. 24.
[41] HAWLEY, CHANGING SHAPE 161.

diction and control of the basic population of each metropolitan area, then, must be sufficiently flexible and capable of growth to assimilate both these kinds of movement.

b. Density

One of the primary identifying characteristics of the metropolitan district is the density of its population, which is greatest in the central city.

The population per square mile within certain selected metropolitan areas is set forth below, followed by the population per square mile within the central city of each such district. The figures are taken from data assembled by the U.S. Bureau of the Census for the year 1960.[42]

TABLE III

Population per Square Mile, Selected Metropolitan Areas and Central Cities

Name of central city	Pop. per sq. mile in met. area	Pop. per sq. mile in central city
Boston	2,673.2	14,585.7
Bridgeport	2,040.1	8,756.9
Chicago	1,675.0	15,835.9
Cleveland	2,611.3	10,788.8
Detroit	1,914.7	11,963.8
Los Angeles	1,392.5	5,638.5
Milwaukee	1,502.3	8,137.5
New York	4,962.5	24,311.1
Philadelphia	1,223.7	15,439.6
Pittsburgh	788.4	11,170.6
San Francisco	840.1	11,037.8
St. Louis	646.4	12,295.5
Washington, D. C.	1,347.7	12,442.3

In 1940, according to Hawley, in the 92 American cities of over 100,000 inhabitants, the density of population was such that a circle of three miles in radius would have encompassed 2,720,800 individuals.

[42] Letter from U. S. Department of Commerce, Bureau of the Census, Public Administration Office, by A. W. von Struve, Feb. 28, 1961.

Never before was it possible for an individual human being to come into physical contact in an hour's time, whether by walking or by riding a wheeled vehicle, with so many other individuals. And never before have the problems of organization, on the one hand, and of adjustment to the land on the other, been so difficult of solution.[43]

The characteristic of density in the metropolitan district suggests a number of distinctive court problems. Most obvious is the great size of caseload. This brings with it the related problems of recruiting personnel and administering work, records, and funds in such a manner as to achieve adequate and expeditious disposition of litigation.

Also notable is the potential lurking in density itself for breeding litigation. Hawley reports that there are certain sectors in our largest cities where the density factor surpasses 100,000 per square mile.[44] Where 100,000 human beings are packed into one square mile, the likelihood of litigation-producing contact may conservatively be described as high.[45]

c. Mobility

To return to a metropolitan characteristic already noted,[46] the mobility of the population in any such area merits closer examination in terms of its bearing upon special metropolitan court conditions. Numerous kinds and levels of migration to and from the core of the metropolitan area occur continually. These tidal waves of human movement are basic

43 HAWLEY, HUMAN ECOLOGY 102.

44 *Id.* at 169.

45 *Id.* at 102. And see HOLBROOK, LOS ANGELES STUDY at 11: "Los Angeles County has one of the largest and most complex combinations of litigation-producing activities in the world. It is the capital of the film industry and rivals New York in radio and television. The automobile factories, steel mills, aircraft plants, clothing manufacturers, a vast network of transportation facilities and moving traffic all provide sources of litigation. Even the 'smog' is a subject of litigation. 'Multi-million dollar lawsuits are commonplace and murder trials are daily occurrences which attract no attention unless a green orchid was found on the corpse.'"

46 *Supra* pp. 9 & 29.

to the existence of the metropolis, and set the unique tone and tempo of its life. "Each great capitol sits like a spider in the midst of its transportation web."[47]

First, consider that even among residents of the metropolitan area, there is continual shifting and changing. In April of 1947, this observer found that over 17 per cent of Detroit residents had moved within the year. In the period April 1958 to April 1959, the mobility rate in urbanized areas of 250,000 to 1,000,000 was 21.5 per cent, according to the U.S. Department of Commerce, Bureau of the Census, *Current Population Reports* (Series P-20, No. 104, September 30, 1960). The figures of the U.S. Bureau of the Census for the year 1955-1956 show that more than 20 per cent of all urban dwellers had moved within that year.[48] More than 10 per cent of these movers came from outside the state. Some of them came from other countries. The attraction exerted by the largest metropolitan centers upon long-range migrants has long been known to and commented upon by population students.[49] This attraction, in turn, results in comparative ethnic heterogeneity within the core city: There is likely to be more foreign-born and nonwhite population and less native-born white population within the city itself. This heterogeneity, in terms of court problems, may be expected to express itself in class and race tension, in increased criminality, and in personal problem litigation arising out of the difficulties experienced by migrants from different ethnic and culture groups to adjust to the demands of the new community. For example, the 1944 race riots on Belle Isle, in Detroit, are said by local court and police personnel to have been the direct result of a clash between native-born Detroit negroes, moving about the city with considerable self-confi-

[47] C. H. Holden, The City of London, a Record of Destruction and Survival 166, as quoted in Owen, The Metropolitan Transportation Problem 65 n. 2 (1956).

[48] Detroit Study 17 n.33. United States Statistical Abstract (1957), Table 38, at 39.

[49] Duncan, Social Characteristics of Urban and Rural Communities 4.

dence and self-respect, and recent migrants brought in for work in automobile plants from rural white settlements in southern and border-southern states. These two groups found themselves jammed together by the hundreds in a crowded public park, on a brutally sultry evening, after several weeks of a debilitating heat wave.

Similar incidents could be adduced concerning Mexicans in the Texas and California metropolitan cities, Puerto Rican migrants in New York, and so on. Such clashes can and often do occur outside metropolitan areas, of course. The point here is that the ever-present large-scale mobility and congestion in any large city make such clashes an integral part of the life of the city and thus are present as permanent elements of its law enforcement and court administration problem.

Next, note that although within each metropolitan area the current strong trend of movement is toward the suburbs, nevertheless the city continues to grow. The congestion at the center is not being relieved, according to observers. Frank Lloyd Wright once inquired whether "a nation born of farms is destined to die of cities."[50]

As Owen points out, the growth of population in the great central cities and their suburbs has resulted in a worsening of transportation problems, magnified and stepped up by the improvement in transportation facilities which has rendered the central city accessible within a day's journey to an ever-widening circle of satellite-dwellers.[51] The problem is not only how to move, but how to find room to move, and how to find a place to stop.[52]

> From 1940 to 1950, when the population increased by 19 millions, 80 per cent of this growth took place in the 168 metropolitan areas. . . . Approximately 46 per cent of the increase was in the 25

[50] Wright, *The Future of the City,* SATURDAY REVIEW OF LITERATURE, May 2, 1955, p. 12, quoted in OWEN, *op. cit. supra* at 17-18.
[51] OWEN, *op. cit. supra* at 2, 3.
[52] *Ibid.*

largest metropolitan concentrations. This growth added 6 million inhabitants to already congested central cities, and another 9 million to the unprepared suburbs. . . .

The result of these trends has been to concentrate the transportation problem in a relatively small number of metropolitan areas.[53]

Owen reports that half of all motor travel is concentrated in the United States in central cities of metropolitan areas, and more than half of all persons entering and leaving metropolitan areas with populations of over 250,000 are moving by automobile. In Washington, D. C., the figure is 58 per cent and in San Francisco and Seattle nearly 65 per cent.[54]

The Hollywood Freeway, which was designed for 100,000 vehicles a day, in a year had reached 168,000 vehicles a day. In New York, the George Washington Bridge carries a daily average of 85,000 cars, whch reaches 134,000 on holiday weekends. In Washington, D. C., the five bridges over the Potomac carry over 200,000 a day.[55]

The peak hour is progressively worsening, according to Owen. He thus shows the problem as observed on a typical business day in New York in 1954, expressed in terms of trans-Hudson movement of passengers.[56]

Means	Passengers in One Direction Total Day (24 hrs.)		Passengers Eastbound Peak Period (7-10 a.m.)	
	Percentage	Number	Number	Percentage
Auto	148,200 passengers	39.6%	27,969	18.4%
Bus	99,278 "	26.5%	49,974	32.8%
Ferry	4,187 "	1.1%	2,567	1.7%
Railway	122,849 "	32.8%	71,537	47.1%
Total	374,514 "	100.0%	152,047	100.0%

[53] *Id.* at 11-12.

[54] *Id.* at 33.

[55] *Id.* at 35.

[56] *Id.* at 82. Bus figures exclude rail passengers delivered in Manhattan by bus. This book, published in 1956, dealt with a "typical day in 1954." By 1960, when this is being written, daily traffic has considerably increased.

Consider, then, the daily commuter: the New Yorker in the five o'clock subway rush, the Angeleno caught in a vast rush-hour traffic jam on the Freeway. These are not occasional traumatic experiences, they are part of the daily pattern of life in a substantial majority of our population.

> The tempo of life is quicker in the community center than in the outlying area. Movements are faster and more frequent, relationships more transitory and doubtless more enervating than elsewhere in the community. . . . There man is in the midst of the most stimulating context that human ingenuity has thus far devised. By bringing into instantaneous focus the opportunities, the risk, and the tragedies of life, man's behavior is made to resemble that of an animal treated to a rapid succession of electric shocks. It is not surprising that the incidence of mental disorder is highest in metropolitan centers.[57]

In addition to the daily commuter, those adding to the rhythm of migration to and from the core cities of metropolitan areas include those attracted there on occasional or semi-occasional business trips (e.g., the buyers, the regional sales managers, the public and private field agents in for reporting and briefing), those brought in by cultural motives (theater and gallery-goers, luxury shoppers, conventioneers, those in need of consultation with experts in a variety of specialized fields), and the throng of vacationing sightseers. From these, we can deduce that the metropolitan court experiences a comparative preponderance of jurisdictional problems arising out of any kind of litigation-producing activity within the city on the part of persons not resident or regularly employed there.

Coming again to the city dweller and city-employed suburban dweller, faced with the countless tangible and intangible frustrations of daily commuting, we may conclude that

[57] HAWLEY, HUMAN ECOLOGY 306-307. Compare WEBER, THE CITY 32 *et seq.*

the metropolitan characteristic of "mobility" will be acted out in litigation in many ways: in a large caseload of traffic and negligence cases, for instance.[58]

In addition to the obvious condition of having to deal with large traffic and negligence caseloads, we might well explore the possibility that the amount of friction generated in commuters by all this movement may express itself, in the metropolitan court's caseload, in a preponderance of cases arising out of or at least triggered by the reaction of the human beings subjected to the movement—the battle fatigue resulting from the long daily struggle to get oneself to and from the office and about one's daily occasions.

Economic factors have an effect upon the metropolitan court, since the metropolis functions as a nerve center for the economic life of areas far beyond its economic boundaries. Metropolitan courts deal with larger numbers of cases testing the banking practices, trading patterns of industry, new thrusts of corporate and other business entities. They most often serve as the battleground for titans of industry and commerce. Related to the concentration of policy-making echelons of business in metropolitan areas is the concentration of their lawyers, skilled in representing large business enterprises. There are more lawyers, and more lawyers who specialize in representing financial institutions, industries, and big business, in metropolitan cities than elsewhere. Their presence is felt in the quantity and quality of metropolitan court litigation. For example, the highly specialized big city lawyer will attract certain types of cases, so that his presence will mean to the court an increased caseload, problems of delay arising out of his multiple engagements, and lengthy court contact for complex test cases.

Another interesting effect of the presence of such counsel in the metropolitan courts is the potentially greater influence

[58] DETROIT STUDY 20; LOS ANGELES STUDY 16-17.

of an important test case if tried in a metropolitan area. Not only is the metropolis the pacesetter for out-lying communities and thus looked to for interesting precedents, but the concentration of communication skills and transmitting devices within such an area makes the influence of such a case easy to spread rapidly and widely.

Section 5. Characteristics of Population

There is some evidence that the ingredients of the total human aggregate in the core city of a metropolitan area differ, and differ in certain specific ways, from the ingredients of the total population of the nonmetropolitan area.

Thus, it is reported that the percentage of native whites decreases as the size of the place increases, that the percentage of foreign born and Negro population increases directly with the size of the place, and that the percentages of single, widowed, and divorced persons are directly related to the size of the place.[59]

McKenzie, in one of the classic older studies,[60] noting the centrifugal movement of metropolitan population,[61] remarked upon the biological selectivity of this movement. He found the proportions of females, foreign-born whites, and Negroes higher in the central cities, while the proportion of children, males, and native white Americans were higher in the suburban territory. He also noted a significant higher percentage of children under 15 years outside the central cities.[62]

Having due regard for the danger of oversimplification, for the variety of population patterning in different metropolitan areas, and for constant shift and change from year to year, it still seems to be fairly well established that the phenomenon of "centrifugal drift" within metropolitan areas

59 Duncan, Social Characteristics of Urban and Rural Communities 33.
60 McKenzie, The Metropolitan Community 178 (1933).
61 See also p. 29 *supra*.
62 McKenzie 178, 180.

marks a strong and consistent trend of stable family groups to withdraw from the central core of the mother-city and seek the greenbelt of suburbia to bring up their children. See, for example, the data in the McKenzie study dealing with the drift of the "more competent families" to take up residence outside the political limits of the city in which they have business and office connections.[63]

As he points out, the

> exodus of the better elements of the city's population—including a wide range of income classes—from the inner to the outer zones is reflected in the cultural life of the community. Measured by almost any index, the city shows a tendency toward increasing wholesomeness and social stability with distance from the center.[64]

The progressive deterioration of neighborhoods near the heart of the central city, in progression from single-family dwelling to boarding house to blighted area to slum, has been diagrammed in a number of studies. Typically, this progress is marked by the influx, in turn, of various ethnic and cultural groups, each crowded out by a successor group less assimilated culturally with the orginal native population of the mother-city, and less able socially and economically to sustain itself while undergoing assimilation.[65]

It is pointed out in a recent series of newspaper articles on gang delinquencies in New York that great mobility of population and disrupted population is always accompanied by the springing up of juvenile gangs to replace the broken stability of the group.[66] It is well known that these lacings of

[63] *Id.* at 185.

[64] *Ibid.*

[65] See, for example, the sections "Distribution of Foreign and Negro Population" and "Succession of Culture Groups in Delinquency Areas" in Shaw's analysis of delinquency areas, pp. 79, 82, *et seq.*, in Shaw & McKay, *Social Factors in Juvenile Delinquency*, in U. S. NATIONAL COMMISSION ON LAW OBSERVANCE AND ENFORCEMENT, REPORT ON THE CAUSES OF CRIME, vol. 13, pt. 2 (1931).

[66] Salisbury, Harrison E., New York Times, "The Shook Up Generation" (March 24-30, 1958), quoting Hugh Johnson of the New York City Youth Board.

different ethnic and social groups, called "interstitial areas" by sociologists, generate conflict. Thus, these articles state that at Red Hook, New York, the Irish-Italian versus Jewish conflict of a generation ago has given way to Negro-Puerto Rican versus Irish-Italian conflict in this generation. Gang warfare by adolescent gangs is only one manifestation of the conflict which may be translated into units in the case-load of the metropolitan courts.

Dependency is another attribute of the population which becomes more and more dominant toward the heart of the mother-city. Rates of destitution, measured by family welfare cases, were found by McKenzie to be greatest in the central area of the mother-city and to decline in proportion to the distance outward from the center.[67]

Shaw's study of areas of juvenile delinquency also has some data indicating that the percentage of families receiving relief from such agencies as United Charities, Jewish Relief, and Mothers' Pension (the predecessor of Aid to Dependent Children) is highest in the congested areas near the core of the mother-city, and that such rates decline in regular progression with distance from such congested areas.[68]

The comparatively high incidence of illegitimate births in metropolitan areas was noted, in the original study in this series, from data assembled by Woolston in his book *Metropolis: A Study of Urban Communities*.[69]

In its monthly county statistics, the Michigan Department of Social Welfare reports that in May of 1958, 41,933 cases received direct relief in the state. Of this number, 16,302 cases were from Wayne County, which is the heart of the Detroit Metropolitan District. Total amount disbursed to all cases in the state was $3,825,961.05, of which

67 McKenzie 185-86, and see table at 182.

68 Shaw & McKay, *supra* note 65, at 74 *et seq.*

69 Detroit Study 27-28. Table II at 28 was taken from Hunter (ed.), Survey of Community Services in Wayne County, Michigan, table 14 at 35 (1948).

$2,062,451.95 went to the Wayne County cases. In the state, 23,593 cases received Aid to Dependent Children for a total of $3,102,800. Of this number, 11,238 cases were in Wayne County, accounting for $1,749,654 of the aid disbursed. The average cost per case is higher in the metropolitan county ($131.51 average per case statewide, $155.69 in Wayne County). Old Age Assistance was granted, in May of 1958, to 66,970 cases throughout Michigan. Of these 18,228 were in Wayne County. The entire state accounted for $4,087,725 disbursed; $1,307,298 of this went to Wayne County clients. The *Editor and Publisher's Yearbook* estimates the population of the respective areas represented above as follows for the date January 1, 1958: Detroit, 2,154,500; Wayne County, 2,925,300; Michigan, 7,700,000.

Please note that Wayne County is not all of the Detroit Metropolitan District, nor is Detroit the only metropolitan district in Michigan. The figures are given for the sole purpose of indicating the great predominance, in the state's public assistance totals, of the caseload from the central core of the largest metropolis.

Other studies also have indicated the predominance of destitution in the congested parts of large urban areas, and this destitution is reported to be directly related, in incidence, to vice, crime, and mobility.[70] It has recently been noted that in New York public housing facilities the policy of screening applicants is such that dependency, destitution, and other factors disruptive of community order are knowingly built into areas served by public housing, thus defeating the purpose of rehabilitation. One New York public housing unit is described as a "$20,000,000 slum."[71]

> . . . the new community is deprived of the normal quota of human talents needed for self-organization, self-discipline and self-improve-

[70] GIST & HALBERT, URBAN SOCIETY 448 *et seq.* (1937), cited by DETROIT STUDY at 30. And see the BURT and GLUECK studies also cited there.
[71] Salisbury, *supra* note 66.

ment. A human catchpool is formed that breeds social ills and requires endless outside assistance.[72]

In the same series of newspaper articles the reporter notes that, at Red Hook House, relief cases constitute about 25 per cent of the 2,900 families in the project.

Another aspect of the concentration of dependency and destitution in the heart of the metropolitan district which is material to this study of court problems is the so-called "multi-problem family." In the Boston studies, the Gluecks found that their 1,000 juvenile delinquents came from families of which 88 per cent were receiving active service from several social agencies.[73]

Thus, it is said that in New York there are approximately 20,000 "multi-problem families," who, although they represent less than 1 per cent of the population, are the source of 75 per cent of all delinquency.[74]

A recent study of St. Paul by Bradley Buell and associates has established the accuracy of the "multi-problem" family concept, and has indicated the extent to which such families consume the funds, time, and energy of community agencies.[75] In this study, it was found that of 41,000 families in St. Paul receiving help from 109 tax-supported and voluntary health and welfare agencies in the area, a "small, hard knot of 6,500," about 6 per cent of the families, accounted for more than half the total caseload served by these agencies. It is these same families that wind endlessly in and out of the metropolitan courts, often in contact with four or five courts at once.

One further point should be mentioned here, as bearing upon the special problems of metropolitan courts. Persons

[72] *Ibid.*

[73] DETROIT STUDY at 30, and see other materials there cited.

[74] Salisbury, *supra* note 66.

[75] BRADLEY BUELL & ASSOCIATES, COMMUNITY PLANNING FOR HUMAN SERVICES (1952). See also LET'S WORK TOGETHER IN COMMUNITY SERVICE, (Public Affairs Pamphlet No. 194, 1953), the latter a summary of the results of studies fully reported in the former.

coming from areas known to contribute more than their share of certain kinds of litigation—say, juvenile delinquency—are subject to what sociologists describe as "categorical risk." That is, a boy coming before a juvenile court, if a member of a certain minority group living in a certain area, has less chance of avoiding a finding of delinquency than would otherwise be the case. Not to mince words, he has two strikes on him.

Within the metropolis we find a population containing more people of marriageable age, but fewer family units. There is more moving about, more crowding, more distance to cover in a day's work, and more friction generated in covering it than outside the metropolis. The stimulations of the metropolitan area are more intense, the competition more fierce, the physical and mental frustrations more continuous and debilitating, the moral and other support from having secure community status less reliable. We find more unstable people in the metropolitan trial court's caseload, as social instability is so measurable: illegitimacy, destitution, dependency, for example.

Within the metropolitan area are the "movers and shakers," the more than ordinarily ambitious, the adventurous, the restless and discontent, in more than ordinary numbers. Some of them, such as recent immigrants and long-range migrants native to cultures greatly differing from that of the metropolis, are subjected to additional stresses in attempting to adjust to and be assimilated by the metropolis. The struggles of newcomers and metropolis one with another are marked by class and race tensions, by progressive deterioration of congested areas, and also by progressive deterioration in factors indicating strength of human spirit—normal family life, economic and social self-reliance, freedom from antisocial aggression.

Within the metropolitan area, mankind is "lost in the mass," as Schweitzer puts it. These characteristics are built-in components of the metropolitan trial court's caseload.

Chapter III

Metropolitan Characteristics Reflected in Metropolitan Court Conditions

Section 1. Immediate Community as Frame of Reference

HAVING defined the "metropolitan community," for purposes of this discussion, as referring to the total community life within a geographic area, it is clear that not only one community is involved, but that so defined the concept includes an infinity of communities. Thus, within any metropolitan area there are increasing numbers of people whose lives and physical comings and goings are guided from a metropolitan center other than the one in which, or near which, these people happen to have legal residence. Airline personnel literally commute to international capitals; those in communications, entertainment, and the top echelons of the industrial, academic, and governmental worlds commute to Washington, New York, and abroad. Some observers suggest that the present trend towards metropolitanization will shortly produce a small group of supermetropolitan areas, which will control the lives of all of us.[1]

Likewise, within the territorial limits of a single metropolitan area, there are an infinite number of lesser communities marked out by business, educational, familial, aesthetic, and cultural categories: the Polish community, the neighborhood community in the "dormitory" suburb, the community of union personnel, the "gown" community in the college or university center, the dwellers in the world of music, and so on. Each of these has its regular orbit, which governs the movement of those tuned to it, within and as a part of the

[1] See *supra* p. 18 at note 14 and authorities cited in note.

vast series of movements which make up the rhythms of the metropolitan community as such.

As more of the population gathers within metropolitan districts, it becomes less realistic to postulate or recommend a solution to court problems by means of designing a single all-encompassing metropolitan court for each entire metropolitan community. The physical distances involved in the larger metropolitan areas are such as to make these courts inaccessible to many litigants, and administratively such a tribunal would be an impossibly unwieldy mass. If the cultural community be regarded as the unit, then there are so many in each geographic metropolitan area that it would be fantastic to think of a court for each.

In order to conduct an intelligible discussion of the "metropolitan court problem" as such, however, we can merely note the existence of an infinity of overlapping cultural communities within each geographic metropolitan area, add this to notice already taken of the multitude of overlapping governmental units within each geographic metropolitan area, and proceed to consider the problem of designing an optimum structure and administrative system for each metropolitan area against this background. What is wanted is a tribunal or group of tribunals so designed and staffed as to make justice readily accessible to each litigant within the area. By "justice" is meant not only sufficiently prompt access to the court to permit disposal of the litigation in time to be of use to the litigants, but also sufficient acquisition and skilled application of knowledge by the court to the problem being litigated to insure a proper quality of disposition.

SECTION 2. MULTIPLICTY OF COURTS

As has been noted, multiplicity of governmental units within the metropolitan area is exhibited in a multiplicity of courts serving the area.[2] Confusion, overlap, and conflict of

[2] *Supra* p. 29.

jurisdiction among these courts is concomitant with multiplicity. This problem is discussed in detail in the Detroit study, as well as in many recent periodicals dealing with court reform projects.[3] As one of the Detroit reporters once remarked, there is likely to be "one court for the corned beef, one for the cabbage."

The structural disadvantages of court multiplicity are first and most obvious the jurisdictional conflict and confusion. These are aggravated by the comparatively great size of caseloads in metropolitan courts, by the large numbers of persons attempting to deal with any given unit in the caseload at any given time, and, in many personal problem cases, by the presence of a neighboring multiplicity of social agencies also concerned with the problem in human maladjustment which has given rise to the litigation, each determined to solve the problem independently. Administratively, then, we are not surprised to find delay and confusion resulting from the coexistence of many courts with duplicating jurisdiction. See, for example, the docket check of the Circuit and Superior Courts of Cook County conducted by this writer for one of the studies in the present series.[4]

Multiplicity of courts has been partially overcome in some metropolitan areas, for example, Los Angeles and San Francisco.[5] In California, a constitutional amendment in 1950 brought about consolidation of most of the inferior tribunals

[3] VIRTUE, DETROIT STUDY chs. 2 & 7. And see for example, Mars, *Court Reorganization in Connecticut,* 41 J. AM. JUD. SOC'Y 6, 8 (1956); *Illinois and Chicago Bars Weigh Merits of Court Reorganization Plan,* 41 J. AM. JUD. SOC'Y 54 (1957); Elliott, *Judicial Administration,* 32 N.Y.U.L. REV. 116, 124 ff., dealing with proposals of Tweed Commission for simplifying court structure in New York.

[4] A.B.A. SEC. OF JUDICIAL ADMINISTRATION, COMMITTEE ON METROPOLITAN TRIAL COURTS, PROGRESS REPORT (June 1953).

[5] CAL. CONST. art. VI; LOS ANGELES STUDY 8-9, 376; Fussell, The Holbrook Report—Eight Months Later 13-14 (1957); Courts Committee, Municipal Court Judges' Association, Los Angeles County, A Proposal for the Consolidation of the Superior and Municipal Courts and an Analysis of the Workability of the Proposal within Los Angeles County.

The California legislature in 1959 addressed itself to some of the problems to which Holbrook called attention. See Stats. 1959, ch. 1371 (defining superior court districts, establishing geographic and population requirements); CAL. GOVT. CODE §§ 69640 *et seq.* (1959 Supp.).

within the metropolitan areas referred to. But note also that the proliferation of branch courts, which concerned Professor Holbrook and his staff in the Los Angeles study, illustrates how the problem crops out in another guise.[6]

It ought to be mentioned here, also, that structural integration in and of itself does not eliminate the disadvantages of multiplicity of courts, for where there are many geographically separate branches of an integrated court, the various branches are sometimes found to conduct themselves as if they were separately existing tribunals with rival jurisdiction. See, for example, the lack of effective cooperation between the Domestic Relations branch of the Superior Court in San Francisco and the Juvenile branch of that same court, as commented on by this writer.[7]

It is indeed a melancholy thought that as early as 1913 Dean Pound, writing of the administration of justice in the modern city, noted the multiplicity of independent tribunals as one of the signal cases of waste of judicial power in large cities.[8] This was decades before the great surge of most of our population into the metropolitan areas.

A recent study by the Council of State Governments describes the process of multiplication of competing or duplicating courts which accompanied the rapidly multiplying urbanization of the American people. The authors list relief of congested calendars, need for better disposition of special types of cases, and far-reaching social changes as causes contributing to the unplanned and fragmentary development of the patchwork upon patchwork which comprises the metropolitan court systems in most of our large cities now.[9]

In addition to the major statewide trial courts of general

[6] Los Angeles Study 11, 376.

[7] Virtue, Family Cases in Court 14, 15 (1956) [hereinafter cited as Family Cases].

[8] Pound, *Administration of Justice in the Modern City,* 26 Harv. L. Rev. 302, 313 (1913), and see examples at 313 and 314 in footnotes.

[9] Frederick & Spector, Trial Courts of General Jurisdiction in the Forty-eight States 2 *et seq.* (Council of State Governments 1951).

jurisdiction, the authors of the last cited study found additional trial courts in metropolitan areas in five states,[10] as well as widespread duplication in statewide court systems and a plethora of petty tribunals in cities.[11]

The American Bar Association, in its minimum standards of judicial administration, has long taken the position that a unified judicial system, such as will eliminate duplication of functions, will permit responsible administrative control of court service, and will nourish uniformity and efficiency in the handling of judicial business, is essential to any adequate system of courts.[12]

SECTION 3. SIZE OF CASELOAD

The most direct reflection of the demographic phenomena referred to as "metropolitanization" as translated into court conditions is the sheer, overwhelming size of the caseloads in metropolitan courts. The avalanche of business under which courts in the great central cities of metropolitan communities lie buried has been the subject of most of the attention directed towards the improvement of metropolitan courts during the last decade. From size of caseload many special metropolitan court problems are derived and will receive further attention. For the moment, attention is directed to size of caseload as such.

In an attempt to estimate the full workload of the entire system of courts serving the City of Detroit in 1947 (the year of field observation for the pilot study in this series), original field notes for that year have been consulted. The

[10] Chicago, Illinois, Superior Court; New Orleans, Louisiana, Civil District Court; Baltimore, Maryland, Supreme Bench; Detroit, Michigan, Recorder's Court; New York, New York, General Sessions.

[11] FREDERICK & SPECTOR, *op. cit. supra,* at 15, 16.

[12] VANDERBILT, MINIMUM STANDARDS OF JUDICIAL ADMINISTRATION 29 (1949) [hereinafter cited as VANDERBILT, MINIMUM STANDARDS]: Recommendation Adopted by the American Bar Association, 1938: "(1) That provision should be made in each state for a unified judicial system with power and responsibility in one of the judges to assign judges to judicial service so as to relieve congestion of dockets and utilize the available judges to the best advantage."

Circuit Court of Wayne County, with general original trial jurisdiction, disposed of 22,195 civil cases in 1947, and of 500 criminal cases arising in the fringe area outside the city but within the county. The Court of Common Pleas of Detroit, a court of limited jurisdiction combining the civil jurisdiction of justices of the peace with increased monetary and other jurisdiction conferred by statute, disposed of 40,466 cases.[13] Recorder's Court of Detroit, with integrated city-wide criminal jurisdiction, disposed of 4,474 high misdemeanors and felonies and 20,428 misdemeanors. The Traffic and Ordinance Division of Recorder's Court disposed of 543,151 traffic cases, both misdemeanor and felony. The Circuit Court commissioners disposed of a total caseload, mostly eviction matters, estimated by them at about 25,000. The Probate Court of Wayne County reported disposition of an approximated 10,000 administrative matters and 800 adoptions. The Juvenile Division of the Probate Court reported 600 unofficial cases, 1,636 delinquency cases, 84 wayward minor cases, 437 dependency and neglect cases, and 4,581 traffic cases.[14]

The total caseload disposed of in 1947 by trial courts sitting in Detroit, on the basis of these figures, is 677,879 cases. The figure is known to be low, since it omits from the Juve-

[13] DETROIT STUDY 48-50.

[14] The jurisdictional pattern of the Court of Common Pleas is described in DETROIT STUDY 48. It was created when in 1929 a legislative enactment consolidated the six independently functioning justices of the peace in the city into a single nine-judge court. The Michigan Supreme Court has said that the statute coordinates the work of the justices of the peace under a single presiding judge, and ". . . continues the justices' courts under another name and does not create a new court." *Kates v. Reading,* 254 Mich. 158, 165-166 (1931). The justices of the peace in Detroit had only civil jurisdiction, since criminal jurisdiction at that level was placed in the Recorder's Court. DETROIT STUDY *op. cit.* 44 *et seq.* In addition to the original civil jurisdiction of justices of the peace, the Court of Common Pleas has additional civil jurisdiction conferred by statute, and, since justices of the peace have the preliminary jurisdiction of magistrates throughout the county, common pleas judges sometimes conduct examinations for persons charged with criminal offenses in Wayne County outside the City of Detroit. DETROIT STUDY 50. And see recent statutory amendments, including Act No. 105, PUBLIC AND LOCAL ACTS OF MICHIGAN 1955, and Act No. 48, PUBLIC AND LOCAL ACTS OF MICHIGAN 1958.

nile Court caseload several hundred adoption cases first referred to that division for investigation and then listed among official dispositions of Probate Court. Also omitted are condemnation cases disposed of by Recorder's Court, and ordinance cases disposed of by the Traffic and Ordinance Division of Recorder's Court. No data could be obtained for the cases so omitted.[15]

In 1956, the Circuit Court of Wayne County disposed of 20,256 cases.[16]

Other areas in Michigan classified as "metropolitan" by the Bureau of the Census, together with cases disposed of by the circuit courts centered in those areas as reported by the Michigan State Court administrator in 1956, follow:

Bay County	639
Jackson	1,418
Kalamazoo	1,365
Lansing (Ingham County)	2,368
Saginaw	1,284
Detroit:	
Wayne	20,256
Oakland	5,211
Macomb	2,421
Total for Detroit metropolitan area	27,888[17]
Grand Rapids	1,878
Flint	3,999

[15] Attention is called to the difficulty of obtaining accurate caseload figures for several of these courts. The problem of accurate records will be dealt with later.

[16] MICH. SUPREME COURT, OFFICE OF THE COURT ADMINISTRATOR, ANNUAL REPORT AND JUDICIAL STATISTICS FOR 1956.

[17] Felony dispositions for Recorder's Court, which are parallel in jurisdiction to criminal dispositions in circuit courts, may be calculated from Table II of the 1956 report at a total of 6,380 dispositions. The court's misdemeanor dispositions (jurisdiction inherited from criminal jurisdiction of justices of the peace) were 20,181 for 1956.

The State Court administrator regards the following areas as also "metropolitan," for purposes of Michigan case reporting:

Berrien	1,146
Muskegon	1,122
Ottowa	850
Washtenaw	1,386
Calhoun	1,184

The largest caseload for the remaining, or nonmetropolitan, circuits in Michigan is St. Clair, with 722 case dispositions reported for 1956.

On the basis of these caseloads, the metropolitan area almost always has the largest caseloads.[18] In the Detroit area, where the concept of "metropolitan area" is exhibited in all its vast bulk, the total caseload is almost four times as large as that of any circuit outside the metropolitan area.

The total cases commenced in all circuit courts in Michigan, as reported by the State Court administrator for 1956, were 59,341. Of these, 19,979 were filed in the Circuit Court of Wayne County, 6,311 in the felony division of Recorder's Court,[19] 2,878 in Macomb County, 5,779 in Oakland County —a total of 34,947 for the entire Detroit metropolitan area, or far more than half the total for the entire state.

Professor Holbrook reports[20] that in the fiscal year 1953-1954 more than 100,000 cases were filed in the Los Angeles Superior Court and 1,154,401 in the Los Angeles Municipal Court that same year.

In 1956, a total of 271,398 cases were filed in all of the California superior courts. In that year, the total filings in the Superior Court of Los Angeles alone were 108,968[21]—

[18] But see Bay City, tabulation *supra*.

[19] With jurisdiction equivalent to that of circuit court over high misdemeanors and felonies arising in the city of Detroit. See DETROIT STUDY 45.

[20] LOS ANGELES STUDY 12 and Table 2 at 14.

[21] JUDICIAL COUNCIL OF CALIFORNIA, SIXTEENTH BIENNIAL REPORT, DEC. 31, 1956, p. 20.

almost half the total for the entire state. This relationship is the more impressive when one recalls that there are several other major metropolitan areas in California, including the San Francisco area, in addition to Los Angeles.

The same table shows a total of 246,477 superior court dispositions for 1956, of which 96,832 were disposed of by the Superior Court of Los Angeles.[22]

In Philadelphia, the Municipal Court[23] alone reported 59,389 total dispositions in 1956, of which 36,295 were by means of formal trials or hearings.[24]

Of the current nine million population of the State of Illinois, 56 per cent reside in Cook County, the heart of the Chicago Metropolitan Area. Sixty per cent of the Supreme Court's business is reported as originating in that area.[25]

Statistics could be multiplied *ad nauseam* without further advancing the point, already driven home by many researchers in various fields: the caseloads of courts in the large central cities of metropolitan areas are of such tremendous size as to confront courts sitting in those areas with conditions quite unlike those anywhere outside such large metropolitan areas.

This characteristic condition—gigantic caseloads—makes

[22] Note the lag. 12,136 fewer cases were disposed of by the Supreme Court of L. A. than were filed in that court during the year.

[23] 43 ANN. REP. OF THE MUNICIPAL COURT OF PHILADELPHIA A3 (ed. Drown & Monahan 1956). This is a court of record having exclusive jurisdiction over dependent, delinquent, and neglected children and children's mental cases; desertion and nonsupport; child custody; wayward children; disorderly street walkers; and adoptions. The court also has concurrent jurisdiction with other courts in the county in civil actions at law and in equity and criminal actions other than those involving grave offenses.

There are also in Philadelphia seven courts of common pleas (civil courts), a court of quarter sessions of the peace (criminal court) a court of oyer and terminer and general jail delivery (criminal court), an orphans' court, and 28 magistrates' courts.

[24] Note the high incidence of dispositions other than by trial or hearing, of which more later. Table V *infra*.

[25] Louis A. Kohn, addressing a meeting of the American Judicature Society in St. Louis, as described by the staff of the American Bar Foundation's court congestion study.

itself felt in the form of many complex structural, administrative, quantitative, and qualitative problems.

As the large metropolitan cities grow, so do the caseloads of their courts. Various suggestions for reducing the size of metropolitan caseloads are now being put forth. Many of them involve "reduction of caseload" as an end in itself, but at the risk of diminishing the prerogative and duty of the court to adjudicate litigation and the right of the litigant to have a judicial determination.

Section 4. Special Types of Cases

a. Introductory Comment.

The special bigness of the metropolitan caseload, then, is a unique and characteristic condition of its courts. Is it also possible to suggest that within this all-pervading climate of special bigness the metropolitan caseload is not just bigger, but different?

Some difference in substance, in social texture, can be noted at the outset, by reason of the fact that the bigger the caseload, the smaller each unit in it must necessarily be in relation to the whole. This fact alone suggests the special duty of the metropolitan court to give more than superficial attention to each individual case while looking to the movement of the aggregate caseload as well. There is a special difficulty in performing the court's function in an adequate manner under conditions in which the total caseload is so large and demanding as to render the individual case all but invisibly small.[26]

But placing aside the problem of difference in caseload as a function of the special relationship between individual case

[26] Weber, The City at 32: ". . . it is important to understand the psychological basis of the metropolitan forms of individuality. . . . The institutions . . . confirm . . . its mentality. . . . Both involve a matter-of-fact attitude. . . . Over-stimulation results in loss of the capacity to respond . . . a blunting of discrimination . . . contacts are superficial. . . ."

and total caseload, there is another way of looking at the difference in substance of the metropolitan caseload.

Numerous studies in various fields have established the fact that there are certain types of cases which predominate, or tend to predominate, in metropolitan areas, particularly in the central cities. Among these are criminal, domestic relations, traffic, mental, and certain other cases which may come into the caseload by reason of the special conditions governing human behavior in metropolitan areas.

b. Criminal Offenses

The Detroit study contains reference to the basic studies establishing the comparatively greater criminality of the metropolitan area per unit of population.[27] As is pointed out there, the metropolitan characteristics of density, anonymity, and mobility combine to produce a milieu providing a maximum of provocation for criminal behavior. The occurrence of "centrifugal drift," which leaves the central city disproportionately occupied by the less stable elements of the population, is relevant, as is neighborhood "blight" with its end product of unassimilated and destitute or near-destitute migrants and maladjusted natives crowded together in great congestion in groups productive of class and race tension.[28] It is also notable that the large metropolitan cities are natural breeding-grounds and headquarters for organized crime.

Not only is crime concentrated in cities, but with some exceptions the larger the type of city the greater the per capita crime rate. For example, in the first half of 1954 the urban complaint rate for robbery rose regularly from a low of 8.2 per 100,000 inhabitants for cities with less than 10,000 population to a high of 64.8 for cities of over 250,000. With unimportant exceptions, the same tendency was re-

[27] DETROIT STUDY 20-23. See especially n. 45 at 21 and authorities there cited. But see HOLBROOK, LOS ANGELES STUDY 16.

[28] *Supra,* Chapter II, § 4, A, B, and C.

ported for the other severe serious felonies for which the FBI furnishes information. . . .[29]

In a recent textbook on criminology[30] Professor Taft discusses the studies of Shaw and others which demonstrated the relationship between rate of crime increase and rate of population density and established "delinquency areas" in certain specific neighborhoods close to the heart of the city. As noted hereinabove,[31] the excessive criminality of these areas has been related to loss of neighborhood controls through group relationships producing a sense of status in one's community, neighborliness, and other supportive attitudes which disappear in the metropolitan milieu.[32] More recent studies, according to Professor Taft, have added the concept of "selective migration" to the delinquency area:

> The neighborhood undoubtedly is a sort of factory manufacturing delinquents, but it is also a receptacle into which drift both delinquents and potential delinquents. . . . Such neighborhoods receive also other social waste—congregations of life's failures. The economically down and out, the relatively unintelligent, the discouraged, the minority group which is unfortunately not welcomed in more reputable areas, and not a few of the genuinely pathological—these types drift to the slum, to the delinquency area. . . . Similarly, the more successful tend to move out of delinquency areas. . . . this movement generally tends to drain off the noncriminal and potentially noncriminal.[33]

Crime reports for 1956 show the urban rate for robbery at 60.0 per hundred thousand population, as compared to a rural rate of 17.2. Similarly, the urban rate for aggravated assault was 87.4 for 1956 as compared to a rural rate of 38.9. The urban rate for burglary and breaking and entering was 449.3 in 1956 as compared to a rural rate of 250.5. The urban rate for larceny in 1956 was 1,228.4 as compared to a rural rate of 339.0. The urban auto theft rate was 389.0 in

[29] TAFT, CRIMINOLOGY 207 (3d. ed. 1956).
[30] *Id.*, 208 *et seq.*
[31] *Supra* Chapter II, § 4.
[32] TAFT, *op. cit. supra* note 29, at 211.
[33] *Id.* at 212.

1956, the rural, 67.0. By 1957, the urban rates show increases in all these categories: aggravated assault, to 90.2; burglary and breaking and entering, 502.9; larceny, 1,317.8; auto theft, 254.7.[34]

Early data suggest that many criminals are nonresidents of the places where their crimes are committed, and that the larger the city, the larger the proportion of nonresident criminals represented in statistics from that city.[35] This condition is what could be expected, reflecting the relatively greater mobility and the larger number of transients moving to and from, and within, the metropolitan area.

Professor Elliott notes that women criminals are chiefly urban in residence, and relates this fact to the predominantly urban phenomenon of organized commercial prostitution.[36] Hawley notes[37] that illicit or criminal occupations of many kinds may constitute permanent and integral functions of the metropolitan community, which serves as a powerful magnet for these as for more constructive activities and organizations.[38]

In the Detroit study, as reported by the Detroit Police Department for the year 1947, it was noted that the first, eighth, and thirteenth precincts, which were then closest to the center of the city and the most densely populated, ac-

[34] U. S. Bureau of the Census, Statistical Abstract of the United States: 1957 through 1960. In the 1957 edition, figures are from Table 170, p. 139. See also 1958 edition at 141, 1959 edition at 140. Crime figures published in the 1960 edition are not comparable with those of previous years. See 1960 edition at 138 and Tables 175-180 at 139 ff.

[35] Elliott, Crime in Modern Society 94, citing Prisoners in State and Federal Prisons and Reformatories, 1929-1930, published by the Bureau of the Census in 1932. So far as could be learned, this is still the best study for the point under discussion.

[36] *Id.* at 94. Detroit police report 1,408 arrests for prostitution in 1957.

[37] Hawley, Human Ecology 217.

[38] Among the best known studies of the problem of organized crime in metropolitan centers are: Steffens, The Shame of the Cities; The Kefauver Report on Organized Crime (U. S. Congress, Senate, Special Committee to Investigate Organized Crime in Interstate Commerce); Landesco, "Organized Crime in Chicago," comprising Part III of the Illinois Crime Survey, Illinois Association for Criminal Justice, in cooperation with The Chicago Crime Commission, pp. 815-1087 (1929).

counted for more than 36 per cent of all charged offenders who were classified as "resulting in prosecution by precinct of arresting officer" throughout the entire city. Of those three precincts, the eighth was the least economically distressed, had more family dwellings, and had fewer different races. A total of 623 offenders were charged from the eighth, as compared with 4,495 from the first and 5,446 from the thirteenth. Precincts one and thirteen together accounted for 34.2 per cent of the total of 29,015 offenders charged resulting in prosecution as so reported. Thus the rate of criminality was shown to be related to closeness to the center of the city, to density of population, and to familial and ethnic placement.[39]

The Michigan State Court administrator, reporting for 1956,[40] notes an increase in the over-all volume of criminal cases. This corresponds with the over-all rise in crime reported nationally by the *Uniform Crime Reports,* which for the year 1956 shows an increase of 23.9 per cent in major crimes in 1956 as above an average for the five years prior to 1956. It is estimated by the FBI that crime is rising four times as fast as the total population is growing.[41]

Scrutinizing current criminal caseloads of Michigan circuit courts to the metropolitan areas in Michigan, the following figures are of interest. The Circuit Court of Wayne County (Detroit) disposed of a total of 916 criminal cases in the year 1956. The Recorder's Court of Detroit (having jurisdiction equivalent to that of the circuit court over high misdemeanors and felonies arising in the City of Detroit) disposed of a total of 6,380 cases in its felony division and of 20,181 cases through its misdemeanor division. The Oakland County Circuit Court disposed of 680 cases, the Macomb

[39] DETROIT STUDY at 22 and sources cited.

[40] MICH. SUPREME COURT, OFFICE OF COURT ADMINISTRATOR, ANNUAL REPORT AND JUDICIAL STATISTICS FOR 1956 at 15.

[41] U.S. FEDERAL BUREAU OF INVESTIGATION, UNIFORM CRIME REPORTS FOR THE UNITED STATES, vol. 27, No. 2 Ann. Bull., at 71, 72 (1956).

County Circuit Court of 379, so that for the entire Detroit metropolitan area as the Bureau of the Census defines it, a total of 28,536 criminal dispositions are reported for 1956.[42]

Turning to other metropolitan areas in Michigan as defined by the Bureau of the Census, we find that the Bay County Circuit Court disposed of 128 criminal cases; the court in Jackson County, 520; Kalamazoo County, 211; Ingham County, 559; Saginaw County, 262; Kent County (Grand Rapids), 183; the Superior Court of Grand Rapids (with jurisdiction equivalent to that of the circuit court for major offenses arising in the City of Grand Rapids), 460, so that the total for the Grand Rapids Area is 643. The Circuit Court of Genesee County (Flint) disposed of 739 criminal cases in 1956.

Rounding out the picture by noting the caseloads of circuit courts in Michigan in areas described by the State Court administrator as "metropolitan," we add the Circuit Court of Berrien County with 284 criminal dispositions; Muskegon, 293; Ottowa, 145; Washtenaw, 391; Calhoun, 214.

The State Court administrator shows total criminal dispositions for the entire state in 1956 at 35,297. The metropolitan dispositions listed hereinabove total 31,364—almost 90 per cent of the criminal dispositions for the entire state.[43]

Caveat: This includes the dispositions in the misdemeanor division of the Recorder's Court of Detroit. These dispositions ought to be related, not to circuit court jurisdiction, but to the jurisdiction of municipal and justice courts, since the court's authority to handle such cases is inherited from that of the criminal justices of the peace of Detroit and is unlike any jurisdiction of the circuit court. Since we have no statistics on criminal dispositions outside metropolitan

[42] MICH. SUPREME COURT, OFFICE OF COURT ADMINISTRATOR, ANNUAL REPORT AND JUDICIAL STATISTICS FOR 1956. Figures shown derived from various portions of this report.

[43] DETROIT STUDY at 44-46.

areas by municipal and justice courts, it is best to eliminate the figure for Recorder's Court Misdemeanor Division.

So eliminating those cases, then, the total for the Detroit Metropolitan Area alone is 7,439; that for all Michigan metropolitan areas, 11,183; and that for the entire state, 15,116. On this basis, criminal dispositions by circuit courts in the Michigan metropolitan areas were more than 75 per cent of the total of such dispositions for the entire state.

The Holbrook study notes, with respect to the extensiveness and rate of increase of criminal litigation,[44] that Los Angeles and San Francisco superior courts considered separately had a higher rate of criminal filings during the course of the study (1953-54) than that typical of the nonurban areas.[45]

With respect to whether the rate of filings increases at a faster rate than resident population growth, Holbrook found that total filings in superior courts in California remained almost the same in volume per thousand population during the period 1940 to 1954, during which the population of the state almost doubled. Criminal cases, however, increased 13 per cent per unit of population during that period, and in Los Angeles there were 33 per cent more criminal filings per 1,000 population in 1954 than in 1940.[46] In Los Angeles there was a 32 per cent increase in the crime rate per thousand population over the fourteen years preceding 1954. The Los Angeles rate for felony filings was higher than the state ratio of felony filings per 100,000 population. Of 19,882 felony filings disposed of in the state in 1954, Los Angeles County disposed of 9,660.[47]

With respect to misdemeanors, criminal filings in all

[44] Los Angeles Study at 289.

[45] *Ibid.* See also *id.* Table No. 23, p. 290. Apart from those two areas, however, a group of twelve predominantly urban counties selected for comparison with twelve rural counties did not bear out the relationship between degree of urbanization and criminal caseload per unit of population.

[46] *Id. at* 294-95.

[47] *Id.* at 311.

twenty-one Los Angeles County municipal courts totalled 1,812,807 in 1953-54, of which 1,024,948 were filed in the Los Angeles Judicial District, representing a 14 per cent increase in the county over the preceding year.

The core of the metropolitan area—the Los Angeles Judicial District—showed only a 9 per cent increase, whereas other municipal courts in the county increased their criminal filings by 20 per cent. This is probably to be expected since the population of the outlying areas is growing at a much faster rate than the central city area.[48]

As has often been pointed out, criminal statistics need to be interpreted *cum grano salis*.[49] At best, they represent the detritus left after many law enforcement officials and other persons have exercised a series of value judgments not reflected in the statistics but governing the components of those statistics.

It is, however, submitted that enough has been set forth here strongly to suggest that the metropolitan court has more of a problem in handling criminal cases than courts elsewhere, not only because there are numerically more criminal cases (as there are numerically more of all kinds of cases) in the total caseload, but because the metropolitan milieu tends to produce more crime per unit of population, while presenting to the court problems of timely and adequate disposition unique to the metropolitan area.

Selecting at random an illustration from the Detroit study, this writer is still impressed with the fact that more than 83 per cent of all defendants represented in 20,428 misdemeanor cases disposed of by Recorder's Court in 1947 were convicted. After six weeks of observation of that court, it was the writer's conclusion, with which court personnel agreed, that at least 80 per cent of the misdemeanors which

[48] *Id.* at 314.

[49] See, for example, VON HENTIG, CRIME: CAUSES AND CONDITIONS 21, 51 (1947); ELLIOTT, CRIME IN MODERN SOCIETY 75; U.S. FEDERAL BUREAU OF INVESTIGATION, UNIFORM CRIME REPORTS FOR THE UNITED STATES, vol. 28, No. 1, at 4, 66 (1957).

are tried, are tried without defense counsel.[50] The report of the court for the year 1957 shows 18,528 misdemeanor dispositions, of which over NINETY PER CENT were disposed of by conviction.

Holbrook's staff found similar cause for concern:

> The volume of dispositions [1,681,708 criminal cases disposed of in 1953-54] does not place as great a burden on the judges as it might first appear to, since 1,654,621 (98 per cent) of the dispositions took place before trial. Of those disposed of before trial . . . 79 per cent were taken care of by bail forfeitures which . . . seldom necessitates appearance of the misdemeanant before a judge.
>
> In 1,324,131 of the cases disposed of in municipal courts in the county, defendants were either convicted or bound over after hearing or forfeited bail. Most of the convictions resulted from bail forfeitures or pleas of guilty. *It is probable that many defendants either take their guilt for granted or plead guilty, even though innocent, to save themselves the time, trouble, and expense of a trial.* Further, of those who do request a trial, 41 per cent appear *in pro per.* . . . Thus, the net result is that only a small proportion of misdemeanor cases go to trial and nearly half of those are without counsel.[51]

A "spot check" of felony cases disposed of by Detroit Recorder's Court in 1957 showed 28 defendants in 87 cases without counsel. A later cross check of fifty more cases showed six defendants unrepresented by counsel. There were, in these cases, two serious felony cases which were tried, and a number of pleas of guilty in cases involving serious offenses by the persons so unrepresented.[52]

This is the more striking in view of the fact that both the Circuit Court of Wayne County and Recorder's Court in Detroit provide by court rule for court-assigned counsel for defense at county expense. In the year in which the above described "spot check" was conducted, Recorder's Court issued 951 vouchers for assigned counsel, totalling $55,385.

[50] DETROIT STUDY 110 *et seq.*

[51] LOS ANGELES STUDY 315-16. Italics supplied by present writer.

[52] DETROIT STUDY 111.

It must be concluded, then, that the court could have provided counsel in the cases referred to.[53]

c. Traffic Cases

The point has already been made[54] that mobility, congestion, and large-scale daily commuting are characteristics of the metropolitan milieu which express themselves in the caseload of the metropolitan court through a predominance of traffic cases.

In the Detroit study, this writer noted that in 1947 Detroit police reported a total number of 535,555 traffic violations known in that year, and Traffic and Ordinance Division of Recorder's Court disposed of 543,151 traffic cases during that year.[55] The report of the Detroit Police Department for the year 1957 shows a total of 1,050,343 traffic violations known to the police. The Traffic and Ordinance Division (which in 1957 had the same number of judges and referees as in 1947) disposed in 1957 of a total of 980,563 cases.

Holbrook reports that in the fiscal year 1953-1954, 1,645,204 traffic cases were filed in the various municipal courts of Los Angeles County, accounting for 82 per cent of all actions filed in those courts. Traffic Divisions of the Los Angeles Municipal Court alone have handled as many as 74,000 cases per month.[56]

The problem of proper disposition of such cases is suggested in a recent article, where the author says: "In the Municipal Court of Chicago, it is common to see each of

[53] *Id.* at 110. A former judge of the Circuit Court of Wayne County, reading this chapter, comments that Detroit is spending enough money to provide defense counsel in criminal cases, and expresses the hope that the problem can be solved without recourse to the public defender system.

[54] *Supra* p. 31 *et seq.*

[55] DETROIT STUDY 20.

[56] LOS ANGELES STUDY 16-17.

the three judges assigned to traffic cases dispose of 600 to 700 cases a day."[57]

In Los Angeles County, Holbrook found the largest motor vehicle registration per capita in the country. As of December 31, 1954, there was approximately one automobile for every two people.[58]

> Traffic citations involving 1,645,204 defendants were filed in Los Angeles County in the fiscal year 1953-54 as compared with only 350,049 filings of all other types of litigation.[59]

It is also notable that the greater rate of growth toward the periphery of the metropolitan area has been spelled out, in the Holbrook study, in the "scatter" of the traffic cases: 44 per cent of the traffic filings in the outlying municipal courts, an increase of 14 per cent from 1942-43 to 1953-54 in outlying municipal courts as compared to 9 per cent increase in the Los Angeles Judicial District filings.[60]

The question of disparity of sentences in these cases gave rise to concern on the part of Holbrook's staff, as did the fact that of a total of 1,012 cases considered, only 27 were dismissed or acquitted, and of those sentenced, only 3 sentences were wholly suspended.[61]

At this point, the problems are merely noted for further exploration. Our present purpose is to relate metropolitan conditions to metropolitan court conditions.

d. Chronic Alcoholism

The problems presented to the metropolitan court by the chronic alcoholic seemed worthy of special note in the Detroit study, as illustrative of a class of petty criminal offen-

[57] Netherton, *Fair Trial in Traffic Court,* 41 MINN. L. REV. 577, 586 (1957), citing WARREN, TRAFFIC COURTS (1942).
[58] LOS ANGELES STUDY 319.
[59] *Ibid.*
[60] *Ibid.*
[61] *Id.* at 320-21.

ders whose offense involves medical and social problems complicating the court's decision concerning the legal nature of the offense, as well as the proper disposition of the convicted defendants. Jurisdictional problems also frequently occur in dealing with this type of case, as where commitment by a civil court dealing with mental problems may appear a more appropriate disposition than imprisonment or probation.[62] The Detroit study offered data concerning the proportionately heavier incidence, in metropolitan areas, of habitual drunkenness than elsewhere.

In inquiries conducted for that study, it was found that in 1946 the highest incidence of arrests for drunkenness resulting in prosecution were from the three precincts closest to the heart of the city and most densely populated: 62.2 per cent of the 9,002 persons so charged in 1946 came from those three precincts. In 1946, 13,600 were detained overnight by the police and released next morning without court action ("golden-ruled"). Of the 1,753 misdemeanor cases disposed of in October 1948 at Recorder's Court, over 32.4 per cent were charged with drunkenness. Other aspects of the problem may be seen in the caseloads of traffic courts.

Holbrook found that apart from traffic violations, intoxication charges accounted for the largest number of misdemeanor filings in the Los Angeles Judicial District in the fiscal year 1954—81,311. He points out that instead of continuing to rise with the rate of population growth, however, intoxication filings have decreased since the peak years of 1946, 1947, and 1948. It will be interesting to compare these peaks with those for divorce cases.[63]

Holbrook found approximately 90 per cent of the persons charged with drunkenness pleading guilty or ultimately convicted, and he thoroughly documented the existence of

[62] DETROIT STUDY 23-25.
[63] LOS ANGELES STUDY 316-18.

the "repeater" problem[64] which, in turn, raises basic questions concerning the development of facilities for chronic alcoholics.

The average length of time given to hearing a plea and passing sentence on persons arrested for intoxication, Holbrook notes, is about one to two minutes. The analogy of the case of Huck Finn's father is appropriately reintroduced here. Can the Los Angeles court, in two minutes, give his case the same quality of disposition as did the court that tried Huck's father?

In view of the conditions confronting such metropolitan courts as Detroit and Los Angeles in dealing with the chronic alcoholic, some discussion of the proper role of probation officers, the use of professional nonlegal experts such as psychologists and medical doctors as court aides, and the extent to which society can afford to extend these expensive services to petty misdemeanants should be included in our discussion of metropolitan court problems.

The *Uniform Crime Reports* for 1956[65] show that in a selected group of cities of over 2,500 population (as of 1950) there were 822,268 arrests for drunkenness alone, of a total of 2,068,677 arrests. This was the highest single category of arrests, the next highest being disorderly conduct with 241,167 arrests. The arrests for drunkenness accounted for 40.2 per cent of all arrests (41.6 per cent male, 28.8 per cent female, 3.4 per cent under 21, 9.7 per cent under 25).[66]

e. Mental Cases

The Detroit[67] and Los Angeles[68] studies have indicated that the rate of admissions to mental institutions is greater

[64] *Id.* at 317.
[65] U.S. Federal Bureau of Investigation, Uniform Crime Reports for the United States, vol. 27, No. 2, Ann. Bull., Table 43 (1956).
[66] See also *id.*, Table 42.
[67] Detroit Study 16-17, and authorities there cited.
[68] Los Angeles Study 15.

inside metropolitan areas than outside them, and that the rate, per unit of population, of psychopathic filings in the courts is greater inside large urban areas than outside them. An old but still sound study of the source of mental cases in the Chicago Metropolitan Area[69] found that high insanity rates cluster in the deteriorated regions in and surrounding the center of the city,[70] showing a regular decrease from the center to the periphery of the city paralleling the distribution pattern shown for other kinds of social and economic breakdown, and pointed out that mental disorders appear to be more prevalent where the population is mobile and heterogeneous than where it is stable and homogeneous and where living conditions are simple and secure.[71]

Of recent years, opinion within the psychiatric profession is said to be divided concerning whether the conditions of life in the metropolitan milieu contribute causally to the predominance of mental commitments occurring there, or whether the apparent predominance results from the greater number of diagnostic facilities available in the metropolis and the greater willingness of the metropolitan population to use them. It is often said that the tolerance of the metropolis to even minor mental abnormalities, such as those occurring in mild senility, is much less than elsewhere. Reasons include the crowded and anonymous conditions in the metropolis and the lack of family and neighborhood interpersonal loyalties, such as are expressed in a feeling of responsibility to look after the mildly senile indigent by means other than filing a petition for commitment to a mental institution. These conditions suggest danger to personal rights.

Whatever the reasons, the great number of mental cases appearing in the caseloads of various courts in the metropolis present special conditions under which those courts

[69] FARIS & DUNHAM, MENTAL DISORDERS IN URBAN AREAS (1939)

[70] *Id.* at 35.

[71] Residences of patients previous to admission were the basis of the findings. See *id.*, ix *et seq.*, 25, 35.

must operate. The difficulty of recognizing a mental case in a crowded docket of petty misdemeanants, or as the causative factor in a domestic relations case, the proper methods of developing court aides or of referring cases to court or noncourt facilities for specialized attention, and the dilemma confronting the court when all available facilities are overcrowded are among the conditions regarded as indicative of special problems.

Holbrook reports 8,920 new cases heard in the Psychopathic Department of the Los Angeles Superior Court in the fiscal year 1953-54 and 4,806 persons committed to state hospitals and veterans' facilities by courts. The average daily psychopathic caseload of this court (about thirty-four cases a day) is high in comparison to all other counties. Three named state hospitals serving the area were housing well over 100 per cent of capacity at the time of the Holbrook study.[72]

f. Domestic Relations Cases

It is fairly well established that divorces occur more often, per unit of population, within metropolitan areas than outside, and that divorce cases are filed more frequently, per unit of population, in metropolitan courts than elsewhere.[73] Peak years for both marriages and divorces coincide with world wars, the last peak occurring in 1946, with rates of 27+ per thousand of population for the State of Michigan.[74] The same peak in 1946 and subsequent drop was found in Los Angeles by Holbrook.[75]

Public health statistics for Michigan show the state's divorce rate for 1954 at 16,281, or 4.6 per thousand popula-

[72] Los Angeles Study 15.
[73] Detroit Study 25 *et seq.*; Los Angeles Study 17, 290.
[74] Mich. Department of Health, Michigan Health Statistics (1954). Current when this chapter was drafted.
[75] Los Angeles Study 290.

tion. The rates for Macomb, Oakland, and Wayne counties, comprising the Detroit metropolitan area, were respectively 4.6, 5.4, and 4.8 for that year. The total number of divorces and annulments reaching final court disposition in Wayne County in 1954 was 6,379, of which 246 were contested—less than 5 per cent. Of these 6,293 were granted—more than 98 per cent—leaving less than 2 per cent denied.

The uncontested divorce presents the court with conditions under which proper qualitative determinations are difficult to achieve. When the cases come in great numbers, in a crowded docket, before persons under pressure to avoid "logjam" or case delay, there is a special problem. Discussion of some of the remedies proposed for these problems, such as specialized courts to deal with family problems, various methods for supplementing the adversary process, multi-jurisdictional problems affecting children in divorce cases, and operative relationships with other court and non-court agencies likewise concerned with family breakdown problems, is reserved. Here the point is merely to note that divorce cases are more of a problem to metropolitan courts than elsewhere, not only because of the delicate and difficult nature of their subject matter, but because there are more of them per unit of population in metropolitan areas.[76] It should be noted here also that divorce cases, since by their nature they postulate and often actually involve continuing court contact over a period of years, represent in each unit a possible geometric progression of future units in the case-load of the metropolitan court. To put it another way, a knowledgeable disposition of the several problems in a divorce case (status of the marriage, property distribution, alimony and child support, child custody) is not only especially difficult to achieve in a rushed and crowded docket of cases in which only one side of the case is presented, but is even more desirable to achieve because the result of inade-

[76] See p. 67 *supra;* p. 70 *infra.*

quate solutions to any of the problems will be future outbreaks of those same problems in the docket. Thus, if a child custody and support order is made other than knowledgeably and wisely, the probable outcome will be a series of motions for modification of custody, for reduction or increase of support, and so on. The more violently outraged the party or parties feel about the disposition of the case, the more likely it is that multiple future litigation in the same or one of several other courts will ensue, until some solution tolerable to all the parties is reached or until one or more of the parties is brought to complete financial, psychological, and legal defeat.

Before leaving the subject of divorce cases, it is perhaps well to point out that the foregoing statistics, which indicate a slightly higher rate of incidence of divorces, per unit of population, within metropolitan areas than outside, deal with divorces reaching final disposition by adjudication—that is, granted or denied. It has been the general experience of those dealing with divorce cases as part of the metropolitan caseload that an over-all one-third of such cases will be dismissed by the parties between filing and court disposition. Therefore, the incidence of original filings is thought to be larger, and to involve problems of predecretal disposition in which the court may or may not have some responsibility, depending on the circumstances in each case.[77]

It has also been suggested, on the basis of several recent studies in various metropolitan areas, that somewhere around half the total caseload of the court of original trial jurisdiction, in each metropolitan area so far studied, is made up of divorce and related domestic relations litigation. Therefore, the conditions under which divorce litigation is handled are thought to be of basic significance to a discussion of special metropolitan court problems.[78]

[77] VIRTUE, FAMILY CASES 13, 73, 132, 213, 236 (1956).
[78] *Id.* at 229 *et seq.*

A rough preliminary exploration of this suggestion was made by comparing the relationship of chancery cases filed to total cases filed for the State of Michigan as a whole, in 1956, with the relationship of chancery cases filed to total cases filed in Wayne County, the core of the Detroit area. Chancery cases, as several judges and court administrators have pointed out recently, may be equated for trend-recognizing purposes with divorce and related domestic relations cases, provided these preliminary soundings are not confused with precise and accurate statistical reports. As reported by the Michigan Court administrator, there were a total of 59,782 cases commenced in all the circuit courts in the state in 1956, and 33,314 of them, or a little more than 55 per cent, were chancery cases.

In Wayne County (Detroit) a total of 19,979 cases were filed in 1956 in the Circuit Court of Wayne County, of which almost 70 per cent, or 13,451, were chancery cases. If we add data from Oakland and Macomb counties, so as to arrive at the totals for the entire Detroit District as the Census Bureau defines it, we find a total of 8,359 cases filed in the three circuit courts serving the district, of which 17,796, or more than 65 per cent, were chancery cases.[79] These figures, then, provide support for the thesis that the domestic relations cases will predominate in the metropolitan area and that their predominance increases toward the core of the area.

Desertion, child abandonment, and the various types of litigation representing the community's attempts to deal with paternity out of wedlock may also be mentioned as presenting peculiar conditions of extent as well as substance to courts in metropolitan areas.

[79] MICH. SUPREME COURT, OFFICE OF THE COURT ADMINISTRATOR, ANNUAL REPORT AND JUDICIAL STATISTICS 7 and Table II beginning at 43 Appendix (1956). In Oakland County, 5,502 cases were filed in circuit court in 1956, of which 2,980 were chancery cases; in Macomb County, 2,978 cases were filed, of which 1,365 were chancery cases.

The proportionately greater incidence of illegitimate births in metropolitan areas was noted in the Detroit study, and data were given on the incidence of illegitimacy in Detroit itself.[80] The Michigan Department of Health in its last published data, covering the year 1954, reports that there were 5,610 illegitimate births in the entire state, of which 2,976 occurred in the city of Detroit.[81]

Such births, representing a complex and delicate problem for the community, are almost certain to be represented at least once each by some kind of litigation: adoption, bastardy, paternity action, juvenile court action. Often such situations are represented over several years by several different kinds of litigation, as various facets of the problem are encountered.

For example, adoption is a frequent means of disposing of the legal aspects of the problems of an illegitimate birth. An adoption involves at least a year of court contact, except in a few emergency cases, and connotes, or should connote, a thorough investigation by court and licensed social agency of both the natural and adoptive parents. The Michigan State Department of Social Welfare reports 4,546 adoptions completed in Michigan in 1957. Of these, 1,418 were completed in Wayne County. Of all adoptions so completed in Michigan, less than half (49.2 per cent) concerned children born in wedlock, and 46.3 per cent concerned children known to have been born out of wedlock.[82]

Cases involving illegitimacy present the court with especially difficult conditions by reason of the nature and complexity of the inquiries and judgments essential to disposition of such cases, and it should be emphasized again that

[80] DETROIT STUDY 28.

[81] MICH. DEPARTMENT OF HEALTH, MICHIGAN HEALTH STATISTICS Table 13 at 84 (1954). The same table shows 323 illegitimate births in Oakland County, 96 in Macomb County, in 1954.

[82] State of Michigan, Adoptions in Michigan in 1957. Compiled and issued by the State Department of Social Welfare in cooperation with the Michigan Association of Probate and Juvenile Court Judges. (Mimeographed).

these difficulties are multiplied when such cases occur in great numbers in the overcrowded dockets of courts in the great metropolitan areas.

g. Multi-Problem Families

Material cited in the Detroit study[83] and hereinabove[84] indicate that social maladjustment such as will produce litigation is likely to occur again and again in certain families, and that these families are found most often in the crowded inner zones of large metropolitan areas. Such social maladjustment exhibits itself through litigation in a variety of ways, including petitions for mental commitment, petty criminal actions involving drunkenness, bastardy and other paternity out of wedlock litigation, juvenile delinquency, divorce, support actions, and the like.

The recent St. Paul study[85] provides supplemental documentation for the hypothesis, emphasized in the first Detroit study, that the multi-problem family, as such, appears more often per unit of population in the metropolitan court's caseload than elsewhere, not only because such families cluster in the deteriorated slum areas in great numbers, but because their social breakdown is reflected in multi-litigious activity occurring again and again over a period of many years.

In assembling background material for the St. Paul study, Bradley Buell and associates obtained a twenty-year study of 560 Connecticut families who had, in 1937, been involved in more than one of the following six categories of social breakdown: crime, delinquency, child neglect, divorce, mental disease, and mental defect. The records of these families were traced back to 1927, and then procedures were devel-

83 DETROIT STUDY 29.
84 See *supra* pp. 42-43.
85 BRADLEY BUELL & ASSOCIATES, COMMUNITY PLANNING FOR HUMAN SERVICES 259 (1952).

oped for continuous and uniform reporting of official cases in the same six categories up to 1947.

The results as reported in the St. Paul study are given in Table IV.[86]

The St. Paul study itself found that, of the 6,466 families with "chronic social maladjustment," there were 9,797 persons with behavior disorders. Of these, almost 25 per cent were mentally defective.[87]

> Of maladjusted families, 1822 persons were reported with diagnosed mental illness or emotional disturbance. Approximately two-thirds of this group were psychotic, most of them in the state mental institutions.[88]
>
> . . . in the St. Paul project. . . , the official evidences of crime, juvenile delinquency, child neglect, illegitimacy, and divorce show a high degree of interlocking in the same families. In other words, it is as if an underlying disorder were breaking out in a variety of symptoms. . . .
>
> A statewide study of juvenile delinquency and juvenile neglect made . . . in Connecticut in 1946 showed that 80 percent of the juvenile offenders on whom there was information came from families with adjustment difficulties. . . . All but 5 of the 51 cases of child neglect reflected a composite of other difficulties, and they averaged nine breakdowns per case. . . . In some 400 neglect cases in Connecticut, 31% of the fathers and 20% of the mothers were divorced or separated, or were absent because of desertion. Similarly a study of aid to dependent children found that in 26 per cent of the cases the father was estranged . . . because of divorce, desertion or separation, or because no marriage had taken place.[89]

Noting that this and other data indicate repeated involvements in various disorders officially defined by society as antisocial, the authors of the St. Paul study point out that even after eliminating traffic violators, the largest group among lawbreakers are persons whose behavior is antisocial, and that most of these go free after paying a fine.

[86] *Id.* at 254.
[87] *Id.* at 259.
[88] *Id.* at 264.
[89] *Id.* at 267.

TABLE IV

Twenty-Year History of 560 Families with Social Breakdown in 1937[a]

	Number of families	Per cent in other categories	Mental disease	Mental deficiency	Divorce	Crime	Delinquency	Child neglect
Mental disease	117	54.7	..	5	11	55	24	6
Mental deficiency	32	90.6	5	..	2	22	21	11
Divorce	90	46.7	11	2	..	31	14	8
Crime	303	67.3	55	22	31	..	143	29
Delinquency	284	58.1	24	21	14	143	..	31
Child neglect	49	89.8	6	11	8	29	31	..
Unduplicated total	560	nr[b]						

[a] Unpublished material collected during a study made in 1946 by Community Research Associates, Inc., for the Connecticut Public Welfare Council.

[b] Not reported.

Source: Bradley Buell & Associates, Community Planning for Human Services. New York: Columbia University Press, 1952. P. 254.

Most of the remaining, those sentenced, remain in the local jail, which contains "the sick and the senile, as well as hardened and experienced criminals. The charges for which the great majority are incarcerated—vagrancy, disorderly conduct, and drunkenness—suggest personality defects rather than professional criminality."[90]

The St. Paul study points out that identification by courts of chronic medical or social problems is an efficient means of singling out persons having these problems. But only occasionally and fortuitously does court contact result in the use of the diagnostic and treatment services of available health and casework systems.[91]

The multi-problem family, then, contributes more than its share to the special conditions under which the metropolitan court operates, for many reasons: there are more of these families, their members appear more often in metropolitan courts, they appear again and again in the same court, they appear simultaneously in various courts having concurrent or duplicating jurisdiction, they involve many competing public and private social agencies which may or may not come into the litigation, they raise problems not readily solved by the adversary process culminating in final judgment at the end of a single day in court, and they suggest far-reaching questions concerning proper jurisdictional bases and methods of operation in metropolitan courts.

Section 5. Summation and Conclusion

It is submitted, on the basis of the foregoing discussion, that an analysis of the problems of metropolitan courts is appropriate because of the great and increasing metropolitanization of the population of the United States, and because the metropolitan areas exert a powerful influence even upon those outside their radii. Certain characteristics of

[90] *Id.* at 259.
[91] *Id.* at 269.

metropolitan areas, such as density, mobility, the recently developing scatter to satellite areas, and the centrifugal drift of stable family units away from the core of the central city, produce conditions in the metropolis which can be seen exhibited in the conditions of metropolitan courts. Certain economic and social problems, such as destitution and dependency, are also regarded as contributing to the special conditions of metropolitan courts.

Translating the factors which distinguish the metropolitan area into conditions controlling the structure and operation of metropolitan courts, we have noted multiplicity of tribunals, fragmented jurisdiction, enormous caseloads, and certain special types of cases tending to predominate in metropolitan areas, as indicative of the special conditions under which courts in those areas do their work.

Using this framework as a scaffold, it is now proposed that consideration be given to identification and analysis of the problems of courts operating under such conditions as those described above within metropolitan areas as heretofore defined.

PART II

THE PROBLEMS OF METROPOLITAN COURTS

CHAPTER IV

What We Know About The Problems of Metropolitan Courts: Basic References

SECTION 1. INTRODUCTION

A GREAT deal of information has been put together about the problems of courts in metropolitan areas. In the literature of judicial administration there is no lack of sage comment and discussion about the components essential to a sound metropolitan court system.

True, these discussions, for the most part, relate to courts as such rather than to metropolitan courts. Mostly, they proceed upon the tacit assumption that there are no special metropolitan court problems, or tend to emphasize a single short-range remedy promising to alleviate certain symptoms —such as logjam—without analysis of the real relationship of such remedy to the well-being of the metropolitan court as a service function for the community it serves.

If we can keep the particular focus of this inquiry in mind, however, there is a good deal of material upon which we can draw in identifying and classifying the problems of metropolitan courts. To this endeavor, the present chapter will be devoted.

SECTION 2. BEFORE 1920

a. *Archeion, or the High Courts of Justice in England*

In a study published in 1635, William Lambarde traces the development of man's various methods of dealing with contention, which "hath benne from the beginning."[1] When all the world consisted of a few householders, the Elder, or

[1] WILLIAM LAMBARDE, London, printed by E.P. for Henry Seile, dwelling at the Tygershead in St. Pauls Churchyard. The quotations are from the

father, exercised authority over his ménage, distributing "reward and paine" among its members after his own discretion. But as "multiplication of families and hamlets" somewhat cooled natural love, and greediness to enjoy the fat of the land increased debate and dissension, the mightier and more mischievous "did gore and grieve the weaker and better sort." The first move was to select someone excelling in virtue, and submit disputes to him, praying that he would "maintaine both the mightiest and the meanest in one indifferencie of right and justice."

Later, when this selected governor either converted his authority to his own gain, or "dealt not a like measure to all," then were laws and rules of justice devised.[2]

Still later,[3] when the number of the suits made it impossible for any one person to judge them or any one place to contain them, jurisdiction was broken into parts,

> the hearing of causes was divided among many persons, and sundry places were appointed to that special end, and service. . . . the Israelites . . . did pronounce their Judgements in the Gates of every Citie, to the end, that both all men might behold the indifference of their proceedings, and that no man should need to goe out of his way to seeke Justice.[4]

The multitude of suits is still increasing with "iniquities and age of the world," Lambarde says, but nevertheless,

> if you will thoroughly behold the matter and subject about which all these Courts are now occupied, you shal perceive, that they are . . . so many branches sprung out of that one Tree. . . . This Court . . . therefore . . . if derived of the Latin *Curia* . . . ,

first few pages. After this chapter was written, Harvard University Press published an edition edited by Charles H. McIlwain and Paul L. Ward (1957). Subsequent page references are to the latter edition, for the more ready convenience of the reader.

[2] *Id.* at 10-11, "within the which . . . the power of Governors should . . . be bounded, and which should have but one tongue and voyce, wherewith to speake to all sorts of Suiters."

[3] *Id.* at 11, ". . . when not only the multitude of men was growne infinite; but wickedness also was much increased with the time; and consequently contentions waxed. . . ."

[4] *Id.* at 11.

which ought to put us on notice, Lambarde says, that "heed and care ought to be taken in the deciding of controversies."[5]

From this, we can with profit note that the metropolitan community ("multiplication of families and hamlets") not only has the inherent universal judicial problem of adequately maintaining "the mightiest and meanest in one indifferencie of right and justice," but also encounters certain special problems such as high caseload and special types of cases ("contentions both manifold in matter and many in number"). This condition results in the breaking up of jurisdiction, which is often referred to as fragmented jurisdiction, multiplicity of courts, multi-judge courts ("the division among many persons of the hearing of causes"), and logjam ("intolerable delay of matters and great vexation of men").

b. Comment on Our Self-Critical Approach to Court Problems

A decade and a half in the vineyards of court survey research has not dulled the wonder of this researcher at the uninhibited enthusiasm with which the American public writes about, criticizes, and plans for its judicial system. The defects of various aspects of judicial administration, and the designing of ideal systems, have been a major preoccupation of journalists, social scientists, and lawyers since the beginning of the twentieth century. A few hours with a legal periodical index and the current bar association reports will yield an impressive list of projects, many representing serious professional effort.

One advantage of this devotion to the American avocation of court reform—or perhaps more accurately, writing and talking about court reform—is the unselfconscious zeal

[5] *Id.* at 12.

with which members of the legal profession, and especially members of the judiciary, enter into and take the lead in calling attention to the need for changes in court structure or procedure and in suggesting remedial measures. Court survey researchers enter American courts confidently, and, once established as to competence and good faith, may expect detailed and scrupulously honest assistance, not only in understanding the mechanics of a given system but also in ferreting out and calling attention to its deficiencies.

There are exceptions, but in the main the climate in which court research operates in the United States is nothing so passive as tolerance, but rather the bracing atmosphere of welcome by knowledgeable, interested, and sometimes inspired court personnel. It has always seemed to this writer that the essential vigor and soundness of our court system, and its place in the democratic process, is nowhere better evidenced than by the sincere cordiality with which our best judges contribute their talents towards improving the system.[6]

It was not until an attempt was made to develop a metropolitan court survey unit in London, England, that the writer fully appreciated the open-handedness of the American judiciary in receiving those seeking to make critical evaluations of the operation of court systems. Though courteous and helpful, the English judges and lawyers were unable fully to conceal their astonishment that such a critical evaluation by persons outside the court system should be seriously suggested.[7] It was difficult for them to imagine that such an inquiry could be projected or received other than as an attack, or at least as an implication that faults existed and should be corrected. To permit such an implication

[6] Why, then do the same problems continue to loom, large and unsolved, after decades of devoted effort by lay and legal people? An attempt will be made, later, to deal with this question. *Infra* pp. 356-57.

[7] One highly placed and distinguished legal scholar remarked to the writer: "My dear woman, if there were such a problem, I should have written a book on it ten years ago!"

might, then, be to offer an affront to the judiciary and might shake public confidence in the British court system.

This is not an untenable or ill-considered approach. Clearly, a serious disadvantage to the American receptivity to criticism of its courts is found in the sometimes harmful effect of uninformed, self-serving, or even hysterical public criticism of courts and of court personnel.[8]

Historians can probably trace the difference back to the chain of events by which the American systems carved out, state by state, the separation of powers,[9] and to close public identification with and feeling of public responsibility for the operation of all three departments of government.

If this is our weakness, it is also our strength.

c. Pound: "Causes of Popular Dissatisfaction with the Administration of Justice"; "Administration of Justice in the Modern American City"

In the first decade of the twentieth century, a single spark was struck that with one flash of light awakened the American legal profession to the problems of judicial administration. Most students feel that our preoccupation with the conditions of our courts, and the tremendous interest and enthusiasm of our best legal minds working for court reform, were kindled when Mr. Roscoe Pound, then of Lincoln, Nebraska, arose in St. Paul on the evening of August 29, 1906, to address the American Bar Association upon "The Causes of Popular Dissatisfaction with the

[8] For example, see CALLISON, COURTS OF INJUSTICE (1956); *Is Stupid Waste of Time Essential?* 4 J. AM. JUD. SOC'Y 155 (1921).

[9] For descriptions of the development of court systems in the various states, see, *inter alia*, CALLENDAR, AMERICAN COURTS: THEIR ORGANIZATION AND PROCEDURE 17 *et seq.*, 31 *et seq.* (1927); SUNDERLAND, CASES AND MATERIALS ON JUDICIAL ADMINISTRATION 22 *et seq.* (2d ed. 1948); VANDERBILT, CASES AND MATERIALS ON MODERN PROCEDURE AND JUDICIAL ADMINISTRATION 53 *et seq.* (1952).

Administration of Justice."[10] The impact upon the audience has been described by Dean Wigmore so vividly that you can feel the St. Paul capitol building rock as you read it.[11] Mr. Justice Vanderbilt recommended that all members of the legal profession be required to reread "Causes" yearly upon returning to work.[12]

All legal systems are the source of dissatisfaction, Pound began, for reasons inherent in all law: mechanical operation of rules, different rate of progress between law and public opinion, popular assumption that anybody is competent to perform the easy task of administering justice, and popular impatience of restraint. The Anglo-American legal system has, in addition, its own causes of dissatisfaction: conflict between the individualistic spirit of the common law and "our collectivist age"; the common law doctrine of contentious procedure, which makes litigation seem like a game; political jealousy of nonjudicial personnel of the advantages enjoyed by judicial personnel from application of the doctrine of supremacy of law; lack of general philosophy resulting in petty tinkering instead of comprehensive reform; and defects of form resulting from overreliance on case law.

With respect to judicial organization and procedure, Pound held that our system of courts was archaic and our procedure behind the times, in multiplicity of courts, in preserving concurrent jurisdictions, and in the waste of judicial power it involves.[13] Judicial power may be wasted,

10 Pound, *The Causes of Popular Dissatisfaction with the Administration of Justice,* 29 A.B.A. REP. 395-417 (pt. I, 1906); reprinted in VANDERBILT, CASES AND MATERIALS . . . 32-49 (1952).

11 Wigmore, introduction to Pound's speech, in VANDERBILT, *op. cit. supra* note 10, at 28.

12 VANDERBILT, MINIMUM STANDARDS xviii-xix (1949).

13 "Uncertainty, delay and expense, and above all, the injustice of deciding cases upon points of practice, which are the mere etiquette of justice, direct results of the organization of our courts and the backwardness of our procedure, have created a deep-seated desire to keep out of court, right or wrong, on the part of every sensible business man in the community." Pound, *op. cit. supra* note 10, at 408-09. (Also in VANDERBILT, CASES AND MATERIALS . . . at 42.)

Pound went on, by rigid districts or courts or jurisdictions by consuming the time of courts with points of pure practice instead of substantial controversy, and by nullifying the results of their action with unnecessary appeals.[14] And finally, he identified six causes of popular dissatisfaction with justice:

> (1) Popular lack of interest in justice, which makes jury service a bore and the vindication of right and law secondary to the trouble and expense involved; (2) the strain put upon law in that it has today to do the work of morals also; (3) the effect of transition to a period of legislation; (4) the putting of our courts into politics; (5) the making of the legal profession into a trade, which has superseded the relation of attorney and client by that of employer and employee; and (6) public ignorance of the real workings of courts due to ignorant and sensational reports in the press.[15]

Pound thought these dissatisfactions in the main to be well-founded.

In 1913, writing for the *Harvard Law Review,* Pound related his analysis specifically to the problems of courts in metropolitan areas, from which comes the pressure for court reform.[16] A particular difficulty, he notes, is that of obtaining the consent of a legislature dominated by non-metropolitan elements to remedial measures designed to solve the special problems of metropolitan courts.[17] Many attributes of the pioneer community which created our antiquated court systems still obtain in them (such as widespread use of lay judges), and the resulting incongruities account for many of our metropolitan court problems. Thus, states Dean Pound, the homogeneous community of the nineteenth century (Huck Finn's home town) created a

[14] *Id.* at 412-16. (In VANDERBILT at 48.)

[15] *Id.* at 415.

[16] Pound, *The Administration of Justice in the Modern City,* 26 HARV. L. REV. 302 (1913).

[17] *Id.* at 325-26. A related difficulty, often overlooked, he says, is that justice in the city is often reviewed by a high court sitting outside the metropolis and manned by justices who looked at the problems of the metropolitan area "through rural spectacles."

judicial system in its own image, with such immediate needs in mind as (1) adapting the eternal verities of English common law to American life as it was in the nineteenth-century small town, through a system of rules; (2) decentralizing justice and bringing it to every man's door; (3) remodeling English criminal law to restrain the occasional crime and the crime of passion, in a society equipped with strong restraints applied through religious conviction and moral training.

The system which was evolved to meet these needs, and under which justice is still administered in metropolitan areas and elsewhere, "presupposes a homogeneous population, jealous of its rights, zealous to enforce law and order, and in sympathy with the law and with the institutions of government."[18]

With respect to the special problems of the administration of justice in a great American city, Dean Pound identifies eight: (1) protection of the moral and social life of every individual under the circumstances of the modern city; (2) organization of judicial administration to dispose of the volume, to deal with the law-enforcement problems, and to safeguard the effectiveness of criminal law, all in such a way as to meet the special conditions of the metropolitan community; (3) adequate provision for petty litigation arising in huge volume so as to prevent grievous denial of justice; (4) application and enforcement of law in a community where law requires sanction beyond a guide to individual conscience; (5) application and enforcement of law in a heterogeneous community, in which classes understand neither one another, nor our tenderness of individual liberty, but are suspicious of authority and of magistrates; (6) administration of punitive justice in a community where the defective, degenerate, and ignorant or enfeebled are exposed to temptations and opportunities existing only in metropolis,

[18] *Id.* at 309.

and where the professional criminal and organized vice must also be reckoned with by the same system; (7) administration of justice in family cases, in a community which by its conditions threatens the security of marriage and the family; (8) the release of judicial administration from the shackles imposed by those who created it, and who in their distrust of remembered royal government sought to make law do the work of administration.[19]

Specific comment is made in more detail upon several special metropolitan court problems:

Logjam: Courts in our great cities . . . are subjected to almost overwhelming pressure by an accumulated mass of litigation. Usually they sit almost the year round, and yet they tire out parties and witnesses with long delays, and . . . dispose of . . . business so hastily or imperfectly that reversals and retrials are continually required. Such a condition may be found in the courts of general jurisdiction in practically all of our cities . . . we must obviate waste of judicial power, save time, and conserve effort. . . . There is often little need of it in the country. . . . In the city, the waste of time and energy in doing things that are wholly unnecessary results in denial of justice.[20]
Multiplicity of courts: . . . in Chicago today, at one and the same time, the Juvenile Court, passing on the delinquent children; a court of equity, entertaining a suit for divorce, alimony and the custody of children; a court of law, entertaining an action for necessaries furnished an abandoned wife by a grocer; and the criminal court or domestic relations court, in a prosecution for desertion of wife and child,—may all be dealing piecemeal at the same time with different phases of the same difficulties of the same family.[21]
Waste of judicial power through rapid rotation: . . . the vicious practice of rapid rotation, which prevails in the great majority of jurisdictions, whereby no one judge acquires a thorough experience of any one class of business, may only be noticed . . . different proceedings in a single cause have been heard before twenty-two different justices. . . .[22]

[19] *Id.* at 310-11.
[20] *Id.* at 312-13.
[21] *Id.* at 313.
[22] *Id.* at 313-14. Citing Kales, *Reorganization of the Circuit and Superior Courts of Cook County*, 7 ILL. L. REV. 218 (1912) (those courts have still not

Petty litigation: . . . It is here that the administration of justice touches immediately the greatest number of people. It is here that the great mass . . . whose experience of the law . . . has been too often experience . . . of the arbitrary experience of police officers, might be made to feel that the law is a living force for securing their individual . . . interests. . . . If the will of the individual is subjected arbitrarily to the will of others because the means of protection are too cumbrous and expensive to be available for one of his means against an aggressive opponent who has the means or the inclination to resist, there is an injury to society at large. The most real grievance of the mass of the people . . . is not with respect to the rules of substantive law, but rather with respect to the enforcing machinery, which too often makes the best of rules nugatory in action.[23]

d. American Judicature Society

The year 1913 was also the year of organization of the American Judicature Society, which devoted several years to intensive study of metropolitan court problems.[24] On January 6, 1914, the directors of the Society presented "an analytical outline of causes for dissatisfaction with the administration of justice in a metropolitan district. . . ."[25] As they then saw it, these causes are "more numerous and more emphatically apparent in a metropolitan district than anywhere else."[26] Six causes are listed: (a) selection, retirement, and discipline of judges; (b) organization of judges; (c) selection, guidance, and use of jurors; (d) rules of practice and procedure; (e) efficiency in court clerks' offices; (f) selection, retirement, discipline, and organization of the bar.[27]

---

been reorganized); and citing at n. 31 a report by a committee of the Bar Association of the City of New York for 1912. Note that in 1958 the legal profession was still trying to accomplish court reform in New York.

23 *Id.* at 315.

24 Among the original directors were Roscoe Pound, John H. Wigmore, Albert Kales, Judge Harry Olson of the Chicago Municipal Court, all major figures in the literature of court reform. The executive secretary was Herbert Harley, for many years the outstanding writer on the subject.

25 1 BULLS. AM. JUD. SOC'Y 1 (Jan. 1914). Reproduced hereinafter as Appendix A.

26 *Ibid.*

27 1 BULLS. AM. JUD. SOC'Y, Bull. I at 2.

The reader is also referred to the Society's "Discussion of the Causes for Dissatisfaction with the Administration of Justice in Metropolitan Districts, by Members of the Council," and "Courts for Smaller Cities, Suggestions Based upon an Investigation of the Administration of Justice in the City of Grand Rapids, Michigan."[28]

The fruit of these studies was a Model Metropolitan Court Act.[29]

e. Reginald Heber Smith: *Justice and the Poor*

As hereinabove noted, Dean Pound in his discussions of metropolitan court problems emphasized the difficulties, in such a court, of seeing to it that the enormous caseload of small claims is expeditiously handled, yet handled with something more than perfunctory routine.

In 1919 the Carnegie Corporation sought a study of legal aid as administered throughout the United States. Originally intended to assist the corporation in evaluating the applications of certain legal aid societies to the corporation for grants, the study, conducted by Reginald Heber Smith of the Boston Bar, has become the classic statement of the problems of dispensing even-handed justice to those who are at an economic, intellectual, or cultural disadvantage in the community in which justice is sought.

As was pointed out in the foreword to the study,

> the question is not primarily one as between rich and poor, but concerns rather the fundamental necessity in a free country to place justice, so far as it is humanly possible to do so, within the reach of those who occupy any station in life. Our civilization rests upon an honest and sincere attempt to realize this ideal.[30]

In theory, the substantive law guarantees to every man, regardless of his rank, wealth, or station, ready access to

[28] 1 BULLS. AM. JUD. SOC'Y, Bull. III at 1-47 (Feb. 14, 1914); Bull. II at 1-24, by Herbert Harley (undated).
[29] Appendix B hereinafter.
[30] SMITH, JUSTICE AND THE POOR xiii (2d ed. 1919).

the judicial process and to justice at its hands. This has been the cornerstone of our legal system since the Magna Carta.[31]

The Smith study demonstrated that in practice there are grave defects in the administration of justice which place certain groups under heavy disadvantage. The resulting bias of judicial administration against the poor, he concludes, comes about not out of the deliberate withholding of justice or the conscious wrongdoing of any individual or group of persons, but because of the lack or inadequacy of machinery able to meet the special needs—particularly in "vast urban populations"—of recent migrants and immigrants, of small wage earners, and of what the current generation calls the indigent.

The major defects found by Smith are delay, court costs and fees, and the expense of counsel. Methods for dealing with the problems, he found, include the channeling of many claimants into noncourt agencies, the development of small claims and domestic relations courts, the emergence of noncourt tribunals, and the growth of legal aid organizations.

With respect to the special metropolitan court problems, the Smith study expressed concern for deliberate preying, in large cities, upon disadvantaged groups by organized business and social predators. Related is the use of usurious interest to exploit them financially.

Court delay, the author concluded, is systematically and consciously manipulated against economically deprived persons to discourage them from persisting in litigation. Thus court delay, deliberately used by those who prey upon the poor, becomes a weapon against them.

31 "To no one will we sell, to no one will we refuse or delay, right or justice." MAGNA CARTA, cap. 40, quoted by SMITH, *op. cit., headnote* ch. I, p. 3. See also BRYCE, AMERICAN COMMONWEALTH 422 (1888), referring to American state constitutions as "the legitimate children of Magna Carta."

Another point made in the Smith study is significant to this inquiry. As early as 1913, he noted the tendency of small claims courts to defeat their own purpose by periodic aggrandizement of monetary jurisdiction, a tendency which in time leaves the court with a large caseload and with practices as rigid and traditional as those of the general trial court it was created to supplement. Designed to remedy the defects of judicial administration in dealing fairly and informally with small claims, the court may finally emerge as a competitor of the general trial court, with duplicating jurisdiction and procedures.

f. Baldwin's *The American Judiciary*

The American Judiciary by Simon E. Baldwin, published in 1905, is notable for its treatment of the historical development of American court systems and of the relationships between trial judges and the bar. Chapter XXIV, dealing with "the law's delays," sounds the familiar theme song of all who write of court problems. It contains interesting factual material on docket conditions then (1905) prevailing in several metropolitan trial courts.[32]

There is also a sagacious analysis of the British trial system, with trials conducted by professional experts in trial procedure before judges themselves drawn from the ranks of those experts. In such an atmosphere, not a word or gesture is wasted: evidence is marshaled with the rapidity of the skilled craftsman; oral arguments go straight to the jugular vein, deliver a killing thrust, and then stop; there is no need to ask that the judge receive further briefing or continue a case while he researches a point. Nor is there any reason why decision should not be pronounced immediately upon completion of the barrister's presentation. Everybody has the sure touch of the master.

[32] BALDWIN, THE AMERICAN JUDICIARY 369 *et seq.* (1905).

This performance is contrasted with that in an American court of Baldwin's period. Trial work then as now was likely to be only one facet of many making up the total professional activity of the lawyer presenting the case. Then as now the judge was not often drawn from among top trial experts; he might, indeed, be entirely unfamiliar with the subject matter and procedure being presented to him. The interplay between counsel and trial judge in such a court is an entirely different key from that heard in the British courts.

The present writer does not accept the premise that mechanical dispatch is the single goal of the judicial process, nor that expertise in trial procedure is an essential qualification for a judge. The Baldwin analysis, however, is recommended as material to the conduct of metropolitan court trials with efficiency and without undue delay. Several problems are suggested in addition to delay, among them the advisability of special courts or special divisions with permanently assigned judges, so as to prevent delay and safeguard quality by producing expert judges; the qualifications and selection of judges; and the proper extent to which the judge should be able to command the method of trial progress. These problems are merely noted here for further treatment later.

g. Other Early Studies

Among other studies made before 1920 which have seemed to this writer to be good basic resources for those interested in metropolitan court problems are Bryce's *American Commonwealth*,[33] Lincoln Steffens' *The Shame of the Cities*,[34] and a few articles in legal periodicals dealing with

[33] Bryce, The American Commonwealth *passim* and, especially, 140 *et seq.;* 225, 237, 255, 299, 481 *et seq.;* 495 *et seq.*, 593 and 606.

[34] Steffens, The Shame of the Cities (1904).

the municipal court movement,[35] with judges,[36] with court organization,[37] and with delay.[38] The last, like the poor, will always be with us—constant companions throughout the course of this study.

Other relevant material published during these two decades either in book or article form will be found in the bibliography following this text. It is also recommended that the *American Bar Association Journal* and the *Journal of the American Judicature Society* be followed throughout the course of their publications. Only major articles from either of these periodicals will hereafter be cited herein, because of space limitations, though both are essential basic references to the subject of metropolitan court problems.

Section 3. The Twenties

a. Introductory Comment

In the second decade of this century, further research was accomplished in the field of court surveys. A special technique began to emerge, combining library research, consultation of court records, direct observation, and interview in order to provide a critical analysis of the entire system. The three crime surveys[39] are the outstanding landmarks in this decade. Two critical studies of the period have had much influence on the literature of judicial administration also, and should be briefly noted at this point.

[35] Langbein, *Municipal Court Rotation as Affecting Jurisdiction and Practice,* 6 Bench & Bar 16 (1906); Olson, *The Municipal Court of Chicago,* 40 Am. Lawyer 111 (1902); Wigmore, *Does Chicago Have the Best Municipal Justice in the United States?,* 3 Ill. L. Rev. 290-92 (1908).

[36] Ellis, *The Criticism of Courts,* 10 Am. Lawyer 111 (1902).

[37] Hartshorne, *How Can We Improve Our Judicial System?,* 27 N.J.L.J. 260, 28 N.J.L.J. 132, 173 (1904-5); Randall, *American Plan of Revision of Our Courts,* 31 N.J.L.J. 130-35 (1908).

[38] Moore, *Avoidable Delay in the Trial Courts,* 18 Yale L.J. 112-20 (1908); W. H. Taft, *The Delays of the Law,* 70 Albany L.J. 300-04 (1908).

[39] *Infra* pp. 98-106.

b. Callender's *American Courts*

Clarence Callender's monograph, *American Courts: Their Organization and Procedure* appeared in 1927.[40] In addition to concise descriptions of the state court systems, the volume contains a good deal of procedural analysis.

The subject of *delays,* Callender found, was the one matter above all others that had received the most attention in any discussion of improving the judicial process. He approaches this problem with caution:

> Delay resembles the many-headed hydra of mythology. It is an evil of many phases and very difficult of extirpation. It may appear at any stage of a lawsuit, be slain by a judicial Hercules, and appear again at a later stage. The many forms which it may assume make it difficult to attack. It is not an isolated problem. The delay may be the result of the procrastination of lawyers; it may be the result of an archaic system of pleading; it may be occasioned by the overcrowded condition of a court's calendar; it may be a consequence of faulty trial procedure; it may be the outcome of inadequate processes for enforcing a judgment; it may be the result of a complex judicial structure; it may be the consequence of a complicated system of appellate procedure, and so on. Accordingly, the problem of delay cannot be attacked as a detached matter. Delays are rather to be considered as reasons why particular phases of judicial procedure should be overhauled. One of the tests to be applied in determining the efficiency of any legal process should be, Does it function expeditiously? If it does not, it is wanting in a very essential particular.[41]

And again, he notes that delays in the administration of justice are not always an evil, but may sometimes be desirable, as by providing adequate time for investigation and preparation, time for parties to "cool off," and perhaps time to induce parties to adjust their differences amicably.

But even after allowing for all these things, he regards

40 CALLENDER, AMERICAN COURTS: THEIR ORGANIZATION AND PROCEDURE (1927). (The author was a member of the Philadelphia bar and Professor of Business Law at the Wharton School of the University of Pennsylvania.)

41 *Id.* at 220.

delay as the basic problem in court reform, notes the widespread dissatisfaction emanating from the bench, the bar, and the public, and looks to the "near future" for definite progress in this regard.

He is equally concerned with procedural reform. ("Procedure is a means, not an end.") He deplores the notion that litigation may be handled by a mechanical process.

> People cling to the notion that if the rules of procedure can only be arranged in such a way as to give the contestants a chance to fight it out, justice will emerge triumphant.[42]

In moving towards procedural reform, according to Callender, a primary consideration is the problem of needlessly complex state court systems.[43] Writing in 1927, he noted that the existence of cumbersome court systems was even then especially notable in large population areas, where "there are several independent trial courts with exactly the same jurisdiction . . . and dozens of justices courts within the same area."

His analysis of the objections to such a "galaxy of courts" is basic to our present inquiry and still worth quoting:

> In the first place, such an elaborate system involves a very wasteful expenditure of public money. Usually it is necessary that separate court rooms be provided; that a complete staff of court officials be employed, and that a complete system of court records be maintained for each court. These things mean a duplication of equipment oftentimes without any compensating benefit to the community. A more serious evil, however, is the effect which a complicated system of independent courts has upon the conduct of litigation. The worst phase of the matter is the endless number of jurisdictional questions which are presented because of it. There is great difficulty in determining whether a certain civil suit or criminal prosecution should be brought in a county, municipal or justice's court, or whether an appeal should be taken to a circuit, superior, or supreme court and so on. If the lawyer makes a wrong selection, the case is thrown out and has to

[42] *Id.* at 223.
[43] *Id.* at 224.

be begun all over again. The case is delayed and additional expense is incurred because there is no method whereby the preliminary proceedings can be saved by a simple transfer of the case from one court to another. The courts are virtually strangers, and each insists that its own procedure be carefully observed. The decentralized system furthermore results in serious inequalities in the distribution of work among the various courts. Some judges are idle during parts of the year, while others are struggling hopelessly with more business than they are able to handle.[44]

Another problem stressed by Callender is inadequate rule-making power in the courts, which he describes as an important reason why American courts fail to function as efficiently as they ought to. At common law, as he points out, courts were regarded as possessing this power. Theoretically they still do, but in practice their authority is much restricted by statute.

In America generally, the policy has been adopted of regulating matters of procedure by detailed practice acts which leave to the courts very little discretion in directing the conduct of their own particular business. It has been assumed that it is possible for a legislature to prescribe a fixed code of procedure which will answer the needs of every type of litigation and provide the means for handling every kind of problem which may arise in the courts. The assumption is an erroneous one and contrary to all judicial experience.

The results are unfortunate. It has relieved the courts of all responsibility for handling their business expeditiously and deprived them of all initiative in devising new methods for improving procedure. The court has become a sort of passive agent for dispensing remedies, rather than an active instrumentality for administering justice. Also, it has deprived the public of ability to fix responsibility. . . . The courts can refute the charge of laxity by asserting that they are merely doing what they are directed to do, and the legislature is too indefinite an aggregation to be held for anything. There the matter rests.[45]

Callender regarded criminal procedure as exhibiting the most serious problems and as most in need of reform. Of

[44] *Id.* at 225.
[45] *Id.* at 229-30.

the magistrate system, he says that it is the consensus of the legal profession that as a class magistrates "are seriously lacking in ability, and, in many instances, in essential honesty," are often hand-picked by political bosses, wield an authority peculiarly susceptible to improper influences, but are not themselves subject to professional control since few of them are qualified lawyers.[46]

c. Willoughby's *Principles of Judicial Administration*[47]

Willoughby, a political scientist, was primarily concerned with the judicial process as part of the total government operation. His analysis of the special function of courts is useful, as is his discussion of the joint law-enforcing responsibility of courts and noncourt administrative agencies. Even as early as 1929, he observed the conflicting pressures towards centralization and decentralization of court systems which have engaged the attention of later researchers working with metropolitan court systems. His materials on special types of courts and cases, such as small claims and family courts and the movements to abolish justice of the peace courts in favor of municipal courts, are germane to any discussion of metropolitan court problems.[48]

[46] *Id.* at 231. See also p. 232 (grand jury, a venerable nuisance, providing delay upon which criminal thrives); pp. 233 *et seq.* (right to refuse to testify, questionable on policy basis; right of appeal, though sound, productive of evils because of method of handling: shields criminal from prompt and certain retribution, because of inadequate control by trial judge over progress of trial, and because of overelaborate and extensive appellate procedures).

[47] WILLOUGHBY, PRINCIPLES OF JUDICIAL ADMINISTRATION (1929).

[48] WILLOUGHBY, *op. cit. supra:* arbitration as a recommended alternative to court disposition (41); conciliation as streamlined device for court cases (41); municipal court movement (281 *et seq.*); justice of peace courts (303 *et seq.*); small claims courts (307 *et seq.*); juvenile and domestic relations courts (329 *et seq.*); business administration of courts (338 *et seq.*); selection and removal of judges (361 *et seq.*); the bar (399 *et seq.*). The most serious charge (417) is that courts tend to be morbidly devoted to narrow procedural rules, to the point of defeating the purpose of substantive law, and the basic duty of the court to see justice done.

d. The Crime Surveys

General description

The three major crime surveys published in the twenties are: *Criminal Justice in Cleveland,* edited by Roscoe Pound and Felix Frankfurter;[49] *The Missouri Crime Survey,* edited by Raymond Moley;[50] and *The Illinois Crime Survey,* edited by John Wigmore.[51] These are all scientific surveys of large scope carried out by teams of experts from various professions, working with ample statistical data assembled from courts under observation. The Missouri and Illinois studies contain some comparison of metropolitan and nonmetropolitan areas, though not as a major focus of the studies.[52] The crime surveys were developed, financed, and supported throughout by numerous civic organizations. The published volumes consist of a series of final reports in monographic or essay form in each of several subject areas, each prepared by an experienced professional and edited by the general editor of each survey.

Pound's analysis of metropolitan court problems, Cleveland survey

In the Cleveland study, Dean Pound discusses the special

[49] CLEVELAND FOUNDATION, CRIMINAL JUSTICE IN CLEVELAND (Pound & Frankfurter eds. 1922) [hereinafter cited as CLEVELAND CRIME SURVEY].

[50] MISSOURI ASSOCIATION FOR CRIMINAL JUSTICE, The MISSOURI CRIME SURVEY (Moley ed. 1926) [hereinafter cited as the MISSOURI CRIME SURVEY].

[51] ILLINOIS ASSOCIATION FOR CRIMINAL JUSTICE, THE ILLINOIS CRIME SURVEY (Wigmore ed. 1929) [hereinafter cited as the ILLINOIS CRIME SURVEY].

[52] In the ILLINOIS CRIME SURVEY, the statistical analysis and general survey (31-103) routinely grouped all data into the following categories: "Total Illinois, Chicago and Cook County, Eight More Urban Counties, Seven Less Urban Counties, Two Strictly Rural Counties, Williamson-Franklin, and Milwaukee." Thus all data are comparable as between metropolitan and rural.

In the ILLINOIS CRIME SURVEY, rural and Chicago police systems are both presented (337-51; 357-72), as are systems of prosecution (249-78, 285-331). See 580-82 for an interesting comparison of the record systems outside and inside Cook County.

In the MISSOURI CRIME SURVEY, the "mortality tables" contain, as do those for Illinois, comparison of terminations of cases at different phases for metropolitan and nonmetropolitan areas (270-336, especially 320 *et seq.*).

problems of metropolitan courts, taking a position much like that of his earlier articles.[53] He develops his thesis more in detail against the rich background of the Cleveland study data. Chief factors in administering justice, he says, are men, machinery, environment, and the realistic bounds within which law can effectively function.[54] Pound quotes Sumner to the effect that some of our worst problems come from transferring to crowded cities maxims and usages which were convenient and harmless in backwoods country towns.[55]

The same thing is true of legal institutions, says Pound, citing the Cleveland materials in substantiation. Metropolitan communities

> have come upon an administrative and judicial machinery made for rural communities and simply added to or patched from time to time to meet special emergencies. The professional criminal and his advisers have learned readily to use this machinery and to make devices intended to temper the application of criminal law to the occasional offender a means of escape for the habitual offender. . . . But the 'Mortality Tables' . . . and the examples of the facility with which old offenders take advantage of the series of mitigating agencies . . . tell the story eloquently.[56]

An inherited system of sheriffs, coroners, and constables resulted in police systems unable to deal with metropolitan criminal problems:

> in holding down the potentially sinful administrative official we give the actually sinful professional criminal his opportunity, and insuring a latitude of free individual self-assertion beyond what they require for the upright, we give a dangerous scope to the corrupt. The local

[53] See *supra,* Section 2, c.

[54] Cleveland Crime Survey 562-63. With respect to the last, there are many conflicting theories about the function of the judicial process which must receive attention. For the moment, we pause to note only that the value judgments of the court observer with respect to what the court ought to be doing set the tone and determine the direction of many conclusions concerning the nature of court problems as well as the efficacy of its performance.

[55] *Id.* at 590.

[56] *Id. at* 592. See also *id.* at 91, 93, and 95.

conditions of cities demand centralization and organization of administrative agencies, coördination of responsibility with power, and reliance upon personality rather than upon checks and balances. . . .[57]

To safeguard the individual from oppression in the guise of prosecution, our criminal trial system is built on a process consisting of many slow steps in prosecution and a trial in which judicial power over jury and over procedure has been curtailed. In metropolitan areas, where a voluminous criminal code is to be enforced against a multitude of offenders, the effect of such a procedure is a serious enfeeblement in the performance of judicial administration, says Pound, citing Table II in the chapter on the criminal courts to show the many phases preliminary to final disposition and the high incidence of escapes from each of these phases.[58]

The operation of the prosecutor's office deeply concerned Pound because of the lack of control over that office, its wide powers, and the extent to which the policy of the prosecutor determines the whole course of law enforcement without leaving a tangible record or being held responsible.[59]

In 1863 there was one county prosecutor to handle 60 indictments and 1,600 arrests. The criminal code then contained 249 sections. In 1921, the year of the Cleveland study, the prosecutor's staff numbered eight, there were 2,700 indictments and 27,000 arrests annually, and the criminal code had 1,053 sections. "But," says Dean Pound,

to put it thus is to divert attention from the most significant fact. What we have to deal with is not merely an . . . increase. . . . It is a radical change in the conditions and character of crimes and in the environment of prosecutions. The multiplication of the number of prosecutors by eight and of the payroll . . . by 24, which has gone

[57] *Id.* at 593.

[58] *Id.* at 593 *et seq.*, citing at 594, *id.* at 236 and 91. See also *id.* at 91, 93, and 95, showing that of city misdemeanor cases, 77.51% were found guilty; sentence was executed in 54.39% of those same cases. Of each 100 state misdemeanor cases, 73 were found guilty, but only 39 sentences were executed. Of felony cases, see *id.* at 95 and explanatory material.

[59] *Id.* at 596. See also *id.* at 85 *et seq.* and 31 *et seq.*

along with the growth in population and in the volume of criminal prosecution, might well have sufficed if there had been a simple question of multiplication. That easy resource has proved unequal to a situation which is not the situation of 1863 multiplied . . . but a wholly new one. . . .

It was well enough then to have no system of segregating cases, to have no system of keeping affidavits, to have no records or file or docket, but rely wholly on the court docket for such information as could not be held in . . . memory, to have no stenographic record of the testimony on preliminary examinations and to make no systematic preparation of the cases prosecuted.[60]

Pound congratulates Bettman on his description of the prosecutor's methods in Cleveland as "a system of serial unpreparedness,"[61] and he concludes that this is aggravated by the practice of deliberately arranging the work of assistants so that the trial prosecutor does not know in advance what case he is to try.[62] This assumption of versatility seriously impairs the efficiency of a complex operation carried on in numerous highly specialized fields by a large number of persons.[63] In Michigan, we refer to this as "the bellhop system."

Want of continuity, rigidity of organization, division of power, diffused and ill-defined responsibility are inevitable in such a system, he says, and give rise to perfunctory routine. The defects cannot readily be corrected because there is no one in a position to study the functioning of the system or to facilitate its rehabilitation, says Pound. The results are visible in the Cleveland study as large-scale perjury, widespread suspicion of the judicial process, and opportunities for favoritism, corruption, abuse, or extortion, particularly in the professional defender of accused persons.[64]

[60] *Id.* at 620-21.
[61] *Id.* at 622.
[62] *Ibid.*
[63] *Id.* at 625. See also *id.* at 208.
[64] *Id. at* 626 and data there cited.

With respect to the structure of the courts, Pound calls attention to the multiplicity of independent tribunals and sees a need for unification before proper attention can be given to special problems encountered in metropolitan areas, such as juvenile and family cases, traffic cases, organized crime, large numbers of recent inmovers unfamiliar with or hostile to traditional legal concepts, and recurrent economic crises affecting the behavior of the population.[65]

The system of electing judges, he feels, is particularly harmful in metropolitan areas, because there this system subjects judges to professional political pressure and produces a bench more narrowly technical than where judges have permanent tenure. He also sees a failure of metropolitan judges to control lawyers, as reflected in unnecessary continuances, wrangling of counsel and ill treatment of witnesses, and relates it to methods of selection of judges. He adds that lawyers may be harder to control in large metropolitan areas, first because the leadership of leading lawyers is withheld from criminal courts, small claims courts, and other tribunals with large caseloads but with infrequent litigation involving wealthy clients. There may be large numbers of poorly trained and badly prepared lawyers in the metropolis, also, who are harder to control and to bring up to standard in the hurry and confusion of a metropolitan court.[66]

Turning to the conduct of business in court, Pound comments:

> The scanty attention to cases . . . in the Municipal Court belongs to the days when the police magistrate knew the town drunkard, as did all his neighbors, and could dispose of the case of Huck Finn's father offhand, with the assurance of one who knew. Today the method persists, but the personal knowledge on the part of the court and of the community which assured that justice would be done is no more. . . . Such things as the shifting of cases from one judge to another,

[65] *Id.* at 597.
[66] *Id.* at 600 *et seq.*

with no effective check . . . grow naturally out of the multiplication of judges, making the court . . . a congeries of coördinate tribunals, each proceeding as if it had before it its own small volume of business, as if it had the intimate personal knowledge of the men and things before it, and was subject to the check of general knowledge . . . by the whole community. . . .[67]

Lack of proper judicial organization in multi-judge courts, as observed in the Cleveland Court of Common Pleas, elicits this comment from Pound:

If some rotation of judges is necessary, there is the more reason why the courts should be so organized that the rotation shall not involve fluctuation in policy, divergence in interpretation . . . , fumbling . . . while the judge . . . is acquiring experience . . . and pressure to put off cases or shift them so as to get them before a judge . . . favorable to . . . the particular accused. . . . [T]he ultimate cure is in unification and thorough organization of the court under responsible administrative leadership.

Organization of courts is defective not only in that there are two courts . . . where one court could deal . . . better, . . . but . . . in that the lines are rigidly laid down by law and do not admit of the judges in the large city doing much to meet the special problems that confront city courts. . . .[68]

The lack of a system of judicial statistics, he feels, ties in with the same general picture of lack of coherent organization with a powerful and responsible executive head. Given such a system, as shown in the Cleveland study, even though it had many conscientious and hard-working men in it, "the system is 'worked for weak spots' by those who know how . . . without anyone in particular being to blame . . . the whole system lends itself to manipulation."[69]

Summing up, Pound finds reform of substantive law needed but beyond the scope of a city. The special metropolitan court problems, as he sees them, are procedural: (1) organization of the administration of the court as a whole

[67] *Id.* at 629.
[68] *Id.* at 630 and materials cited.
[69] *Id.* at 632-33.

and in all its branches; (2) pruning the accumulation of checks and mitigating agencies through which many guilty persons escape; (3) coordinating responsibility and power, centralizing responsibility for the functioning of criminal justice; (4) directing correlation between administrative and judicial agencies.[70]

This discussion by Pound of the special problems of metropolitan courts, as found in the Cleveland study, has been examined in detail because it is the only intensive discussion of the special metropolitan court problems in the literature, so far as the writer can discover, other than those conducted by the Section of Judicial Administration for the present study.

Moley's comment on metropolitan problems in the Missouri study

Raymond Moley, in his foreword to the *Missouri Crime Survey,* is impressed with the statistical showing as to how many cases disappear at various stages of the judicial process. These are the famous "mortality tables," from which the efficacy of a system of criminal justice was evaluated in terms of the percentage of sentences carried out, as over against the number of prosecutions originally initiated.[71]

He takes issue with Pound's theory of old-fashioned small-town justice dispensed in a metropolitan setting:

> The survey gives an exceptional opportunity to compare the results of the administration of justice . . . especially to compare urban with rural areas. . . . We found the inadequacy of the explanation that the trouble with the administration of justice in the United States is the persistence of rural institutions in modern urban conditions. This explanation ignores facts which are much more important. In many respects the City of St. Louis stands out in happy contrast with rural areas. Certain institutions coming down through the ages and surely

[70] *Id.* at 605 *et seq.*
[71] MISSOURI CRIME SURVEY 4-5.

devised for rural conditions are better administered in cities than country. The coroner's office, for example, is operating as well in the largest city as anywhere.[72]

Moley notes that most sentences come after a guilty plea, not after trial by jury, and questions the accuracy of the general impression of the jury as basic to the criminal trial. Like Pound, he is impressed with the enormous unchecked power of the prosecutor to dispose of case without trial, and with the lack of skill and preparation shown by the prosecutor's staff.[73]

Though professing to disagree with Pound, he comes out astonishingly close to the same place in final summation:

> . . . generally the machinery of justice is too cumbersome; . . . there is too little co-ordination and co-operation among the various agencies working to the same end . . . there are too many laws standing in the way of prosecution and conviction of persons guilty of crime; . . . there is too much lost motion and unnecessary expense in procedure; . . . there is laxity in prosecutions; . . . there is altogether too much leniency exhibited in the granting of pardons, paroles and commutations.[74]

Lashly's comment on the Illinois study

Lashly, summarizing the results of the Illinois survey, regards the failure of justice as traceable more often to administrative defects than to weaknesses in the laws.[75] The weakest spot, he says, is in the detection and apprehension of criminals: for example, in 1926, 21,301 robberies and burglaries were committed, but during that period only 4,129 robbery and burglary prosecutions were started," indicating 80.61 per cent of persons committing those offenses were never caught." A total of 1,177 persons charged with those offenses in 1926 were punished, which is only 5.52 per cent of those committing these crimes. Lashly states that

72 *Id.* at 5.
73 *Id.* at 5, 6.
74 *Id.* at 7.
75 Lashly, *Director's Introduction*, ILLINOIS CRIME SURVEY 16.

similar records in other large cities, when compared, are not at variance.[76]

The major focus of attention in the *Illinois Crime Survey* is the material on organized crime. Lashly concludes that organized crime presents the worst problem in the metropolis of Chicago. During the period of this study, the traffic in intoxicating liquor provided a center around which organized crime built its empire, with the revenues from this and other illegal traffics acting as a powerful growth stimulant, and with criminal gangs perfecting the technique of the gang murder as a tool for community control.

Although the fully overlapping jurisdiction of circuit and superior courts in Cook County was then, as now, an outstanding feature of the court structure of the Chicago metropolitan area, the Illinois study team did not relate the low level of the judicial performance there to the structural pattern of the courts.

e. Other Studies Made in the Twenties

Schramm's Piedpoudre Courts

Like *Justice and the Poor,*[77] Schramm's study of small claims litigants in the Pittsburgh district, published in 1928, was sponsored by the Legal Aid Societies, and reflected their need to solve the problems inherent in achieving prompt, just, and final disposition of the court problems of poor litigants in a large metropolitan area. This study is extensive: it continued for over three years, covered over eighteen thousand case records in a single populous county, and made use of questionnaires, interview, and conscientious library research.[78]

[76] *Id.* at 17. Note the tacit assumption that punishment is the objective of criminal judicial administration, and the conclusion that to the extent those charged are not punished, the judicial process has broken down.

[77] *Supra,* Chapter IV, §2 (E).

[78] SCHRAMM, PIEDPOUDRE COURTS (1928).

Tracing the *piedpoudre,* or *dustyfoot,* court back to the special court established each fair day in England during the middle ages, Schramm notes that its purpose was originally to provide a petty claims tribunal convenient to many litigants and capable of operating with a dispatch amenable to the movements of many transitory suitors, so that their disputes might be adjusted even before the dust of travel fell from their feet. In the surging of modern population in and out of metropolitan areas, Schramm notes a similar need.[79]

Reviewing the legal machinery, Schramm notes the many overlapping courts[80] and the large number of judges empowered to act: 311 in Allegheny County alone, or 391 if the mayors, burgesses, and police magistrates were included.[81] There was no current list of all these judges extant.

Describing the handling of claims not exceeding $300, Schramm found that squires freely refused to accept cases where neither party was able to put up the costs, despite a statutory mandate requiring acceptance of all cases.[82] The process of "calling the list" of 150 or 200 cases in the county court, with automatic continuances upon request, was depressingly familiar to the present writer. So, also, was the passage describing the discontinuance, because of at-

[79] For history of the development of the justice of the peace system, see BEARD, THE OFFICE OF JUSTICE OF THE PEACE IN ENGLAND AND ITS ORIGIN AND DEVELOPMENT (1904).

[80] SCHRAMM, *op. cit. supra,* at 10, chart fig. 1 at 11 (state courts); Allegheny County Courts at 16; fig. 2 at 17. *Id.* at 22-24: "Obviously, there is no unity of administration possible with so large a number in authority with uncorrelated procedure. . . . The sponsors of the so-called Metropolitan Plan insist that in Allegheny County the general governmental system . . . needs reorganization; to this we wish to add and emphasize that the administration of justice in the country . . . demands immediate and thorough investigation as a basis for reorganization," citing REPORT OF THE COMMISSION TO STUDY MUNICIPAL CONSOLIDATION IN COUNTIES OF THE SECOND CLASS TO THE GOVERNOR AND GENERAL ASSEMBLY (Feb. 15, 1927) and 8 J. AM. JUD. SOC'Y 191 (1925).

[81] SCHRAMM, *op. cit. supra,* at 22.

[82] *Id.* at 26, 93. And see Maguire, *Poverty and Civil Litigation,* 36 HARV. L. REV. 361, 402 (1923).

torneys' objections, of the practice of calling dilatory parties before the court to clear up the list of delayed cases.[83]

Schramm compares the simplicity and swiftness of the then new county court with the procedure in the Court of Common Pleas in Philadelphia, which he found full of meaningless confusion and delay. He noted with concern, however, the tendency of the county court to follow in the footsteps of the court next above it by developing a formalistic ritual of its own, rather than to fulfill its original purpose of becoming an informal, prompt, and effective "piedpoudre court."[84]

Schramm noted and commented upon one factor, important to us, which is not noted elsewhere except in the sociological literature, so far as this writer can learn: the effect of urbanizing tendencies upon the performance of courts within the entire area, even outside the metropolitan area—an instance of the "magnetizing" influence of the metropolis noted in the introductory chapters.[85]

With respect to civil cases, he found that judgment was awarded by default in 97.4 per cent of his sampling of 1,000 cases.[86] The vast majority of cases (81.5 per cent) were brought before urban rather than rural squires, though the rural areas contained almost half the population of the county.[87]

[83] *Id.* at 31, 32. Compare *In re* Huff, 352 Mich. 402, 91 NW 2d 613 (1958). In Detroit, the Circuit Court of Wayne County's "no progress" docket exhibits an efficient method of solving the problem. See DETROIT STUDY 196.

[84] SCHRAMM, *op. cit. supra* note 78, at 33.

[85] *Id.* at 48, and *supra* at 8-9.

[86] SCHRAMM, *op. cit. supra,* at 47. Compare DETROIT STODY 116, 131-35.

[87] SCHRAMM, *op. cit. supra,* at 49. "While the population of the four cities in the county is only a trifle more than one-half of the entire County, 46 aldermen had 13,781 cases of the 16,341 appealed, or 81.5 per cent, and the 242 justices of the peace had only 2,560 cases, or 18.5 of the total. . . . It may be argued that appeals are easier to file from an urban alderman's office than from that of a country squire. . . . from all the evidence . . . it seems evident that the aldermen secure the great bulk of this litigation . . . the writer . . . was impressed with the concentration of cases in a few downtown aldermen's offices. . . ." (Note: the aldermen are city squires, the term applied to justices of the peace in the cities.)

He describes the squire as a "mere fee-collecting, time-delaying automaton."[88]

With respect to cases appealed to the county court, Schramm came up with one paradoxical bit of material about jury trials. Though the line of least resistance was *against* use of juries (waived, if no demand), he found a marked trend *towards* jury trials.[89]

With respect to disposition of appeals, he notes that in more than two-thirds of cases appealed to the county court, the defendant was finally victorious—a dramatic contrast with the findings as to results of cases originally brought before the squire, where the defendant won in less than 1 per cent of the cases appealed. "Surely there is something wrong somewhere in the system."[90]

Schramm's conclusions:

1. The squire's system is unadapted to the trial of civil litigation in our modern industrial society. It has developed into an automatic, time-delaying, fee-collecting mechanism, and tends to destroy respect for the judiciary among the people.
2. The county court which was organized to offset and minimize the baleful effects of the squire's system and to provide a swift, sure, informal and inexpensive method of appeal, by being a real piedpoudre or small claims court, has not become such a court. . . .[91]

He recommends abolishing or curtailing the jurisdiction of the squire, abolishing the fee system, integrating the administration of all justice courts in the area, eliminating partisanship, requiring legal qualifications, and adapting the county court to its real function, that of handling small claims.[92]

Connecticut court studies

Judge Charles E. Clark, formerly Dean of Yale Law School, when professor at the school in 1928 reported on the

[88] *Id.* at 52.
[89] *Id.* at 71 *et seq.*
[90] *Id.* at 98 and see discussion beginning at 84.
[91] *Id.* at 106.
[92] *Id.* at 107 *et seq.*

beginning of a series of experiments in court survey research which later developed into several major projects.[93] The first report covered nearly 9,000 cases in trial courts of general jurisdiction in three Connecticut counties. The purpose was to experiment towards development of adequate statistical information on court business, to aid in evaluating administration, structure, and policy.

In this study, it was found that divorce cases were most numerous, comprising over one-fourth of total caseload. In 94 per cent of these cases, the divorce was granted. Most were tried within three to six months of commencement of litigation, practically all of them within a year, practically none of them in contested proceedings.

Next most numerous were negligence cases involving traffic accidents: 1,325 actions brought, only 207 of which resulted in a contested trial, with 119 victories for plaintiff, 78 for defendants. "Apparently the chief function of the court," comments Clark, "was to afford a place for the parties to arrange a settlement." Uncontested foreclosures, contract, and debt cases constituted the other large categories of business. As to the latter, Clark points out that the "function of the court to act as a collection agency was quite apparent." Data on the small use of juries, its negligible effect on the general run of dispositions, are worthy of our note.[94]

Small claims and conciliation courts

The success of the Chicago Municipal Court,[95] and the wide public interest in *Justice and the Poor* and other studies accelerated interest in legal circles concerned with

[93] Clark, *An Experiment in Studying the Business of Courts of a State,* 14 A.B.A.J. 318 (1928).

[94] And see also Clark, *Yale Study of Connecticut Courts,* 15 A.B.A.J. 326-27 (1929).

[95] A good description may be found at 1 J. AM. JUD. SOC'Y 133-47 (1918) in an article captioned *Success of Organized Court,* which includes a discussion of the Chicago Municipal Court.

improvement of courts of inferior jurisdiction. Some New York judges expressed resentment towards the Smith study.[96] A group of New York lawyers and other community leaders, however, developed a plan for a "poor man's court" for New York, designed to give destitute litigants the benefit of the special skills of lawyers and judges, as they felt arbitration could not.[97] In Chicago, a plan was developed to consolidate all the Chicago courts into a single circuit court with its own chief justice. This plan went down to defeat with the rest of a proposed judicial constitutional reform for Illinois.[98]

A good survey of the incidence of small claims courts in the United States as of 1920 may be found in two articles in the *Columbia Law Review*. In the latter of the two cited notes,[99] concern is expressed over the trend to permit claim-

[96] *Court Resents Criticism,* 3 J. AM. JUD. SOC'Y 154 (1920).

[97] *Necessary Courts for Large Cities,* 11 VA. L. REG. (n.s.) 507 (1925).

[98] 6 J. AM. JUD. SOC'Y 3-6 (1922). The courts proposed to be merged were: circuit court, superior court, municipal court, probate court, criminal court, county court, and the city court of Chicago Heights. There were eighty judges then in those courts, including nine who would have been made permanent judges of the new appellate court had the plan gone into effect. The article contains an interesting description of the compromise plan arrived at after incumbent judges registered objections to the "metropolitan trial court plan" as proposed by the American Judicature Society. See Appendix B *infra.*

[99] 20 COLUM. L. REV. 901-06 (1920); 21 COLUM. L. REV. 481-82 (1921). The periodical literature of the decade reflects the interest of the profession in municipal, small claims, and conciliation courts. See, for example, *Why Tolerate Inferior Courts?,* 4 J. AM. JUD. SOC'Y 22-24 (1920); *Report of Small Claims and Conciliations Procedure,* 10 A.B.A.J. 828-32 (1924); *Business Principals in City Court,* 7 J. AM. JUD. SOC'Y 166-75 (7924); Ryan, *Shall Municipal Courts with Limited Concurrent Jurisdiction with Circuit Courts Be Abolished?* 9 MARQ. L. REV. 33 (1924); *Ohio Conciliation Courts,* 12 A.B.A.J. 500 (1926); *Municipal Court of New York,* 12 J. AM. JUD. SOC'Y 116 (1928); Clark & Connell, *The Working of the Hartford Small Claims Court,* 3 CONN. B.J. 123-29 (1929).

In 14 J. AM. JUD. SOC'Y 15-16 (1930) may be found a most interesting account of a survey of the municipal court of Philadelphia by the Bureau of Municipal Research, financed by a foundation. The court was created in 1912 "when there was no higher conception in judicial organization than to create a new court of special powers to perform neglected functions. . . . Starting with . . . narrower jurisdiction, the Philadelphia court rapidly expanded its volume of work, until, with no more than ten judges, it had over five hundred on its payroll. B. . . . its civil jurisdiction was raised to $2,500.

ants in small claims cases to be represented by other than qualified lawyers. In certain states, lawyers were actually excluded from such courts.

Other special types of courts

Lou's classic study of juvenile courts appeared in 1927.[100] The growth of juvenile courts is basic to our study of special metropolitan court problems, since in general it has been in metropolitan areas that the full-fledged juvenile court, with its battery of specialized services and its liaison with surrounding noncourt child-serving agencies, has developed.[101] Certain courts of limited criminal jurisdiction began, in metropolitan areas, to establish specialized divisions or dockets geared, as the juvenile courts are geared, towards reclaiming offenders. See, for example, an article describing the Pittsburgh "morals court," "with no more legal basis than the magistrate's court," with a caseload of 14,000 cases annually, and with an approach geared to maximum cooperation with various social and community agencies offering assistance in the rehabilitation of young offenders.[102]

By the twenties, also, the concept of the "family court" was beginning to make itself widely felt. An article by E. F. Waite in the *Minnesota Law Review* in 1921 contains a good survey of various statutes then in force providing a single tribunal for handling desertion and nonsupport, illegitimacy, juvenile delinquency, and neglect, adoption,

---

Its most extensive and dramatic field was developed in the case of juveniles and minors. . . , in adoption, domestic relations, and misdemeanors. . . .

"The present survey appears . . . competent. . . . But it will fall short . . . if it does not present . . . a plan for wiping out competition between local tribunals by the establishment of one trial court with functional divisions and control through a council of judges who are heads of divisions."

[100] Lou, Juvenile Courts in the United States (1927).

[101] *Id.* at 33 n. 1. See, for example the list of juvenile courts created by special laws to serve large cities or counties.

[102] 12 J. Crim. L. 412-15 (1921).

divorce, and alimony, or any partial combination of such cases.[103]

General trends in court reform literature

During this period, there was manifestation of interest in unification of courts on a statewide as well as a citywide basis, as a method for improving judicial administration.[104] Attention was focused on procedural aspects of judicial ad-administration as well: rule-making and other powers of judges,[105] the use of specialized facilities to assist the trial court in certain types of cases,[106] and, of particular interest to us, the development of special assignment and judicial

[103] Waite, *Courts of Domestic Relations,* 5 MINN. L. REV. 161 (1921). See also, *Courts of Conciliation,* 52 AM. L. REV. 617-20 (1918); *Domestic Relations Court of Cincinnati,* 3 U. CINC. L. REV. 444 (1929).

[104] Kales, *The English Judicature Acts: Concise Description of Statutes Which Unified Numerous Courts,* 4 J. AM. JUD. SOC'Y 133 (1921); Wilcox, *Simplifiying the Organization of the Courts of the State,* 9 MARQ. L. REV. 25 (1924), but see a spirited rebuttal in the same issue at 33: Ryan, *Shall Municipal Courts Which Have Limited Concurrent Jurisdiction with the Circuit Courts Be Abolished?; Missouri Judicial System Unified in Revised Constitution,* 7 J. AM. JUD. SOC'Y 117 (1923); Miller, *Would Improve Iowa Courts,* 7 J. AM. JUD. SOC'Y 17 (1923) (address by president of Iowa Bar Association); *Suggestions for Improving Court Procedure in Texas,* 1 TEX. L. REV. 67-75 (1922); *Texas Unifies Trial Courts,* 11 J. AM. JUD. SOC'Y 38 (judicial districts, assignment of judges under presiding judge, judicial conference) (1927); Goodrich, *Judicial Council for Michigan,* 6 MICH. S.B.J. 201 (1927); *Detroit Circuit Court Integrated,* 14 AM. JUD. SOC'Y 175 (1931) (describes the pre-trial system, the Friend of the Court, as well as the development of the strong presiding judge); *Detroit's Unified Criminal Court,* 14 J. AM. JUD. SOC'Y 180 (1931); *California Judicial Council Unifies California Courts,* 12 J. AM. JUD. SOC'Y 18 (1928).

[105] Pound, *A Bibliography of Procedural Reform; Including Organization of Courts,* 5 MASS. L.Q. 332-45 (1920); *Morgan, Judicial Regulation of Court Procedure,* 2 MINN. L. REV. 81-96 (1918); Taft, *Possible and Needed Reforms in Administration of Justice in Federal Courts,* 8 A.B.A.J. 601 (1922), see also 625 (comments on article); Webster, *The Courts and Procedural Reform,* 6 MICH. *S.B.J.* 191-201 (1927); Sunderland, *An Appraisal of the English Procedure,* 24 MICH. L. *Rev.* 109-29 (1925). And see, generally, Pound, *Judicial Power,* 35 HARV. L. REV. 787-96 (1922); Potter, *Judicial Power in the United States,* 27 MICH. L. REV. 1-21 (1928); 167-90 (1928); 285-313 (1929).

[106] Adler, *Medical Science and Criminal Justice,* in THE CLEVELAND CRIME SURVEY 349 *et seq.;* Bliss, *Mental Disorder, Crime and the Law,* in THE MISSOURI CRIME SURVEY 399 *et seq.;* Singer, *The Deranged or Defective Delinquent,* in THE ILLINOIS CRIME SURVEY 737 *et seq.;* Perkins, *The Need for Socializing Court Procedure in Commitments to the State Training Schools*

administrative systems to obtain prompt and orderly attention to cases in large metropolitan trial court systems.[107]

f. Comment on Opinion Concerning Metropolitan Court Problems by the End of the Twenties

Summing up the purport of the materials available to the student of metropolitan court problems by the end of the twenties, we have found a good deal of work done on the general problem of judicial administration, motivated by judicial and legal recognition of public dissatisfaction with the operation of courts, and by their recognition of the duty of the legal profession to bring the actuality closer to the high ideal demanded of the trial court by both the general public and the profession itself.

In general, most observers agreed that American courts were working under several disadvantages inherent in their structure and control: for example, though required to discharge the same functions as the English courts on which they were patterned, many American state courts were stripped of much of the British judge's power to exercise authoritative control over the conduct of the judicial process. Legislatures sought by this means to avoid autocratic control by a small professional elite, which was repugnant to those desiring to develop true democratic processes in a heterogeneous community. But thereby they had also eliminated the prompt efficiency possible in a court system operated entirely by an authoritative group of ex-

---

for the Feeble-Minded, 26 J. CRIM. L. 589 *et. seq.* (1926); Calhoun, *Domestic Relations Courts,* 7 ST. LOUIS LAW REV. 152 (1922); *Detroit Circuit Court Integrated* 14 J. AM. JUD. SOC'Y 175 (business-manager judge) 177 (Friend of Court: "debunking alimony applications") (1931).

107 Powell, (Cleveland assignment system) *Justice without Denial or Delay,* 10 A.B.A.J. 188 (1924); *High Efficiency in Cleveland Court,* 11 J. AM. JUD. SOC'Y (1927); PRELIMINARY REPORT OF SPECIAL COMMITTEE ON CONGESTED CALENDARS, PROCEEDING OF BAR ASSOCIATION OF CITY OF NEW YORK 379-97 (1926); *Time to Speed Up,* 8 A.B.A.J. 64 (1922) (discussing delay of 2-5 years in St. Louis trial courts); Cain, *Laws' Delays and Proposed Remedies,* 90 CENT. L.J. 333-42 (1920).

perts fully in control of the system and free from the questions and criticisms of the masses.

Other problems, it was perceived, confronted the American court system because of changing concepts regarding its function: the movement towards individualized justice raised questions concerning the role of the judge as an adjuster of personal relations and a rehabilitator of the socially disadvantaged as well as, or perhaps in place of, a decider of conflicts presented through the adversary process alone. Writers about court problems in the late twenties had not reached consensus on the proper role of the trial court, though there was by that time a developing trend to encourage benign and even therapeutic handling of juvenile cases, and to tolerate the beginnings of a trend towards development of specialized courts, such as family courts, staffed by judges with sympathy and special knowledge of such cases and by administrative aides with various skills for diagnosing and solving litigants' problems.

In general, court reform movements in this period centered about restoration of rule-making power to judges, examination of methods for recruiting judges, unification of courts on a statewide basis, and consideration of various methods for dealing with "delay," but the catch phrase, "delay," then, as now, meant all things to all lawyers, and has been variously used to describe observers' conclusions towards the court structure, the qualifications of the judiciary, the industry or contentiousness of trial counsel, or the administrative machinery by which the court's business is done.

The problems of metropolitan courts had received a good deal of thoughtful and professional attention by the end of the twenties. The movement of population into teeming metropolitan centers had helped to focus public attention upon the problem of judicial administration as such, particularly in the areas of criminal cases and of small claims matters and other litigation involving the indigent. It was perceived by Smith and Schramm, among others, that the public image of justice as a guarantor of fair play for everyone is essential to our concept of a working democracy. Their studies show the disadvantages of a multiplicity of courts, staffed by unqualified judges, administered without business efficiency, and operated on a push-button basis with no real effort to safeguard rights or to take cognizance of the real situation of indigent or near-indigent litigants.

Attention to small claims courts was general, but opinion as to corrective measures was divided between those who recommended a conciliation court, in essence a case-settling device administered by a judge, and those who recommended a municipal court as such. Both devices were popular, and the Municipal Court of Chicago was, in this period, probably the most successful and widely respected achievement in court reform. It is notable that this court made use of unification on a citywide basis, that it worked with highly qualified judges, and that it developed businesslike administrative methods for assigning cases, for ordering their progress, and for seeing that all comers found justice evenhanded.

Among the great landmarks in the literature of court reform are the three crime surveys, and these are landmarks also for the student of the metropolitan court's special problems. The multiplicity of courts and of cases in a metropolis causes problems, particularly to the prosecution, exhibited in lack of consistent responsible control of large staffs with a heavy workload. These same conditions not only handicap the court, but are encountered in the court also. The result is ineffectual and results in superficial routine contact with each case, rather than a planned and skillful application of the case for the prosecution, with the rights of the defendant safeguarded adequately, but not to the extent of paralyzing the trial process. For the metropolitan court student, it is interesting that the crime studies show in detail how the special sociological conditions found in the metropolis (e.g., mobility, organized crime, social maladjustment of disadvantaged individuals) further confuse and confound the metropolitan court in its attempts to deal with the tremendous criminal caseload.

That delay in reaching the cases is a problem, all observers agree. They do not agree on the cause of the delay nor how to solve the problem. One theory is that metropolitan courts are handicapped most because they must use a mechanism designed for another generation and another way of life. Another is that the basic system is healthy enough, justice being justice whether on the prairie or on Times Square, if only the proper people were given the proper authority to operate the mechanism.

Some writers found the jury outmoded and in the way, others regarded its threatened disappearance as a grave omen, and still others viewed with alarm the steady growth of the use of juries. Some desired to eliminate lawyers from participation in certain types of cases—juvenile and small claims cases, for example; others regarded lack of participation by lawyers in all cases whatsoever as one of the worst symptoms of malfunctioning in metropolitan courts.

These differences in evaluation seem symptomatic of a lack of agreement as to the basic role of the metropolitan trial court. One writer put his finger on the crux of the disagreement: To what extent, he asked, can justice be individualized without invading the constitutional rights of due process?[108]

Section 4. The Thirties

a. The Johns Hopkins Studies

A number of court studies were undertaken at Johns Hopkins University in the thirties. One of them, a study by

[108] Waite, *How Far Can Court Procedure Be Socialized Without Impairing Individual Rights?* 12 J. Crim. Law & Criminology 339 (1921).

William J. Blackburn, Jr., of the administration of justice in the Columbus, Ohio, metropolitan area, is especially useful to the present inquiry.[109] The Columbus area is one of unusual geographic and cultural stability.[110] For this reason, it provides an interesting contrast to, say, Detroit, with its wide and strong cultural and racial tensions. Blackburn mounted factual material, directly observed, on a framework of data obtained by legal and by some sociological research. Emphasis is placed upon the justice of the peace system outside the city,[111] for which Blackburn suggests a unified minor county court.[112] He concludes the Municipal Court has need for vigorous administrative supervision by a presiding judge, and stresses liaison between court and prosecutor together with improvement in the offices of public defender and adult probation. As have all other studies of criminal justice, this one dwells on the major role played by the police in conditioning the climate of justice in a large city.[113]

In the court of common pleas (the general trial court), functional organization was found overlapping and inefficient, and need was felt for a modern and efficient system of recording, bookkeeping, and reporting. The domestic relations court is described, and fuller use of its therapeutic philosophy recommended. A related recommendation is that for wider and more expertly supervised use of adult probation and more attention to the need for counsel in criminal cases. The Columbus court at that time had no delay problem worthy of the term as we now use it—median time interval from filing of transcript to termination of case was

[109] BLACKBURN, THE ADMINISTRATION OF CRIMINAL JUSTICE IN FRANKLIN COUNTY, OHIO (1935).

[110] *Id.* at 14-15.

[111] *Id.* at 243: "tangled . . . lack of system, lack of cooperation, overlapping jurisdiction, and sometimes distinctly mercenary atmosphere."

[112] *Id.* at 244, citing *Unification of the Judiciary,* J. AM. JUD. SOC'Y (1927 and 1928).

[113] *Id.* at 246.

41 days for those who pled guilty and 62 days for those tried and convicted.[114] But, *caveat,* most criminal defendants in Columbus, as elsewhere, were not disposed of by means of trial, but pled guilty: more than 85 per cent throughout Franklin County.[115]

A statistical study of *Criminal Actions in the Common Pleas Courts of Ohio,*[116] based on data collected for the first six months of 1930 by court officials on authority of the Judicial Council of Ohio, contains some general comment of interest to us, as well as a rich source of statistical information for the period. Gehlke notes that although these statistics show differences between urban and rural justice, there is nothing in the figures to indicate which kind of justice is "superior."[117]

He challenges the concept that the court is an appropriate agency to determine the treatment of the offender.

> Certainly there is nothing known about the way men's minds work which would give any aid or comfort to those who believe that a mere balancing of punishment against crime is now or has been effective.[118]

Another conclusion of the Gehlke study, underlining that of Blackburn just commented on, is that "justice of the trial is the exception, justice of the conference the rule. Of the 7,505 defendants, just 772 were tried."[119] And, commenting on the disuse of the elaborate safeguards except in about 10 per cent of the cases, he points out:

> . . . we have turned the operation of the courts over to one elected official, the prosecutor. . . . Whereas another elected official of the court, the judge, functions pretty largely in the glare of the court

[114] *Id.* at 97.
[115] *Id.* at 249. Compare DETROIT STUDY 216; LOS ANGELES STUDY 313.
[116] GEHLKE, CRIMINAL ACTIONS IN THE COMMON PLEAS COURTS OF OHIO 290 (1936).
[117] *Id.* at 289. "The ultimate aim of courts is justice. Justice, like truth, is an eternal question."
[118] *Id.* at 290.
[119] *Ibid.*

room, the prosecutor may make his secret way for the great bulk of the cases.[120]

Gehlke, who is not a lawyer, comments from basic premises not acceptable to most lawyers, including this writer. Attention is called, however, to the fact that Gehlke, like several other writers in this field, notes that the prosecutor is forced to take sole responsibility for prosecution and disposition of the great mass of criminal cases. Working closely with prosecutors, this writer knows they merit respect for conscientious application to duty and principle. Nevertheless, the problem exists: the traditional safeguards of due process are in fact not operating in criminal cases. Instead, most of these cases proceed from charge to final disposition with no critical evaluation and no challenge of the state's case. This is not the way it is supposed to work. Compare Chapter IV of the *Detroit Study.*

The Johns Hopkins studies also include the famous Maryland and Ohio divorce studies of Marshall and May,[121] which demonstrated many significant things, including the fact that almost no divorce cases involve any real adversary proceeding—or, to put it another way, the court, though responsible for terminating the marriage and safeguarding the welfare of the children, in actuality almost never has facts before it upon which knowledgeable decision can be based.[122] The authors called attention to the extreme variations from one community to another in all aspects of divorce litigation, inexplicable except in terms of different community attitudes. These studies are among the few to point out that the dynamics of timing is evaluated in accordance with the basic philosophy of the observer; one's conclusion regarding the proper timing of divorce litigation depends on whether one favors quick divorce with no real inquiry by

[120] *Id.* at 291.

[121] MARSHALL & MAY, THE DIVORCE COURT, 2 vols. (1932).

[122] See, for example *id.,* vol. I at 226: of 3,306 cases filed in Maryland in 1929, there were a total of less than 150 contests.

the court. When does proper attention to the case leave off and "delay" begin? It depends on who is observing.[123]

b. The Yale Studies of Clark and Shulman

In 1937, the Yale Law School published a part of the results of a ten-year factual study in depth which its faculty had been making in Connecticut courts during that period. This was an experimental study of the "day to day activities of various selected trial courts," with the emphasis upon the activity of the court as a governmental unit.[124] The range and complexity of this detailed presentation permits of no one-sentence generalization, save as it may be identified as a major reference resource for any student of the operation of metropolitan trial courts. Its findings include total caseload, types of cases, and duration of cases, with special emphasis on use of juries and certain special categories of cases.

c. Lepawsky's Chicago Study

"Volume, variety and expansion are the outstanding features of metropolitan judicial work," observes Albert Lepawsky in his study of the judicial system of Metropolitan Chicago.[125]

> The courts of the Chicago area are mainly concerned with traffic violations, minor business claims, and family problems . . . many cases are disposed of merely by the payment of a fine before the cashier's cage, by a proceeding which does not even require parties to appear in court, or by a probation officer's visit at the home of a delinquent

[123] See, for example, INSTITUTE OF JUDICIAL ADMINISTRATION, DELAY AND CONGESTION IN THE SUPERIOR COURT OF MARICOPA COUNTY, ARIZONA, A SURVEY (1955) [hereinafter cited as PHOENIX STUDY] at 27, where it is recommended that since divorce cases seldom involve a serious contest as to whether a divorce should be granted, it would improve judicial administration to require the filing of affidavits regarding property and income, thus enabling the court to dispense with any trial at all in the vast bulk of such cases.

[124] CLARK & SHULMAN, A STUDY OF LAW ADMINISTRATION IN CONNECTICUT (1937).

[125] LEPAWSKY, THE JUDICIAL SYSTEM OF METROPOLITAN CHICAGO 1 (1932).

youth. The orthodox conception of judicial organization is an orderly system of lesser powers and appellate authorities. But in the Chicago region we find, instead, a confusing array of overlapping courts.[126]

Lepawsky's view is that self-government should be given to the metropolitan area, which could then design a court structure in terms of the pattern of its special problems. Details of court organization should be worked out by judicial and not by legislative authority, he holds.[127] Unlike the Yale studies, which are restricted to operational data, the Lepawsky study utilizes research techniques from several professions to place the Chicago metropolitan district in its political and cultural setting, then moves on to describe and analyze the outstanding features of its judicial system as seen in action. Outside the contemporary studies undertaken by the Section of Judicial Administration for the specific purpose of examining the special problems of metropolitan courts, the Lepawsky study is the only major effort known which is also focused on the metropolitan court system as a function of the metropolitan community.

d. General Comment

Court survey research reached a zenith of sorts in the thirties, with the constellation of studies carried on at Yale and at Johns Hopkins. This writer, a student at Yale Law School during the early thirties, was like many other students of the period caught up in the intellectual excitement of the attempt to see clearly the dynamics of judicial administration in action. Old class notebooks, even in such classes as torts and procedure, indicate that the sense of large discovery with which Dean Clark and Professor Shulman were then burning tended to permeate the classrooms and commons rooms no matter what the subject at hand.

126 *Ibid.*
127 *Id.* at 104-05.

Throughout the task of preparing this report, this writer has had the repeated experience of creating some gem of a conclusion here, some jewel of implication there, with a feeling of triumph and insight—only to find the identical treasure, more clearly and succinctly stated, tucked away in some footnote of Clark's or Shulman's, some entirely unrelated article of Hamilton's or Arnold's—or, most eerie of all—even in an article prepared by a research associate working on the traffic studies with Underhill Moore. Court survey research was in the air we breathed. *Lux et veritas!*

Even at our most manic, however, we felt a healthy respect for the necessity of keeping in central focus the qualitative factor—the evaluative grain of salt without which large-scale fact studies are likely to prove more destructive than helpful.

Please note again that the grand spectacular studies of the thirties—cut down in their splendor by the Depression and not yet duplicated in scope, creativity, or capital investment—were all conducted by seasoned professionals who continually warned against the dangerous cutting edge of the statistical tool.

We have pride in the Anglo-Saxon ideal of a fair trial for Everyman, with each accorded his day in court, the judge so conducting the procedures that truth emerges triumphant from the adversary process. But Gehlke points out that this ideal is not realized by a system of criminal trials in which few criminal defendants are tried, a system in which the real course and outcome of each case is decided by the prosecutor, outside the system of checks and balances supposed to safeguard the trial process, and beyond the reach of the judge in all but a handful of cases. In divorce actions, as Marshall and May demonstrated, almost all the divorce cases that go to final decree are uncontested, so that the court has no opportunity to know the case, its sole duty being to give official sanction to what the plaintiff has asked for. Lepawsky shows that Chicago courts are mainly concerned with traffic, small claims, and family problems, and calls attention to the fact that in all these categories the full-scale trial is a very rare bird indeed. Clark and Shulman had found the Connecticut trial courts debt-collecting, mortgage-enforcing, compensation-awarding, marriage-dissolution-approving agencies, rather than case-trying agencies. These conclusions fortified those of earlier studies by Smith and Schramm, which had shown small claims and petty misdemeanor litigation to be almost entirely a push-button performance.

By the end of the thirties, then, there was ample factual material in which the problems of trial courts, and particularly metropolitan trial courts, had been exhibited. Much of this material demonstrated the extent to which the vast caseloads of Metropolis are disposed of *other* than by trial. Basic questions, then, concerning the role of the trial court and the state of health of the ideal of due process had been raised. These questions were thought to loom largest in metropolitan areas, not only because of the large proportion of the total caseload carried by metropolitan courts, but also because the metropolitan environment makes conditions of litigation there such as to require special attention to safeguard due process, to protect both the individual and the community.[128]

[128] See also MORSE & BEATTIE, THE ADMINISTRATION OF CRIMINAL JUSTICE IN OREGON (1932); Shaw & McKay, *Social Factors in Juvenile Delinquency* in U.S. NATIONAL COMMISSION ON LAW OBSERVANCE AND ENFORCEMENT, REPORT ON THE CAUSES OF CRIME, (vol. 13, pt. 2 1931); Sunderland, *The Efficiency of Justices' Courts in Michigan* in 4 MICH. JUDICIAL COUNCIL REPORT at 169-172 (1934).

The various publications of the Yale studies are cited in footnotes in the introductory chapter of CLARK & SHULMAN, *op. cit. supra* note 124. The various publications in the Johns Hopkins series are listed in the back pages of GEHLKE, *op. cit. supra* note 116.

Of special interest to this study are the two studies of Paul J. Douglass for the Johns Hopkins series: THE JUSTICE OF THE PEACE COURTS OF HAMILTON COUNTY, conclusions at pp. 109 *et seq.* (1932); and THE MAYORS' COURTS OF HAMILTON COUNTY, OHIO (1933). See also MARTIN, THE WAIVER OF JURY TRIAL IN CRIMINAL CASES IN OHIO (1933).

Section 5. The Forties

a. Warren's *Traffic Courts*

In 1942 appeared the report of an extensive study of traffic courts prepared by George Warren of the Trenton, New Jersey, bar for the National Committee on Traffic Law Enforcement.[129] His research technique included questionnaires, correspondence, and a field period of a year. His recommendations and conclusions were scrutinized by the members of the committee, and his report was approved by a number of national organizations.[130] The Warren study was successful in focusing wide public attention, both in the legal profession and elsewhere, upon the importance of police courts and justice of peace courts in formulating the public image of justice as dispensed by American courts.[131]

He proposed a statewide traffic court, organized on a flexible district basis, with qualified and especially trained judges devoting full time to traffic cases. This court was to be part of a statewide unified court, if possible. In addition to considerable financial economies, he suggests that this type of judicial organization would bring about: (1) good personnel, (2) impartiality, (3) availability, (4) speedy procedure, (5) dignity, (6) predictability, and (7) accountability. These are the indispensable prerequisites for a good court system, he says.[132] His plan presupposes the use of a violations bureau, and includes the approximation of the separate traffic court, in sparsely populated areas or in areas where the unified court plan is not acceptable, by means of a distinct

[129] WARREN, TRAFFIC COURTS (1942).

[130] National Conference of Judicial Councils, American Bar Association and its sections of Judicial Administration and of Criminal Law, and later, the International Association of Chiefs of Police.

[131] See comment, VANDERBILT, MINIMUM STANDARDS at xxv: "For the first time it came to be realized that for almost all of our citizens those local courts of first instance are in fact the courts of first and last resort. It is in these courts that most of our citizens gain their ideas of American justice and acquire—or lose—their respect for law."

[132] WARREN, *op. cit supra,* at 238.

docket heard apart from other criminal violations as a separate session of court.[133]

The Warren study was followed by the establishment of a separate committee on traffic courts within the American Bar Association. Through the work of this committee, which has specialized in the conducting of short-range studies for interested communities and in the awarding of certificates for outstanding courts, the handling of traffic cases in many cities has been modernized along the lines of the Warren recommendation. In terms of active results, the Warren study is an outstanding accomplishment.

b. Vanderbilt's Study: *Minimum Standards*

In 1940, the Section of Judicial Administration of the American Bar Association, working with the Special Committee on Improving the Administration of Justice, initiated the broad program of which the present report is a part, in response to the adoption by the American Bar Association in 1938 of the minimum standards of judicial administration. Its first major effort was a broad factual survey in the field of procedural reform, involving members of the faculties of several law schools and large numbers of judges and lawyers.[134] The report, prepared under the direction of the late Chief Justice Arthur T. Vanderbilt of New Jersey and edited by him,[135] is a survey of the extent to which the standards accepted by the American Bar Association as essential have been accepted throughout the United States.

Its major categories include judicial selection, conduct, and tenure; managing the business of the courts; judicial regulation of proceedings by rule-making; selection and service of juries; pretrial conferences; traffic and justice of peace courts; evidence; appellate practice; and state administrative agencies and tribunals.

[133] *Id.* at 236-37.
[134] VANDERBILT, MINIMUM STANDARDS at xxvi.
[135] *Ibid.*

Through the use of annual questionnaires distributed to committeemen in each state, the Section of Judicial Administration has sought to maintain the level of data contained in the monumental *Minimum Standards* by preparing annual reports indicating for each year the progress made in all states towards the standards adopted by the American Bar Association as constituting the minimum essential for proper judicial administration.[136]

c. Other References from the Forties

In 1940, Dean Pound published his *Organization of Courts,* outlining the development of American court systems, reviewing present defects, and setting forth principles for and an outline of a modern organization, comprising a statewide unified court system concentrating all judicial power in one court, with local units, procedures, and personnel subject exclusively to the authority of the Chief Justice. The system he outlined would be alterable from time to time by court rule. Special divisions, for example, could be set up for certain categories of cases such as family and traffic cases.[137]

During the same decade, Professor Edson R. Sunderland of the University of Michigan continued his work in judicial administration, which included a series of fact studies of the workings of justice of the peace courts and of courts dealing with mental cases. The latter is especially notable.[138]

A good small study is Porter's inquiry into the problems

[136] The latest, at time of writing, is JUSTICE CALLING, 1958, A.B.A., Section of Judicial Administration (4th ed. 1958). And see THE IMPROVEMENT OF THE ADMINISTRATION OF JUSTICE, a Handbook prepared by the Section of Judicial Administration (3d ed. 1952). As set forth at p. 3 therein, the handbook was designed to supplement the information contained in MINIMUM STANDARDS. In recent years, the annual reports have served the same purpose, indicating from time to time the extent to which the standards have been adopted.

[137] POUND, ORGANIZATION OF COURTS (1940). See ch. 8, pp. 273 *et seq.*, for recommendations.

[138] By Sunderland: *A Study of Justices of the Peace and Other Minor Courts: Requisites for an Adequate State-wide Minor Court System,* 15 MICH. JUDICIAL COUNCIL REPORT 53-118 (1945); *Territorial Jurisdiction of*

of the Cincinnati courts. In a frank and forthright report, he stated that he found: (1) too many judges for the caseload; (2) too many court employees; (3) underworked, overpaid court appraisers; (4) a system of judicial rotation productive of divergence in handling cases, opportunistic shifting, and lack of expertise with regard to special types of cases; (5) a bail bond system undermined by excessive forfeitures; (6) a lack of pretrial procedure; (7) indigent defendants represented by appointed attorneys unequal to their opponents on the prosecuting side; (7) an unjudicial atmosphere in the municipal criminal courts, produced by such habits as rude and familiar treatment of defendants, witnesses, and spectators; sloppy dress and demeanor of court clerks; crowding of spectators behind the bench; inadequate time for hearings because of desire for speed; (8) too lenient municipal judges in gambling and traffic cases; (9) lack of effective organization. Porter, then a third-year student at Harvard Law School, placed the responsibility for these defects on political necessity and the passivism of the bar.[139]

A well-known British monograph, Jackson's *Machinery of Justice in England,* appeared in 1940. Its chapter on "The Outlook for Reform" is perhaps especially relevant, but the entire volume is indispensable.[140]

Minor Courts, 29 J. AM. JUD. SOC'Y 147-55 (1946); *Subject Matter Jurisdiction of Minor Courts,* 29 J. AM. JUD. SOC'Y 175-85 (1946) (the last two cited are adaptations of the report published in the Judicial Council report); with Campbell, *Michigan Probate Procedure for the Commitment of Insane, Feeble-minded and Epileptic Persons to Institutions for Their Care, and the Release of Such Persons,* 13 MICH. JUDICIAL COUNCIL REPORT 57-198 (1943).

139 Porter, *Defects in the Administration of Justice in Hamilton County (Cincinnati), Ohio,* 32 J. AM. JUD. SOC'Y 14-22 (1948). At 3, Glenn R. Winters, the editor, comments that Cincinnati is not a horrible example, but compares very favorably with other cities, which in itself makes this report good reading. The *Cincinnati Enquirer,* he goes on, went out of its way to scoff at Porter, who was belittled because of his youth, his crew cut, and his student status. ". . . [I]deas are entitled to a hearing on their intrinsic merits whatever their source, and the truth is the truth, whether spoken by sage, stripling or ouija board."

140 JACKSON, Solicitor of the Supreme Court, Lecturer in Law at the University of Cambridge, MACHINERY OF JUSTICE IN ENGLAND (1940).

Finally, it was late in the forties that the Section launched its inquiry into the special problems of metropolitan courts, which began with a two-year library and fact study conducted in Detroit. Its hypothesis has already been stated.[141]

SECTION 6. THE FIFTIES

a. The Institute of Judicial Administration

Other projects have recently been undertaken, in addition to the activities of the Section of Judicial Administration just described, which have brought into the field other agencies interested in and working towards the solving of metropolitan court problems.

Chief among these agencies is the Institute of Judicial Administration, established at New York University School of Law through the efforts of the late Chief Justice Arthur T. Vanderbilt of the Supreme Court of New Jersey. The Institute has conducted and made available a series of inquiries into various problems in judicial administration.[142] Its annual report on delay in the principal trial courts, as measured by the interval from "at issue" to trial, are particularly interesting.[143] From the 1958 calendar status report:

[141] DETROIT STUDY. See also IMPROVEMENT OF THE ADMINISTRATION OF JUSTICE, 90 *et. seq.* (3rd ed. 1952); Jayne and Virtue, *Survey of Metropolitan Courts: Detroit Area,* 37 A.B.A.J. 444 (1951); *Administration of Justice in Metropolitan Areas as Studied in New Survey of Detroit Area Courts,* 34 J. AM. JUD. SOC'Y 111 (1950); *The Detroit Court Survey* (summary by the author), 90 MICH. STATE BAR J. 40-44 (1951); Virtue, *The Court Problem in Detroit,* 20 THE DETROIT LAWYER 15-18 (Feb. 1952). See pp. 1 *et seq. supra,* herein.

[142] E.g., Court Administration (Aug. 1, 1955, mimeo.); Small Claims Courts in the United States (Aug. 10, 1955, mimeo.); Compulsory Arbitration and Court Congestion, The Pennsylvania Compulsory Arbitration Statute, Delay and Congestion—Suggested Remedies Series No. 11 (July 1, 1956, mimeo.); Check-List Summary of 1958 Developments in Judicial Administration (July 15, 1958, mimeo.). Others will be cited in connection with analysis of the subject matter concerned.

[143] This series began in 1953 and has been made available in mimeograph form each year since, under the title "State Trial Courts of General Jurisdiction, Calendar Status Study," followed by the year. In 1957 and 1958, the

As in past years, there is a correlation between population and calendar congestion. . . . Only six courts appear on this year's list of jurisdictions having delay of over twenty-five months, and all are situated in counties with populations of over 500,000.[144]

The six courts are Superior Court, Cook County, Illinois (57.3 months); Circuit Court, Cook County, Illinois (38.2 months); Supreme Court, Queens County, New York City (38 months); Superior Court, Fairfield County (Bridgeport), Connecticut (31.5 months); Superior Court, Hartford County (Hartford), Connecticut (38.5 months); Court of Common Pleas, Cuyahoga County (Cleveland), Ohio (26.5 months).[145]

The Director of the Institute, Shelden Elliott, prepares an annual checklist summary of developments in judicial administration, which in article form appears in the *Annual Survey of American Law* published by the New York University School of Law.[146]

b. Council of State Governments and Public Administration Service

Both the Council of State Governments and the Public Administration Service have a sustained professional interest in the operation of courts and have made several

---

subtitle is added, "Personal Injury Jury Cases." This reflects the decision of the Institute to disregard all cases but personal injury jury cases in reporting on calendar status. Their reason (p. v, 1958 study): "As a result of experience, as well as of conferences and discussions with court administrators and others, it was determined that personal injury jury cases were the principal source of calendar delay. Further, it was concluded that time intervals in personal injury jury cases are correlated with intervals in other cases, and therefore furnish an index of calendar congestion in general." Compare the same Institute's PHOENIX STUDY, *op. cit. supra* note 123, at 51, exhibit A, showing comparative intervals from filing to trial, including: negligent homicide, 142 days; personal injury civil cases, 20.4 months; other torts, 26.5 months; others, 25 months; divorce, 10.4 months. And see 254 *et seq.*, *infra.*

144 State Trial Courts of General Jurisdiction, Calendar Status Report at ii, iii (1958).

145 *Id.* at iii.

146 At the time of writing, the last published is found in 1959 ANNUAL SURVEY OF AMERICAN LAW at 593.

studies of metropolitan courts in action as the political scientist views them.[147] The Maricopa County (Phoenix) and Milwaukee studies are especially interesting because some of their findings present an interesting basis for comparison with studies made of the same court systems by legal personnel: in the case of Phoenix, by the Institute of Judicial Administration; in the case of Milwaukee, by several researchers, including the present writer. There is something about Milwaukee which has always challenged court survey researchers: despite a structural and administrative system having as many imperfections as most, its total performance is so strikingly superior to most in terms of civilized interdepartmental cooperation and humane disposition of problems as to confound the IBM system of analysis. Though this writer is not prepared to offer scientific proof, she has from time to time entertained the suspicion that this quality may not be unrelated to the behavior patterns of the population of Milwaukee, which is unusually homogeneous, law-abiding, and socially well oriented.

c. Other Recent Studies

In many states, studies are being made or have recently been made in connection with reform programs in those states. Some of these studies will be mentioned later in connection with a discussion of possible remedies for court problems in metropolitan areas. The New York studies of the Tweed Commission are sufficiently extensive and provocative to deserve consultation beyond the immediate legislative program in New York.[148] Another New York study, that of

[147] E.g., Public Administration Service, Judicial Administration in Puerto Rico, A Survey Report (1952), 59 pp.; The Organization and Methods of the Office of the Clerk of Superior Court, Maricopa County, Arizona (1953) 32 pp.; The Administration of Court and Legal Services in the Government of Milwaukee County (1955) 66 pp., mimeographed; and see Council of State Governments, State Court Systems, Revised (1953) mimeographed; Trial Courts of General Jurisdiction in the Forty-Eight States (Sept. 1951) mimeographed.

[148] New York Temporary Commission on the Courts, 1957 Report: I, *A Recommendation for a Simplified State-Wide Court System;* II, *Recom-*

the Association of the Bar of the City of New York entitled *Bad Housekeeping*, is a major resource to the student of metropolitan court problems.[149]

In 1956 the Attorney General of the United States held a conference on court congestion and delay in litigation. The published proceedings contain much useful discussion appropriate to the problems of state trial courts in metropolitan areas. Major studies of the problem of delay have just been completed at the University of Chicago and at the University of Pennsylvania.[150]

In the field of family litigation, two studies of the operation of courts in New York City have been completed recently: one by a professional social worker, the other by a member of the faculty of the Columbia Law School. There is less disagreement between them than one would have supposed possible.[151]

One of the Metropolitan Trial Court Committee studies into the metropolitan court problem is that of the Los Angeles courts published in 1956.[152] Another, unpublished,

---

mendations for Amendments to Youth Court Act; III, *First Preliminary Report of the Advisory Committee on Practice and Procedure;* IV, *Recommendations Respecting Calendar Congestion and Delay.* Supporting studies are included with the report.

149 Ass'n of the Bar of the City of New York, Bad Housekeeping: The Administration of the New York Courts (1955) [hereinafter cited as Bad Housekeeping]. Unification of structure and organization is the basic recommendation.

150 Zeisel, Kalven, and Buchholz, Delay in the Court (1959); Levin & Wooley, Dispatch and Delay: A Field Study of Judicial Administration in Pennsylvania (1961).

151 Kahn, A Court for Children: A Study of the New York Children's Court under the auspices of the Citizens' Committee on Children of New York City, Inc. (1953); Gellhorn, Children and Families in the Courts of New York City, A Report by a Special Committee of the Association of the Bar of the City of New York on the Administration of Laws Relating to the Family in the City of New York (1954).

152 Los Angeles Study. See also Fussell, The Holbrook Report—Eight Months Later (summary of action taken on Holbrook's recommendations) (1957) 81 pp., mimeographed, with bibliography by Fannie J. Klein; A Proposal for the Consolidation of the Superior and Municipal Courts of Los Angeles by the Municipal Courts Committee of the Conference of California Judges (Sept. 10, 1957) 74 pp., exhibits, mimeographed; Los Angeles (County) Superior Court Statement . . . in Opposition to the Proposed

is the report of a month's observation of the courts of London, England, conducted by this writer. Other efforts of the committee have included reconnaissance surveys in New York City, Chicago, Kansas City, and Los Angeles by this writer, who also conducted for the committee a study of the condition of dockets in Chicago, a general questionnaire and library study of delay, and a study of the professional qualifications of judges,[153] as well as an Interim Report for 1953. This writer has also prepared, for the Interprofessional Commission on Marriage and Divorce Laws, a series of court studies looking to the actual operation of several metropolitan courts in family litigation, and a study of various court and other services for children.[154]

d. Comment on the Forties and Fifties

Though there has been no dearth of research in the last two decades, the emphasis has shifted from the bold, intensive analytical approach of the thirties, with its imaginative thrust and reach, to studies directed towards searching out all the facts. The more modern studies have some important advantages: they now involve many, if not most, of the personnel actually responsible for operating the court. They have made good use of new systems analysis techniques by which it is possible to obtain vast harvests of factual data from every part of the country and to correlate data by various intricate mechanical means. These later studies evidence more and more interest in the problems of judicial adminis-

---

"single trial court" for Los Angeles County (Apr. 28, 1958) 44 pp., mimeographed, by the Committee on Court Organization of the Superior Court of Los Angeles.

[153] Jayne and Virtue, Progress Report, Committee on Metropolitan Trial Courts (June 1953) 49 pp.; Virtue, Interim Report, Director of State Committees (March 25, 1955, typescript, unpublished); *What Is the Logjam Problem?* 15 F.R.D. 207 (1954); *Improving the Structure of Courts,* 287 ANNALS 141-46 (1953).

[154] VIRTUE, FAMILY CASES IN COURT (1956); BASIC STRUCTURE FOR CHILDREN'S SERVICES IN MICHIGAN (1953).

tration on the part of court and legal personnel, and some have the keen interest of influential lay and professional groups to assist in reaching solutions for these problems. It is wonderfully easy to send out a nationwide questionnaire, to get its data processed by IBM, to call a conference of outstanding experts to discuss the results, to tape-record their comments, and to distribute the end product on a wide scale.

The studies produced in the last two decades have, however, at least in the view of this writer, tended towards a pattern which also has some disadvantages. For example, the full participation of judicial and other court personnel in a court survey research project *ipso facto* makes it difficult forcibly to state conclusions which might threaten the *status quo*. It can be and has been done, as recourse to the studies cited will show: the point is that the awareness of the difficulty automatically conditions the shape and momentum of the study, and various reactions to it. Some will be overdefensive; others will mistake tact for whitewash.

Along somewhat the same line, the present climate of opinion is not conducive to the trumpeting forth of conclusions about controversial questions. It is, the writer suggests, inherent in the contemporary cultural landscape to avoid the controversial whenever possible, to eschew the negative approach, and ever to have a watchful eye out for public relations. These objectives are not always achieved by the same means which produce the best job of court survey research.

Still another difficulty inherent in the availability of the rich resources of duplicating, dictating, distributing, and data-processing machines is that almost inevitably the habitual use of these techniques produces a tendency to ask questions of such a nature as to be fully understood and accepted by anybody at all anywhere in the country, to elicit a simple and quickly prepared response (so as not to scare off one's local committeemen from mailing back the questionnaires), and to limit one's conclusions to the statement of the results so obtained. There is a tendency, to put it bluntly, to substitute mere fact for truth, without acknowledging or even being fully aware of the substitution.

This troubled the late Chief Justice Vanderbilt exceedingly. In a series of letters exchanged early in the fifties with this writer, he commented on the frequency with which factual data, oversimply stated, are misinterpreted during the summarizing process, so that the final generalization made in the study report becomes entirely misleading even on a superficial factual level. It was his feeling that many modern large-scale "fact" studies "paint with too large a brush" and suffer from inadequate qualitative selection and analysis. He pointed out, however, that these deficiencies will disappear as we become more proficient in communicating through the new techniques and more sagacious in evaluating data so collected. The gain in broad-scale interest and participation and in knowledge of what the facts really are far more than offset these disadvantages, he felt.

However that may be, the purpose of the present comment is to invite attention to the contrast between the studies of the last two decades, and those preceding, in terms of the disadvantages just outlined. The differences in inherent quality are striking, are they not?

Section 7. Enumeration of Metropolitan Court Problems

a. Preliminary Note on Basis of Inclusion

In the first part of this study, the metropolitan community was defined and certain metropolitan characteristics mentioned which are reflected in the conditions encountered in metropolitan courts. In the second portion, now moving towards conclusion, the objective has been to select from the entire literature of judicial administration those threads which can be woven usefully into our final grouping of problems peculiar to or more extensively encountered in metropolitan trial courts. Where the problem is included by reason of incidence rather than peculiarity, its appropriateness to this discussion will rest upon the necessity, in metropolitan areas, of evolving special facilities to deal with it—such as are not essential or appropriate outside the metropolitan areas.

b. Metropolitan Court Problems Specified

Group one: structural and jurisdictional problems

1. *Multiplicity of separate trial courts,* including justice and other "inferior" courts, including
   a. *many separate courts in Metropolis*
   b. *an immense totality of separate courts in the entire metropolitan area, including the satellite territory*

(Note: All studies of metropolitan court systems have shared the conclusion that a multiplicity of separate courts, with great overlap, duplication, waste, and confusion of jurisdiction, is the basic structural problem. This multiplicity includes not only the plethora of special purpose courts in Metropolis, but also the scatter of one-man justice and other "inferior" courts dotted throughout the satellite region on the fringes of Metropolis' legal boundaries, though within the real geographic community.)

2. *Inadequate or inappropriate jurisdiction to serve the metropolitan community promptly and efficiently,* as by
   a. *geographically inadequate jurisdiction*
   b. *duplicating or concurrent jurisdiction of two or more courts with partly or wholly overlapping jurisdiction*
   c. *fragmented, conflicting, or otherwise confused jurisdiction*

d. *lack of specialized jurisdiction to deal properly with special cases*

3. *Restraints upon judicial control essential to proper disposition of cases,* as by constitutional, legislative, or other shackling of power of court
4. *Modernization or replacements for justice of peace system*

(Note: Ill-fitting jurisdiction, noted by all observers of metropolitan courts, is productive of controversy about implications and remedies. For example, a small claims court usually shares with the general court of original trial jurisdiction a certain monetary bracket of jurisdiction in the higher reaches of small claims. Some regard this as a healthy choice of tribunals, others as a waste of judicial resources and an invitation to petty status-seeking attorneys to crowd their way into the higher court, thus clogging its dockets. Again, replacement of the multitudes of one-man justice courts by a unified municipal or small claims court is resisted as substituting a monstrous impersonal judicial bureaucracy for the friendly neighborhood court essential to bring readily available and effective "people's courts" to those who need them.

The question of the proper design for a jurisdictional pattern for Metropolitan Court, then, bristles with conflicting value judgments related to various basic premises about the role of the court.)

Group two: special types of cases

(Note: We touched on this problem in *2d* above. The special case problem, however, is not inherently one of jurisdiction, but rather that of finding the best way to handle the large caseloads of special types of cases requiring special handling, such as criminal, traffic, small claims, domestic relations, mental and borderline mental cases. This is a very complex problem. Observers try to steer between the Scylla of "push-button" processing of delicate personal problem cases and the Charybdis of transforming the judicial process into a medical or social work clinic exclusively preoccupied with personal rehabilitation.

There seems to be a pattern of progress through successive stages: first, a specialized docket or calendar; second, a specialized judge; third, development from a separate docket to a separate division, or part, with a specialized staff under a specialized judge; fourth, change from specialized separate division to separate specialized court. At this phase, we encounter the problem of multiplicity of courts in the making.

There are conflicting opinions about the advisability of specialization and also about the way to develop a specialized court facility. The complexity and extent of the problem seem to demand that we give it a separate grouping and look at it closely.)

5. *Separate specialized subject-matter courts*
6. *Specialized divisions or parts, technically within a general court, but actually operating separately*
7. *Specialized or separate dockets or calendars in general courts*
8. *Number of individual specialized judges to handle special subject-matter caseloads*
9. *Recruitment of specialized judges*
    a. *election to designated specialized judgeship*
    b. *assigned by presiding judge on long-term basis*
    c. *assigned on rotating basis*
    d. *other methods (appointment, importation from outside, etc.)*
10. *Family courts*
    a. *geographic jurisdiction (state, metropolitan area, Metropolis)*

b. *subject-matter jurisdiction*

I. *divorce and child custody*

II. *separate maintenance*

III. *misdemeanor and felony cases (abandonment, etc.)*

IV. *juvenile cases, dependency, neglect, delinquency*

V. *paternity out of wedlock*

VI. *adoption*

VII. *guardianships of minors*

VIII. *other*, e.g., *mental*

Group three: personnel

(Note: The problem of obtaining qualified and competent judicial and other court personnel emerges from many of the studies as a major problem of metropolitan courts. This problem is not exclusive to metropolitan courts, but has a special impact there because of the difficulty of obtaining, identifying, and keeping the competent, and of eliminating the incompetent, in the infinitely crowded and complex milieu of Metropolis.)

11. *Total number of judges in Metropolis and in metropolitan area*

12. *Judges compensated wholly or in part on a fee basis*
    a. *in Metropolis*
    b. *in satellite area*

13. *Qualifiations required of judges*
    a. *in Metropolis*
    b. *in satellite area*

14. *Number of judges not legally qualified*
    a. *in Metropolis*
    b. *in satellite area*

15. *Judicial retirement systems*
    a. *in Metropolis*
    b. *in satellite area*

16. *Age of judges*
    a. *in Metropolis*
    b. *in satellite area*
17. *Quasi-judicial personnel exercising decision-making authority*
    a. *referees*
    b. *commissioners*
    c. *other*
18. *Number of quasi-judicial officers not legally qualified*
19. *Provisions for obtaining counsel for indigent litigants*
    a. *criminal cases*
    b. *small claims cases*
    c. *civil cases*
    d. *juvenile cases*
20. *Use of nonlegal professionals (marriage counselors, social workers, psychologists, psychiatrists, etc.)*
    a. *as full-time court paid staff members in*
        I. *criminal court*
        II. *juvenile court*
        III. *family*
        IV. *other*
    b. *on a case by case basis by a*
        I. *criminal court*
        II. *juvenile court*
        III. *family*
        IV. *other*
    c. *on a referral basis by a*
        I. *criminal court*
        II. *juvenile court*
        III. *family*
        IV. *other*
21. *Methods of obtaining juries*
22. *Qualifications for jurors*
23. *Occupational and other bias on part of juries*
24. *Total number of court employees (full-time basis)*

a. *judicial capacity*
b. *quasi-judicial capacity*
c. *professional capacity other than legal*
d. *executive or administrative capacity*
e. *stenographic and clerical*
f. *other*

25. *Tenure of employees (civil service)*
26. *Special problems in selection and tenure of judges*
    a. *appointment*
    b. *election on partisan basis*
    c. *election on nonpartisan basis*

Group four: machinery for handling dockets and disposing of caseload

27. *Judicial responsibility for case progress in multi-judge courts of general original trial jurisdiction*
    a. *presiding judge, executive judge, other*
    b. *method of recruitment and length of term of presiding judge*
28. *Methods of assigning cases for trial and other disposition*
    a. *assignment clerk*
    b. *centralized written assignment system (Cleveland system)*
    c. *personally by presiding judge, as by calling docket each day*
29. *Extent of use of pretrial*
    a. *in all or selected civil cases*
    b. *in all or selected criminal cases*
    c. *by court rule*
    d. *by agreement of counsel*
    e. *otherwise*
    f. *percentage of caseload disposed of at pretrial hearings*
30. *Total caseload in trial court of general jurisdiction in*

Metropolis and caseload per metropolitan judge as compared to that of other judges

31. *Delay in metropolitan courts*
    a. *Average length of time between date case at issue and date final disposition in*
        I. *all cases*
        II. *chancery (equity) cases*
        III. *criminal cases, jury and nonjury*
        IV. *law cases, jury and nonjury*
        V. *negligence cases as such, jury and nonjury*
    b. *Other information concerning delay*
        I. *date filing to disposition*
        II. *oldest and youngest case method*
        III. *length of detention of jailed prisoners compared with bailed defendants in criminal cases*
        IV. *other*
32. *Illusory nature and implications of "delay" problem*
33. *Percentage of total caseload disposed of other than by trial*
34. *Percentage of total tried cases tried to jury*
35. *Encouragement to waive juries by assigning priority to nonjury cases*
36. *Incidence and implications of delay problem*
37. *Major cause or causes of delay*
    a. *insufficient judges*
    b. *incompetent or undiligent judges*
    c. *defects in structure of court system*
    d. *inadequate system for handling docket, calendar, and assignment problems*
    e. *deliberate maneuvering by counsel, or procrastination*
38. *Measures currently employed to control delay*
39. *Measures currently regarded as most effective against* delay
40. *Relationship of "quick justice" (perfunctory routine*

disposition of cases) and pressure upon metropolitan judges to avoid delay

41. *Relationship of amount of control of judge over procedure and ability of judge to control delay*
    a. *judicial prerogative to require that case be disposed of at a certain time*
    b. *prerogative of attorney to determine procedure in relation to that of judge*
42. *Relationship of views concerning role of trial judge and attitudes towards delay*

Group five: effective integration and cooperation among various courts and related agencies within a metropolitan area

(Note: Several of the studies of metropolitan courts have found that the effective operation of the entire system as a function of the metropolitan area is hampered by the existence of many independent courts (with confused, overlapping, competing or duplicating functions, as in Group One, *supra,* each jealous of its own autonomous status, the whole without integration or cooperation throughout the metropolitan area. The following do not exhaust the subject but are selected as useful for testing the existence and depth of the need for administrative or structural unification at various locations in the judicial process.)

43. *Court administrator*
    a. *state court administrator (or similar state level integrator) as coordinator for metropolitan area viewed as a function*
    b. *metropolitan area court administrator as coordinator for various court activities within area*
44. *Methods of coordinating specific court activities throughout Metropolis and throughout entire metropolitan area*
    a. *court records*
    b. *money and financial records*

c. *probation records and work of probation officers*
d. *other aspects of judicial administration*

45. *Separate jury commissions serving various courts within same Metropolis or metropolitan area*
46. *Separate probation departments*
    a. *in Metropolis*
    b. *in entire metropolitan area*
    c. *extent of cooperation among these departments*
47. *Arrangements for coordinating efforts of various courts dealing with personal problem cases,* e.g., *family, juvenile, mental and criminal cases involving maladjustment rather than willful violation of law*
    a. *in Metropolis*
    b. *throughout metropolitan area*
48. *Arrangements for effecting liaison among various courts dealing with types of cases noted in 47,* supra, *and the various public and private social agencies which may also be involved with the same problems*
49. *Advantages and disadvantages of single integrated court for the entire metropolitan area, in terms of achieving more efficient disposition of all or any part of the caseload*

Group six: safeguarding due process

(Note: Several observers have reached the conclusion that safeguarding due process is one of the most serious of metropolitan court problems. Among the factors mentioned as contributing to this problem are the complexity of the court systems, the confusions arising out of the size and complexity of the administrative staff, the pressures towards perfunctory routine disposition of each case in the large caseload, the tendency to reduce caseload by screening out cases for disposition other than by judicial process, and, in personal problem cases, the tendency for the court to assume functions not appropriate to its role either by (a) withdrawing in favor of expert nonlegal professionals who may or may not be available, or (b) by attempting to perform services other than judicial.)

50. *Number of litigants who go to final disposition in Metropolis without benefit of counsel*
    a. *traffic cases*
    b. *criminal cases*
    c. *juvenile cases*
    d. *small claims cases*
    e. *domestic relations cases*
    f. *mental cases*
    g. *other*
51. *Extent and propriety of efforts by courts handling divorce cases to obtain objective evaluations in child custody and support matters from persons other than litigants and their counsel*
    a. *in contested cases*
    b. *in uncontested cases*
    c. *regarding possibility of reconciliation in divorce cases*
    d. *assumption by court of supervision of collection of child support and/or custody orders, after disposition of divorce case*
        I. *propriety of court exercising function of surveillance over welfare of children*
        II. *relationship between pressure on courts to avoid delay and perfunctory routine disposition of cases involving the welfare of children in divorce and other family cases*
52. *Removal of criminal cases from orbit of judicial authority by prosecutor, as by nolle pros, bargaining for guilty plea or plea to lesser charge, or by other means*
    a. *extent of problem of due process arising out of these practices, through deprivation of full use of judge's knowledge and discretion*

b. *extent of due process problem arising out of deprivation of public trial*
c. *extent of problem where defendant is without counsel*
b. *extent of problem in misdemeanor as distinguished from felony cases*
e. *relationship of problem to over-all percentage of guilty pleas in Metropolis*

53. *Extent of procedures in mental cases affording full hearing in commitment cases, inside and outside Metropolis*
    a. *total caseload of mental cases in Metropolis*
    b. *extent of requirement that persons alleged to be in need of confinement in mental hospitals be represented by counsel*
    c. *extent of requirement of testimony by qualified psychiatrists*
    d. *diagnostic commitment statutes*
    e. *use of juries in mental cases*
    f. *extent to which elderly indigent, needing custodial care, are committed to mental hospitals, for want of a better place, in order to relieve local public authorities of financial and other responsibility for their care.*
    g. *advisability of handling all mental commitments other than by judicial hearing, with decision to be made by psychiatrist, and with no provision for judicial hearing except after commitment and upon demand by patient.*
    h. *relationship of due process and medical problems under statutes substituting psychiatric diagnosis and treatment for trial in such cases as those involving criminal sexual psychopaths*

54. *Use of "unofficial" category in juvenile cases*

(Note: In handling juvenile cases, some courts routinely

set up an "unofficial" category, into which some cases are channeled and maintained, sometimes for several years. In these cases, the court accepts no petition, but court-employed caseworkers make a file and provide direction and supervision. This technique saves the judge's time and prevents overwhelming him with a large caseload, avoids the making of a record against the juvenile, and enables the social workers to establish and maintain better rapport with the juveniles and their families.)

a. *propriety and effectiveness of "unofficial" category of juvenile (or other) cases in terms of providing community with best possible court services*
b. *propriety and implications of "unofficial" category in terms of due process problem*
c. *implications of "unofficial" category in terms of distinguishing identity and function of judicial process from that of nonjudicial administrative agency*
d. *extent to which "unofficial category" problem assumes special quality in Metropolis*

55. *Use of marriage counselors as court employees*
 a. *propriety and effectiveness of requiring counselor to see*
  I. *all cases coming before court on compulsory basis*
  II. *persons with cases before court who desire to avail themselves of counselor's services*
  III. *persons referred by judge at his discretion*
 b. *propriety and effectiveness of extending court marriage counselor's services to persons not involved in litigation*
 c. *propriety of court employee spending some or a substantial part of his time in counseling persons not involved in litigation before the employing court*

I. *where there are other counseling agencies in the community*

II. *where the court is the only agency in the community offering marriage counseling*

d. *function of court marriage counseling in terms of assisting court to achieve better performance of court's function*

56. *Extent to which traffic and small claims cases in Metropolis go to final disposition without any challenge of the moving party's statement of the case*

57. *Extent of public trust, in Metropolis and in metropolitan area, of the integrity of*
    a. *traffic policemen*
    b. *justices of the peace*
    c. *small claims court judges*

58. *Extent of danger of loss of traditional function of courts by "push-button" handling of traffic and installment credit in terms of relationship of such cases to total caseload of Metropolis*

59. *Extent of responsibility of legal profession to safeguard due process in traffic and small claims cases*

60. *Public image, in Metropolis, of judge as*
    a. *one who sees that justice is done to and for each individual*
    b. *one who sees that traditional legal procedures are followed, no matter what happens to the people*
    c. *one who provides a fair opportunity for trial lawyers to safeguard their clients' interests as they see fit*
    d. *one who sees that cases are disposed of promptly and in an orderly manner*
    e. *a member of a distinguished and privileged gentlemen's club*
    f. *a showman, grandstanding for the reporters, with an eye on the next election*

(Note: The intent is to focus on the problems created for the judge, the profession, and the community by reason of the nature of the public image of the judge, in Metropolis, as distinguished from the real function performed by the occupant of the bench. Reason for believing that the gap between the image and the reality are wider and more dangerous in Metropolis will be found in the first part of this study.)

61. *Consensus, in opinion of legal profession, and in opinion of general public, concerning identity and extent of major problems of metropolitan courts*

PART III

DISCUSSION OF MAJOR PROBLEMS

Prefatory Note to Part III

IN Part II, an attempt was made to survey the literature of judicial administration for the purpose of searching out and analyzing any and all material bearing upon the special problems of metropolitan trial courts in the state court systems, but excluding federal courts, as required by the frame of reference of the Metropolitan Trial Court Committee for this series of studies.

Part III will contain an intensive discussion of certain metropolitan trial court problems as just enumerated.[1] The foundation for this discussion is the series of fact studies carried out for the Metropolitan Trial Court Committee and other recent fact studies in which the present writer has participated since 1947.[2] In addition, material will be included from replies to questionnaires prepared for this study, and directed to section committeemen and selected court personnel in metropolitan areas.[3] These questionnaires were forwarded to recipients on April 1, 1959, and from time to time thereafter during the next year to recipients who had not replied or to new recipients recommended by section personnel. The closing date for receipt of answered questionnaires was set at April 1, 1960. At that time, questionnaires had been received from the following metropolitan areas:

Baltimore, Maryland
Baton Rouge, Louisiana
Biloxi, Mississippi
Binghamton, New York
Boise, Idaho
Brocton, Massachusetts

[1] *Supra* pp. 136-49.
[2] *Supra* pp. 132-33.
[3] Appendix E.

Burlington, Vermont
Charleston, South Carolina
Charleston, West Virginia
Chattanooga, Tennessee
Cheyenne, Wyoming
Cleveland, Ohio
Des Moines, Iowa (two questionnaires)
Eugene, Oregon
Grand Forks, North Dakota
Huron, South Dakota
Las Vegas, Nevada
Miami, Florida
Milwaukee, Wisconsin
Minneapolis, Minnesota
Newark, New Jersey
Philadelphia, Pennsylvania
Phoenix, Arizona
Pueblo, Colorado
Rutland, Vermont
San Jose, California
St. Paul, Minnesota (two questionnaires)
Sioux Falls, South Dakota
Washington (questionnaire answered on statewide basis)
Wichita Falls, Texas

Although other materials may appear in brief citation from time to time, the basis for Part III is the author's direct experience with the recent fact studies of courts in action. This is in contrast with Part II, where the basis was a historical survey of library materials in the literature of judicial administration.

CHAPTER V

Structural Problems

SECTION 1. MULTIPLICITY OF SEPARATE TRIAL COURTS

a. Many Separate Courts in Metropolis

WITH the possible exception of delay, multiplicity of separate trial courts is the court problem identified as typical of metropolitan court systems by virtually all writers. From Archeion through Pound to the Tweed Commission, all have been concerned with the vast confusion of multifarious tribunals serving large population centers.

Typical is a recent comment of The Honorable David W. Peck, former Presiding Judge of the Supreme Court of the State of New York, Appellate Division:

> The historic practice, particularly in the large cities, has been to splinter and parcel out fields of jurisdiction among many courts of limited jurisdiction. The trend for a century has been to create rather than consolidate courts, to narrow rather than broaden jurisdiction, to divide rather than concentrate administrative authority. The result, in many places, is a conglomeration of courts, each autonomous in administration, confined but overlapping in jurisdiction.
>
> In many cities administration of the criminal law has been separated from administration of the civil law. Separate courts have been created for probate and estate proceedings and for domestic relations. There has even been an elaborate stratification of courts in the same legal line. New York City, for example, has three layers of courts in both the civil and criminal lines. The civil courts are divided by monetary limits. The criminal courts are divided by degrees of crime.
>
> Such a fragmented court organization, without flexibility in moving judges and cases about to achieve balance in distribution, and without centralization of administrative authority, lacks the elementary essentials of a court system. It is not a court system.[1]

[1] Peck, *Court Organization and Procedures to Meet the Needs of Modern Society*, 33 IND. L.J. 182, 183 (1958).

As noted hereinabove,[2] fact studies conducted for the Section of Judicial Administration by this and other writers have confirmed other data demonstrating the existence of a plethora of autonomous judicial tribunals in most states—with California and New Jersey the notable exceptions—and that this multiplicity is most exaggerated in metropolitan areas.

> Reasons for the costly and inefficient piling up of courts include (1) retention of the outmoded justice of the peace system, (2) population shifts resulting in demand for new courts, and (3) ephemeral local pressures to create a new court for each specialized set of issues. . . . 'Sibling rivalry' among . . . governmental units, and heavy case loads in congested population centers, also contribute to the pressure for more courts.[3]

Examples may be found in *Family Cases in Court*[4] and *Children and Families in the Courts of New York City*,[5] *inter alia*, to indicate proliferation of narrowly specialized courts. It is notable that in most large metropolitan cities, however, the problem of the unreconstructed one-man lay justice court has not persisted. In that area, court reform has been at least nominally successful: in general, the munic-

[2] See pp. 29, 45-47 *supra* and studies there cited. Worth repeating: Lepawsky found 556 autonomous tribunals in Chicago metropolitan area in 1932, 205 in Cook County alone. Virtue found 145 independent judicial tribunals in the Detroit metropolitan area in 1948-50. Compare HOLBROOK, LOS ANGELES STUDY 8-9, having in mind that the major trial courts in California have recently been unified. Jackson notes 20,000 male magistrates and 3,000 women magistrates with over 1,000 courts; and, in addition, twenty-seven police magistrates in the County of London, and eighteen Stipendiary Magistrates. JACKSON, MACHINERY OF JUSTICE IN ENGLAND 130, 82-83 (1940). See BAD HOUSEKEEPING 1 *et seq.* (over 250 judges in New York City alone); and see this writer's FAMILY CASES IN COURT at 53, Chart II (Court System of Cook County, Illinois); 5, Chart I (Court System of California); 116, Chart III (Court System of Indianapolis); 175 *et seq.* (narrative description of court structural systems affecting family cases in Milwaukee, Ohio, Michigan); TALBOTT, INTERGOVERNMENTAL RELATIONS AND THE COURTS, a study of Minnesota Courts, especially 23 *et seq.*, 47 *et seq.* (1950).

[3] Virtue, *Improving the Structure of Courts*, 287 ANNALS 141 (1953).

[4] See, for example, VIRTUE, FAMILY CASES 178-79 (1956).

[5] GELLHORN, CHILDREN AND FAMILIES IN THE COURTS OF NEW YORK CITY 25 *et seq.* (1954).

ipal court as such has superseded the original justice courts, within the mother city itself.[6]

The problem of multiplicity within the mother city seems to consist partly of duplicating general trial courts set up to ease congestion, and partly of a piling up of separate highly specialized courts.

We have already noted that the problem of the specialized court wears two faces: to some extent, specialization is an informed recognition of the need for specialized attention to certain types of cases. But its other aspect presents the disadvantages of freezing specialized parts or departments of the general court into aggressively independent autonomies, narrowly specialized and so confirmed in their procedures and provincial in their specialties as to have defeated the original purpose of improving the quality of disposition of cases by segregating certain cases for specialized handling. Instead, at this extreme phase, we have all the disadvantages of multiplicity: waste, inefficiency, bureaucratism, lack of communication with other parts of government, and loss of public confidence.

It is this writer's conclusion, based on total contact with the court research projects, including discussions with lay and legal personnel, that the loss of confidence problem is in large part based on inadequate, cavalier, or fumbling attention to specialized cases by overspecialized personnel.[7] It

[6] VANDERBILT, MINIMUM STANDARDS 309 *et. seq.* (1949); and annual reports of the Director of State Committees of the Section of Judicial Administration supplementing Standards. The 1952 edition was published in paperback form as IMPROVEMENT OF THE ADMINISTRATION OF JUSTICE (handbook).

[7] Examples: the refusal by a juvenile court referee to give to a divorce court investigator any information concerning the existence or nature of juvenile court contact with two boys who were subjects of divorce court concern because of change of custody proceedings (Detroit); insistence by a mental division administrative clerk that a dubious commitment proceeding be consummated by immediate transfer of patient to state mental facility, for the reason that the local hospital needed the space (Detroit); a violent tongue-lashing administered by a traffic court judge to a nice elderly lady with a New England accent who had dared to request a court hearing (Los Angeles).

may be significant that this particular aspect of the problem also occurs in the subject areas (small claims, family cases, petty criminal cases, mental cases) where one finds the largest part of the metropolitan caseload and where the service of attorneys are likely not to be a routine part of the court contact.[8]

In any event, the existence of a multiplicity of separate courts as a special metropolitan court problem appears to be fully accepted, and we may leave further discussion of its implications for the time.

b. Multiplicity of Courts in the Entire Metropolitan Area, Including the Satellite Area

The large number of total courts existing in the entire metropolitan area is in good part comprised of one-man justice courts which continue to exist in their original state—one-man, fee'd, lay justice courts—in the nonurban and even some of the urban territory satellite to Metropolis.

No doubt most readers have encountered this phenomenon directly, as in traffic cases. Its relation to the special metropolitan court problem is the existence, within a single metropolitan area, of large numbers of these anachronistic tribunals. Their presence preserves waste and confusion, assures inadequate handling of large numbers of cases, and provides the self-seeking, ambitious, or unscrupulous with a ready means of avoiding or negating the control of an efficient and modern court designed to serve the metropolitan community.

For example, the writer had a case in which suburban police officers in the Detroit area were angered at the lack of cooperation displayed by a mother after her daughter "escaped" from a girls' training school. She did not report the escape to the police, and, though she misrepresented no

[8] *Supra* p. 53 *et seq.*

facts, did nothing to make apprehension of the girl easy for the officers. They took her before a township justice in a neighboring noncity area, charged her with abetting the escape of a criminal, and held her in jail for more than two weeks. At the time the charges were quashed by the Circuit Court in Detroit, it was brought out that the officers' selection of the justice court, which bound her over and held her in custody without bail, was related to their objective in this case: to make an example of one who had "got wise with the cops."

In a poll of state committee personnel of the Section of Judicial Administration made in 1953 by this writer, Delaware reported that recommendations were being made for improvements in the justice system by reduction in number, by requiring qualifications, eliminating the fee system, and modernizing procedural and process-serving methods.[9]

Florida recommended abolishment of the justice system. Georgia reported dissatisfaction with handling of small claims and traffic cases by justices of the peace, particularly where city policemen made an arrest and arranged for trial before a noncity justice. Illinois at that time had 2,950 justices of the peace, including 150 justices of the peace and 100 police magistrates in Cook County.

Indiana reported between 500 and 600 justices of the peace and indicated a general feeling that revision of this system, especially in and near cities, is essential. A traffic study commission was preparing to recommend constitutional revision abolishing justices of the peace.

Michigan reported 2,795 justices of the peace in the state.[10]

[9] A.B.A. Section of Judicial Administration, Interim Report, Director of State Committees (March 1955) (unpublished typescript).

[10] Milton Bachmann, executive secretary of the State Bar of Michigan, remarked that the numerical strength of Michigan J.P.'s is known because "Mr. Harlon Mark of this office personally counted them from a register in the office of the Secretary of State." He also calls attention to Professor Edson R. Sunderland's studies and recommendations for a county court:

In Minnesota, elimination of justice courts and creation of municipal courts has been done "very piecemeal," according to our report. Our committeeman cautioned that often a so-called "municipal court" may be an unreconstructed justice of the peace under a modern name. "It seems the end result is practically the same sort of animal that existed before they were called Municipal courts."

Missouri had abolished its justices of the peace. Ohio still had 41 counties with both the justice and the municipal court system, despite its dense population and acknowledged leadership in municipal court reform. Thirty-eight counties had justices but no municipal courts. There were, in 1953, approximately 1,300 justices of the peace in Ohio.[11]

The Pennsylvania committeeman reported that there are a tremendous but unknown number of petty courts in that state, called justice of the peace courts in county districts, and called Magistrates' Courts in Philadelphia.[12]

SECTION 2. INADEQUATE OR INAPPROPRIATE JURISDICTION TO SERVE THE METROPOLITAN COMMUNITY PROMPTLY AND EFFICIENTLY

a. Geographically Inadequate Jurisdiction

Where the geographic community we call the metropolitan area has outgrown its original legal governmental

---

Sunderland, *The Efficiency of Justices' Courts in Michigan*, 4 MICH. JUDICIAL COUNCIL REPORT 169 (1934); *A Study of Justices of the Peace and other Minor Courts—Requisites for an Adequate State-wide Minor Court System*, 15 MICH. JUDICIAL COUNCIL REPORT (1944); *Tentative Draft of an Act to Establish County Courts of Record*, 16 MICH. JUDICIAL COUNCIL REPORT (1945). Mr. Bachmann points out that the State Bar of Michigan introduced a county court bill in 1947 and 1951, but that it did not pass. The organization of justices of the peace in Michigan is active and effective.

[11] For a description of the relationship between the lay magistrates and stipendiary magistrates in the London area, see REPORT OF THE DEPARTMENTAL COMMITTEE ON COURTS OF SUMMARY JURISDICTION IN THE METROPOLITAN AREA (LONDON), (1947); GILES, MAGISTRATES' COURTS, and THE DAILY MIRROR'S SPOTLIGHT ON JUSTICE 20 *et seq.* (Cave ed. Nov. 1954).

[12] The 1950 reorganization of most of the courts of limited jurisdiction in California has been referred to *supra* p. 46. And see LOS ANGELES STUDY 8-9.

boundaries, and where the courts serving the area are restricted geographically to the original legal boundaries, the result is inadequate geographic jurisdiction. This is the typical condition of almost all metropolitan communities. Examples are given hereinabove[13] in terms of the larger metropolitan areas which now include several counties, several states, or, in a few cases, two countries.

The Port Authority of New York, developed by interstate compact to meet this problem of inadequate geographic jurisdiction, is the classic example. The Michigan legislature has recently extended the Uniform Reciprocal Enforcement of Support act beyond the territorial limits of the United States, in order that Detroit and Ontario may enforce the liability to support of persons who presently avoid the exercise of jurisdiction by courts of their native land by crossing the international boundary (Detroit-Windsor) and taking up temporary residence and employment across the line.[14]

Law enforcement officers and prosecutors operating in metropolitan areas are continually harassed by the difficulties of pursuing law violators beyond the territorial jurisdiction of the local government in which the offense was committed, apprehending them, and establishing a jurisdictional basis to bring them to trial. Most readers have doubtless been made aware of the jurisdictional difficulties as between state, township, and city police in dealing with a problem which can reasonably be identified with any of the three.

Recorder's Court in the City of Detroit, for example, has jurisdiction over all criminal offenses committed within the City of Detroit. Where an offense is committed just across the city line in Wayne County, the Recorder's Court

[13] *Supra* p. 26 *et seq.*

[14] Act No. 191, Public Acts of 1959. Interstate agreements: e.g., Naujoks, *Compacts and Agreements Between States and Between States and a Foreign Power*, 36 MARQ. L. REV. 219-47 (1952-53) and see authorities cited 219 n. 2; *Interstate Compact: A Survey*, 27 TEMPLE L.Q., 320-29 (1954).

has no jurisdiction, but such offenses must be brought before a justice or municipal court, if a low misdemeanor, or before the Circuit Court of Wayne County, if a high misdemeanor or felony.[15]

California, which reorganized its court system in 1950, has to some extent solved this problem of inadequate geographic jurisdiction by providing for statewide jurisdiction, as opposed to venue, not only in superior (general trial) courts but also in municipal and justice courts.[16] In nonstate criminal cases, the jurisdiction is local. But, as Holbrook points out,[17] the unification of the superior court is being hampered administratively by the rapid proliferation of separate branch courts.[18] Separate municipal courts serving the Los Angeles area are increasing as the population level here and there increases to the point of qualifying more and more communities for municipal courts. This proliferation of separate municipal courts is, in turn, creating a need for consolidation thereof. Holbrook recommends a moratorium on the creation of further superior court branches and municipal courts and the consolidation of all municipal courts in the county into one tribunal.[19]

b. Duplicating or Concurrent Jurisdiction of Two or More Courts with Partly or Wholly Overlapping Jurisdiction

In several metropolitan areas, special metropolitan courts exist with geographical jurisdiction duplicating that of the local branch of the general trial court of the state court system. The Council of State Governments cites the following:

[15] DETROIT STUDY 35, 45.
[16] LOS ANGELES STUDY 36-37.
[17] *Id.* at 375.
[18] Certain 1959 legislation is said to have ameliorated this problem to some extent.
[19] LOS ANGELES STUDY 376-78.

Illinois	Chicago	Superior
Louisiana	New Orleans	Civil District
		Criminal District
Maryland	Baltimore	Supreme Bench
Michigan	Detroit	Recorder's
New York	New York	General Sessions[20]

The circuit and superior courts of Cook County have received considerable attention as outstanding examples of competing or duplicating jurisdiction. The section observed these courts for a study of factors in delay in 1953.[21] The several layers of duplicating jurisdiction in New York have been dealt with by the Tweed Commission and by the Association of the Bar of the City of New York, *inter alia.*[22]

The most conspicuous defect in the coexistence of duplicate courts is waste: waste of financial resources and personnel, waste of judicial attention to cases, waste of quality of disposition and of public confidence.

Occasionally the argument is encountered that the fully duplicate court bestows the advantage of "choice of tribunal" upon the lawyer. Reasons given for desiring to preserve the choice include doubt concerning the jurisdiction of one court, preference for procedural policies in one court, more or less congestion in one court (either may be ad-

[20] COUNCIL OF STATE GOVERNMENTS, TRIAL COURTS OF GENERAL JURISDICTION IN THE FORTY-EIGHT STATES (Sept. 1951) and see 1953 supplement.

[21] A.B.A. Section of Judicial Administration, Committee on Metropolitan Trial Courts, Progress Report, docket study of circuit and superior courts, Cook County, beginning page 26 (June 1953). And see LEPAWSKY, THE JUDICIAL SYSTEM OF METROPOLITAN CHICAGO 14 *et seq.* (1932); Cedarquist, *The Continuing Need for Judicial Reform in Illinois,* 4 DEPAUL L. REV. (1955); *An Analysis of the Illinois Court System* (10 lectures), 46 ILL. B. J. 571-632 (1958); VIRTUE, FAMILY CASES 54.

[22] Report, Temporary Commission on the Courts (1957), Recommendation for Simplified State-Wide Court System, and earlier reports cited; BAD HOUSEKEEPING, ch. beginning at 21; ASS'N OF THE BAR OF THE CITY OF NEW YORK, SPECIAL COMMITTEE ON THE ADMINISTRATION OF JUSTICE, THE CITIZENS AND THE COURTS, A Report on a Proposed Simplified State-Wide Court System (1956).

vantageous to a lawyer under special circumstances), personal preference of lawyer for a certain judge.

These reasons seem very feeble when laid over against the disadvantages. The best answer is that made in the Wisconsin memoranda:[23] nobody has a right to a trial before any particular court. Expression of the "choice of tribunal" argument seems to be founded upon the tacit premise that the court system exists for the convenience of the lawyer. Though this is a philosophy not infrequently encountered in the legal literature, the writer assumes any serious student of metropolitan court systems will regard it as a luxury we cannot afford, and as irrelevant to a consideration of the metropolitan court system as a service function for the community.

c. Partly Overlapping Jurisdiction

Partial overlap is more frequently encountered than duplicating jurisdiction *in toto*. This condition is by no means confined to metropolitan areas, but abounds there because of the chaotic and unplanned manner in which special purpose and special district courts come into existence in metropolitan areas. Examples are contained in the study made by the Council of State Governments.[24] The Detroit study contains discussion of overlapping jurisdiction in Detroit courts. There the term was used to include not only formal overlap but also actual overlap, as where the same set of facts, if labeled "custody," may lie in one court, but if called "neglect" or "improper guardianship," may lie in

[23] Court Organization Studies, Wisconsin Judicial Council (1954) (mimeographed pages dated "5/3/54" and entitled "Memo re Choice of Courts by Lawyers.") Compare DETROIT STUDY 203. Exercise of the right to maneuver for or away from a particular judge in a multi-judge court, however, may be basic to the proper exercise of the lawyer's duty.

[24] COUNCIL OF STATE GOVERNMENTS, *op. cit. supra* note 20, at 61, tabulation beginning 64.

another.[25] Most of the jurisdictional difficulties encountered in fitting a particular human controversy into the categories available in any given metropolitan court system are discussed in the following section, dealing with confused and fractionated jurisdiction.

One aspect of overlap, however, seems basically significant to the condition of the metropolitan court system. This is the area of concurrence between the small claims court in a metropolitan area, on the one hand, and the general trial court, on the other. Allusion to the problem has been made heretofore.[26] Several earlier studies, as well as the Detroit study, expressed concern about the tendency to increase the jurisdiction of small claims courts. Reasons for increase, which is very widespread, usually are stated as: (1) the desire to upgrade the monetary jurisdiction to keep pace with inflation; (2) the desire to decrease delay in the general trial court by diverting some of its caseload to courts of limited jurisdiction.

The latter expedient has been reported as achieving remarkable results in New Jersey,[27] and it has been recommended in New York[28] and in California,[29] as well as in other areas.

In 1955, a Minnesota judge reported to the Section of Judicial Administration that the filing of small claims suits in District Court rather than in Municipal Court was a serious problem in Minneapolis.

With respect to personal injury suits in the Los Angeles area, Holbrook writes:

[25] DETROIT STUDY, section beginning 219. The LOS ANGELES STUDY did not deal with these problems, though a close reading of its data will disclose much which is relevant to the problem, e.g., 25, 33-34, 297, 304. And see FAMILY CASES 56, 107, 164, 175.

[26] *Supra* pp. 92, 106. And see ZEISEL, DELAY IN THE COURT 111 (1959).

[27] LOS ANGELES STUDY 297.

[28] ZEISEL, *op. cit. supra*, at 209 *et seq.*

[29] LOS ANGELES STUDY, recommendations L and N at 388-90.

It was the opinion of many judges that frequently personal injury suits were filed in the superior court which should have been filed in the municipal court. In personal injury cases during 1954, 43 per cent of the jury verdicts and 44 per cent of the non-jury judgments in the superior court were for amounts below the jurisdiction of the court. These cases consumed an amount of time equivalent to the full time of six judges. The average recovery of the lowest twenty-five jury verdicts was $340. The average demand for the same twenty-five cases was $30,426.

The explanation for this arises from various causes. In some of these cases the possible damages would be so close to the $3,000 borderline that an estimate with reasonable certainty would be impossible; in justice to the client, the attorney would have to seek the court of higher jurisdiction. Another group of cases arise from the desire to preserve bargaining power. . . .

Nevertheless, there are many instances in which counsel should not file suit in the superior court because it should be apparent to him that the recovery is almost certain to be below the jurisdictional minimum of that court. In such instances, attorneys may file in the superior court purely for prestige purposes. There are many attorneys who proudly claim that all their work is in the superior court implying that they are all "big cases." Perhaps pretrial conference will accomplish some weeding out of these latter cases, but the problem is an exceedingly difficult one to solve without the possibility of doing real injustice.

The New Jersey system permits a judge at pretrial to remand a case to an inferior court, but provides that the inferior court may render a judgment for an amount above the usual jurisdictional limit if the evidence reveals that the higher amount is warranted. . . . It was reported that during one year in New Jersey, 2,443 personal injury cases were transferred to a lower court, and a backlog of 11,500 civil cases awaiting trial in superior courts was reduced to approximately 9,300 cases in eight months.[30]

The same problem is encountered in England, according to Jackson[31] and *The London Daily Mirror*.[32] The latter remarks the number of cases within the range of overlap that continue to be filed in the High Court, despite cost and

[30] *Id.* at 297.
[31] JACKSON, MACHINERY OF JUSTICE IN ENGLAND 30-32 (1940).
[32] DAILY MIRROR SPOTLIGHT ON JUSTICE 6-7 (Cave ed. 1954).

delay, rather than in the less costly and more prompt county court:

> Legal Snobbishness is one of the main causes of the trouble. It is akin to people who cannot afford it insisting on having what is often described as a 'slap-up' funeral for one of their relatives. They must have the best. It is the same in law. Amazing as it may seem there are plaintiffs who insist on having a 'slap-up' trial.

It is important that the litigant feel that he has had his day in court. An experienced judge or lawyer has long learned that a case won is often less satisfactory to the client, if he feels his problem has not had the conscientious attention of judge and counsel, than a case lost after proceedings in which the client has been made to feel that he has had a real "run for his money." The psychological dynamics of the minimum essentials necessary to make the litigant feel so might be the subject of a useful study.

Some increase in the monetary limits of small claims courts is only facing the facts of recent inflation. But it would be disadvantageous to mistake a slight economic adjustment as a basic tool of court reform.

The possible disadvantages of referring cases from the general trial court to the small claims court deserve some mention. The ingenuity of counsel is such that, where "high filing" takes place for status-seeking purposes, a method of getting around the diversionary system will sooner or later be found by such counsel. The effort bestowed upon diverting cases to a lower court may, furthermore, result in blurring and confusing professional efforts to find more basically effective solutions to the problem of delay.

In its study of the Phoenix courts, the Institute of Judicial Administration recommended *against* increasing the jurisdiction of justice courts and against removing drunk driving cases from the superior court. Both recommendations were based upon the conclusion that the desirability of maintaining proper quality of disposition outweighed possible advantages of relieving the superior court of those cases.[33]

Disadvantages of diversion, then, are these:

(1) Tendency for an increased jurisdiction to be accompanied by a rigidifying of procedures, turning the original small claims court into a duplicate of the general trial court, ill-adapted to the handling of many small claims. Then, the small claims litigant, particularly if indigent or near-indigent, is left, as he was when Smith and Schramm called attention to his plight, no better off than under the original justice system—that is, without access to a real day in court.

(2) Danger of relegating a class of cases from a higher to a lower quality of judicial process, solely on the basis of the monetary value of the claim. This would entail great injustice in individual cases, as Holbrook points out, and is in conflict with the principle of "equal justice for all."

(3) The illusion that the problem of delay in the general trial court is solved or even much alleviated by diverting the lower monetary brackets of its civil caseload to the "small claims court." As Zeisel points out,[34] this smacks of shifting the weight of the backlog from one court to another, without improving the opportunity of all litigants to be sure of an adequate day in court. If the two courts involved are entirely separate, the problem of denial of justice is more observable than where the interchange of cases is part of an integrated administration of a single system.

In any event, the problem of overlap as such would yield its disadvantages under a unified court, with judicial discretion to assign cases to their proper monetary level within

[33] PHOENIX STUDY at 47-48.

[34] ZEISEL, *op. cit. supra* note 26, at 211. In the New York system the court by internal rule classifies cases which could have been filed in the lower court as unpreferred for trial—i.e., such cases would never be reached for trial. Not the amount claimed, but the higher court's judgment concerning the probable amount of the judgment, is the basis for assigning preference. This is constitutional: Plachte v. Bancroft, 3 App. Div. 2d 437, 441-42, 161 N.Y.S. 2d 892, 896-97 (1st Dept. 1957).

the court, and with procedures so designed as to assure a real "day in court" at either level.

d. Fragmented, Conflicting, or Otherwise Confused Jurisdiction

This subheading is used here to designate any condition experienced as confusion about which court has authority to make final determination of a problem in litigation. Thus, it includes some of the jurisdictional problems already referred to, such as multiplicity of separate courts, geographic inadequacy, and overlap of jurisdiction. It looms large in this writer's list of special difficulties making up the climate of metropolitan courts.

A number of examples were given in the Detroit study, including small claims cases,[35] rent cases,[36] trials *de novo* on appeals,[37] mental cases,[38] chronic alcoholics,[39] criminal cases,[40] cases involving minors,[41] and domestic cases generally.[42] As was there noted, there are five different legal procedures for handling paternity out of wedlock.[43] The area of family cases displays confused jurisdiction at its most chaotic, not only in Detroit,[44] but elsewhere.

The section committeeman from Pennsylvania reported in 1953:

> The only current agitation in Philadelphia is the establishment of a Family Court. Today the Common Pleas Court has jurisdiction over divorce proceedings, the Domestic Relations Division of the Municipal Court over support or maintenance orders, the Juvenile Division of

[35] DETROIT STUDY *at* 219. And see *supra* section c on "overlap."
[36] DETROIT STUDY at 222.
[37] *Ibid.*
[38] *Id.* at 223.
[39] *Ibid.*
[40] *Id.* at 225.
[41] *Id.* at 226.
[42] *Id.* at 233 *et seq.*
[43] *Id.* at 231-32. And see Alexander, *Family Court of the Future*, 36 J. AM. JUD. SOC'Y 39 (1952).
[44] DETROIT STUDY 231 *et seq.*

the Municipal Court over delinquent and deserted minors under the age of 18, the Orphans' Court has jurisdiction over the appointment of guardians for the person as well as the property of minors, and the Municipal Court, as above indicated, has jurisdiction over adoption proceedings.[45]

The District of Columbia was at that time working for the passage of a family court act, which has since been accomplished.

The pinnacle of confusion of jurisdiction is probably reached in New York.[46] But the same problem has been noted in virtually all other metropolitan areas studied: London,[47] Los Angeles and San Francisco,[48] Chicago,[49] Indianapolis,[50] various Ohio areas,[51] and Milwaukee,[52] for example. But we have no evidence of jurisdictional conflict arising out of family cases in Phoenix.

Note that the existence of a unified court system in Phoenix (the Superior Court has jurisdiction over bastardy, adoption, juvenile and divorce cases) may account for this.[53] Unification of the statewide court system does not, however, prevent jurisdictional confusion in family cases: compare California and New Jersey.[54]

45 Virtue, Interim Report, Director of State Committees 111 (March 5, 1955).

46 GELLHORN, CHILDREN AND FAMILIES IN THE COURTS OF NEW YORK CITY 382 *et seq.;* BAD HOUSEKEEPING 21-37; Community Services Society of New York, Bureau of Public Affairs, A New Pattern for Family Justice 65, especially app. B thereof (1954).

47 See, for example, ROYAL COMMISSION ON MARRIAGE AND DIVORCE, REPORT 1951-1955, 196-97.

48 LOS ANGELES STUDY 300; FAMILY CASES 46 *et seq.*

49 FAMILY CASES 46 *et seq.;* LEPAWSKY, HOME RULE FOR METROPOLITAN CHICAGO 54 *et seq.*, 81 *et seq.* (1935).

50 FAMILY CASES 170 *et. seq.*

51 *Id.* at 175-76.

52 *Id.* at 178 *et seq.;* and see Lehmann, Findings and Recommendations on Court Services, a Division Report of the Milwaukee County Survey of Social Welfare and Health Services, Inc. (July, 1959) (unpublished); Public Administration Service, Administration of Court and Legal Services in the Government of Milwaukee County 2, 44 (1955) mimeographed.

53 PHOENIX STUDY 9 *et seq.*

54 Report of the New Jersey Supreme Court's Committee on Juvenile and Domestic Relations Courts (April 19, 1956) (mimeographed, pages unnumbered); California, see *supra* note 48.

Other areas in which confusion of jurisdiction has been especially noted are: traffic-juvenile,[55] mental,[56] and criminal.[57]

This problem, that of confused jurisdiction, may be said to be aggravated, in metropolitan areas, by the presence there of many independently existing special purpose courts, with jagged fragments of jurisdiction confusing even to experienced metropolitan attorneys. In Detroit, for example, there is perennial confusion about whether the Common Pleas Court (a consolidation of justices of the peace which inherited the civil jurisdiction of city justices of the peace remaining when the criminal jurisdiction was transferred to a predecessor of Recorder's Court)[58] still retains authority to exercise preliminary criminal jurisdiction to arraign, examine, and bind over, by virtue of the continuing status of Common Pleas judges as "justices of the peace." A similar area of confusion exists in attempting to determine the jurisdiction, if any, of the Recorder's Court *qua* circuit court to entertain appeals from its own misdemeanor division, or the jurisdiction of Wayne County Circuit Court to exercise such jurisdiction.[59] Such special problems usually accompany the establishment of a complex court system and may be regarded as typical of most metropolitan areas.

Finally, the presence in metropolitan areas of large numbers of unassimilated recent migrants, when combined with the relatively predominant caseloads of personal problem, traffic, and small claims cases, in which attorneys often do not participate, contributes to and exaggerates the incidence and impact of jurisdictional confusion upon the metropolitan courts.

[55] Los Angeles Study 322, 290.

[56] Public Administration Service, Administration of Court and Legal Services in the Government of Milwaukee County 63.

[57] See, for example, Lepawsky, *op. cit. supra* note 49, at 58 *et seq.*

[58] *Supra* p. 49, note 14.

[59] Detroit Study 45-46, 50.

e. Lack of Specialized Jurisdiction to Deal Properly with Special Cases

This caption describes, not so much a category separate from those just discussed, but rather another facet of the specific disadvantages encountered in a multiple court system with a multiplicity of special purpose courts. A few examples will suggest the nature of the problem. Where a defendant in a criminal court appears to be suffering from what seems to be a mental illness, the metropolitan criminal court has difficulty in determining its proper course of action. If the case happens to fall within the category of murder or certain sex offenses, the court may be able to reach the problem by invoking certain specialized statutes permitting the use of a sanity commission and of hospitalization instead of trial and conviction in those cases. Where, however, the case falls into no such category, there is difficulty.

Suppose that a traffic court defendant, examined by Recorder's Court Psychopathic Clinic in Detroit, is found to be psychotic? Or suppose that an assault case, involving a beating administered by a son to his aged mother, suggests that the son needs immediate psychiatric hospitalization?

As noted in the Detroit study, Recorder's Court has evolved an ingenious method of solving the problem by deputizing one of its psychologists as a deputy sheriff and by having her file mental petitions on such cases, meanwhile continuing the criminal matter pending outcome of commitment proceedings in the probate court. The legal risks of such a course are obvious enough; the necessity of taking them is also. The metropolitan community particularly has the need to assure itself that such special problems will be met: because of its crowds and confusions, the community has more to fear from the insane driver and the assaultive son, and for the same reasons, there is less likelihood that resources in the community outside the criminal court will meet the need.

Similar problems are encountered in the lack of jurisdiction of a divorce court to place children in facilities available to the juvenile court, where separate from the divorce court; in the lack of jurisdiction of a criminal court to enforce restitution where such enforcement will converge upon another court's jurisdiction of a civil suit; and in the lack of jurisdiction of a criminal court confronted with a "contributing"[60] case to deal with the problems of the exploited minors.

Section 3. Restraints upon Judicial Control Essential to Proper Disposition of Cases

A consideration of jurisdictional problems of metropolitan trial courts would be incomplete and unrealistic without some attention to the real effectiveness of the court's authority to dispose of cases. This power, as has been noted,[61] is in most American jurisdictions more or less hamstrung by constitutional or legislative systems which deny full rule-making power to judges. Detailed practice acts and codes of procedure are often mentioned as depriving the trial judge of necessary power by restricting his discretion to regulate the conduct of judicial business.

The general problem is discussed in *Minimum Standards,* where the general trend is noted of broadening rule-making and supervisory power in the state court of last resort.[62]

It is suggested that in a multi-judge court in a large metropolitan area the lack of authority in the trial court to deal with its special problems (e.g., docket delay, high-filing,

[60] Usually the court with jurisdiction over criminal offenses will deal with persons charged with contributing to the delinquency of a minor apart from the court with jurisdiction over the juvenile.

[61] *Supra* p. 96.

[62] Vanderbilt, Minimum Standards 140. See also annual reports of A.B.A. Section of Judicial Administration for developments subsequent to publication of Minimum Standards in 1949.

splintering) through an experienced presiding judge should be viewed as a lack of essential authority. In Detroit Recorder's Court, for example, an experienced criminal lawyer can easily delay trial indefinitely or maneuver his case before a judge known to be cooperative by a little adroit footwork at the time the case is assigned.[63] In the Superior Court of Chicago, this writer was impressed by the way in which a case, finally discontinued for want of progress after several years of continuances granted at counsel's request, was promptly reinstated, as of right, by filing the case anew. If the court is so helpless to rid its docket of deadwood, can we properly hold the court responsible for the docket delay?

Along the same line, it was noted that the system which prevailed in Milwaukee for docketing cases during the time of this writer's observation (May 1953) required that an attorney request the setting of a case for trial before the case could be set. To put it another way, the procedural rules were such that until counsel signified readiness to go to trial, there was said to be nothing the judges could do about hastening the progress of any case, nor could they discontinue it for no progress. At that time, there was a delay of more than two years in reaching divorce cases, including uncontested cases, for hearing, and this time is measured from and after the filing of the praecipe.[64] Predecretal motions, as for temporary support and custody, required more than three months from the time they were ready for hearing in order to reach hearing by a referee. If a judicial hearing was required, the time was much longer.

Another example of lack of adequate judicial control over the metropolitan court caseload has been touched upon in the discussion of "high filing" hereinabove. Outside New York and New Jersey, we have heard of no metropolitan area in which any attempt has been made to achieve ade-

[63] Detroit Study 203.
[64] Family Cases 212.

quate centralized judicial authority to evaluate each case at pretrial and to assign it to the appropriate level for trial.

We suggest, then, that the problems of the metropolitan trial court are complicated by the lack of real power of the trial judges to control the place of filing of the case, the pretrial progress of the case, the conduct of the trial, and other aspects of judicial business. This lack of power varies from place to place, but no metropolitan area is known where all the components of the metropolitan trial court system are under the control of a bench directed by a presiding or executive judge with adequate authority over the system as such.

SECTION 4. MODERN REPLACEMENTS FOR THE JUSTICE OF PEACE SYSTEM

Earlier in this chapter,[65] the large number of unreconstructed lay justice courts operating in metropolitan areas were mentioned in the context of their relationship to the problem of multiplicity of courts. Within the mother-cities themselves, as distinguished from the satellite area outside, some progress has been made towards replacing the individual justice of the peace system.

In 1938, the American Bar Association adopted as one of its minimum standards for the administration of justice the abolition of justices of the peace as individual courts, substituting therefor

> municipal courts or courts with wider territorial jurisdiction, properly organized and housed, having trained and salaried judges, competent clerks, office equipment sufficient for keeping proper records, and sitting, so far as practical, at such times and places as the needs of a community indicate.[66]

Most of the effort of the American Bar Association has been concentrated, since 1938, upon the modernization of

[65] *Supra* p. 158 *et seq.*
[66] MINIMUM STANDARDS 264.

courts dealing with traffic offenses, dealt with hereinafter.

In the survey of justice of the peace courts made by Warren for the American Bar Association, the final report contains the following comment by Chief Justice Vanderbilt:

> The justice of the peace is one of the major problems in the field of the administration of justice. Inherited from the English judiciary the office was intended to provide a ready means for the settlement of petty complaints. . . . Its ineffectiveness . . . can be traced to two factors: *first,* in adopting the justice court . . . the colonists neglected to take with it the safeguards there provided; *second,* the change from rural to urban civilization found it poorly fitted to meet the new requirements.[67]

The safeguards he referred to were, first, qualification of judges, and, second, supervision with respect to records, funds, and procedural practices.[68]

The same report quotes the late Edson R. Sunderland:

> The administration of justice is not properly a city (or local) function, but an obligation of the state, and jurisdictional barriers around incorporated cities, with the resulting inequitable discrepancies between urban and rural justice, are out of place in a modern commonwealth.[69]

Within the mother-cities themselves, and in many of the larger satellite cities within the metropolitan areas, the municipal court movement has eliminated the original individual justice courts, substituting for them municipal or mayors' or city justice or small claims courts, with jurisdiction over small claims, petty criminal offenses, or both.[70]

[67] *Id.* at 678.

[68] *Id.* at 264.

[69] *Id.* at 263, quoting *Efficiency of Justice Courts in Michigan,* 4 MICH. JUDICIAL COUNCIL REPORT (1934).

[70] See POUND, ORGANIZATION OF COURTS 245, 263 *et seq.* (1940). For the present status, see SMALL CLAIMS COURTS, IN THE UNITED STATES, a recent study of the Institute of Judicial Administration, No. 3-U6 (Aug. 10, 1955) and a 1958 supplement thereto, as well as the current reports of the A.B.A. Section of Judicial Administration and Traffic Committee. See also the excellent brief survey, *Metropolitan Criminal Courts of First Instance,* 70 HARV. L. REV. 320 (Note) (1956).

So far there has been little indication of success, though some interest has been expressed, in extending geographic jurisdiction of municipal courts into the area lying beyond the limits of the mother-city but within the geographic limits of its population community. A recent exception is the new Metropolitan Court of Miami, Florida.

The modernization of the justice of the peace system within Metropolis presents certain problems of effective control. The façade of reform has sometimes been found to conceal inadequacies such as unqualified personnel, superficial or otherwise inadequate attention to cases, pressure to relieve delay in the upper layer of the trial court by becoming a duplicate of that court, lurking corruption, physical inaccessibility, and loss of public confidence.[71] These are particularly sensitive problems in the metropolitan areas because they are harder to root out and determine responsibility and because they have impact upon such large numbers of litigants.

Section 5. Summation

Summing up, then, it is suggested that the special jurisdictional problem of the metropolitan trial court system, yet largely unsolved, is that of providing a tribunal or series of tribunals (a) with adequate geographic jurisdiction to reach the real as opposed to the original legal community, and yet be readily accessible to all; (b) with a means of integrating jurisdictional control so as to avoid conflicting, confused, or competing jurisdiction, and yet provide for informed attention to special types of cases; (c) with sufficient inherent power in the judiciary to permit control by the court

[71] See, for example, Pound, *op. cit. supra* note 70, at 264; comment of Minnesota committeeman, *supra* p. 160. Los Angeles Study recommendation ZZ at 404. During brief observation in Los Angeles, this writer noted the problem of physical inaccessibility of municipal courts in suburbs there as one of significance to the structural system. See the Detroit Study 214 *et seq.* dealing with the Detroit Court of Common Pleas and the Early Sessions (misdemeanor) Division of Recorder's Court.

of all aspects of judicial business, and yet protect the prerogatives of counsel and the right to due process of every litigant; (d) with sufficient centralized control to achieve responsible knowledge of and control over each unit in the caseload, and yet preserve full relationship to the over-all hierarchy of judicial control in the state trial court system of which the metropolitan trial court system is a part.

CHAPTER VI

Special Types of Cases

SECTION 1. SEPARATE COURTS FOR SPECIALIZED SUBJECT MATTER

a. Introductory Note

As has been pointed out in earlier portions of this study, the predominance of certain types of cases occurring in metropolitan areas has resulted in the need to isolate certain cases by subject matter, in an attempt to achieve more knowledgeable and expeditious disposition.[1] This need has variously expressed itself in (1) the establishment of entirely separate courts of specialized subject-matter jurisdiction; (2) the development of specialized divisions or parts of general courts, sometimes manned by specialized judges; or (3) the segregation of certain cases by subject matter into specialized dockets or calendars. These categories are not always easy to differentiate. A tribunal established by statute as a division of another court may, upon close analysis, turn out to be in every sense a fully separate court, while what looks, on paper, like a separate court may turn out, as administered, to be fully integrated with some or all of the rest of the court system.

The material in this chapter is therefore presented with the *caveat* that a change in personnel, administrative practices, court rule, or any combination of these, may alter the actual character of any court mentioned insofar as these three classifications are concerned.

b. Small Claims and Conciliation Courts

Early studies emphasizing the unsatisfactory performance of lay justices of the peace resulted in a movement to develop

[1] *Supra* pp. 54-72, 110-13, 125, and 155.

municipal courts and other modern substitutes for the original justice of the peace system, to handle small civil claims and petty criminal cases.[2] Substantial replacement, within the mother-cities of metropolitan areas, of individual justices of the peace by some form of municipal tribunal has been mentioned.[3] The extent and prevailing form of the "small claims court" movement, including conciliation (informal settlement), is tabulated in a recent publication of the Institute of Judicial Administration.[4] Examples of the independent small claims court include the Court of Common Pleas of the City of Detroit (civil justice jurisdiction throughout the city), the Municipal Court of St. Paul, special act courts in Hartford, Stamford, and Baltimore, the Municipal Court of Chicago (special branch of which is devoted to small claims), the Municipal Court of the District of Columbia (special branch for small claims), and the Minneapolis Conciliation Court, established in 1955.[5] None of these courts is statewide; none is structurally integrated into the state court system. Miami and Wichita Falls, Texas, are the only metropolitan areas which, in response to our questionnaire, reported a separate small claims court.

c. Separate Traffic Courts

Warren recommended separate traffic courts, organized by districts as part of a statewide traffic court system. So far as we can learn, this recommendation has not been adopted in any state, so that Mr. Justice Vanderbilt's statement in *Minimum Standards* is still correct.[6] Sixteen states,

[2] *Supra* pp. 110-11.
[3] See *supra* p. 175.
[4] INSTITUTE OF JUDICIAL ADMINISTRATION, SMALL CLAIMS COURTS IN THE UNITED STATES, No. 3-U6 (Aug. 10, 1955), Conciliation Procedures at 5; detailed listing and analysis at Appendix B, beginning at 41.
[5] MINN. LAWS 1955, ch. 129.
[6] WARREN, TRAFFIC COURTS, (Judicial Administrative Series) n. 10 at 237 (1942); VANDERBILT, MINIMUM STANDARDS 287.

according to *Minimum Standards,* permit the establishment of separate traffic courts, and that source states that there are many separate full-time traffic courts under a variety of names.[7]

Responding to our questionnaire, Miami reports a separate Metropolitan Traffic Court.[8] In Detroit, the Traffic and Ordinance Division of Recorder's Court is housed in a separate building with its own staff, records, and financial resources. Its jurisdiction and caseload are distinct from that of the parent court, and it has been judicially recognized as a separate entity.[9]

Ordinance cases other than traffic ordinance cases, in this court, are routinely handled by a referee and are insignificant in incidence compared to the traffic caseload. Therefore, it may be regarded as a separate specialized traffic court. The total disposition of cases in this court for the calendar year 1957 is as follows:

felony and high misdemeanors	94
state misdemeanors	5,457
accident (ordinance)	21,772
moving (ordinance)	458,413
parking (ordinance)	482,705
miscellaneous (ordinance)	12,122
	980,563

A recent study of courts in the State of New York reports a separate traffic court for Albany.[10] We have not been able to learn of other structurally separate metropolitan traffic courts, though no doubt there are many traffic divisions of other courts which, upon analysis, would emerge as separate in administration. Readers interested in this

[7] *Ibid.*
[8] And see 187, *infra.*
[9] BAD HOUSEKEEPING 37.
[10] MINIMUM STANDARDS 290 *et seq.*

subject are referred to the American Bar Association's special Traffic Courts Committee and its reports.[11]

d. Separate Courts for Criminal Cases

The outstanding example of a fully specialized criminal court, with exclusive and complete jurisdiction over all offenses occurring within the city, is the Recorder's Court of Detroit, described in detail in the first study of the present series.[12] This court inherited jurisdiction from city police justices, from the city recorder (ordinance violations), and from the circuit court (branch of state court of original trial jurisdiction), and thus has jurisdiction over all criminal cases, including misdemeanor and felony cases, and ordinance violations occurring within the city limits. It is a combined city and state court, having ten judges in the Recorder's Court proper and two (plus four referees) in its Traffic and Ordinance Division, which, as has been noted, [13] is actually a separate court. So far as we can learn, this tribunal is unique in its structure and jurisdiction.

The Chicago area has a specialized criminal court, the Criminal Court of Cook County, with jurisdiction concurrent with that of justices of the peace in minor criminal actions. The Court of Special Sessions of New York County is specialized with jurisdiction in the misdemeanor bracket. In addition, there are forty-nine city magistrates in New York City, with general jurisdiction over such criminal offenses as disorderly conduct, vagrancy, public intoxication, and ordinance violations other than misdemeanors.[14]

The Council of State Governments reports the existence

[11] In many large cities there are separate violations bureaus which perform the functions of separate traffic courts, though some of them are under the jurisdiction—not of judges—but of police departments, court clerks, and other nonjudicial city officials. This presents a due process problem.

[12] DETROIT STUDY 44-46 *et passim*.

[13] *Supra* pp. 49-50; DETROIT STUDY 46-47.

[14] See BAD HOUSEKEEPING 33.

of special separate criminal trial courts in various cities in the following states: Florida, Indiana, Tennessee, and Texas.[15] The legislative history of the specialized criminal court is touched upon by Pound.[16] Many cities have police judges, or magistrates, or other petty tribunals devoted to the lower range of offenses, such as ordinance violations and petty criminal offenses. These are variously called magistrates', mayors', recorders', or police courts, and occur in great variety and profusion throughout the metropolitan areas.

In London, the Metropolitan Police Courts (magistrates) and the Central Criminal Court (the Old Bailey) provide good examples of the establishment of separate criminal tribunals in metropolitan centers.[17]

e. Separate Juvenile and Family Courts

The family cases present complexity, multiplicity, and complication at its worst. It has been well noted that a single family problem frequently is expressed in half a dozen different metropolitan courts at once.[18] In most metropolitan areas examined during this study, the special nature of the juvenile and domestic relations caseload has led to the establishment of specialized facilities to deal with them.

The Institute of Judicial Administration reports structurally separate juvenile courts covering some or all areas in twenty-one states.[19] According to the same source, juvenile

[15] Trial Courts of General Jurisdiction in the Forty-Eight States 15 (mimeographed, 1951).

[16] POUND, ORGANIZATION OF COURTS 245 (1940).

[17] JACKSON, MACHINERY OF JUSTICE IN ENGLAND 82-87 (1940). For an excellent discussion and analysis of the structure of metropolitan criminal courts, see 70 HARV. L. REV. 320 (Note) (1956).

[18] Pound, *Administration of Justice in the Modern City*, 26 HARV. L. REV. 302, 313 (1913); Alexander, *The Family Court of the Future*, 36 J. AM. JUD. SOC'Y 38 (1952); DETROIT STUDY 231; Sicher, N.Y. LAW J. (Sept. 19, 1949), *inter alia*.

[19] INSTITUTE OF JUDICIAL ADMINISTRATION, JUVENILE COURTS—JURISDICTION No. 2-U21 (March 18, 1954).

courts have been established as separate entities in certain cities or on a population basis in Colorado, Delaware, Indiana, Louisiana, New York, Oklahoma, South Carolina, and Virginia. A separate juvenile court established for Indianapolis (Marion County, Indiana) in 1945 has been described in a recent study,[20] as has the Milwaukee County juvenile court.[21]

Structurally separate courts variously described as "juvenile," "family," or "domestic relations" courts are reported by the Institute of Judicial Administration in twenty-one states.[22] Many of these are established in metropolitan areas, either on the basis of population or in certain cities.

In Jackson, Jefferson, and Mobile counties in Alabama, there is a statutory court having jurisdiction over juvenile (neglect, dependency, delinquency), contributing-to-delinquency, school and child labor law violations, and certain domestic criminal cases such as child abandonment, assault and battery, and cruelty to children. In Delaware, courts in three populous counties have jurisdiction including, besides juvenile cases, custody matters in separation cases, proceedings to test custody, support, and certain family offenses. The District of Columbia has a fairly new "family court," with paternity and support matters added to jurisdiction over juvenile cases, but without jurisdiction over custody or adoption. In Florida, Broward and Dade counties have special courts with custody and support jurisdiction and with general chancery power over persons and estates of minors, guardianship, and such criminal matters as cruelty to children and child labor violations, in addition to jurisdiction over juvenile cases (dependency, neglect, delinquency).

Separate courts with some aspects of jurisdiction over family cases, in addition to the basic jurisdiction over juve-

[20] VIRTUE, FAMILY CASES 114.

[21] *Id.* at 179.

[22] INSTITUTE OF JUDICIAL ADMINISTRATION, JUVENILE, FAMILY AND DOMESTIC RELATIONS COURTS, SEPARATELY CONSTITUTED No. 3-U28 (Sept. 1, 1955).

nile cases, are shown by this same report to have been established on a population or city basis in the following areas: Georgia (county of 50,000 or more); Indiana (county of 250,000 or more); Louisiana (constitutional family court, East Baton Rouge Parish);[23] Massachusetts (Boston); New Jersey (county of 600,000 or more);[24] New York (children's Court in certain counties; Domestic Relations Court of City of New York, with Children's Court Division and Family Court Division); North Carolina (certain counties and cities of 5,000 or more, discretion of county commissioners); Pennsylvania (Allegheny County); South Carolina (Domestic Relations Court established in each county containing city of over 70,000; Juvenile Domestic Relations Court in each county containing city of 60,000–70,000 population; each court has Children's Court Division and Domestic Relations Division); Texas (Potter, Lubbock, Harris, Starr counties); Utah (public welfare commission may establish districts with gubernatorial approval; Virginia (each county and city, or combination);[25] West Virginia (Cabell and Kanawha counties); Wisconsin (each county of 500,000 or more).

SECTION 2. SEPARATELY FUNCTIONING DIVISIONS, OR PARTS

a. Small Claims

Most metropolitan court systems make provisions for special handling of small claims. The typical arrangement

[23] The Baton Rouge Family Court, which was established in 1954, has unusually complete jurisdiction over all aspects of family litigation. The jurisdiction is spelled out in detail in the constitutional provision establishing the court, LA. CONST. art. VII, §53a. And see LA. REV. STAT. ANN. tit. 13, ch. 6 (1951).

[24] See N. J. STAT. ANN. tit. 2A, ch. 4 (1952); N. J. STAT. ANN. tit. 2A, ch. 4 (Supp. 1954) ("In each county with population of 600,000 or more, and, in discretion of governor with consent of senate, in each county of not less than 305,000 nor more than 370,000 population. In any other county or combination of counties, upon petition of 5% of registered voters of county or counties or resolution by board or boards of chosen freeholders, and majority vote by voters of county or counties.")

[25] *Op. cit. supra* note 22, at 6.

is a small claims, or conciliation, division in a municipal court. The Small Claims Division of the Municipal Court of Chicago, established by court rule, is well known, as is the Cleveland conciliation branch.[26] A tabular presentation of specialized divisions or branches dealing with small claims has been made available.[27] How many of these tribunals have specialized judges, we have no way of knowing, but we have formed the impression that the attendance of a long-term specialized judge is usually the boundary dividing the specialized docket, or part, from the specialized division. This is the point where the latter begins to emerge as a separate operating unit.

The Municipal Court of New York City, itself restricted to claims for less than $3,000, has a small claims part for actions not in excess of $100. In Detroit, the Court of Common Pleas, a nine-judge court consolidating the jurisdiction of the former city civil justices of the peace, has jurisdiction up to $3,000. It used to have an active conciliation division, which fell into disuse after the depression and now exists in name only.[28] This illustrates one advantage of the specialized division over the separate specialized court—when the special need ceases to exist or to justify full-scale operation of the specialized division, the facilities can be absorbed elsewhere in the court, to be reinvoked by court rule whenever and to whatever extent the future caseload makes advisable.

The Los Angeles study shows twenty-one municipal court judicial districts in Los Angeles County. The largest, the Los Angeles Municipal Court, is a forty-two judge court with various divisions; the others are autonomous. Within the Los Angeles court, the small claims court consists of two full-time divisions of the municipal court, located in a

[26] POUND, *op. cit. supra* note 16, at 266 *et seq.*

[27] INSTITUTE OF JUDICIAL ADMINISTRATION, *op. cit. supra* note 4, app. B, beginning p. 41.

[28] DETROIT STUDY 88-90.

separate building apart from the other municipal courtrooms. The operation is described in the Holbrook study.[29] More than one-third of all civil filings in municipal courts in Los Angeles County are small claims actions (demand not over $100). In 1953-1954 in the Los Angeles Municipal Court alone there were 49,235 such cases filed. No attorneys are permitted, and the question has been raised whether sufficient time is given to each litigant to convince him that he has had his day in court.[30] This operation is so specialized that a special calendar has been set up within the specialized division, known as "store day," and reserved for stores and other businesses.

b. Traffic

It is the conclusion of this writer, based on observation, library research, and questionnaire reports received for this study, that in most metropolitan areas traffic cases are physically and administratively separated from the rest of the caseload of the municipal, police, or magistrates' court which handles traffic cases. Although the specialized facility for handling such traffic cases is often called a "traffic court" (as in Miami), the entity so designated is most often not structurally a separate court but rather a specialized appendage of a court with more general jurisdiction.

The specializing process is described in part as follows in the recent *Harvard Law Review* survey of metropolitan criminal courts:

> Criminal courts of first instance have tended in large cities to become specialized in their handling of cases, and these specialized courts have been vested with city-wide rather than police-district jurisdiction. Traffic is generally the first area of specialization and is the only area which has been established as a separate city-wide division in Philadelphia, New Orleans, and Atlanta. . . .[31]

[29] LOS ANGELES STUDY 272, 274, 282.
[30] *Id.* at 304, and see tables following.
[31] *Metropolitan Criminal Courts,* 70 HARV. L. REV. 320, 322 (Note) (1956).

The Warren study reported that of fifty-six populous cities in the various states surveyed, ten had municipal courts with several branches, one or more of which was devoted exclusively to traffic, and eleven either set separate days for traffic cases or heard them during special hours.[32]

Direct observation for this series of studies showed that in Detroit traffic cases are handled by a fully separate court, linked in name only to the Recorder's Court.[33] In Los Angeles, four courtrooms in the Los Angeles court are designated as traffic divisions and are housed in the Traffic Courts Building, handling traffic offenses committed within the City of Los Angeles. The four branch courts in the judicial district handle offenses committed in each respective district. All jury trials arising out of traffic violations committed within the judicial district (barring San Pedro, Van Nuys, and San Fernando) are sent through the misdemeanor master calendar division at the Civic Center. "Of the four traffic divisions at the Civic Center, one is designated as the traffic arraignment division, another as the traffic master calendar division." Most traffic cases are disposed of without court appearances.[34]

In New York City, the City Magistrates' Court (forty-nine magistrates) is divided into court districts in each borough other than the Bronx. In addition, the court sits in twelve divisions, one of which is known as the "traffic court."

c. Juvenile and Family Cases

The best known special divisions handling family cases are probably the Ohio "family courts." Each is established as a separate division of the Court of Common Pleas, each has its own separately elected specialist judge, and each

[32] Vanderbilt, Minimum Standards 647, app. C.
[33] *Supra* p. 182.
[34] Los Angeles Study 277.

contains within itself separate departments for juvenile and for domestic relations cases. Such courts have been established in Cincinnati, Dayton, Columbus, Toledo, Akron, Canton. Youngstown, and Warren. The operation of the Toledo and Cincinnati courts has been described as observed by this writer in another study.[35] Their jurisdiction includes divorce, juvenile, and bastardy cases.

Responding to questionnaire for this study, the following metropolitan areas report specialized divisions handling family cases within more generalized courts:

Cleveland reports a separate domestic relations branch of the Court of Common Pleas (but in 1961, a new statutory family court will be established there). Las Vegas reports a separate juvenile division (called "juvenile court") in the district court. St. Paul reports a juvenile branch of the district court, while Philadelphia reports several divisions within the municipal court, i.e., juvenile division, domestic relations division, adoption division, and division for delinquent women.

Minneapolis has recently set up a specialized juvenile division and a family division in the district court; Boise has a juvenile division in the probate court.[36]

Special divisions created by statute within specialized courts occur in several large metropolitan areas, for example, New York City and Charleston, South Carolina.[37]

Recorder's Court in Detroit has recently established a Youth Division by court rule; Juvenile Division of Probate Court of Wayne County (Detroit) has separate divisions for neglect, girls' delinquency, and boys' delinquency cases;

[35] FAMILY CASES 175 *et seq.*

[36] For other "juvenile courts" which are appellations applied to probate or other courts while engaged in handling juvenile cases, see INSTITUTE OF JUDICIAL ADMINISTRATION, JUVENILE COURTS—JURISDICTION, No. 2-U21 (March 18, 1954); SIMES, MODEL PROBATE CODE 462 and statutes cited (1946).

[37] For descriptions of the labyrinth of courts and divisions handling family cases in New York, see KAHN, A COURT FOR CHILDREN (1953); GELLHORN, CHILDREN AND FAMILIES IN THE COURTS OF NEW YORK CITY (1954); BAD HOUSEKEEPING 32 *et seq.*

Municipal Court in Chicago has a Boys' Court, a Women's Court, and a Family Court as separate divisions.

In Los Angeles, the judges have invoked their constitutional and statutory authority to create a separate conciliation division (meaning, in this context, reconciliation of divorcing spouses) in the Superior Court.[38] The operation of this division has been described by this writer as it existed prior to 1953,[39] and by Judge Louis H. Burke, now presiding judge of the Superior Court of Los Angeles, as it developed under his guidance from 1953 on.[40]

d. Other

It is not unusual to find that where jurisdiction of criminal cases is placed in a court of more general jurisdiction, the actual handling of such cases in metropolitan cities is arranged within a specialized division of that court, either by court rule or statute, with its own physical facilities and full-time staff. Thus, for example, in Los Angeles' Civic Center, the Superior Court of Los Angeles County has established a criminal division with its own master calendar, with eight[41] departments devoting full time to criminal cases, and with its own presiding judge. Holbrook reports that all informations, indictments, and accusations are assigned automatically to the master calendar department of the criminal division, and all proceedings prior to trial are heard and determined in this division.[42]

The specialized division for chancery and probate cases

[38] CAL. CONST. art. VI, §7; CAL. CIV. CODE §§ 1730-1772.

[39] FAMILY CASES 7-10; 254-58.

[40] Burke, Problems of Court Administration in a Metropolitan Court XII at 10 *et seq.* (Nov. 23, 1959) (typescript of address delivered before the National Conference on Judicial Selection and Court Administration, Chicago) also in 43 J. AM. JUD SOC'Y 190 (1960). See also BURKE, WITH THIS RING (1958).

[41] This was the number reported by Holbrook. Judge Burke, in the address cited in note 40 *supra,* reports fourteen criminal departments in 1960.

[42] LOS ANGELES STUDY 141 *et seq.*

is also common. An example is the separate probate division of the Superior Court of Los Angeles. In some places (for example, Chattanooga) we are told that probate matters are handled as part of the business of one division of the chancery court.[43]

Owing to the dominance of negligence cases in most law-jury caseloads and the relatively longer trial length of such cases, investigators of court delay have emphasized the importance of giving special attention to such cases. So far as we have been able to learn, there are no specialized divisions exclusively designed to handle negligence cases alone. The negligence case emerges as a special problem because of its special trial time requirements, and hence is an administrative problem related to case progress in metropolitan areas, rather than a problem of structure.

In several large metropolitan areas, it has been observed or reported that city transit cases loom large enough in the caseload of the general trial court to be separately docketed and often assigned to specialist judges and prosecutors or assistant city attorneys.

Section 3. Specialized Dockets or Calendars

a. Introductory Note

The term "specialized dockets or calendars" is used here to differentiate between an operation administered as a self-contained unit focused on a specialized caseload (though structurally part of a court of wider jurisdiction), on the one hand, and a more informal segregation of certain types of cases for expeditious handling within an operation geared to a miscellaneous caseload, on the other.

The former, discussed in the preceding section, shows an adaptation of the entire judicial mechanism to the needs of a particular type of case. The latter may be no more than

[43] Information received by questionnaire.

a clerical or docketing device by which certain types of cases are segregated for more convenient processing. The latter, then, displays a simpler and less differentiated response to the metropolitan need for specialized attention to certain types of cases.

The meaningful use of the distinction depends on practice, not on nomenclature. Such words as "court," "part," "division," "calendar," "dockets," and so on, are used in widely varying senses and are subject to interchangeable usage. The reader is cautioned that except where based on actual observation, the designation of any operation as belonging in this section rather than the preceding is based on nomenclature used in library research or reports received and should be read as subject to further analysis in light of the actual nature of the operation.

b. Examples of Specialized Dockets or Calendars

In the small claims area, it is probable that some of the examples already given of conciliation and/or small claims "divisions" within larger courts might prove, upon observation, to be mere calendaring devices without real specialized administration. It is interesting to contrast the machinery for handling small claims within the City of Los Angeles with that employed in outlying branches of the municipal court, where the judges hear all types of cases, and where small claims are heard on Thursday afternoons, traffic cases for half an hour every morning, and civil trials every Monday and Thursday.

Responding to questionnaire, St. Paul reports that its municipal court has separate calendars for conciliation, traffic, and criminal cases.

In the State of Washington, it is reported that family, juvenile, and probate work in the metropolitan areas is segregated into specialized dockets, each of which is assigned to one judge for a limited time, then rotated. In Cleveland and Minneapolis, rapid transit cases are assembled into separate dockets. Milwaukee separates contested divorces and uncontested divorces, and rotates these two special dockets among the judges.[44] In Milwaukee, ordinance violation cases coming into district court are by statute heard in branch "2" of that court, and misdemeanors in branch "1," unless transferred for prejudice.

Several cities report separate calendars for criminal and divorce cases. In Des Moines, Iowa, the district court handles juvenile cases in one specialized docket, domestic relations cases in another. In Phoenix, juvenile work in the superior court is assigned to one judge full time, for a minimum time of one to three years, but other domestic relations cases are handled by judges on general assignment.

The separate domestic relations dockets in San Francisco and Los Angeles have been described for this series of studies.[45]

In New York, there are many specialized calendars and dockets within the bewildering complication of courts serving the city. Typical are the Girls' Term of the Magistrates' Court and the "Social Court for Men" "intended for the arraignment of defendants arrested for disorderly conduct due to intoxication, whose condition indicates that social treatment is necessary for their rehabilitation."[46]

The psychopathic department of the superior court of Los Angeles, established by court rule, is located in the county hospital, and the judge assigned to that department handles all proceedings, other than guardianship, relating

[44] And see FAMILY CASES 178 *et seq.*, 204 *et seq.*

[45] LOS ANGELES STUDY 232-33; FAMILY CASES 10 *et seq.*, 23 *et seq.*

[46] *Metropolitan Criminal Courts*, 70 HARV. L. REV. 332 n. 74 (1956). For a discussion of the problems of dealing with the alcoholic in court see *id.* at 330 *et seq.;* and Foote, *Vagrancy-Type Law and Its Administration*, 104 U. PA. L. REV. 603, 631 (1956); Lacey, *Vagrancy and Other Crimes of Personal Condition*, 66 HARV. L. REV. 1203, 1218-19 (1953); TAPPAN, A STUDY OF THE WAYWARD MINOR COURT OF NEW YORK (1947); WORTHINGTON & TOPPING, SPECIALIZED COURTS DEALING WITH SEX DELINQUENCY (1925).

to the care, supervision, treatment, and restraint of alleged mentally ill persons, feeble-minded persons, drug or narcotic users, inebriates, users of stimulants, and mentally abnormal sex offenders.[47] A similar specialized assignment, with the hearings actually taking place in the hospital, was observed in San Francisco. It seems to this writer that this is the most successful method of handling mental cases (no matter how they have reached the litigation process) to obtain adequate medical evaluation, to protect the dignity and morale of the patient, and at the same time to observe the requirements of due process. In neither Los Angeles nor San Francisco is the judge assigned to the psychopathic department a permanent or specialized judge, but merely receives this assignment in rotation in his turn. Recent developments in the Los Angeles court include a prelitigation screening device consisting of a professional evaluation of the mental condition of persons alleged to be in need of commitment prior to court hearing.[48]

Other examples of specialized calendaring may be found in profusion in the literature of court administration.

Section 4. Specialized Judges

There is a good deal of controversy about the proper relationship of the judge to the specialized court, or division, or docket. On the one hand, it is asserted that prolonged assignment to a single subject matter, such as criminal cases, is unwise.[49] On the other, it is argued that it is useless to provide specialized dockets, administrative personnel, and expert professional consultants, unless the judge is permitted to become thoroughly familiar with and knowledgeable about the specialty.[50]

[47] Los Angeles Study 242.
[48] Burke, Problems of Court Administration, cited *supra* note 40, at 14-15.
[49] See, e.g., Criminal Justice in Cleveland 629 (Pound & Frankfurter eds. 1922). And see Los Angeles Study 56.
[50] Pound, Organization of Courts 258 (1940).

Dean Pound has been a persuasive advocate for the specialized judge, rather than the specialized court, as a remedy for waste of judicial manpower, for multiplicity of courts, and for perfunctory or otherwise inefficient disposition of special problem cases.

> . . . where separate courts are set up, jurisdictional lines become necessary which are not easy to draw in advance of experience. Such courts do not need to be separate in order to secure the services of specialist judges. As has been said before and cannot be said too often, specialized courts should be replaced by specialist judges sitting in branches or departments of unified courts.[51]

Observation has finally convinced this writer that successful specialization in such fields as juvenile and domestic relations cases is best accomplished where a specialized judge is made part of the unit handling the specialized cases.[52] The best known example, perhaps, is Judge Paul Alexander, of the Toledo Family Court, who is elected to that particular judgeship.

The more usually encountered method of selecting a specialist judge is that employed by the superior and municipal courts in Los Angeles, where the presiding judge of the particular court assigns judges to certain specialized assignments. In Los Angeles, the fixed policy is reported to favor periodic rotation of all assignments in order to avoid overspecialization and to avoid overtaxing certain judges with the "mankiller" assignments.[53] The unwillingness of many judges to accept a steady diet of divorce or juvenile cases is well known. This sometimes results, however, in prolonged assignment of a temperamentally well-qualified judge to a specialized family problem caseload, as observed in Los Angeles and Detroit. Holbrook notes that the dislike of municipal judges for the "Sunrise Court" (mostly arraignments for intoxication) is a motivating factor in deter-

[51] *Id.* at 271-72.
[52] For the reason given by Dean Pound, ORGANIZATION OF COURTS 272.
[53] LOS ANGELES STUDY 59-60.

mining the strict rotation policy of all assignments, including the "bête noire" assignments.

Another reason often given for avoiding overspecialization is the disadvantage of leaving the specialized court without knowledgeable judicial manpower when the long-term specialist finally retires. Several such situations have been encountered during observation.

Our information suggests the trend is towards specialized judgeships in the large metropolitan areas for traffic and juvenile cases, with other specialties occurring sporadically as the needs and personalities inspire them.

The Institute of Judicial Administration[54] notes judges specially elected or appointed for specialized juvenile, domestic relations, or family courts in approximately a dozen states. Those responding to our questionnaires report specialist judges selected for specialized family courts in Cleveland,[55] in Minneapolis, and in Charleston, South Carolina. The same persons report specialist judges assigned by presiding judges for fixed terms to full-time work in specialized divisions or dockets in Des Moines (juvenile, domestic relations), Baton Rouge (family), Phoenix (juvenile), Minneapolis (traffic, small claims, family court), St. Paul (juvenile), Las Vegas (juvenile, small claims), and Newark (juvenile, domestic relations).

During observation, a few elected specialists were encountered, but in the main the impression formed was that specialists develop after assignment on a routine rotation basis, and eventually become virtuosos in their specialties by leave of their colleagues. This occurs most often in the "personal problem" case area, where judges temperamentally suited to such a caseload are rare and, where found, have little competition from their brothers on the bench. Honesty compels the statement, however, that one or two

[54] JUVENILE, FAMILY AND DOMESTIC RELATIONS COURTS, *op. cit. supra* note 22.
[55] A newly created court, scheduled to commence operations in 1961.

juvenile court judges were encountered who gave the impression of having sought and kept that office because of the political advantages of appearing to be affectionately concerned with the needs of children.

There is controversy about the best method for selecting a specialist judge. This writer has formed the opinion that appointment by a presiding judge is, on the whole, the method offering more advantages and fewer disadvantages than other methods employed. This method places responsibility for selecting the specialist, and for determining the length of his assignment, upon the judge responsible for administration of the entire court. The advantages are integration of the specialty with the entire court administration problem, flexibility, and avoidance of the dangers of empire building, multiplicity of overspecialized courts, unavailability of or waste of judicial manpower, and retention of ultimate control of the specialty, along with other aspects of court administration, by the judicial officer responsible for the administration of the total court.

Section 5. Summation

Material gathered for this series of studies and all other material available to the writer show a strong trend, in virtually all metropolitan areas, towards the development of some type of specialized facilities for dealing with certain types of cases, notably traffic, criminal, small claims, and family cases. The need for such special facilities has increased the tendency towards the occurrence of a multiplicity of separate courts, the principal structural disadvantage of metropolitan court systems.

The special division within a larger court system, where such division is operated as a unit with specialized personnel but is integrated with the general court system under a presiding judge, appears to offer the most promising method of meeting the needs of special types of cases without incurring waste, multiplicity, and confusion.

Special devices for docketing or calendaring certain types of cases are often encountered. These are too ephemeral to offer grounds for generalization. The special docket does seem to be a typical first step towards real specialization when operated by a judge temperamentally well suited to a specialized caseload under a presiding judge sympathetic to development of the specialty.

It is the writer's impression that the establishment of specialized courts or divisions by constitutional provision or statute has fallen out of professional favor, and that the contemporary preference is for the use of court rule for this purpose.

CHAPTER VII

Personnel

SECTION 1. JUDICIAL PERSONNEL

a. The Multi-Judge Court of Metropolis

THE metropolitan court is virtually always a multi-judge court.[1] The relationship of such a court to the community is inherently a different thing from that of the one-judge court which tried Huck Finn's father. Certain problems, such as selection and tenure, are the same in kind as those encountered anywhere but are aggravated in metropolitan areas by the size and complexity of the community, with attendant difficulties in communicating with the public. It is not easy for a citizen of New York or Los Angeles to obtain enough information about a judge's qualifications to evaluate him effectively.

Certain problems, such as division of judicial labor, development of administrative mechanisms, and determining responsibility for certain judicial acts, are not merely aggravations of similar problems occurring anywhere, but are peculiar to the multi-judge courts of the large metropolitan cities. Consider, for example, the Los Angeles voter, asked to choose between one judicial candidate advocating full integration of municipal branch courts, and another, who opposes this plan. The best informed and most conscientious scholars and judges disagree: how is the voter to express his preference on the basis of this issue?

Or suppose a voter is asked to choose between a judge who advocates compulsory pretrial and another who opposes

[1] For example (chosen at random from our questionnaires) there are 24 judges in the City of Cleveland, 6 in Baton Rouge, 22 in Milwaukee, 13 in Chattanooga, 12 in Des Moines, 46 in Miami, 40 in Philadelphia.

it? Or between a candidate who advocates a family court and another who opposes it as contributing to further fragmentation and overspecialization?

In a metropolitan area, as anywhere, the conscientious voter will make an attempt to get at the facts. But in a metropolitan area, with its multi-judge court, the facts when obtained are so complex, so confusing, and so controversial, even among judges and lawyers, that the judge-community relationship—basic to performance of courts under our scheme of government—is especially difficult.

b. Selection of Judges

Judges are still elected in most states. The American Bar Association has long given support to the American Bar plan, or Missouri plan, whereby judges are initially selected by a commission made up of representatives of the executive branch of government, the bar association, and the lay public, with reappointment or election of each judge upon his record.[2] This plan has been regarded in some quarters as subject to the disadvantage of bias towards the *status quo* through probable domination by the most conservative wing of the bar. However this may be, there is great concern in all the metropolitan areas known to these studies to obtain the best qualified judges on a basis other than that of political partisanship and to retain them in office free from pressures of a partisan political nature. Encountered everywhere, these pressures are badly aggravated in metropolitan courts because of the difficulty of tracing and identifying them, and the size and influence of the metropolitan political machine. Even in areas where judges are selected on a so-

[2] Vanderbilt, Minimum Standards. The plan is discussed in Chapter I. See also reports issued annually by the Section of Judicial Administration, and various reports in the Journal of the American Judicature Society, on the progress of various states and cities in improving their judicial selection methods.

called "nonpartisan" basis, as in Detroit, the selection is often regarded as political.[3]

The hopeless anonymity surrounding the metropolitan citizen in relation to his judge is underlined by the fact that in many places the so-called "elective" system for selecting judges comes down, in practice, to an appointive system, with successive re-elections almost assured to candidates designated "incumbent." In Los Angeles, there were seventy-eight superior court judges in office when the Holbrook questionnaires were distributed.[4] Of these, seventy were originally appointed by the governor, later succeeding themselves in elections. Holbrook comments that while in theory each judge has the potential threat of opposition, in practice the incumbent is rarely defeated. This appears to be the case in most metropolitan areas and underlines the special problems of devising a system of selection for metropolitan judges.

The California judges in the Los Angeles area were universally regarded, by the bar, as having unimpeachable integrity.[5] This has not always been the case with other metropolitan areas known to the survey. It is the writer's impression that one of the most serious problems of metropolitan courts is the difficulty of persuading first-rate men to become candidates for judgeships in areas where, rightly or wrongly, segments of the public regard the judiciary as susceptible to pressure by political factions. The kind of seasoned professional lawyer, with a marked flair for administration, who is most needed on the bench of the Metropolitan Court, is a sagacious man, and well he knows that no matter how high his ideals and scrupulous his performance, he will sometimes be accused of being a tool of the party bosses. Many judges overcome this factor by sheer

[3] DETROIT STUDY 63 *et seq.;* and see n. 25, p. 68.
[4] LOS ANGELES STUDY 47.
[5] *Id.* at 41.

moral energy and ability. The point is that it is there to be overcome.

c. Qualifications

In the Jacksonian era, belief that every man was fit to hold any public office, including judicial office, became part of the machinery for selecting judges. The Council of State Governments, in a recent comprehensive study, has set forth the general requirements for judges.[6] In most states, there are minimum age, residence, and citizenship requirements for all occupants of the bench. The Council reports that in twenty-nine states, judges of trial courts of general jurisdiction are required to have had legal experience as lawyers or judges.[7] In ten other states, they must be learned in the law. In the other nine, it is theoretically possible for persons without legal experience or learning to serve as judges in the major trial courts. California is one of the states in which all judges of trial courts are required to be attorneys, and this state also requires municipal court judges to be members of the bar. Justices of the peace must either be lawyers admitted to the California bar or judges of a superseded court or have passed a qualifying examination under regulations prescribed by the Judicial Council.[8] In Los Angeles County, Holbrook found that all the judges were legally qualified except for one individual, formerly a justice of the peace, who was blanketed in when his court became a municipal court.

In Michigan, although circuit court judges must be lawyers, neither probate court judges nor justices of the peace must be lawyers. Despite the lack of statutory requirements, however, we found no laymen occupying the bench in the

[6] Council of State Governments, Trial Courts of General Jurisdiction in the Forty-Eight States, Table 6 (1951).

[7] *Id.* at 35.

[8] Los Angeles Study 43.

City of Detroit (though outside Detroit only three out of eighteen city justices of the peace in the metropolitan area were members of the bar).[9]

The questionnaires returned for this study confirm the general impression that although there are still a few lay justices holding forth in the rural portions of the satellite part of the metropolitan districts, courts in the central cities of such areas are, for the most part, occupied by members of the bar. Lay justices of the peace, magistrates, police judges, or others in the same bracket of jurisdiction are reported in metropolitan districts as follows: Grand Forks, North Dakota, 2; Phoenix, Arizona, 1; Charleston, North Carolina, 2 in the city, 9 in the satellite area; Wichita Falls, Texas, 2; Milwaukee, 11 to 14 (estimate); Las Vegas, Nevada, 2 in Las Vegas, 6 in the satellite area; Boise, Idaho, 4 in the satellite area. Although no judge in Tennessee is required to be a lawyer, all in fact are.[10]

The problems of obtaining qualified judges for metropolitan courts are not, as we view them, centered around requiring that judges be lawyers (though this should, of course, be a minimum essential), but around insuring certain types of previous legal experience, specialized training, or

[9] A 1935 statute requiring circuit judges to be experienced practicing attorneys was held unconstitutional in 1937: Attorney General, *ex rel.* Cook, v. O'Neill, 280 Mich. 649 (1937). Thereafter, MICH. CONST. art. VII, §17 was amended in 1955 to require that justices of the Supreme Court and judges of the Circuit Courts be licensed to practice law. Municipal court judges in Michigan are required to be qualified lawyers. See authorities cited in DETROIT STUDY at 62, and see [1957-1958] 1 MICH. ATT'Y GEN. BIENNIAL REP. 37 (1957), discussing the various statutes. Act 5 of the Public Acts of 1956, as last amended by Act 209 of the Public Acts of 1959, Mich. Stat. Ann. (1959 rev.) §27.3937 (1), subpara. (8) requires home rule cities adopting municipal court provisions under that statute to provide for legally qualified judges. Since the MICH. CONST. (art. VII, §15) permits the legislature to make requirements for justices of the peace, it is thought likely that these statutory and charter requirements will survive court test. See, for example, People *ex rel.* Wexford County Prosecuting Attorney, v. Kearney, 345 Mich. 680 (1956). There is considerable controversy regarding the effect of statutory requirements for qualified judges of municipal or city justice courts.

[10] Examples selected from questionnaires returned by section committee personnel for this study.

experience in special types of cases, and around such basic intangibles as judicial temperament, good public presence, and both the ability and reputation for withstanding pressures of all kinds.[11]

d. Compensation

The fee system

Where justices of the peace are paid wholly or in part on a fee basis, a close working relationship with police or principal plaintiff-litigants is facilitated, and questions occur with respect to the integrity of the judicial process in this regard. We asked our committeemen, therefore, to what extent the fee system still prevails anywhere in the metropolitan areas. Of thirty answers received at the time this chapter was written, most reported that the fee system has been fully abolished throughout the metropolitan area.

In the following metropolitan districts, fee'd justices of the peace are reported found within the central city itself: Des Moines (approximation only), 12; Miami (number not given, fee to fixed maximum); Wichita Falls, Texas, 2; Grand Falls, North Dakota, 4 (fee system abolished 7-1-61); Biloxi, 2; St. Paul, 4; Charleston, 4; Rutland, 3 or 4; Burlington (Vermont), 15 have authority, but only 5 or 6 exercise it.

In the following areas, fee'd justices of the peace are found in the satellite area surrounding the city: Wichita Falls, 2; Sioux Falls, 5 or 6; Miami, number not given (fee to fixed maximum salary); Grand Forks, 1 (fee system

[11] Los Angeles Study 42. Holbrook comments that many Los Angeles attorneys express the view that at least five years in private practice should be a prerequisite for judges, as a guard against recruitment from governmental agencies of persons without sufficient trial experience. The same thought was frequently expressed during the 1959 Conference on Judicial Selection. The present writer does not regard long trial experience as an essential qualification for all occupants of the bench, but concludes that a large portion of the active bar does so regard it.

abolished 7-1-61); St. Paul, 5; Philadelphia ("intolerable and inexcusable"); Baton Rouge, 2; Milwaukee, 26 (includes police judge, salary plus fees); Charleston, 16; Rutland, 18 or 20; Burlington, 1 or 2.

A few fee'd justices were found in townships, and there were even a few city justices paid by fee noted in the Detroit study.[12] Holbrook found that in Los Angeles the salaries of justices of the peace are fixed by the board of supervisors of the county and vary with the population and workload in each judicial district. He points out, however, that some of them spend only part time at their judicial work and are privileged to engage in the practice of law in other courts.[13]

The fee system, then, with its attendant evils, appears to be on the way out, with two or three astonishing exceptions. Therefore we may still identify abolishment of the fee system as a problem worthy of attention in metropolitan areas.

Salary of general trial court judges

In Los Angeles and Detroit, like many other metropolitan areas, the salaries of trial court judges are paid in part by the state, in part by a local unit of government such as the county or municipality.[14] Rapid successive increases in compensation for judges at this level have occurred in most large metropolitan areas. This is thought to reflect the increase in population and caseload as well as the inflationary rise in living costs. According to the *Book of the States for 1958-1959,* action to provide judicial salaries more commensurate with the current importance of judicial office has been extensive throughout the states at various judicial levels. This source shows that at least twenty-five states increased salaries of justices of courts of last resort,

[12] DETROIT STUDY 71.
[13] LOS ANGELES STUDY 50.
[14] DETROIT STUDY 68 *et seq.;* LOS ANGELES STUDY 49.

and twenty-seven increased the salaries of their judges of trial courts of general jurisdiction. The median now approximates $12,500.

The compensation of judges of limited jurisdiction, however, regarded as a special metropolitan court problem because of the vast metropolitan caseload and the difficulty of detecting substandard judicial performance in such courts, has not fared so well. With the shining exceptions of New Jersey and Pennsylvania, which have provided high salaries for their courts of limited jurisdiction,[15] most are still provided with salaries regarded as low even for preinflationary professional men, or with fees.[16]

Adequate compensation for judges was regarded, by the participants at the 1959 Conference on Judicial Selection and Court Administration, as an important basic ingredient of the problem of recruiting first-rate candidates for judicial office. In metropolitan districts, they felt, the hazards of recruitment are intensified by the comparatively greater sacrifice required of a candidate in giving up a potentially much more lucrative practice in return for a potentially much more difficult and occasionally frustrating activity.

e. Retirement Problems

Closely related to the problem of obtaining adequate compensation for judges is that of obtaining for them and their dependents some measure of security. Judicial retirement plans have been adopted by the federal government and by forty-eight states, the latter covering state appellate

[15] THE BOOK OF THE STATES, 1958-1959, Table 6. New Jersey: up to $13,000, $16,000, $10,000, for probate, county and municipal courts respectively; Pennsylvania: $18,000-$25,000.

[16] Table 6, cited *supra* note 6. Fees listed for justice, magistrate, or police courts in Alabama, Colorado, Idaho, Illinois, Iowa, Michigan, Minnesota, Mississippi, Montana (to $3,600), Nebraska (to $2,400), New Mexico, North Carolina, Oklahoma, Rhode Island, South Dakota, Tennessee, Utah, West Virginia, Wisconsin.

and trial court judges.[17] Coverage for judges of courts of limited jurisdiction is not so common as such, but many judges may obtain coverage through general retirement plans covering all employees of the county, township, or municipality serviced by the particular court.

Judicial retirement plans have, in fact, become so widespread that concern is now expressed at the rapidity with which judges paid from more than one level of government are perfecting retirement accounts with two or more retirement systems. More than one state is known to perceive difficult legal and financial problems resulting from multiple participation in retirement plans by judges and others. Many judicial pension plans now cover dependents of judges.[18]

The desirability of making judicial retirement compulsory (openly or covertly) on a calendar age basis, once widely accepted, is now under question. For a time, it was the fashion for those concerned with the court delay or logjam problem to propose compulsory retirement of judges as the cure-all for justice delayed. Compulsory retirement on a basis of age is now provided for in a number of states, including Connecticut, Idaho, Kansas, Louisiana, Maine, Maryland, Michigan, Minnesota, Mississippi, Missouri, Nebraska, New Hampshire, New Jersey, New York, Ohio, South Carolina, Vermont, Virginia, Washington, and Wisconsin.[19] In some of these states, not only is a judge required to step down upon achieving a certain number of days on earth, but is subjected to pressure not to engage in the practice of law thereafter, on the basis that his prestige might subject opposing counsel to unfair competition or,

[17] See INSTITUTE OF JUDICIAL ADMINISTRATION, JUDICIAL RETIREMENT: STATUTORY PROVISIONS AND COMMENT, No. 4-U51 (May 8, 1956); THE BOOK OF THE STATES, 1958-1959, pp. 98-99 and Table 5, pp. 104-05.

[18] THE BOOK OF THE STATES, 1958-1959, at 99; INSTITUTE OF JUDICIAL ADMINISTRATION, PENSIONS AND BENEFITS FOR JUDICIAL DEPENDENTS, No. 4-U68 (Aug. 17, 1956).

[19] JUDICIAL RETIREMENT, *op. cit. supra* note 17, Chart C, beginning at 24.

sometimes, that he is morally obligated to subsist upon his retirement pension without any attempt to augment it.[20]

Thus does a grateful community reward the accumulated wisdom and experience of a lifetime on the bench!

Whatever may be said in favor of this policy, as that it spares someone the responsibility of basing an individual's retirement upon specific circumstances rather than upon a general quantitative rule, it surely does not encourage first-rate men to renounce private practice in favor of a judicial career. Assurance of subsistence in idleness after age 70 will not attract superior career judges.

Recently, judges in retirement status have been recruited to augment judicial manpower so as to alleviate the logjam problem, whether as referees, visiting judges, or judges at large.[21] In the metropolitan districts, where logjam is most acute and specialized caseloads most often encountered, it would seem more sensible to leave an experienced judge, if fit at 70, upon the bench where his experience can be most effectively brought to bear upon the logjam problem. In England, for example, judges at certain levels may remain upon the bench after 70, upon annual review, at the discretion of the Lord Chancellor.

To get a preliminary indication of the extent to which superannuation is a problem in metropolitan districts, we reviewed the earlier studies and asked the section committeemen to comment. The Detroit study found the age of the median Detroit judge at somewhere between 50 and 60 in 1948.[22] It had dropped several years at the time of this writing in 1960, due to numerous recent appointments of young men. From Holbrook's findings it can be calculated

[20] *Id.* at 43-47, Chart E; and see "Expressions of opinion on the practice of law by retired justices and judges who are receiving pension allowances," and an explanation of Chart E at 40-42.

[21] *Id.* at Chart D; and see THE BOOK OF THE STATES, 1958-1959, at 98, listing Louisiana, Minnesota and Oregon as having recently taken measures to re-enlist retired judges. See also LOS ANGELES STUDY 52-53.

[22] DETROIT STUDY 63.

that during his study the age of the median Los Angeles judge at that time was somewhere between 50 and 59.[23] Of the thirty questionnaires at hand while this chapter was being written, seven contain no estimate of the average age of judges within the metropolis. The others contain estimates ranging from 36 (Boise, Idaho) to over 60 (three districts), with five falling in the 40-49 age group and most (fourteen) falling between age 50 and 59. This small group of figures has no statistical value. They are estimates made by persons familiar with the machinery of justice in individual metropolitan areas. As such, however, the figures do suggest that in these areas there is no great problem of judicial superannuation.

Section 2. Quasi-Judicial Personnel

While working on the Detroit study, the present writer was struck with the establishment of specialized personnel and facilities which, in some instances, had taken over activities usually regarded as judicial in response to the tremendous needs and pressures of the metropolitan caseload.[24] Sometimes, as where a commissioner assembles information or works out a solution under judicial supervision, this seemed a legitimate method of stretching the judge's reach. Sometimes, as where juvenile court personnel administratively designated "referees" dispose of all cases falling within a certain classification without any real judicial supervision, it seemed a usurpation of the judicial function by personnel untrained in legal disciplines and unaware of the indispensability of due process.

It was hoped that subsequent studies would develop further information from which an objective analysis could be made of the extent to which judicial manpower can be

[23] Los Angeles Study 43.
[24] Detroit Study 100 *et seq.*

augmented, in metropolitan areas, by the use of masters, commissioners, referees, and the like, without surrender of essential judicial safeguards by reason of the large caseloads, extensive departmentalization, and special types of problems there encountered.

The Holbrook study did not look at this problem, nor have other committee inquiries made for the committee provided enough information for proper analysis. Yet the general topic seems basic to a discussion of special metropolitan court problems. Nothing more can be done in this study than call attention to the existence of the question and invite others to go further.

Of thirty questionnaires at hand when this chapter was written, seven reported no quasi-judicial personnel exercising decision-making authority within the respective metropolitan districts represented. Two mentioned bankruptcy referees, two auditors, one an examiner, six listed commissioners, and five mentioned masters or special masters. Philadelphia has a criminal court administrator. Two or three mentioned probate court referees. Half a dozen mentioned juvenile court referees, one referred to a family court referee, and one to a sanity commission. Almost all the above were listed as legally trained, with the exception of the juvenile and family court referees and the sanity commission.

It was pointed out in the Detroit study that circuit court commissioners there, unlike those outside the metropolitan area, have their own clerical staff, central record system, and individual courtrooms. In dealing with landlord-tenant cases, they operate quite distinctly from the circuit court; in fact, when a case goes from the commissioners to the circuit court, it is officially designated an "appeal."[25]

On the other hand, the Friend of the Court in Detroit, though it is extensively staffed and has authority to act as referee in certain domestic relations matters, appeared to

[25] *Id.* at 100.

the writer to be fully under the supervision and control of the circuit judges.[26]

Traffic court referees, in Detroit, seemed to be additional judges, for all practical purposes.[27]

The use of social workers called "referees" in juvenile courts in a number of communities seems to raise questions concerning surrender of judicial prerogative, and this is an area where such questions are intensified by differences of opinion between administrative and legal personnel concerning their proper respective prerogatives.[28]

In Indianapolis, the use of substitute judges recruited from the bar was interesting.[29] In a number of communities the writer has observed court clerks and top supervisory department personnel acting in judicial capacity with respect to court cases.[30]

Other examples may be found in "youth bureaus," or similar activities, carried on by some metropolitan police departments. Some of them actually act out a trial process in which the officer presiding is called "Your Honor," and "judge," ostensibly to impress and hence constructively to influence the behavior of persons brought in for questioning and possible further legal action. One such police department bureau observed conducts a successful television program carrying these kangaroo court sessions "live."[31]

Much precourt screening and delegation of judicial function to nonjudicial personnel is, of course, necessary and

[26] *Id.* at 101.
[27] *Ibid.*
[28] *Id.* at 102 *et seq.*
[29] FAMILY CASES 140 *et seq.*
[30] E.g., FAMILY CASES, the case history, 140 *et seq.*
[31] See the discussion by Holbrook of the disposition of juvenile traffic cases by the Juvenile Traffic Detail of the Los Angeles and San Fernando Police Departments which disposed of these cases, though without authority to do so, using the juvenile court as a threat with which to induce cooperation from juveniles and their parents. Contrast San Francisco, where juvenile traffic cases are handled in the juvenile court. LOS ANGELES STUDY 28 n. 47. As of November 1960, it is reported that the juvenile traffic cases are no longer being so handled.

desirable in any large city; without it, the judicial function would stifle in the vast mass of the caseload.

But these extensions to the judicial arm, occurring in Metropolis by reason of the special conditions there obtaining, also raise special problems for bench and bar in preserving the integrity of the judicial process by insuring proper judicial control of these extensions.

Section 3. Attorneys

The role of both prosecutor and defense counsel in shaping the course of judicial contact with criminal cases has been described in several studies referred to previously, notably the crime surveys of the twenties, which document in detail the way in which the prosecutor's policy not to pursue certain cases, or to bargain for guilty pleas, or nolle pros, can establish a pattern of criminal justice. These studies show, too, how trial prosecutors, by their skill or lack thereof, can either bring judicial control into full play or virtually prevent it from operating at all.

In the Detroit study, the infrequency with which either prosecution or defense counsel appeared in misdemeanor cases was pointed out, and the possibility suggested that this was related to the high (85 per cent) percentage of convictions.[32] Defense right to counsel appears well established both by constitution and statute in Michigan. Still, serious felony cases were found going through the full trial process without counsel,[33] and counsel appear most infrequently in Traffic and Ordinance Division of Recorder's Court, even at felony level.[34] Probate court clerks were observed to act as counsel for litigants as a matter of course, even preparing their pleadings.[35] It was noted that the

[32] Detroit Study 108

[33] *Id.* at 111-12.

[34] *Id.* at 114.

[35] *Ibid.*

Legal Aid Bureau of Detroit refrained from representing persons involved in mental cases, that there was virtual disuse of counsel in juvenile and small claims cases,[36] and that the cases in which counsel were not found predominate numerically in the metropolitan caseload.

It is the view of the writer that participation by attorneys is indispensable to the operation of the judicial process, and that guaranteed access to the judicial process for all litigants, including petty and "social problem" litigants, is a minimum standard for any metropolitan court system. Accordingly, further attention to the problem of the role of attorneys in metropolitan court systems was invited.

Holbrook, in the Los Angeles study, estimated that most of the cases defaulted in both municipal and superior courts in Los Angeles (Civic Center buildings) were cases in which the defendants were without attorneys, but found that attorneys appear for both litigants in most civil cases which go to trial in the superior court.[37]

In contrast to Detroit, the Los Angeles system has a county public defender who represented almost half the defendants who went through felony trials during the year of the Los Angeles survey. Only about fifty defendants went to trial without counsel, and because of the machinery for insuring the right to counsel, it would appear that Holbrook is sound in concluding that these fifty preferred not to have counsel.[38]

Holbrook is of the view that some of the "social" cases do not require the advice and appearance of attorneys—e.g., domestic relations matters preliminary to divorce, conciliation cases, juvenile and mental cases.[39] In Los Angeles, as in Detroit, parties in such cases are not often represented by counsel, but unlike Mr. Holbrook the present writer is

[36] *Id.* at 116.
[37] Los Angeles Study 77.
[38] *Id.* at 78.
[39] *Ibid.*

concerned by their absence. It is interesting to note that in Los Angeles, both parties, that is, adopting and natural parents, in adoption cases are reported as represented by counsel in almost every case.[40] Would that this were so in other metropolitan areas!

The statute provides that attorneys are not permitted to appear in the small claims courts in metropolitan areas in California.[41] With respect to other courts Holbrook estimates that in about one-eighth of the cases assigned for trial in the Los Angeles municipal court divisions housed at the Civic Center, one or both parties is without counsel; that very few attorneys appear for traffic violators except that in serious cases about one-third of the cases are manned by attorneys.[42] Of 1800 "drunk" cases handled in the Los Angeles municipal court (Civic Center building) in an average week, only two or three defendants have counsel. As to misdemeanors other than traffic or intoxication, six to ten defendants are represented by private counsel out of an average of seventy-six to one hundred cases per day. But the city public defender assigns a deputy to each of this court's divisions to represent the defendants as a group.[43]

The Holbrook study contains excellent descriptions of the duties and operations of county counsel, district attorney, county and city public defenders (all of whom are under civil service), city attorney, assigned defense counsel, and legal aid. The Los Angeles county public defender's office, established in 1913, was the first in the United States. Legal professional coverage in the Los Angeles area is clearly far more complete than in the Detroit area, yet problems exist there.

We asked our correspondents what facilities exist for furnishing indigents with counsel in criminal, small claims, civil,

[40] *Ibid.*
[41] *Ibid.*
[42] *Ibid.*
[43] *Id.* at 79.

and juvenile cases. Of thirty responses at hand when this chapter was written, only Baton Rouge reports no coverage for any criminal cases. In Biloxi, court-appointed defense counsel are reported available in capital cases only, and five other districts report that the court will appoint defense counsel in felony cases only. Court-appointed counsel in selected criminal cases are reported by seventeen metropolitan districts. One correspondent adds that no compensation is offered, another that compensation is poor, a third refers to court-appointed defense counsel as "victim," a fourth comments that the leading lawyers are not available for such work. Public defenders were reported in only two reporting districts—St. Paul and Miami—but two others report legal aid available for criminal cases. The rotation system is in use in two districts reporting, one of them being Newark, New Jersey, with a modernized rotation assignment system which has received favorable comment.[44] In it, each attorney in turn is assigned a case by alphabetical order.

In Philadelphia, both the public defender and legal aid societies are voluntary; the former is available for criminal cases, according to the report received.

Respecting small claims cases, the correspondent answering from San Jose, California, reports that attorneys are prohibited by law from appearing in such cases (as is the case in Los Angeles). Correspondents from seventeen answering districts report that no machinery exists for supplying counsel in such cases, and the other thirteen responding report legal aid available in selected cases. As to civil cases generally, sixteen districts report no machinery, one indicates the court will appoint in proper cases, and seven that legal aid can be supplied.

[44] BEANEY, THE RIGHT TO COUNSEL IN AMERICAN COURTS 233 (1955). *Supra* p. 61 for comment on criminal cases without counsel in Detroit, and comment that public money is available for counsel in such cases.

In juvenile cases, thirteen districts report no counsel for indigents, one supplies public defenders in felony cases involving juveniles, five supply court-appointed counsel in "selected cases," and the other eleven responding report that legal aid, either voluntary or full time, can be obtained.

A comprehensive discussion of the coverage of various types of legal aid and public defender systems, together with a thorough analysis of the problems, may be found in Brownell's recent survey, *Legal Aid in the United States*.[45] The official position of the American Bar Association has always been that no one should be denied access to justice, including counsel, by reason of poverty, and that the method and instrumentality of securing adequate representation be regarded by the Association as a local question for determination in light of local conditions, needs, and wishes.[46]

On the basis of experience with the studies conducted for this series, it is the writer's conclusion that enforcement of the right of each litigant to counsel is a problem of serious proportions in metropolitan districts, having a special incidence in such districts not only by reason of the predominance in metropolitan caseloads of the types of cases in which litigants are most likely to require supplied counsel, but also because of the special need for counsel's services in metropolitan areas to avoid perfunctory routine attention to any single case in the vast caseload.

Further attention is invited to some aspects of the problem, such as the availability of counsel from the beginning in criminal cases, so that pleas may be decided on, examinations waived, and other significant decisions made the purport of which only a lawyer can evaluate. Similarly, the

[45] BROWNELL, LEGAL AID IN THE UNITED STATES (1951). See, especially Table III at 36, listing cities providing service as of 1916 and 1947; Table XVI at 130, jurisdiction of public and private agencies offering service; extent of need in criminal cases at 83; need in civil cases at 85. See also INSTITUTE OF JUDICIAL ADMINISTRATION, PUBLIC DEFENDERS, No. 3-U48 (May 18, 1956).

[46] BROWNELL, *op. cit. supra*, 65.

need of fuller participation by counsel in juvenile, mental, and support cases seems worthy of further intensive study.[47]

SECTION 4. JURIES

It has always been thought by students of court problems that the task of selecting qualified and conscientious jurymen and keeping them free from improper pressures is especially difficult in metropolitan districts by reason of the size of such areas and the relatively greater difficulty in selecting and supervising the jury.

The "key number system," the method employed in Detroit Recorder's Court and the Los Angeles Superior Court, and the Detroit jury questionnaire, which is available to the attorneys, has received favorable attention as a good way of meeting the problem. It is described in both studies.[48] In essence, this is a selection of names from eligible lists by application of a number determined by dividing the lists by the number of jurors needed and then applying this key number sequentially to the entire list. Thus, if the number is seven, every seventh name is selected.

Another problem, however, emerged from the Detroit study: the coexistence of several entirely separate systems for obtaining juries, each with its own philosophy and apparatus, and each a charge upon the community. It is interesting that at this writing, a decade after publication of the Detroit study, with attendant publicizing of this multiplicity, no change has yet been made.

Holbrook, in the Los Angeles study, was much interested in the jury system.[49] He has included a section full of fas-

[47] For a good basic study of the entire problem, the reader is referred to a recent monograph, THE RIGHT TO COUNSEL IN AMERICAN COURTS, *op. cit. supra* note 44; and for a description of the English legal aid system, see JACKSON, THE MACHINERY OF JUSTICE IN ENGLAND 253 *et seq.* (1940). The system he describes has since been extended. For description of the Legal Aid and Advice Act see Voorhees, *Lawyer Referral Service and the British Aid and Advice Act*, 44 A.B.A.J. 418 (1958).

[48] DETROIT STUDY 119 *et seq.*

[49] LOS ANGELES STUDY 97 *et seq.*

cinating and richly suggestive data. Justice courts have a system different from the key number system obtaining in both superior and municipal courts, but juries are little used in justice courts. It is notable that until 1955 branch municipal courts conducted no jury trials, but trials where juries were requested were transferred to downtown Los Angeles.

The composition of juries received considerable attention in the Los Angeles study.[50] Most of the trial attorneys and judges interviewed thought that juries do not comprise a reasonable community cross section, but overrepresent housewives and retirees while underrepresenting executives and craftsmen.[51] Preliminary instruction booklets are furnished to jurymen in Los Angeles to supplement the oral address by the presiding judge, as in Detroit. As in Detroit, also, there is lively interest in the use or misuse of the *voir dire* as related to the problem of delay. The use of commercial jury books, containing information about individual jurors for use of counsel, is unique in Los Angeles so far as we know.

In dealing with instructions to juries, Holbrook describes the device, now well known, originating in and widely employed by Los Angeles judges and counsel, namely two books containing approved instructions for criminal and civil cases, respectively. These are numbered, and an attorney can request a particular instruction by number from the court clerk, who will hand him a printed form to be attached to the attorney's request. It is said that use of these form, or canned, instructions has saved trial judges in Los Angeles much time. There is controversy concerning the value and implications of such a device.

Holbrook explored the question of the comprehensibility of instructions given to jurors. He found that 96 per cent of the jurors thought they themselves understood all right,

[50] *Id.* at 107 *et seq.*

[51] See *id.* at 108 *et seq.* for detailed material on excusals, age, marital, educational, and occupational groupings of jurors.

but that about half were sure that some of their fellow jurymen had failed to understand the instructions![52]

Los Angeles county was found by Holbrook to have a lower percentage of jury trials than the rest of the state, especially in criminal cases, insofar as superior court cases were concerned.[53] The same did not hold true of municipal courts. The average jury trial took four days in Superior Court; there were 594 criminal and 1,159 civil jury trials in the year 1953-1954.[54]

Looking at comparative results, Holbrook found juries more acquittal-minded than judges in criminal cases. Use of juries is now very high in personal injury cases (76 per cent in 1954). In tort cases tried in calendar 1952, judges gave judgment for plaintiff in 64 per cent of the 352 cases tried by judges; juries in 54 per cent of the 712 cases tried by juries. In personal injury cases tried in calendar 1954, judges gave plaintiff judgment in 54 per cent of 254 cases tried by judges; juries gave judgment in 46 per cent of 814 cases tried by juries. Commenting, Holbrook refers to an earlier study of Sunderland, concluding that there is little difference in comparative results in civil cases as between judges and juries, either as to result or assessment of damages, except in situations in which a strong emotional appeal is inherent in the type of case.[55]

A question addressed to our correspondents respecting methods of selecting juries elicited no information worthy of analysis in this study. The answers confirmed what has often been stated: that methods of selection and qualifications for jurors are incredibly various and sporadic, ranging from random selection of passers-by near the courthouse to elaborate wheel and key number systems applied by jury

[52] Los Angeles Study 120.

[53] *Ibid.*

[54] See *id.* at 122-23, Tables 10 and 11, for comparative use of juries in superior and municipal courts.

[55] Los Angeles Study 125, citing *Trial by Jury*, 11 U. Cinn. L. Rev. 120 (1937).

commissions to lists assembled from various places. One committeeman reports that in his district each *judge* has his own jury commission. But only in Milwaukee can we find evidence of an integrated system, with one jury commission which makes up a panel from which all courts in the metropolis then draw. It is the uniqueness of this report from Milwaukee, among metropolitan districts known to or observed by these studies, which is most striking.

One trend deserves mention: instead of decreasing, as this writer thought it would at the time of the Detroit study, use of juries in both civil and criminal cases has been sharply increasing in Detroit and elsewhere.[56] This is often attributed to the increase in negligence and accident cases in both civil and criminal phases, and to the growing size and sagacity of a specialized bar dedicated to the pursuit of such cases.

The relationship of the jury trial to the problem of case delay, or logjam, is often mentioned, and various suggestions made for accelerating the total performance of a court by means of devices designed to discourage or eliminate jury trials. The problem of delay as such is discussed elsewhere.[57]

The American Bar Association has long recommended the use of the key number system in metropolitan centers,[58] permissive conduct of *voir dire* by judges,[59] and the impaneling of one or more extra jurors in certain cases.[60] The key number system was first brought to the bar's attention after its adoption by Cleveland.[61]

[56] See, e.g., MICH. OFFICE OF THE COURT ADMINISTRATOR, SUPREME COURT OF MICHIGAN, ANNUAL REPORT AND JUDICIAL STATISTICS FOR 1956 at 17, Table 8.

[57] *Infra.* p. 254.

[58] VANDERBILT, MINIMUM STANDARDS, chapter beginning p. 147, recommendation quoted p. 146.

[59] *Ibid.*

[60] *Ibid.*

[61] A full survey of various systems for selecting and instructing juries will be found in Vanderbilt's MINIMUM STANDARDS, and recent trends can be

SECTION 5. NONLEGAL PROFESSIONAL PERSONNEL

In the Detroit study, the extensive development of court departments staffed with specialized nonlegal professional personnel to deal with special types of cases was exhibited as characteristic of metropolitan court systems, which were thought to develop such facilities as a means of meeting the subject matter and the conditions of metropolitan court work. Examples are the Friend of the Court of the Circuit Court of Wayne County, with more than a hundred employees, dealing with investigation and supervision of custody and support matters in divorce and other cases involving children;[62] the psychiatric clinic at Recorder's Court, which furnishes the criminal court with diagnoses and prognoses in referred cases;[63] the precourt adjustment division at Recorder's Court, which works out and enforces voluntary support settlements so as to prevent criminal nonsupport litigation;[64] the elaborate probation departments of various courts;[65] and the extensive staff of the juvenile court.[66]

Such developments are most interesting in terms of the metropolitan court problem for several reasons: they increase the total number of court employees and the complexity of its machinery, and thus are an important factor in shaping the administrative problem of the entire metropolitan court system. They raise problems of judicial control and due process, since they involve nonlegal professionals

---

found by consulting the annual reports of the Section of Judicial Administration supplementing MINIMUM STANDARDS.

The Institute of Judicial Administration has three recent surveys of particular aspects of the jury problem: JURY COSTS, No. 3-U2 (Aug. 15, 1955); WAIVER OF JURY TRIAL IN FELONY CASES: AN ANALYSIS OF THE APPLICABLE CONSTITUTIONAL AND STATUTORY PROVISIONS IN THE FORTY-EIGHT STATES, No. 3-U53 (Jul. 25, 1955); STATUTORY RIGHT OF JURY TO FIX PUNISHMENT IN CRIMINAL CASES, No. 3-U1 (Jul. 7, 1955).

62 DETROIT STUDY 173-80.

63 *Id.* at 181-83, 235-36.

64 *Id.* at 157-59.

65 *Id.* at 149-72.

66 *Id.* at 165-70.

unschooled in the traditions of legal procedure. But they constitute an essential and practical method for guarding against perfunctory routine disposition of the personal and social problem cases, and thus offer a way of making judicial process effective to achieve workable dispositions in a range of cases otherwise not easily managed.

The Holbrook study contains descriptions of several Los Angeles court departments which make use of nonlegal professional personnel on a full-time basis, including the marriage counselors and commissioners in the conciliation court,[67] adoption workers,[68] the staffs of the two juvenile court departments,[69] the counselor of mental health and staff of the psychopathic department of superior court,[70] the domestic relations investigators and commissioners assigned to that department,[71] and others.

The domestic relations investigators of the Superior Court of San Francisco,[72] various professional departments in the Toledo Family Court,[73] Cincinnati Family Court,[74] the Divorce Counsel and Domestic Conciliation Department in Milwaukee,[75] and the marriage counselor and Friend of the Court in Ann Arbor[76] have been discussed by the present writer in a recent series of studies of metropolitan trial courts in relation to the handling of domestic relations cases.

We asked our correspondents to comment on the number of full-time nonlegal professionals employed by various metropolitan court systems either full-time, on a case by

[67] Los Angeles Study 234.
[68] *Id.* at 237.
[69] *Id.* at 154, 238.
[70] *Id.* at 153, 242.
[71] *Id.* at 151, 300. It has been reported that in 1960, all commissioners were lawyers.
[72] Family Cases in Court 14 *et seq.*
[73] *Id.* at 184 *et seq.*
[74] *Id.* at 201 *et seq.*
[75] *Id.* at 204 *et seq.*
[76] *Id.* at 215 *et seq.*

case basis, or indirectly on a referral basis to noncourt agencies or personnel. The responses, though without statistical value, support our impression that extensive use of nonlegal professionals in family and social cases is typical of the larger metropolitan cities.

Pueblo, Colorado; Charleston, West Virginia; Rutland and Burlington, Vermont; Huron, South Dakota; Cheyenne and Casper, Wyoming; Boise, Idaho: all reported that no nonlegal professionals are employed by the court system. On the other hand, so did Chattanooga, a center large enough, one would have supposed, to support the type of facility under discussion.

Biloxi, Mississippi, reports one full-time juvenile court officer; Brocton, Massachusetts, indicates that juvenile cases are referred to professionals on a case by case basis; Baltimore employs a full-time psychiatrist for criminal cases. Several courts in the state of Washington use nonlegal professionals in criminal and juvenile cases both on a full-time and referral basis. Wichita Falls, Texas, has full-time staff for criminal and juvenile cases. Sioux Falls, South Dakota, employs social workers and also refers certain juvenile cases to professionals on a case by case basis. Charleston, South Carolina, has full-time nonlegal personnel for criminal and juvenile cases. Grand Forks, North Dakota, has a juvenile court commissioner and reports that criminal cases are referred to nonlegal professionals by district court.

Las Vegas employs a staff of social workers in its juvenile court for juvenile and adoption cases, and certain criminal and mental cases are referred to nonlegal professionals on a case by case basis. St. Paul, Minnesota, has full-time nonlegal professionals employed for cases in criminal and juvenile courts. On a case by case basis, criminal, juvenile delinquency, and mental cases are referred, sometimes to the 25-man staff of probation officers. San Jose, California, has a staff of 30 deputy juvenile court probation officers, 17 adult probation officers, and 64 juvenile custodial personnel. Philadelphia has a full-time staff for criminal and juvenile cases, and also uses referrals. Minneapolis employs a full-time staff for criminal, juvenile, and family cases. Baton Rouge employs nonlegal professionals full time in juvenile court, on a case by case basis for criminal and juvenile cases, and also refers some such cases. The family court of Baton Rouge has a staff of 9, including social workers and clerical help.

The Milwaukee staff has been referred to just above. Briefly, Milwaukee employs a Divorce Counsel and staff and a Department of Conciliation and staff for circuit court, a case and detention staff at juvenile court, and refers on a case by case basis criminal and juvenile cases.[77] Des Moines has a full-time juvenile court staff, and also uses the referral and case by case system. A probation department, consisting of one chief officer and nine full-time and one part-time officers, does investigations and supervises children. We had two answers to the questionnaire from Des Moines. One correspondent reports that these officers are professionally qualified, the other that they are not.

Phoenix, Arizona, has a large juvenile court staff. Miami has a staff of social workers to investigate and report to the court in juvenile cases. Criminal and juvenile cases are also referred, or handled on a case by case basis.

In New Jersey, the probation office of the county serves all courts in criminal cases. A reconciliation program, using professional marriage counselors, is now proceeding on an experimental basis in some courts.

Thus we may conclude that extensive use of nonlegal professionals in personal problem cases is found more often than not in metropolitan cities, and that the use of such personnel tends to become more frequent as the size of the metropolitan city increases. But this is not always the case. The lack of use of nonlegal professionals in family cases in

[77] *Id.* at 204 *et seq.*

Chicago and Indianapolis, for example, is rather striking.[78] It is the conclusion of the present writer, on the basis of all studies available, that the contrast in quality of performance between cities which do provide these specialized facilities and those which do not, is also striking.[79]

SECTION 6. TOTAL STAFF OF COURT EMPLOYEES

It was pointed out in the Detroit study that the size of the personnel attached to metropolitan courts, like the size of the caseload, itself creates a unique kind of administrative, mechanical, and supervisory problem for metropolitan courts, and also complicates the basic task of the judge with respect to each individual case for which he is responsible. In 1948, more than 900 persons were employed full time by courts sitting in the City of Detroit.[80]

In *Bad Housekeeping,* the Association of the Bar of the City of New York notes that no one possessed a fair working knowledge of the personnel of all the courts of New York City, though it costs more money to run those courts each year than it does to operate the entire federal judicial system.

> Even more astounding—after much research and investigation it is still impossible to state with any degree of accuracy the size of the clerical and administrative staff of the New York courts.

The reasons given for this state of affairs apply as well to Detroit, Los Angeles, and other large metropolitan cities.

> (1) There is no central administrative organization within the judicial branch of our state government which is charged with super-

[78] *Id.* at 125 *et seq.,* 77 *et seq.*

[79] Among recent studies which contain detailed analyses of the functioning of specialized court departments in large metropolitan cities are GELLHORN, CHILDREN AND FAMILIES IN THE COURTS OF NEW YORK, a study sponsored by the Association of the Bar of the City of New York (1954). And see the companion study, A COURT FOR CHILDREN by Alfred J. Kahn, a professional social worker (1953).

[80] DETROIT STUDY 193.

vising the work of the courts and . . . the collection of relevant statistical information;

(2) To a considerable degree each court is autonomous;

(3) The courts are financed by more than one unit of government; and

(4) The . . . budgets . . . and other financial data for different courts are not published or otherwise made available in detail, and many of those that are available do not contain line items. . . .[81]

To suggest the magnitude of the problem, the New York study notes that the 1954 budget appropriation for salaries for courts in New York city alone totaled almost twenty-four million dollars. This did not include the maintenance staffs nor did it include the state portion of salaries of judges of the Supreme Court in New York City.

There were more than 300 judges and official referees in New York City at the time of this study, and almost 3,500 people were employed on the staffs of the eight courts in the city.[82]

At the time of the Los Angeles study, there were 82 judges in the Superior Court at Los Angeles. The number has since been increased to 102.[83] The personnel of that court alone includes 246 employees other than judges, commissioners, bailiffs, and court clerks. At the time of the Holbrook study, the Clerk of the Superior Court at Los Angeles employed more than 400 persons, the probation department more than 1,100 persons of whom 430 were deputy probation officers. Of these, 82 men and 59 women were assigned to juvenile court. Juvenile Hall itself had a staff of 300. There were at that time 42 judges in the Los Angeles Municipal court (exclusive of branch court personnel) and the clerk of that court employed 302 persons.[84]

[81] BAD HOUSEKEEPING 48-49.

[82] *Id.* at 50.

[83] Burke, *Problems of Court Administration in a Metropolitan Court,* 43 J. AM. JUD. SOC'Y 190 (1960); LOS ANGELES STUDY 342-43.

[84] LOS ANGELES STUDY *passim.* Municipal judges, p. 58; administrative and clerical personnel, superior courts, p. 129 *et seq.;* municipal courts, p. 165 *et seq.*

Lepawsky, in his study of courts in the metropolitan district of Chicago, found 556 independent courts employing 3,415 "judicial officers"[85] in the region; 205 separate courts employing 2,257 officers in Cook County alone; and 10 independent tribunals within the city limits of Chicago, even after integration of inferior tribunals there under the celebrated Municipal Court System.[86]

Principally to check the availability of information on total court staff, we asked our correspondents to indicate the total number of people employed by courts on a full-time basis in the metropolis and in the satellite area in the following capacities:

1. judicial
2. quasi-judicial
3. professional capacities other than legal
4. executive or administrative
5. stenographic and clerical
6. other

A typical answer came from Newark, New Jersey, a state which has achieved maximum court integration and modernization: "Can't answer; separate payrolls for state, county and municipality."

Other answers indicate variations in interpreting the question, as in including bailiffs, probation officers, and so on. The data should therefore be approached with more than usual caution. At most, the answers suggest the direction of the correspondent's reaction to a question about the overall size of the court staff in the central city of the metropolis.

They range all the way from "1 judge, 1 part-time stenographer" (Casper, Wyoming) to the total of 283 reported from San Jose, California, as follows:

[85] LEPAWSKY, THE JUDICIAL SYSTEM OF METROPOLITAN CHICAGO 106 (1932), persons aside from attorneys officially engaged in performing judicial services.

[86] *Id.* at 219.

judicial	17
quasi-judicial	1
nonlegal professional	1
executive, administrative	5
stenographic, clerical	131
other:	
bailiffs	17
adult probation officers	17
juvenile probation officers	30
juvenile institute	64

Philadelphia did not answer, nor did Milwaukee. In the case of the latter, however, a recent study of the Council of State Governments provided information relevant to the inquiry.[87] It shows 22 judicial personnel in the following courts: civil, 6; circuit, 10; county, 2; municipal, 1; district, 2; children's court, 1; 68 total judges' personnel;[88] and 144 other personnel. Note that the information is given on a county, not a city or metropolitan district, basis.

Other totals shown by our correspondents include the following: Pueblo, Colorado, 16 (including 3 judges); Baltimore, 125 (15 judges); Las Vegas, 14 (6 judges); St. Paul, 85 (13 judges); Boise, 15 (6 judges); Baton Rouge, 23 (6 judges); Cleveland, 154 (including judges); Chattanooga, 67 (13 judges); Charleston, West Virginia, 44 (10 judges); Rutland, 7 (3 judges); Burlington, 12 (2 judges); Wichita Falls, 21 (7 judges); Sioux Falls, 16 (5 judges); Charleston, South Carolina, 9 (8 judges); Des Moines, 65 (12 judges); Cheyenne, 12 (4 judges); Miami, 261 (46 judges); Sioux Falls, South Dakota, 5 (2 judges).

Clearly, the problems of Casper and of Los Angeles,

87 Public Administration Service, The Administration of Court and Legal Services in the Government of Milwaukee County 21, Table 11 (mimeographed, 1955).

88 Total staff serving courts, including clerks, bailiffs, *et al.* as well as judicial personnel, i.e., those performing judicial functions.

though both are classified as metropolitan districts, have a different texture as well as a different size. It begins to emerge that the metropolitan problems as the committee seeks to explore them are the problems of the large metropolitan cities.

Of all districts reporting, only Cleveland and San Jose, California, have civil service staffs.[89] In Detroit, some courts are partially covered.

Phoenix, Arizona, which is outstanding among metropolitan districts for the simplicity of its court structure above the justice court level (but has no means of integration between general trial courts and the justice courts, so far as we can learn), reported only 14 judges.[90]

There it is shown that a single clerk's office serves all the courts of original trial jurisdiction in the city, above the justice court level. An elected official, he appoints his own staff, which at the time of the study numbered 37, including courtroom clerks. Bailiffs and maintenance personnel and court reporters are not included in this Council study.

The American Bar Association has long recommended that provision be made in each state for a unified judicial system, that state judicial councils be established, and that quarterly judicial statistics be required.[91] State court administrators are now provided in 18 states, as reported by the Institute of Judicial Administration.[92]

The problem of integration of all the staff serving trial courts in a single metropolitan city, however, has not been given much attention. The proposed Detroit Metropolitan Court plan, reproduced in Appendix C, takes a good-sized step in this direction, but is still in the planning stage. The

[89] Holbrook reported civil service coverage of Los Angeles courts.

[90] But see a recent study of the Council of State Governments which gives further information, THE ORGANIZATION AND METHODS OF THE OFFICE OF THE CLERK OF THE SUPERIOR COURT, MARICOPA COUNTY, ARIZONA (Aug. 1953).

[91] VANDERBILT, MINIMUM STANDARDS 29.

[92] INSTITUTE OF JUDICIAL ADMINISTRATION, COURT ADMINISTRATION, No. 3-U8 (Aug. 1, 1955).

size and complexity of the personnel groupings given hereinabove, together with this writer's observation of the confusion, conflict, and waste resulting from lack of integration from court to court within the city, suggest that such administrative integration should be considered. In 1957,[93] California established an executive officer for the Superior Court of Los Angeles County. Note that this officer does not attempt to correlate the work of superior with that of municipal courts within the county.

In Illinois, the state court administrator has recently appointed a deputy administrator for the Chicago metropolitan area. So far as we can learn, this is the only current attempt by anyone with supervisory authority to obtain information on the basis of which adequate supervision of court staff could be exercised horizontally, throughout the trial court system of a metropolitan area, so as to control efficient use of staff throughout the area.

It is the conclusion of the writer that, until such supervision is mounted and vigorously exercised, court administration in metropolitan areas, particularly in the large cities, will continue to be in need of reform.

[93] CAL. STAT. ch. 1221 (1957).

CHAPTER VIII

Machinery for Handling Docket and Caseload

SECTION 1. THE ROLE OF THE JUDGE

ALL observers agree that within the limits set by the caliber of the bar the standards of performance in metropolitan courts are set by the judges. But there appears to be a divergence of views within the legal profession about the proper function of the metropolitan trial court judge. To some, he appears to be primarily a trial-presiding functionary present to serve the convenience of trial counsel. To some, he is personally responsible for all consequences resulting from litigation. To some, he is the administrator of a complex governmental operation. Each court observer projects his judgments about what the judge should be doing in his views about the efficiency of the court system under observation.

If one thinks, for example, that a judge is only performing as such when actively engaged in trying a fully contested case, then such activities as those of presiding judge, pretrial judge, or conciliation judge will not be highly evaluated. Some of the most recent studies of delay proceed from the premise that the *trial* of contested cases is the real and proper business of the court and its judges, and that the performance of the court is to be measured by the efficiency and dispatch with which the trial process is reached and concluded.

The great majority of dispositions reached in metropolitan trial courts, however, are reached other than by trial. In the Detroit study, for example, it was shown that in

Wayne County the circuit court tried only 6.4 per cent of the cases it disposed of (as compared with 14.4 per cent tried by circuit courts outside Wayne County).[1] Other courts in the Detroit area below the circuit court level, such as those disposing of petty misdemeanors, mental and juvenile cases, and small claims cases, showed an even greater load of cases disposed of without trial. More than 95 per cent of the caseload of the Detroit Court of Common Pleas was shown to have been disposed of by default.[2] Other examples have been given in earlier chapters. The Los Angeles study shows that of all criminal actions in the municipal courts in Los Angeles county more than 98 per cent of the dispositions took place at a phase before trial.[3]

The great preponderance of dispositions occurring other than by trial seems, therefore, of great significance to any analysis of the special problems of metropolitan courts because of the preponderance of dispositions other than by trial in the metropolitan areas. Therefore, correspondents were asked to indicate percentage of caseload disposed of other than by trial in various metropolitan areas. The results are presented in Table V.

It seems clear that most of the work for which the metropolitan trial courts is responsible does not consist of trying cases. Does the public think of the judge as a case-trying functionary? Because of the significance of the evaluation of the judge's role in evaluating metropolitan court performance, we asked our correspondents what they think the public expects of judges.

In 27 areas, those responding to the questionnaires state that the public looks to the judge primarily to see that justice is done to each individual. This represents all but two of the questionnaires containing answers to that question. One selected "giving a fair opportunity to lawyers to represent

[1] DETROIT STUDY 215.
[2] *Id.* at 216.
[3] LOS ANGELES STUDY 315.

TABLE V

Percentage of Caseload Disposed of Other Than by Trial in Various Metropolitan Cities

City	Total	Chancery	Criminal	Law	Negligence	Other
Baltimore	(Approximately 50% disposed of prior to trial. Of total 6,762 cases, 3,399 disposed of before trial, 3,237 after trial began, 126 after trial.)					
Baton Rouge	85%	85%	90%	90%	..	..
Boise	82%	..	90%	..	..	..
Burlington	75%	?	90%	75%	75%	..
Binghamton	90% plus	75%	90%	90%	90%	90% (estimates)
Casper	..	95%	90%	80%	..	..
Charleston, W. Va.	85%	50%	75%	50%	..	..
Cheyenne	(About 75%. Probably 60% of filings are default divorce or collections.)					
Cleveland	93%	..	..	..	..	..
Des Moines	90%	85%	90%	92%	92%	..
Grand Forks	80% (estimate)					
Miami	85% (estimate)					
Milwaukee	50%					
Minneapolis	72% civil ("regrettable")		95% (Depends on how good prosecutor is, defendant's estimate of chances of winning.)			
Newark			county 86%	superior county 79%		
Philadelphia	85% or more					
San Jose	90%	95.5%	85.5%	70%	94%	99% (mental)
Sioux Falls	50%					
Washington (state)	90% (estimate)					
Wichita Falls	..	..	75%	60-75%	75%	..

their clients' interest" as the paramount judicial role. The other reports that in his area the public looks upon judges primarily as individuals who grandstand for the reporters, with one eye on the next election. He adds:

> Our present judges are honest, if incompetent, but the public doesn't know the difference and the newspapers foster the grandstand position, presenting, as news, only gory details of criminal cases, reversals of judges by the Supreme Court, and the like.

One of our problems in this area, he points out, is to educate both the public and the courts, as well as lawyers, to the real duties and functions of courts and lawyers.

Ranking second as the most commonly accepted public image of judges is that of one whose primary function is to dispose of cases promptly and efficiently. Thirteen correspondents so reported. One ranked this function first:

> That part of the 'public' which consists of upright, intelligent citizens, believes as I do [that the judge's primary functions are to "see that cases are disposed of promptly and in an orderly manner" and to "provide a fair opportunity for trial lawyers to represent their clients' interests"]. These people, after living a short time in a small or larger sized community, know quite accurately whether their judges are good or not: but unfortunately these people constitute a minority of the 'public.'

This correspondent suggests we should do as the English do, appoint a judge for his "judicial" attributes only.

Correspondents from seven metropolitan areas reported "prompt and orderly disposition of cases" as the third most important judicial function, as viewed by the public, while two areas ranked this function fourth.

In two areas, the public reportedly ranks the following of traditional legal procedures, regardless of outcome, as the second most important judicial function. Five areas placed this function third; eight placed it fourth.

"Giving a fair opportunity to lawyers to represent their

clients' interests" was reported as the second most important function of judges, in the public view, from eleven metropolitan areas. This function was reported third from eleven areas, and fourth from two areas.

"Prompt disposition of cases" ranked first in one metropolitan area, second in fourteen, third in eight, fourth in two.

Two categories, inserted to provoke response on the degree of understanding by the public of the role of the judiciary, were "to join and enjoy the privileges of a gentleman's club," and "to grandstand for the reporters, with an eye on the next election." With the exception of the one area which put "grandstanding" first, most correspondents gave these questions the silent treatment; a few ranked them last without comment; others indicated they were not properly within the scope of the question.

It is concluded, then, that the general public in metropolitan areas is like the general public elsewhere in that it expects its judges to see justice done, whether by trial or otherwise. Our correspondents believe that the public also widely appreciates that judges must see that lawyers have a fair chance to serve their clients, and that it is up to the judge to see that cases are disposed of promptly and in an orderly manner. As was expected, there is some, but not universal, appreciation of the judge's responsibility to follow traditional legal procedures, without regard to the result in an individual case.

Most correspondents felt that the judges in their areas are living up to the expectations of the public. One from a very large metropolitan city, however, says:

> Until the method of selection of our judges in the great metropolitan centers is taken out of the hands of politicians, we will not have the caliber of judges we should have and the public image of the judge is affected thereby.

Several mentioned the importance of keeping the public informed concerning the real problems and functions of the judiciary. One commented that the easy and melodramatic handling of cases in radio and television has increased the difficulties experienced by lawyers and judges in explaining procedural requirements.

Summing up, then, it is the experience of the survey as a whole that both the lay public and the profession look to the judge to uphold justice. This is a larger role than acting as referee to competing trial counsel, and the role of the judge must be regarded as encompassing any activity necessary to achieve justice. Therefore, in considering the special problems of metropolitan trial judges, we must give attention to those activities which are thrust upon metropolitan judges by reason of the milieu in which they operate. These include the purely administrative activities necessary to keep a tremendous organization going; the distribution of judicial and other manpower; the shepherding of each case through various phases of court contact, together with whatever application of judicial skill is necessary to bring each case to a just disposition, whether by trial, settlement, pretrial, conciliation, transfer to another court, reference to a noncourt agency, or other means. Because of the extent to which metropolitan cases are terminated other than by full contested trial, it seems important to call attention to the extent of the nontrial functions performed by metropolitan judges.

Section 2. Organization of Judicial Personnel

a. Presiding Judge

In most, if not all, metropolitan cities, the trial courts are multi-judge courts. Whenever a court has more than one judge, problems of administration, of division of labor, of point of view, and of supervision arise. We found no unanimity of opinion or practice with respect to the best method of fixing responsibility for the work of the court among the judges in a multi-judge court. In some quite large metropolitan areas, such as Indianapolis and Philadelphia, multi-judge courts still operate on the principle that each individual should in effect run his own autonomous court, disposing of his numerical share of all litigation filed and being fully responsible as an individual to the community.[4]

In other areas, such as Detroit, administrative problems are the responsibility of a presiding or executive judge, selected by and responsible to the occupants of the bench. The advantage of the presiding judge system is that it centralizes in one judicial officer the control of case movement and progress, permitting a knowledgeable and consistent system for the assignment and disposition of cases to be developed even in the largest courts. Where, as in Detroit, the presiding judge is selected by his colleagues and his tenure is subject to their periodic review, a judge with administrative ability can develop an assignment system capable of making the best use of the special abilities on the bench and of dealing with the ever-shifting workload within the court.[5] He can design and develop appropriate systems for obtaining reports and statistics and for coping with sudden changes in workload or personnel.

The other view, that the position of presiding judge should be rotated after a short period of time as a matter of democratic principle, was still being expressed in Los Angeles at the time of that survey.[6]

But we note that in Los Angeles as in Detroit, where a judge with superior administrative ability appears, the objections to allowing him to remain as presiding judge tend to diminish and the assignment system tends to improve as

[4] FAMILY CASES 117 *et seq.*

[5] DETROIT STUDY 75 *et seq.* Compare the Circuit Court of Wayne County, with a strong presiding judge, and the Detroit Recorder's Court, with a system for rotating the presiding judge every month.

[6] Los Angeles Study 55 *et seq.*

he remains on the job long enough to grasp all the complexities of the court's administrative problems and to develop techniques to deal with its total caseload.[7]

Our correspondents report by questionnaire that in New Jersey the presiding judge of the general trial court is appointed by the Chief Justice of the state supreme court and serves at his pleasure. In San Jose, California, the presiding judge is selected by a majority of his colleagues on a six months' rotation basis. Pueblo, Colorado, with three judges, has no presiding judge. But Brocton, Massachusetts, with two judges, has a presiding judge appointed for life. In Baltimore, with fifteen judges, the presiding judge is appointed by the governor for a term of fifteen years. Las Vegas, with six judges, chooses its presiding judge for an indefinite period by concurrence of all the judges. In St. Paul, with thirteen judges, the presiding judge serves from year to year upon vote of the entire bench. In this court, the presiding judge used to be selected on the basis of seniority.

In Minneapolis, the chief judge is selected by the judges, but in fact does not act as the court's executive officer, we are advised. In Boise, with three judges, the presiding judge is elected for six years, and in Baton Rouge, with six judges, he is elected for four years. In Cleveland, with twenty-four judges, the presiding judge is selected by the judges for six years, but in Chattanooga (thirteen judges) there is no presiding judge, nor is there a presiding judge in Milwaukee (twenty-two judges).

In Wichita Falls, Texas (four judges) the office of presiding judge rotates every six months. In Huron, South Dakota, the judges alternate; in Charleston, the presiding judge is elected by the state legislature for a four-year term. In Des Moines, the presiding judge is elected by the judges

[7] See Burke, *Problems of Court Administration in a Metropolitan Court,* 43 AM. JUD. SOC'Y 190 (1960). Judge Burke has recently been re-elected for an unprecedented third term as presiding judge of the Superior Court of Los Angeles.

and the office rotates. In Cheyenne, with two judges, each judge takes all cases filed in his half of each month and deals with those cases in lieu of designating either as presiding judge. In Phoenix, an assignment judge is selected by other judges, and the office rotates every six months. In Miami, a presiding judge is elected each year by fellow trial judges, but in practice he is usually re-elected. In Sioux Falls, a presiding judge is elected for six years.

On the basis of the data submitted by our correspondents and from the total experience of the survey, it is the writer's conclusion that no adquate control can be achieved over the total performance of a large multi-judge court without the service of a long-term presiding judge with thorough knowledge and understanding of the complex personnel and assignment problems and with adequate authority to deal with these problems. The trend seems to be in this direction. Professor Holbrook commented, with respect to Los Angeles:

> It will be noted that the presiding judge's functions are set forth in very general terms and with no implementing authority or sanctions to impose his will. As one former municipal court presiding judge pictured it, he was 'an impressario with forty-two prima donnas and no power.' Perhaps this slightly overstates the case but the problem calls for the efforts of a diplomat of no mean skill. Observation has convinced us more and more clearly that a key figure in the successful administration of the large court is the presiding judge.[8]

He also notes that "the presiding judge is the administrative head of a gigantic business and we doubt that any major industry elects to change its managing head with such frequency."[9]

The fallacy in the idea that each judge should be king in his own courtroom with respect to his numerical share of the total caseload may be illustrated by noting what happens when one of the judges in a large metropolitan court gets a

[8] Los Angeles Study 54.
[9] *Ibid.*

really complicated antitrust case. Some such cases take more than a decade to try; almost any antitrust case—or other case involving the industrial structure or practices of a large industry—will take the better part of a year to try.

To say that the best system of administration in a multijudge court in a large city is to leave each judge with his numerical share of the caseload seems to this writer like saying that the best way of piloting a large transatlantic airliner is to assign to each member of the crew his numerical share of the payload and to leave that member fully responsible for bringing that share safely to destination.

b. Specialized Judges, Divisions, and Calendars

The segregation of cases by subject matter (and the use of specialized judicial personnel to handle them) is itself an important aspect of any discussion of machinery for handling docket and caseload. Overuse of these devices may result in fragmenting the caseload and thus impede docket control. Underuse may also impede proper handling of cases by preventing knowledgeable attention to the component parts of the docket.[10]

Section 3. Methods of Assigning Cases

a. Introductory Comment

Various methods of assigning cases have been described in the Detroit and Los Angeles surveys and in other materials previously referred to hereinabove.[11]

[10] Los Angeles Study 54 *et seq*; Detroit Study 72 *et seq; supra* p. 179 *et seq.*

[11] Los Angeles Study 218, 270 *et seq.; Detroit Study 195 *et seq.;* Progress Report, Committee on Metropolitan Trial Courts 27 *et seq.* (June 1953); Phoenix Study 9 *et seq.;* Family Cases, San Francisco 10 *et seq.*, Chicago 69 *et seq.*, Indianapolis 128 *et seq.*, Milwaukee 212; Public Administration Service, Administration of Court and Legal Services in the Government of Milwaukee County 8 (mimeographed, 1955).

In some courts, each case after being filed with the clerk is immediately assigned to the judge who is to handle it, and he becomes solely responsible for its progress thereafter. In Chattanooga, each judge calls his own trial docket three times a term. In Boise, the two judges take alternate cases. In Indianapolis, each case when filed is assigned in rotation to one of the judges by means of a chronological numbering system, supposed to guard against manipulation by attorneys seeking to reach or avoid a particular judge. Like other purely mechanical systems observed, this method can readily be manipulated by the attorneys.[12] It is interesting that Milwaukee, which had a serious delay problem when observed by this writer,[13] is reported to have since dropped the system requiring that counsel apply to have each case moved onto a trial docket, in favor of a so-called "lottery" system supposedly foolproof against the machinations of counsel.[14]

b. Presiding Judge, Daily Docket Call

In some courts having a presiding judge responsible for the assignment of cases, the presiding judge "sounds" the docket every day, or every week.[15] To "sound," or "call," the docket is to ascertain the number of cases ready for judicial attention from among those listed as ready. This is often done in large cities (e.g., Detroit) by an assignment clerk, by telephone, or by requiring attorneys to report to the clerk, rather than by response to oral inquiry from the bench. Emergency matters are, of course, handled by the judge assigned to this function. This may be the presiding judge or

[12] FAMILY CASES 128-30.

[13] *Id.* at 212.

[14] The Administration of Court and Legal Services in the Government of Milwaukee County, *op. cit. supra* note 11, at 11.

[15] E.g., Philadelphia, trial commissioner; Boise, presiding judge; San Jose, trial calendar judge. Presiding judge: Sioux Falls, Biloxi, Brocton, Binghamton, Pueblo, Newark (information supplied by questionnaire).

his designee. But in some large metropolitan cities, such as Chicago, there are still courts in which the presiding judge still spends much time literally calling cases one by one and assigning them in open court after conference with counsel as they respond to each such call. This seems not only a waste of judicial time and brainpower but also may produce a confused and inefficient case system. As observed, it contrasts strikingly with the orderly progress of cases under an experienced presiding judge and assignment clerk using the central assignment system.[16] There will always be emergency adjustments requiring the attention of the presiding judge, of course, but under the master calendar system, if well handled, the daily emergencies are handled by the assignment clerk after conference with the presiding judge, or by motion presented to the presiding judge by counsel.

c. Assignment Clerk

The employment of a full-time assignment clerk acting under the supervision of the presiding or assignment judge is beneficial to orderly administration of a metropolitan assignment system and is thought essential in a large multi-judge court with a heavy caseload. The work of the Los Angeles and Detroit assignment clerks has been described in earlier studies. St. Paul, Miami, Charleston, Baton Rouge, and Minneapolis report using assignment clerks. In 1958, the presiding judge of the Superior Court of Los Angeles instituted the procedure of using a court commissioner to call the calendar and to hear the regular motions presented in the master calendar department. Philadelphia also has a trial commissioner.[17]

[16] E.g., DETROIT STUDY 195; LOS ANGELES STUDY 218, 270; and see Burke, *supra* note 7.

[17] Information obtained by questionnaire.

d. Master Calendar System

The most appropriate way of assigning cases in a large metropolitan trial court, in the opinion of this writer, is the Cleveland, or central assignment, or master calendar system. This provides a central written assignment plan for all cases, directly supervised by the presiding judge, who is thus at all times familiar with and in control of the entire mechanism of the court's total caseload. From the master calendar, cases move into various calendars and divisions and dockets, but at all times are under the scrutiny and authority of the judge responsible for the whole. The advantage of the system is that it permits the development of centralized responsibility, knowledge, and control of the entire caseload. Development of proper statistics, personnel and record practices, and administrative techniques can only take place where responsibility is thus centered.

In highly developed systems, the over-all master calendar is subdivided, as in Los Angeles, where there is a criminal master calendar and a civil master calendar. The former is delegated by the presiding judge to another judge, and the latter is handled by the presiding judge with the assistance of the new calendar commissioner.[18]

The use of some variation of the master calendar system is reported by Cleveland, Baltimore, and Phoenix through questionnaires distributed for this study. There are many individual variations. In Phoenix, it is reported that civil cases are set about sixty days in advance, with such allowance for dropouts as experience suggests. Each day, depending on judicial manpower available the following day, the assignment judge refers out criminal, domestic relations, motions, and other matters not set in advance.

In Des Moines, cases work up a list from "ready" to "on call." The assignment judge applies his attention to law

[18] Burke, *supra* note 7.

cases "on call," as the state of the docket requires. The judge assigned to equity division and the one assigned to the criminal division each handles his own docket problems, after the original assignment to the specialized division.

e. Concluding Comment

It is the conclusion of this writer that the problems of a large multi-judge metropolitan trial court require the use of some version of a centralized assignment system, operated by an experienced presiding judge with authority over the entire caseload. In no other way, it is submitted, can adequate records, statistics, and knowledge be developed, and skill to control the entire load be acquired and maintained.

SECTION 4. PRETRIAL

a. Background

Though not confined to the United States,[19] the emergence of the pretrial hearing as a major device for insuring the orderly and efficient progress of cases in a large metropolitan court has been an American procedural achievement. The development of the pretrial conference by Judge Ira W. Jayne, the chairman of the committee responsible for the present study, has been described many times.[20] It was made a regular feature of court practice for the first time by Judge Jayne in Detroit.[21]

As Judge Murrah points out, Judge Jayne discovered in 1929 that he could dispose of considerably more cases and

[19] FINAL REPORT OF THE COMMITTEE ON SUPREME COURT PRACTICE AND PROCEDURE (usually and hereinafter referred to as the EVERSHED REPORT), CMD. No. 8878, at 73 *et seq.* (1953).

[20] E.g., Brand, 16 J. AM. JUD. SOC'Y (1942); foreword by Judge Jayne, 17 OHIO STATE L. J. 160-62 (Autumn 1956 symposium); Judge Alfred Murrah, *Pre-trial Procedure,* 328 ANNALS 70 (March 1960 symposium). And see NIMS, PRE-TRIAL (1950).

[21] Murrah, *op. cit. supra,* 71.

manage his business more effectively by calling a conference prior to trial, to dispose of uncontested issues and eliminate waste trial motions. He also noted that the catalytic effect of confronting the parties and attorneys with the problems of the case disposed them to make decisions concerning those problems, with the result that many cases were settled without trial.

From Detroit, the pretrial conference spread to Boston, Cleveland, and other large metropolitan centers. It became a "fundamental cornerstone of the Federal Rules of Civil Procedure" and, as Federal Rule 16, has influenced the development of pretrial in state court systems also.[22]

The use of the pretrial conference in metropolitan areas and elsewhere has been officially recommended by the American Bar Association as part of the judicial reform program developed by the Section of Judicial Administration.[23]

As defined by the Section of Judicial Administration:

> The pre-trial conference is one held prior to the trial of a pending case, conducted by a judge and attended by counsel for the parties and sometimes by the litigants. The purpose of the conference is to simplify the issues, to obtain admissions and stipulations to avoid unnecessary proof, to discuss limitation of the number of expert witnesses and to explore the possibility of compromise, adjustment, or settlement.[24]

The use of pretrial became compulsory in all cases in Detroit in 1931, and in 1952 a discovery procedure was added for the purpose of exploring all cases as soon as they came to issue in order that the pretrial judge may include all undisputed facts in his pretrial statement.[25] The use of pretrial

[22] *Id.* at 71, 72.

[23] VANDERBILT, MINIMUM STANDARDS 206; THE IMPROVEMENT OF THE ADMINISTRATION OF JUSTICE 51 (a handbook prepared by the Section of Judicial Administration) (3d ed. 1952).

[24] *Ibid.*

[25] Jayne *op. cit. supra* note 20, at 162.

in the Circuit Court of Wayne County, Michigan, was described in detail in the Detroit study.[26]

At the time of the Los Angeles study, pretrial was in an early stage of development.[27] At about the same time, the Section of Judicial Administration issued a *Judge's Handbook of Pretrial Procedure* prepared by Judge Clarence Kincaid, then Chairman of the Pretrial Committee of the California Judicial Council and Judge of the Los Angeles Superior Court. In a recent address the present presiding judge of the Superior Court of Los Angeles states that pretrial is now mandatory in Los Angeles.

> Our judges are in general agreement that the pretrial procedure is an efficient tool not only to reduce or prevent court congestion, but to assure the advanced preparation of cases for trial.
>
> From two to four judges are regularly assigned on fulltime duty in the Pretrial Department. In addition, we have a panel of fifteen civil trial court judges who hear one pretrial matter every morning . . . before the start of their regular trial work. The more complicated pretrial matters are kept in the fulltime pretrial departments. . . . In our state, pretrial has been mandatory for several years, and the pretrial judge does not assign a trial date to an action until the pretrial rules have been fully complied with. This means that by and large all discovery proceedings will have been completed, the joint pretrial statement agreed upon and submitted, and a pretrial order made *before* a case will be given a trial date.[28]

In addition to this compulsory pretrial, the Los Angeles Superior Court has devised a program for the early settlement of personal injury cases through offering to attorneys the services of a special pretrial personal injury settlement calendar operated by a special panel of eight judges. Notices are sent by the court to all counsels in personal injury cases a month in advance of the normal notice of a pretrial hearing. Judge Burke reports that the initial reluctance of counsel early disappeared, and by November 1959, 25 per cent

[26] DETROIT STUDY 78-79, 194-95, 273-74.
[27] LOS ANGELES STUDY 260 *et seq.*
[28] Burke, *supra* note 7.

of such cases were requested by both counsels to be referred to this special docket, resulting in settlement of 60 per cent of those referred. This figure is thought by Judge Burke to be slanted low, because it does not include cases settled after the pretrial conference but as a result of it.

b. Extent of Use

Pretrial is now officially authorized in most jurisdictions.[29] Our correspondents were asked to comment on several aspects of the use of pretrial in various metropolitan areas. Pretrial is reported as compulsory in general trial courts in the following cities (in addition to Detroit, Boston, and Los Angeles): Philadelphia (recent); Charleston, S. C.; St. Paul;[30] San Jose;[31] Cleveland.[32] A compulsory pretrial system is reported under study in Newark, New Jersey. All civil cases in municipal court in St. Paul are subjected to pretrial, according to our correspondent.

The use of pretrial in selected civil cases by court rule, by agreement of counsel, or both, is reported in Milwaukee; Minneapolis (seldom used); Boise; Baton Rouge (state district court, not municipal court); Rutland and Burlington, Vermont; Wichita Falls ("when courts deem necessary"); Sioux Falls ("motion of counsel, not much used"); Huron ("agreement of counsel, not much used"); Cheyenne; Pueblo ("practically abandoned"); Miami ("all by some

[29] Clark, *Objectives of Pre-trial Procedure* 17 OHIO STATE L. J. 163 (1956); VANDERBILT, MINIMUM STANDARDS 206-18; A.B.A. SECTION OF JUDICIAL ADMINISTRATION, REPORT OF PRE-TRIAL COMMITTEE; INSTITUTE OF JUDICIAL ADMINISTRATION, PRE-TRIAL RULES, No. 2-U22 (Dec. 11, 1953).

[30] Was compulsory in 1952, was abandoned, and became compulsory again in 1959.

[31] As in all California Courts, by rule of State Judicial Council.

[32] See Report and Recommendations on Trial Delay in the Common Pleas Court of Cuyahoga County, Ohio, by the Committee on Court Congestion and Delay in Litigation, Cleveland Bar Association 22 *et seq.* (1958); Shumaker, *An Appraisal of Pre-trial in Ohio,* 17 OHIO ST. L. J. (1956); Woodle, *Discovery Practice in Ohio—Pathway to Progress,* 8 W. RES. L. REV. 117 (March 1957), 456 (Sept. 1957).

judges, selective by others"); Grand Forks; Binghamton; Eugene, Oregon; Baltimore; Las Vegas; Phoenix.

The selective use of pretrial in criminal cases—an interesting recent development—is reported from Rutland and Burlington in Vermont, and also from Des Moines and Las Vegas.

c. Percentage of Caseload Disposed of at Pretrial

The percentage of total caseload reported disposed of at pretrial in the Circuit Court of Wayne County (Detroit) rose from 40 per cent in 1935 to 76.06 per cent in 1948.[33] In 1956, the Court Administrator of Michigan reported that of 11,574 cases assigned for final action after reaching issue in the Circuit Court of Wayne County, 86.01 per cent were disposed of without trial, mostly through "administrative devices (discovery and pretrial conferences) employed by the Wayne Circuit Court."[34] No other court, the figures of which have been made known to the study, approaches these figures.

Binghamton reports 50 per cent pretrial dispositions; Des Moines, 30 per cent civil, 5-10 per cent criminal; Cleveland and Cheyenne, 20 per cent; Las Vegas, 25 per cent; Charleston, 15 per cent; Casper, 3 per cent; San Jose, 1 per cent;[35] Minneapolis, "tiny." In Philadelphia, the use of pretrial is too recent to provide a statistical basis, and in other areas those responding to the questionnaire did not feel able to hazard an estimate. It will be noted from the above information that compulsory pretrial does not necessarily result

[33] DETROIT STUDY 195.

[34] ANNUAL REPORT AND JUDICIAL STATISTICS FOR 1956, at 21. The latest report at date of this writing is 1958, which shows (Appendix, Table IV), the types of disposition for various types of cases in each circuit, but does not indicate the percentage of pretrial hearing dispositions.

[35] This apparently does not include cases settled after conference as a result thereof. The same correspondent reports 90% of cases in the general trial court disposed of other than by trial.

in a high percentage of pretrial dispositions. On the other hand, voluntary use of pretrial by agreement of counsel cannot always be equated with a low percentage of dispositions at a phase prior to trial. Much depends on the skill of the judge, in either case. The use of a "blitz" type of special pretrial effort to clear the docket of ancient cases in the United States District Court for the Southern District of New York, though beyond the scope of this study as affecting a federal court, is relevant to the extent of pretrial dispositions. Here a special committee of judges canvassed the nonjury cases and called pretrial meetings between the judge and the lawyers and litigants, with the result that most of the backlog was wiped out and currency restored.[36]

d. Acceptance

With respect to the desirability of pretrial, the comments from correspondents were most strongly in favor of the device, as saving time and money and assisting the court to render true justice in each case. One commented that its broad use will "promote justice, eliminate waste of time, cut down the waiting period getting to trial, shorten trials." Several recommended compulsory pretrial as essential to efficient operation in metropolitan trial courts to determine basic issues and agree to or order whatever will be essential to the trial.

Several point out that pretrial is useful only in the hands of a competent judge. Two or three feel that pretrial is helpful in complex cases, but not where the issues are simple and the facts easy to ascertain. One cautions sharply against use of pretrial as a lever to force settlement. One, from a jurisdiction where pretrial is compulsory, expresses the view that a majority of judges and attorneys would welcome its

[36] Kaufman, *Decongestion Through Calendar Controls*, 328 ANNALS 84 *et seq.* (March 1960) (symposium on *Lagging Justice*).

abolition or a reduction of its application, particularly in divorce and personal injury cases.

Three correspondents indicate that since pretrial is time-consuming, there is a problem of arriving at the proper allocation of time and judicial manpower for this purpose. In an excellent study of the mechanical problems of delay in bringing cases to trial, the view is expressed that pretrial can reduce delay only if the judicial manhours utilized for pretrial result in the pretrial disposition of enough cases to overbalance the judicial time which would have been used in trying those cases.[37] Such a view rests upon the premise that delay is the equivalent of delay in reaching trial, and that the function of the pretrial hearing is to prevent cases from reaching the trial stage by settling them, thus preserving the judges for their real business: trying cases.

If, however, the premise is adopted that the judicial process is something more than a mechanical device for trying cases, the validity of evaluating pretrial by the amount of judicial trial time it displaces disappears.

It is the premise of this study that the metropolitan court has a responsibility to each of the cases in its caseload, and that this responsibility is to apply skilled judicial attention to each case at such time, and in such intensity, as will dispose of each case in an appropriate and just manner, whether by trial or otherwise. It is submitted that a judge is discharging his function just as much when dismissing a case or pretrying one as when trying one, if in each case he reaches the best solution. As has been shown, only a small fraction of dispositions in any trial court is by trial, and the larger the metropolitan area, the smaller the fraction.

Therefore, it is submitted that pretrial should be evaluated in terms of whether it can assist judges to maintain full control over the progress of the entire caseload and to deal meaningfully with each case to the end that justice may be

[37] ZEISEL, DELAY IN THE COURT 141 *et seq.* (1959).

done to each litigant. There is abundant evidence that it can.

The real objectives of pretrial are set forth in Federal Rule 16.[38] As Judge Clark has said:

> . . . the central purpose of it all . . . is, as I like to view it, the individualization of the case, so that it may be separated for its own particular treatment from the vast grist of cases passing throughout courts in daily routine toward negotiation and settlement and, occasionally, trial. . . . To me successful pre-trial represents the perfection of the judicial art; and the trial judge who is skillful in piloting a case thus promptly and effectively, either to speedy disposition on the merits or to settlement, has shown himself more effective in his work than one who may be able to turn out well-rounded opinions, but has not the tact and temper for the pre-trial conference.[39]

Another eminent jurist, Judge Murrah, has recently stated, "Pretrial recognizes the current conception of a lawsuit: one free from surprise, with all triable issues exposed prior to the courtroom."[40]

The experience of the group of studies being summarized has been that the significance of pretrial to the metropolitan trial court rests not only upon its effectiveness in reducing delay and confusion, but also upon its usefulness in enabling the metropolitan trial judge, and particularly the presiding judge, to achieve knowledge of and maintain mastery over the entire caseload at an earlier phase, and to organize the court to deal with its components. It is this quality which has resulted in the rapid increase in the use of pretrial during the last decade. It is perhaps the outstanding device now available to deal with a major special metropolitan court problem: that of coping with the total caseload while re-

[38] Murrah, *supra* note 20, quotes the rule at 72.

[39] Clark, *supra* note 29 at 163. See also NIMS, PRE-TRIAL (1950); RAGLAND, DISCOVERY BEFORE TRIAL (1932); Sunderland, *The Theory and Practice of Pre-Trial Procedure*, 36 MICH. L. REV. 215, 21 J. AM. JUD. SOC'Y 125 (1937).

[40] Murrah, *supra* note 20, at 70. And see Yankwich, *Crystallization of Issues by Pretrial: A Judge's View*, 58 COLUM. L. REV. 470 (1958) in a symposium devoted to pretrial and discovery in the federal courts.

taining awareness of and ability to deal justly with each individual case.

Section 5. Statistics

a. Recommendation of American Bar Association

The importance of developing an adequate system of statistics for all courts has been stressed by most writers on judicial reform.[41] In 1938, the American Bar Association, as part of its comprehensive program for improving judicial administration, adopted the following recommendation: "That quarterly judicial statistics should be required."[42]

This recommendation was linked with two others related to management of court business: provision for unified state judicial system with power to assign judges for best use of available manpower to relieve congestion, and provision for a statewide Judicial Council.

The need for adequate statistics reported periodically is especially important to efficient operation of the large multi-judge trial court, since in such a court the presiding judge must rely to a great extent on statistical information in evaluating case progress, dealing with delay, and making judicial assignments.

b. Caseload per Judge

In the Detroit study, some information was given on caseload per judge in various trial courts in the Detroit area.[43] In the Los Angeles study, Holbrook commented in some detail on the difficulty of arriving at a method of reporting

[41] E.g., Sunderland, *Defects of English and American Statistics,* 16 A.B.A.J. 773-75 (1950); Vanderbilt, Minimum Standards 89; Thiel, *Judicial Statistics,* 328 Annals 94 (March 1960); Bad Housekeeping 136 *et seq.;* The Improvement of the Administration of Justice, *supra* note 23, at 34 *et seq.* (3d ed. 1952).

[42] Vanderbilt, Minimum Standards and see The Improvement of the Administration of Justice 34 *et seq.*

[43] Detroit Study 96-100.

caseload per judge for purposes of evaluating the work of the judge.[44] Thus, the taking of a summary judgment or disposing of a case on motion is less time-consuming than the trial of a fully contested case. It is not clear that such dispositions involve less judicial skill, however; in fact, they may well demonstrate a very high degree of judicial performance.

For many purposes, general figures on caseload per judge are not useful and may even be misleading. Still, over a year, and for purposes of general information, the caseload per judge figure—like other statistics—is useful if not overread or misread.

Therefore, we asked our correspondents to comment on caseload per judge in various metropolitan courts, having particularly in mind the extent of development of the individual court's machinery for keeping track of the work of each of its judges from time to time.

In Detroit, the caseload per judge in the Circuit Court of Wayne County, an eighteen-judge court, was 1,255 in calendar 1947; in 1958, it was 1,324.[45] In Los Angeles in 1953-1954, then an eighty-judge court, it was 947 cases.[46]

Of those reporting for this study, only ten were able to give any information on caseload per judge. Philadelphia reports that there exists no data on the basis of which caseload per judge can be calculated! Miami showed total dispositions per judge for 1958 of 1,142; San Jose, 1,136; Cheyenne, one judge 900, the other 200 (total 1,100); Cleveland, 737; Des Moines, 600; Boise, 484; Newark, 357; Milwaukee, 595; Minneapolis, 575 (counting 12 judges only, the other 2 being otherwise assigned). This information strongly suggests that there are differences in

[44] LOS ANGELES STUDY 65 *et seq.*
[45] DETROIT STUDY 97; MICH. OFFICE OF COURT ADMINISTRATOR, SUPREME COURT OF MICHIGAN ANNUAL REPORT AND JUDICIAL STATISTICS FOR 1958 at 12. The figure for 1959, found at 24 of REPORT FOR 1959, was 1,319.
[46] LOS ANGELES STUDY 66.

the matters reported as "dispositions." For this reason, it is again emphasized that no conclusions are justified concerning the comparative diligence or productivity of the judges concerned.

The more interesting conclusion, for purposes of this study, is the comparative absence of any statistical tool by which presiding judges, assignment clerks, and state court administrators can measure the actual and potential productivity of available judgepower in their work of attempting to evolve efficient methods for handling docket and calendar problems.

SECTION 6. DELAY

a. Definition

A precise definition of "delay" is hard to come by, partly because of the extent to which subjective philosophy concerning the trial judge's role influences the interpretation of logjam data, and partly because of the lack of workable statistics. Adequate statistics are not available internally in many courts. We know of no adequate metropolitan-wide statistical system for all trial courts in any metropolitan area. In some states, state court administrators have developed good systems of statistics for all trial courts in the state. It has been found difficult to generalize about delay from these, because of the variations in use of such terms as "total caseload," "at issue," and "disposition." Finally, there is no nationally agreed upon statistical base from which delay can be measured. The only approach to such a definition is the annual report of the Institute of Judicial Administration, which is restricted to personal injury jury cases and therefore rules out the overwhelming majority of dispositions for which any single metropolitan trial court is responsible.[47]

[47] STATE TRIAL COURTS OF GENERAL JURISDICTION, CALENDAR STATUS STUDY, 1958. And see ZEISEL, DELAY IN THE COURT 29 *et seq.*, pointing out that the

For purposes of this study, the interval from "at issue" to "final disposition" has been regarded as the most workable existing rule of thumb for measuring logjam in trial courts. The period between "filing" and "at issue" was considered and finally excluded, after much soul searching, on the ground that it is not legitimate to hold the court responsible for delays occurring during this period. That is, the consensus of those consulted is that bringing a case to issue is the responsibility of the parties. Where parties have not brought the case to issue within the period required by statute or court rule, it is concluded that in most courts the case can be defaulted or disposed of for no progress. In some courts, however, it was noted with interest that the court was itself powerless to rid itself of docket deadwood. Thus, in Milwaukee, much of the serious delay observed several years ago was attributed by local personnel, and by the observer, to the circumstance that no case could reach disposition until counsel had requested that it be placed on a trial docket. Where no such request was filed, there was no machinery by which the court could get rid of the case.[48] In a study of Chicago courts several years ago, this observer found several ancient cases, which had been dismissed by the court for no progress, only to be reinstated by counsel, where they continued on the docket, undisposed of, for several more years. Such findings suggest a lack of effective power in the court to control its load.[49]

Granting, then, that the elimination of cases filed but never brought to issue is related to delay in the sense that courts must have effective authority, by statute or court rule, to eliminate cases not brought promptly to issue, we have

---

delay in the personal injury calendar in New York has been created by the system of calendaring and assigning such cases. The same could be said of several other courts, with resulting false emphasis upon these cases.

[48] Family Cases 213.

[49] Progress Report, *supra* note 11, at 26 *et seq.*, 30 *et seq.*, 38-39 (table), cases A and D (1953).

nevertheless reached the conclusion that the interval from "at issue" to "final disposition" is the most direct measure of the *court's* efficiency in dealing with cases. Caution is advised in interpreting any such data because of variations in the functional use of the term "at issue," and because of the tendency to exclude from total figures such cases as are disposed of summarily or without trial. As has been said, we are unable to accept such exclusions because this survey has proceeded on the premise that every litigant is entitled to the best attention the court can give, and to receive that disposition which is most appropriate in each individual case, in the considered judgment of a thoughtful and diligent judge.

b. Extent of Delay

There are many well-known studies of delay in trial courts, some of them recent, some not yet complete. These have been described in a recent issue of the ANNALS.[50] Many of the classic studies have been cited earlier in this monograph.[51] Both the Detroit and Los Angeles studies contain discussions of delay.[52] No attempt will be made at this point to review or further document this material.

We asked our correspondents for the average length of time between "date case at issue" and date of final disposition for all cases, and for the same figure broken down by chancery (equity) cases, criminal jury and nonjury, law jury and nonjury, and negligence cases jury and nonjury. Of thirty questionnaires at hand when this chapter was written, those from five metropolitan areas gave no answer to this question: Boise, Pueblo, Baltimore, Biloxi, and Rutland. Huron, South Dakota, reported "no court congestion."

Grand Forks, North Dakota, estimated a 5-month interval

[50] *Lagging Justice,* 328 ANNALS (March 1960).

[51] *Inter alia:* pp. 87, 89, 92, 94, 99 *et seq.,* 129, 131-32.

[52] DETROIT STUDY 205 *et seq.;* LOS ANGELES STUDY 221 *et seq.* Discussions of delay by the present writer include 15 F.R.D. 207 (1954); FAMILY CASES, *passim;* PROGRESS REPORT, *supra* note 11.

for all cases. Phoenix, Arizona, reported that in all civil cases the interval from issue to *trial* has increased to close to 15 months, and that criminal cases have an average interval from filing of information to trial of 3 to 4 months (constitutional right to trial in 60 days in criminal case often waived). Newark, New Jersey, reports reaching all criminal cases within 4 months 17 days from indictment; all law cases within 25 days from commencement of suit (filing complaint, serving summons).

The answers of other correspondents are presented in Table VI, with the caution that the sampling is too small and the questioning technique too primitive to support generalization.

Thus, an over-all delay of a year or more is reported from San Jose; Charleston, S. C.; Milwaukee; Cleveland; Minneapolis and Phoenix (civil cases). This supports the general consensus that delay is a normal part of the environment of the large metropolitan trial court, regardless of structural pattern or administrative machinery.[53] But note Miami in Table VI.

[53] The age of cases problem has been discussed in the DETROIT STUDY at 205 *et seq.;* LOS ANGELES STUDY 220-21 *et seq.* See also PROGRESS REPORT, COMMITTEE ON METROPOLITAN TRIAL COURTS (1953); FAMILY CASES 74 *et seq.,* 212 *inter alia.*

The problem of delay in Phoenix was analyzed in the PHOENIX STUDY, a report of a survey made by the Institute of Judicial Administration: DELAY AND CONGESTION IN THE SUPERIOR COURT OF MARICOPA COUNTY, ARIZONA (1955). With regard to Milwaukee, see, in addition to the FAMILY CASES IN COURT reference, Public Administration Service The Administration of Court and Legal Services in the Government of Milwaukee County (1955). The Cleveland Bar Association has recently (May 1958) published an excellent REPORT (*supra.* note 32) as made by its Committee on Court Congestion and Delay in Litigation. Delay in the various courts in London, England, has been discussed in the DAILY MIRROR SPOTLIGHT ON JUSTICE (1954), and in the classic studies: FINAL REPORT OF THE COMMITTEE ON SUPREME COURT PRACTICE AND PROCEDURE, CMD. No. 8878 (1953) (EVERSHED REPORT); REPORT OF THE ROYAL COMMISSION ON THE DISPATCH OF BUSINESS AT COMMON LAW (1934-36). Reports of delay in New York courts abound, and include the 1957 REPORT OF THE TEMPORARY COMMISSION ON THE COURTS, BAD HOUSEKEEPING, and DELAY IN THE COURT by ZEISEL, all as previously cited herein. A study of delay in Pennsylvania courts is in preparation, and other appropriate materials may be found cited in *Lagging Justice, supra* note 50, or by inquiring of the librarian at the American Bar Center.

TABLE VI

Average Elapsed Time Between Date Case at Issue and Date Final Disposition, Various Metropolitan Cities

Metropolis	All	Chancery	Crim. jury	Crim. nonjury	Law jury	Law nonjury	Neg. jury	Neg. nonjury
Baton Rouge		same as law	6 mo.	60 days	9 mo.	6 mo.	not separated	
Binghamton	(estimate not more than 6 months if counsel is diligent)							
Brocton	..	current	current	1 yr.	1 yr.	current	..	
Burlington	6 mo.	6-12 mo.	2 mo.	1 mo.	6 mo.	6 mo.	..	..
Charleston, S. C.	12 mo.							
Charleston, W. Va.	8 mo.	2 yrs.	14 mo.	3 mo.	6 mo.	..	6 mo.	12 mo.
Cheyenne	4 mo.	..	3 mo.	15 days	6 mo.	2 mo.	2 mo. for all negligence unseparated	
Cleveland[a]	18 mo.	18 mo.	4 mo.	3 mo.	18 mo.	18 mo.	18 mo.	18 mo.
Des Moines[b]	2½ mo.	3 mo.	2 mo.	2½ mo.	2 mo.	3 mo.	2 mo.	3 mo.
Eugene, Ore.[c]	8 mo.	90 days	60 days	60 days	8 mo.	8 mo.	8 mo.	8 mo.
Las Vegas[d]	9 mo.	8 mo.	9 mo.	2 mo.	9 mo.	2 mo.	9 mo.	2 mo.
Miami	6 mo.	5 mo.	2 mo.	3 mo.	7 mo.	6 mo.	7 mo.	6 mo.
Minneapolis	13 mo.	..	almost immediately	same as jury	..	..	..	..

TABLE VI (*Continued*)

Metropolis	All	Chancery	Crim. jury	Crim. nonjury	Law jury	Law nonjury	Neg. jury	Neg. nonjury
Milwaukee[e]	..	..	..	..	..	..	..	..
Philadelphia	6 mo.	..	..	..	23 mo.	6 mo.	..	..
San Jose	12 mo.	4 mo. (includes eminent domain)	3 mo.	1 mo.	18 mo.	5 mo. plus	18 mo.	5 mo. plus
Sioux Falls, S. D.	3 mo.	3 mo.	3 mo.	3 mo.	3 mo.	3 mo.	3 mo.	3 mo.
St. Paul	all jury 8 mo. nonjury sep. calendar 3 mo.		immediate	immediate	8 mo.	..		
Washington (state)	varies with jurisdiction, from 1 to 2 weeks in smaller areas to 3 months from issue in larger areas, 4 to 7 months in one area							
Wichita Falls, Tex.	probably 6 mo.	blended system	2-6 mo.	2-6 mo.	6 mo.	2 mo.	..	..

[a] And see *Report and Recommendations on Trial Delay* in the Common Pleas Court of Cuyahoga County, Ohio, Cleveland Bar Association, Committee on Court Congestion and Delay in Litigation, May 1958.

[b] Two questionnaires were received from Des Moines. One answered as above set forth; the other answered "4 months" to all questions.

[c] Industrial accident cases are given preferential docket position, disposed of in about 60-90 days; uncontested divorce in about 60 days, immediately after termination of statutory waiting period.

[d] "We have kept no statistics exactly. If, for instance, 4,400 divorce cases are filed in one year, 3,100 of them will be heard in court. The remainder are usually abandoned. Negligence cases are very frequently settled by the parties just before trial, especially where we can get early settings after the case comes to issue."

[e] A total of 859 cases have been ready for trial between 1 and 2 years; 284 between 2 and 3 years; 205 more than 3 years.

These figures provide evidence against the statement, encountered in a recent study, that there is no delay problem in chancery cases. This observer found protracted delay in chancery cases in Chicago in 1953, and found in Milwaukee a docket congestion so serious that even uncontested motions for temporary alimony or custody could not be reached for more than three months, and divorce cases both contested and uncontested required more than two years to reach hearing after being brought to issue and moved onto the trial calendar.[54]

The figures set forth in Table VI also support the conclusion, drawn from previous experience with these studies, that delay is not confined to negligence cases or to jury cases.

The data on jury trials show an interesting disparity. During observation in Detroit and elsewhere, this observer noted that litigants were encouraged, either openly or by awareness of docket conditions, to waive jury trials in order to avoid delay. Consultants were divided as to the advantage to be gained by this device when weighed against the potential threat to the constitutional right of trial by jury. Correspondents were invited to comment on the percentage of tried cases which are being tried to juries. Responses are summarized herewith:

Baton Rouge tries less than 1 per cent of its law cases to juries, and no other cases, because the civil law system, permitting appellate courts to reverse the facts, makes jury trials less attractive to litigants and hence seldom encountered. No metropolitan area reported more than 50 per cent; Eugene, Oregon, reported 50 per cent of all tried cases tried to juries; Miami, 35 per cent; Washington state, 28 per cent; Grand Forks, 25 per cent; Huron, 33⅓ per cent; Burlington, 20 per cent; San Jose, 7.3 per cent; Binghamton, 10 per cent; Boise, 3 per cent.

[54] Family Cases 212.

Only one area, Burlington, Vermont, reported chancery cases tried to juries, 50 per cent; all others reporting reported "none" or "virtually none."

Reporting on percentage of tried criminal cases tried to juries, Charleston, S. C., Cheyenne, and Miami all reported 100 per cent; Sioux Falls, 99 per cent; and Eugene, Oregon, 95 per cent. Washington state reported 76 per cent; San Jose, 55.2 per cent. Burlington, Vermont, shows 20-25 per cent; Boise and Des Moines, 10 per cent; Baton Rouge and Binghamton, 5 per cent.

Of tried law cases tried to juries, Baton Rouge reports less than 1 per cent; Charleston, S. C., "virtually all"; Cheyenne, 20 per cent; Cleveland, 3 per cent; Des Moines, 5-6 per cent on one questionnaire, 70 per cent on the other; Eugene, 90 per cent; Miami, 35 per cent; San Jose, 7.5 per cent; Sioux Falls, 60 per cent; Wichita Falls, 20 per cent.

Of tried negligence cases tried to juries, those answering reported as follows: Binghamton, 10 per cent; Charleston, S. C., "virtually all"; Charleston, W. Va., 33 per cent; Des Moines, 5-6 per cent on one questionnaire, 90 per cent on the other; Eugene, 99 per cent; Miami, "most all"; San Jose, 97.5 per cent; Sioux Falls, 95 per cent; Wichita Falls, 75 per cent.

These figures, whatever they do not suggest, do seem to indicate that it is unwise to hypothesize that jury trials are falling into disuse, that their use is related to size of community, or that their disuse can be correlated with extent of delay. The sizeable percentages in negligence cases are notable.

We asked correspondents to indicate whether litigants are encouraged to waive jury trials to avoid delay. Brocton, Philadelphia, Pueblo, San Jose, and Newark answered affirmatively. Newark added: "nonjury cases are encouraged and do receive earlier trial but no special list or priority is provided in Superior and County Court."

The writer's feeling about jury waiver as a method of controlling delay is negative, in part because of the hunch that at best it would shortly result in bogging down the nonjury docket, in part because of the implicit threat to the constitutional right of trial by jury. In similar vein, Zeisel *et al.* comment:

> Whether at least one party elects a jury trial depends . . . on whether juries . . . decide cases the same way judges would. On the best available evidence, it appears that they do not, and that the bar recognizes they do not . . . the decisive difficulty with remedies designed to increase the waiver ratio is that the consumer won't buy them.
>
> It is true of course that remedies can be devised which would price the jury trial out of the market, as for example sharply raised fees and costs. But such remedies, since they involve penalizing those who wish a jury trial, are really coercive. . . .[55]

There is furthermore the danger that, by directly or indirectly encouraging waivers, courts will place themselves in the position of threatening, or seeming to threaten, that which it is their function to protect, namely, the right of all litigants to all safeguards afforded by the judicial process, including a jury trial for those who want it.

Most court surveyors have regarded delay as *the* characterizing problem in metropolitan trial courts. To test this, correspondents were asked to state whether or not they felt that their areas had a delay problem, and, if so, whether it was serious or minor as of 1959. Baton Rouge, Binghamton ("fairly serious"), Charleston, S. C., Chattanooga, Cleveland, Miami, Milwaukee, Minneapolis,[56] Newark, Philadelphia, Phoenix, Pueblo, San Jose, and Wichita Falls[57] describe the delay problem as serious. Washington state reports that its delay problem is confined to the most populous

[55] ZEISEL, DELAY IN THE COURT 9-10.

[56] "Serious, but not as bad as in other places of comparable size."

[57] "Nature of problem in dispute, at times serious, remains somewhat serious."

county. Baltimore,[58] Boise, Burlington, Casper, Charleston, W. Va., Eugene, Las Vegas, and Rutland regard the problem as minor. Brocton, Cheyenne, Grand Forks, Huron, St. Paul, and Sioux Falls find no delay problem. Biloxi gave no answer.[59]

With the curious exception of Las Vegas, the large metropolitan areas represented are sensitized to the problem, and most regard it as serious, including those who have it best under control. It is fair, then, to identify delay as a characteristic problem of metropolitan trial courts and to conclude that in general its incidence is correlated with the size of the population center. It is also demonstrable that, even in a large and growing metropolis, delay can be controlled.

c. Major Causes of Delay

From direct observation for this and other court surveys, and from the literature, the conclusion had been formulated that one major cause of delay in metropolitan trial courts is the environment creating and conditioning the metropolis. This has already been dealt with, so far as a lawyer can deal with it in a study such as this.[60]

Sociological aspects aside, the major causes of delay can be enumerated as follows:

a. insufficient judges
b. incompetent or undiligent judges
c. defects in structure of court system
d. inadequate administrative system of handling docket, calendar, and assignment problems
e. deliberate maneuvering by counsel

[58] "And only at end of term."
[59] Note the disparity of views as to delay, in terms of the reported intervals, at Table VI.
[60] *Supra*, Part I.

Invited to comment on these and to rate them in order of rank, correspondents responded thus:

"Insufficient judges" was ranked as the major cause of delay by nine correspondents,[61] ranked third by one, Wichita Falls, and checked without rating by nine.[62]

"Incompetent or undiligent judges" was ranked first by only one (a west coast area), mentioned by Philadelphia and St. Paul without ranking, placed fifth by a southwestern city, and mentioned with qualification (undiligent only) by one small western metropolitan city.

"Court structure" was not regarded as the major cause of delay by any correspondent, was ranked second by Binghamton and Wichita Falls, ranked fifth by Baton Rouge, and mentioned without rating by Milwaukee, Philadelphia, and Pueblo ("partly").

"Inadequate administrative system for handling calendar and docket" was ranked first by Chattanooga, Washington state, and Wichita Falls; second by Baton Rouge and Charleston, W. Va.; third by Binghamton; and mentioned without rating by Des Moines, Grand Forks, Milwaukee, Philadelphia, and Pueblo ("partly").

"Maneuvering by counsel" was ranked as the major cause of delay by Biloxi and Grand Forks; second by Minneapolis, San Jose, Washington state; third by Charleston, W. Va.; fourth by Wichita Falls; and mentioned without rating by Charleston, S. C., Las Vegas, and St. Paul.

Correspondents were asked to list any other causes of delay. Of nine who did, five mentioned "overcommitted trial counsel" as a major cause of delay.[63]

[61] Baton Rouge, Binghamton, Boise, Brocton, Charleston (W. Va.), Minneapolis, Newark, Pueblo.

[62] Boise (another questionnaire), Cleveland, Des Moines ("now remedied"), Eugene ("improving with new judges"), Grand Forks, Miami, Phoenix, St. Paul (another questionnaire).

[63] Boise: "laches, trial counsel"; Burlington: "Overcommitted trial counsel"; Casper: "Busy practice of counsel requires settings to conform with schedule which results in delays"; Philadelphia: too few trial counsel. Com-

Other causes mentioned were lack of courtroom facilities (Las Vegas), explosive population growth (Miami); neglect of settlement opportunities at pretrial (San Jose), and improper districting of state (Washington state).

Holbrook found more delay in Los Angeles county than in less metropolitanized counties. In Los Angeles delay cannot be attributed primarily to structural defects, because California has one of the most completely unified court systems of any state. Nor can it be attributed to inadequate administrative control over calendar and docket, for Los Angeles has adopted the master calendar system. Lack of a long-range presiding judge in Los Angeles has seemed to this writer worth noting, but was not found significant by Holbrook. He did note that judges and attorneys found considerable fault with each other in answering questionnaires for his study, and concluded that trials are prolonged for many reasons that are not a result of the calendar system.[64]

It was this writer's conclusion as to Detroit that the delay found during observation was in large measure due to the overlapping and confused court structure within Detroit and to the lack of effective administrative coordination from court to court. Another factor was thought to be procrastination or maneuvering of trial counsel, and growth of caseload resulting from growth of the population center.

In a recent study of Phoenix, the Institute of Judicial Administration found an inadequate administrative system (assignment, statistics), recommended a statewide court ad-

---

pare ZEISEL, DELAY IN THE COURT 190 *et seq.* Should the trial bar "require" the court to set cases to conform to the attorneys' schedule, or should the court "require" the attorneys to try, or have associates try, cases when set by court?

[64] LOS ANGELES STUDY 225 *et seq.*, and see index for discussion of other aspects of delay problem. Instead of a multiplicity of several trial courts with overlapping jurisdiction, there is in Los Angeles County a single Superior Court, with specialized subject matter handled by separate divisions or calendars rather than by separate courts. Consolidation of most of the courts of limited jurisdiction in California has been referred to hereinabove at 46.

ministrator, better selection and compensation of judges, curtailment of jury trials, use of standardized instructions, and some structural changes.[65] In Cleveland, which has long enjoyed the benefit of a learned and diligent bench and bar with leadership in judicial administration, the most recent report analyzes the factors herein discussed and concludes that additional judges to relieve the civil dockets are the immediate need in that metropolis.[66]

d. Measures Currently Employed to Control Delay

Hans Zeisel, Harry Kalven, Jr., and Bernard Buchholz, in their epoch-making current study of delay in the court, enumerate the following measures now being employed or recommended to control logjam and achieve timely disposition of cases: reducing trial time, as by abolishing the jury, increasing jury waivers, or speeding up the jury trial;[67] increasing settlements, as by use of impartial medical experts, including interest from day of accident in negligence cases, use of pretrial, use of certificate of readiness;[68] obtaining more judge time, by increasing number of court days, increasing hours per day, enlarging trial bar, leveling the calendar, and increasing the number of judges or quasi-judicial personnel.[69]

Current measures employed in Los Angeles, as described by Presiding Judge Burke in a recent address,[70] include a newly appointed court executive, use of the master calendar, use of a commissioner to call the calendar (to relieve the

[65] PHOENIX STUDY.

[66] CLEVELAND B. ASS'N COMM. ON COURT CONGESTION AND DELAY IN LITIGATION, REPORT AND RECOMMENDATIONS ON TRIAL DELAY (1958). Other causes of delay, as analyzed from time to time in various cities, have been referred to throughout this study.

[67] ZEISEL, DELAY IN THE COURT 71-94.

[68] *Id.* at 111-55.

[69] *Id.* at 173-206.

[70] Burke, *Problems of Court Administration in a Metropolitan Court*, 43 J. AM. JUD. SOC'Y 190 (1960).

presiding judge of this work), expanded use of pretrial, a pilot experiment with the "impartial medical expert" plan developed in New York, use of approved printed jury instructions, specialized procedures for domestic relations, use of commissioners and *pro tem* judges to "piece out" the judicial personnel, fuller use of specialized departments or panels, and recruitment of a full-time statistician. It is also notable that Judge Burke, by his spectacular example, has overcome previous objections to more than a year's tenure in the presiding judgeship and has been re-elected. Thus, it is fair to add that Los Angeles has an experienced presiding judge to list among current measures for control of delay.

Correspondents were requested to indicate what measures are now in use for control of delay in general trial courts in their metropolitan cities. The answers are reported hereinafter.

An accomplished or proposed increase in the number of judges was reported by Baltimore, Binghamton, Boise, Cleveland, Des Moines, Eugene, and Milwaukee. Use of visiting judges to augment resident judges was mentioned by Minneapolis and the state of Washington. Increased activity on the part of judges (as by extra sessions, longer hours) is reported by Brocton and Miami.

Changes in court structure were reported as current delay control measures by only two correspondents: Charleston, West Virginia, which has a new juvenile court, and Milwaukee, where several statutory courts are being combined into one county court having both civil and criminal jurisdiction concurrent with that of the general trial court.

Several correspondents indicate that judges are exerting more control over counsel to alleviate delay. Thus, in Burlington, the judge sets matters regularly and requires real basis for postponement; in Cleveland, a certificate of readiness is prerequisite to admission to a trial docket, and judges have restrained postponements in pleadings and trial dates.

In Minneapolis, a judge is assigned to "continually press lawyers [and] judges to move things along."

The use of the impartial medical testimony plan is proposed in Cleveland. Phoenix and Des Moines mention increased rule-making power. Newark and Pueblo point to current studies: the former, that of the Columbia University Project for Effective Justice; the latter, to the statewide study of the administration of justice in Colorado directed by the Colorado Legislative Council, which includes intensive docket analyses in various courts.

Las Vegas has a new courthouse under construction.

Several correspondents indicate awareness that the explosive population growth common to almost all metropolitan areas during the last decade is a basic factor underlying the impact of delay.

When asked to state their opinions as to the most promising measures now in use or recommended to control delay, the correspondents did not restrict themselves to a single panacea, but most of them included structural, procedural, administrative, and personnel recommendations, each adapting those specifically applicable to his area. Thus, some recommended more judges.[71] Others sought to increase judicial manpower by other means, such as visiting judges,[72] the Pennsylvania arbitration system,[73] or stricter discipline for judges already on the bench.[74]

Addition of a state court administrator was suggested by some;[75] others suggested that area administrators, or presiding judges, also be made available in each district so as to create a responsible authority on an areawide basis.[76] This is similar to the court administrator plan now being

[71] Baton Rouge; Boise; Cleveland; Minneapolis.

[72] Philadelphia; Washington State; Minneapolis.

[73] Philadelphia; Miami.

[74] Des Moines (strong presiding judge, weekly workload reports); Sioux Falls.

[75] Minneapolis; Philadelphia.

[76] Washington State; Milwaukee.

adopted in Chicago and seems to this writer one of the most promising developments on the horizon.

Structural reform, as by a fully integrated court system, was mentioned by Binghamton, Pueblo, Des Moines, and Milwaukee.[77] One of the best thought-out recommendations came from Milwaukee where the correspondent suggested that if we had a fully integrated court system with a state court administrator at its pinnacle, with a metropolitan-area administrator in each district, and with a strong presiding judge with power to assign judges to specialized divisions as conditions warrant, then we would have a system providing maximum control and integration, yet with sufficient flexibility to serve the changing needs of any local community.

Procedural reform by adoption of federal rules or increasing rule-making power generally was among the recommendations, as was increasing use of pretrial, use of readiness certificate before access to trial docket, and appointment and control of clerks by judges.[78] These suggestions all rest on the premise that the judge should be "in complete control of his courtroom," as one correspondent put it. This premise also underlies recommendations for a strong presiding judge, for weekly workload reports by judges, for "more effective and forceful administration by judges," for "more courageous judges who will force counsel to trial". . . , and for "judges who will make lawyers try cases when assigned," will require lawyers to attend to local cases, and will require lawyers to "spread out" the negligence cases.[79]

On the other hand, the idea that the lawyer should have control over the timing of his case is also reflected in the correspondents' answers: for example, Phoenix suggests that

[77] Pueblo suggests combining justice and county courts, the adoption of the Missouri plan for selecting judges, and development of a family court.

[78] Charleston, S. C.; Boise; Eugene; Minneapolis; Washington State.

[79] Individual identification withheld as a courtesy to correspondents.

the county attorney exercise greater selectivity in filing cases. Baltimore suggests that lawyers can get on if they really want to. And one correspondent frankly says he cannot honestly make any recommendation: "After 14 years at the bar and 29 on the bench, I'm giving my considered judgment. Lawyers will not settle their cases before the pressure is applied."

These two types of answers suggest that there is a basic dichotomy in professional thinking about delay: we want the judge to see the docket keeps moving, but none of us wants our case to be forced to trial until we are ready to try it, and when we are ready, we want all the time we feel we need. As one correspondent points out, there are few things more frustrating than to wait for an important case to come up, only to have the judge hustle you through it so that he can get on to some other case.

And yet, if the bar is going to insist on its rightful prerogative to take such time as the lawyer feels is necessary, then it must follow that the bar should not hold the judge responsible for, or define as "court delay," such time as is attributable to the lawyer's preparation.

There is another intangible, of which this writer has become much more vividly aware during the last five years while acting as Assistant Attorney General and thus having the opportunity to work with many different judges in many parts of the state. The presence and participation—even the silent listening participation—of a judge acts as a catalytic agent on the attorneys. Until the catalyzing influence is added, the substance of the final disposition does not come into existence, even where both lawyers are honestly trying to work out a settlement. The addition of judicial skill and creativity to the brew which counsel has set to simmering is an indispensable ingredient of justice. Its timing is a delicate and individual matter, finally depending on the precise circumstances and questions in each case, the degree of heat being used, the relative skill and aggressiveness of counsel, the rate at which counsels' and judge's intellectual gears mesh, and other nonquantitative factors. No mechanical device, system of statistics, or other such measure can or should substitute, shape, or even be permitted to inhibit the free exercise of such judicial discretion.

As one correspondent says, statistics are meaningless unless rigidly subordinated to the system of values they are supposed to serve. This correspondent, a richly experienced trial court judge himself, says he has often had the experience of working longer and harder over a motion to dismiss than over a full jury trial lasting more than a week. Any good judge could say the same.

This writer does not recommend debasing the currency of our judicial system by substituting time-interval statistics for the professional judgment of lawyers and judges as to the timing which best serves justice in each individual case, whether or not the case is disposed of by trial.

e. Relationship of Other Court Problems to Delay

To test the penetration of fear lest current emphasis on control of delay is developing a threat to the safeguards of due process, correspondents were requested to comment on whether they see a problem of "quick justice," or perfunctory routine disposition of cases, resulting from pressure upon judges to maintain prompt disposition of caseload.

Eighteen negative answers were received;[80] six affirmative.[81] Several others answered on a basis of individual personalities or with qualified comments. Philadelphia comments that pretrial should not be a vehicle to pressure settle-

[80] Baltimore; Baton Rouge; Binghamton; Boise; Burlington; Casper; Charleston, S.C.; Charleston, W.Va.; Chattanooga; Des Moines; Grand Forks; Eugene; Las Vegas; Newark; Phoenix; St. Paul; San Jose; and Washington State.

[81] Brocton; Cleveland; Cheyenne; Miami; Minneapolis; Pueblo.

ment. Phoenix says that although its docket is falling behind, the judges are resisting the temptation to relax safeguards in any case. St. Paul points out that if counsel and judge are both able and businesslike, there is no problem, no matter how much time is consumed.[82]

The correspondent from San Jose feels that the problem is in bringing cases *to* trial, not *through* trial. Sioux Falls: "They know whether they are doing the case justice—and they must!"

On the affirmative side, Brocton describes the present system of calling six or more superior court cases for trial on the same day as resulting in litigants "having their day in court and a week in the corridor." Minneapolis: "There is a temptation toward arbitrariness and to measure our accomplishments statistically. Here I criticize [naming a recent writer] for statistical emphasis." Miami: "The current emphasis on speed may result in 'drum-head justice.' Trial judges need more help and more authority to meet this problem."

It is interesting that the affirmative answers tended to come from the more densely populated areas. It is the writer's conclusion, based on observation and interview for this and other court studies, that most if not all judges of trial courts in large metropolitan areas are very highly sensitized to professional and public demand for bringing the problem of court delay under control. The good judges respond to this stimulus by inventing devices for increasing the administrative efficiency of the machinery they have, and by working harder, without relaxing their vigilance to protect the rights of each litigant. Without exception, all of them with whom the writer has discussed the problem perceive danger that the more sensitive the judiciary grows to the problem of "delay" viewed as a purely quantitative phenomenon, the more difficult it will be for the judge to dis-

[82] And if there is no counsel? See 298 *infra*.

charge his basic function—to see that justice is done in each case. The population growth, and hence the growth of caseload, in metropolitan areas, intensifies and focuses this danger.

Probing further into the dynamics of the judge's role, as viewed by our correspondents in the context of the "delay" problem, we asked whether they feel it is the prerogative of the judge to require that a case be disposed of at a certain time, whether the exercise of such prerogative will interfere with the attorney's prerogative to take the time he needs, and finally what, in their opinion, is the basic function of a trial judge.[83]

Nineteen correspondents believe that the trial judge should have power to require disposition at a certain time.[84] There were four qualified affirmatives.[85] Of those who answered "yes" either with or without qualification, eight believe that there is danger that the exercise of such judicial prerogative will interfere with the prerogative of the attorney with respect to the time of disposition. Des Moines comments that if the judge is a real judge, there is no problem, but if he is a tyrant, danger exists.

Seven correspondents do not believe it is the prerogative of the trial judge to require that a case be disposed of at a given time.[86] These answers point up the confusion, even within the profession, as to the basic role of the trial judge, and the difficulty of analyzing the problem of court delay

[83] This question is focused on the basic function of a trial judge, in the opinion of legal professionals, in the context of delay control, as contrasted with the previous question (*supra* p. 271) focused on general judicial function in public opinion.

[84] Baltimore; Baton Rouge; Biloxi; Binghamton; Burlington; Casper; Chattanooga; Cheyenne; Cleveland; Des Moines; Grand Forks; Milwaukee; Newark; Philadelphia; Pueblo; Rutland; San Jose; Washington State; Wichita Falls.

[85] Boise (within limits); Des Moines (exercised gingerly due to politics); Phoenix (limited); St. Paul (not ordinarily).

[86] Boise; Brocton; Charleston, S.C.; Charleston, W.Va.; Eugene; Huron; Las Vegas; Minneapolis; St. Paul (not ordinarily).

until the profession has taken a clear position on the extent of the authority and responsibility of the judge.

With respect to the basic function of the trial judge as viewed in this connection, there is an interesting group of comments.

Some, adhering to the immediate context, answered in terms of the procedures used in conducting the trial:

Baltimore: "to rule on evidence, prevent waste of time, apply or instruct on law"
Casper: "to rule on the admission of evidence and testimony"
Charleston, W. Va.: "to rule intelligently and justly on questions of law and evidence"
Chattanooga: "in jury cases to see that the trial proceeds in an orderly and legal manner. In a nonjury case the same with the additional duties . . ."
Grand Forks: "quick termination of litigation"
Wichita Falls: "preside over the introduction of evidence in a judicious manner with equality of manner, attitude and expression towards counsel, the jury and the parties"

Others raised their eyes a little farther:

Baton Rouge: "give fair hearing, render decision according to weight of evidence and applicable rule of law"
Binghamton: "preside over trial calendar, dispose of as many cases as possible by trial or settlement without either forcing settlement by judicial pressure or fostering unnecessary trials by failing to comment upon value because of undue timidity or disinterest"
Brocton: "preside impartially and see that the case progresses expeditiously, but not to detriment of anyone's rights"
Burlington: "keep docket reasonably current; accommodate counsel in assignment of cases for trial so far as can properly be done; at trial, to preside and make proper rulings and charge, but permit counsel to try his case without interference of court"
Cheyenne: "try cases as soon as at issue unless delay is necessary because of discovery, working out possible settlement or to determine extent of injury, etc.
Des Moines: "administer all the business of the court promptly and efficiently in accordance with the terms of his oath"

Las Vegas: "preside with fairness to all; be courteous but firm; have an above average knowledge of the law; maintain dignity; decide the cases submitted with reasonable dispatch"
Philadelphia: "Our trial judges possess all the powers of trial judges at common law and may freely discuss the evidence, its weight, the credibility of witnesses and like matters, provided always that the ultimate decision is left to the jury. We also have a n.o.v. procedure, where notwithstanding the verdict, the trial court may enter judgment as legal principles involved require."
San Jose: "admit and consider proper evidence, to apply the law to that evidence, and to render a decision accordingly, having due regard at all times during the trial to the rights of witnesses and the parties"
Sioux Falls: "To make just decisions according to law. In jury cases he should be an unbiased referee, seeing to it that the rules are complied with and the law enforced. He should not comment on the evidence or in any manner influence the jury."
State of Washington: "to hear and decide questions of law and fact all directed toward resolving the dispute under the law of the jurisdiction"

A few correspondents perceived the ultimate destination of the question and met the challenge head-on:

Boise: "To evaluate the contentions of opposing parties and their counsel. Whether the judge should go beyond the issues and arguments so presented to any appreciable extent in order to achieve justice is questionable."
Cleveland: "I subscribe to Justice Vanderbilt's definition: a judge should be in complete control of his courtroom."
Miami: "To listen attentively and decide cases fairly, without indecent haste on the one hand, or undue delay on the other. I believe in the adversary system, with active learned counsel for the respective parties enlightening the court by their incisive presentations, and thus making possible prompt, correct decisions, after careful consideration and due deliberation by the court. Judges should not try to practice law in cases pending before them. I believe in the common law court rather than the civil code court concept."
Minneapolis: "To accomplish justice in each particular case and to accomplish it in as many cases as he can do well . . . litigants and attorneys should be made comfortable as that is possible in the court,

and should leave feeling within themselves that they have been fairly heard and the court will do its best to arrive at a proper solution."

Pueblo: "to see that litigants receive speedy fair trial at which he presides as arbiter in judicial role only"

Rutland: "to see that justice is done"

St. Paul: "He should be able, industrious and patient. He should be on the job daily, all day. He should be available to and approachable by every lawyer having real business. His job is to terminate disputes, patiently and businesslike, under the law as he sees it. He should try to do justice within the law; but he is seldom sure of that. In short, his basic function is to *try* to do so."

Attention is directed to the Minneapolis comment, which takes cognizance of the litigants' desire to be fully heard and their sense of having had a day in court. Judges and experienced trial counsel will agree, the writer is sure, that this feeling is close to the heartbeat of justice.

Delay, then, comes back again to the skill and dedication of the judge. Calamandrei, in *Eulogy of Judges*, describes the great judge as one in whose presence awareness of the personalities, the pressures, the maneuvering and fine phrases fades away, to be replaced by an overwhelming sense of being in the presence of justice. To invoke this presence is the sole purpose of all the calendar-managing, delay-controlling devices.[87]

[87] Readers who are interested in further exploration of the analysis of the nature of the judicial function may be interested in these references, found particularly invigorating to this writer: CALAMANDREI, A EULOGY OF JUDGES (1942); CARDOZO, THE NATURE OF THE JUDICIAL PROCESS (1937); BRUCE, THE AMERICAN JUDGE (1942); LUMMUS, THE TRIAL JUDGE (1937); DAWSON, JUDGES: THE ORACLES OF THE LAW (1959 Thomas M. Cooley Lectures, to be published); AUMANN, THE INSTRUMENTALITIES OF JUSTICE: THEIR FORMS, FUNCTIONS AND LIMITATIONS (1956).

CHAPTER IX

Effective Coordination and Cooperation Among Various Courts and Related Agencies Within the Metropolitan Area

SECTION 1. INTRODUCTORY COMMENT

IN the Detroit study, an attempt was made to anatomize the structural and administrative confusion and conflict among Detroit courts, the lack of effective cooperation among courts, and the existence of strong policies *against* cooperation among courts and social agencies dealing with the same caseload and, in many instances, with the same problems of the same people.[1] The types of cases affected by conflicting jurisdiction and lack of cooperation are the same cases which tend to predominate, numerically, in the metropolitan area.[2] Therefore, the cumulative effect of structural complexity, of jurisdictional confusion, and of lack of cooperation among agencies in the same metropolitan area is regarded as typical of metropolitan court problems and as one of the most serious distinctive problems encountered. The same condition has been found to exist elsewhere: for example, in New York,[3] Chicago,[4] and Milwaukee.[5]

Yet despite wide recognition of the need for integration of court services throughout each metropolitan area, it is the writer's impression that very little progress has been

[1] DETROIT STUDY 219 *et seq.*

[2] *Supra* p. 53 *et seq.*

[3] BAD HOUSEKEEPING 1 *et seq.;* Peck, *Court Organization and Procedures to Meet the Needs of Modern Society,* 33 IND. L.J. 183 (1958).

[4] LEPAWSKY, THE JUDICIAL SYSTEM OF METROPOLITAN CHICAGO 200 *et seq.* (1932).

[5] Lehmann, Findings and Recommendations on Court Services, Division Report of Milwaukee County Survey of Social Welfare and Health Services, Inc. (1949).

made, in the decade since the Detroit study, in this promising direction.

Therefore it seemed wise to seek, from our correspondents, further information concerning the status of some typical methods for achieving greater integration among the multiplicity of autonomous agencies serving the metropolitan caseload. This chapter consists of reports made by these correspondents with respect to metropolitan-wide integration.

SECTION 2. COURT ADMINISTRATOR

a. State Court Administrator

The pattern for unifying administration of all courts on a statewide basis through the office of court administrator is discussed by Leland Tolman, a member of the council of the Section of Judicial Administration and an experienced court administrator, in a recent symposium.[6] He reports that twenty-two states have followed the original New Jersey pattern. In 1948, a year after the New Jersey constitutional court reforms, the National Conference of Commissioners on Uniform State Laws prepared and approved a Model Court Administrator Act, designed to "weld all of the courts of the system into a single administrative unit, with strong centralized direction centering in the highest judicial officer."[7]

Some version of this plan, differing greatly from state to state in the particularity with which the powers are enumerated and exercised, has been enacted in Alaska, California, Colorado, Connecticut, Idaho, Illinois, Iowa, Kentucky, Louisiana, Maryland, Massachusetts, Michigan, Missouri, New Jersey, New Mexico, New York, North Carolina, Ohio, Oregon, Puerto Rico, Rhode Island, Virginia, Wash-

[6] Tolman, *Court Administration: Housekeeping for the Judiciary*, 328 ANNALS 105 (March 1960).

[7] *Id.* at 109.

ington, Wisconsin, the District of Columbia, the United States Courts, and Hawaii (forthcoming).[8] Mr. Tolman also describes the slightly different pattern for the courts of the United States.[9]

b. Court Administrator for Individual Metropolitan Area or Metropolis

An administrator of the state court system provides an excellent method for ameliorating structural defects even without structural reorganization, as Tolman points out.[10] In and of itself, however, it does not get at the distinctive problems of the metropolitan trial court, nor assist the various individual courts within a metropolitan area to improve their interaction. The existence of the office of the state court administrator does furnish a framework from which a more specialized instrument can be constructed to integrate administration of all trial courts within a given metropolis or metropolitan area.

Our primary concern here is the extent to which metropolitan area-wide court administration, or at least metropolis-wide court administration, is being provided to meet the problems of confusion, lack of communication, and delay among the courts within any one such area.

The court system of New York, if that vast proliferation can be called such, has been divided into four roughly autonomous judicial departments—two in the metropolitan area of New York City, two in the upstate areas. Each such department has its own intermediate appellate court, with administrative control over trial courts under it. This sets the basis for the Judicial Conference of the State of New

[8] *Id.* at 110, and see INSTITUTE OF JUDICIAL ADMINISTRATION, COURT ADMINISTRATION (1959) for details of their powers.

[9] Tolman, *supra* note 6, at 108.

[10] *Id.* at 109, citing Michigan and Maryland.

York, established in 1955, which comprises the foundation for the hoped-for administrative structure under the pending amendment to the judicial article of the New York state constitution.[11]

The Superior Court of Los Angeles has recently created an executive officer for that court, as authorized by the legislature.[12] Considering the vast size and jurisdiction of the Superior Court of Los Angeles, this must be considered a giant step forward in bringing together all departments of that court. The article does not indicate to what extent the branches of the Superior Court have been affected by the work of the new executive. The present writer's observations in Los Angeles several years ago and her reading of the Holbrook report left the impression that administrative difficulties due to the geographic distance of the branches from the Civic Center tended to occur with respect to filings, time of assignment for trial in the branches, adequacy of staff serving certain branch judges, disproportionate branch assignments of certain types of cases, and other such problems.[13] So far as could be learned, the establishment of Executive Officer of the Superior Court of Los Angeles has not resulted in structural or administrative consolidation of the municipal or justice courts with the Superior Court. It has been suggested that a consolidation of the Superior and Municipal Courts in Los Angeles County, with provision for absorbing the outlying justice courts, would eliminate "duplication of judicial effort, and overlapping and con-

[11] *Id.* at 108 and authorities cited n.5.

[12] Burke, *Problems of Court Administration in a Metropolitan Court,* 43 J. AM. JUD. SOC'Y 191 (1960).

[13] LOS ANGELES STUDY 135, 157, 216-17, 288, and index references, 376. At that time the Superior Court had ten branches and several special departments. When Holbrook wrote there were twenty-one municipal courts in the county, including the Los Angeles Municipal Court with four branches and forty-two divisions. The other twenty are called "outlying" municipal courts. At that time there were five justice courts in the area, in five judicial districts, each with one judge.

current and confusing jurisdictional differences."[14] But the 1959 legislation referred to hereinabove is said to have alleviated these problems to some extent.[15] And in 1960, a constitutional amendment was adopted providing for an Administrative Director of the Courts.[16]

In Cleveland, it is reported that the Court of Common Pleas has an administration restricted to that court only. Ohio also has a state court administrator.

In Chicago, a deputy state court administrator for the Chicago metropolitan area, under the state supreme court, constitutes a development offering a real opportunity to improve court administration in that problem area. This device was adopted in Illinois as an alternative to the basic reorganization of courts through constitutional amendment, which was to have unified the conflicted structural system in the Chicago metropolitan area.[17]

Newark, New Jersey, reports that the State Director has power to integrate all the courts within a given metropolitan area. So far as we can learn, this power has not in fact been exercised so as to bring the lower level of courts, such as traffic and juvenile courts, within a unified administrative system with the general trial courts of any metropolitan area.

Philadelphia answers "yes, of a kind" to the question whether there is a court administrator for the Philadelphia metropolitan area. No doubt this is a reference to the Trial Commissioner and the Administrator for Criminal Courts,

[14] See Court Committee, Municipal Judges' Association, Los Angeles County, A Proposal for the Consolidation of the Superior and the Municipal Courts and an Analysis of the Workability of the Proposal Within Los Angeles County (1958).

[15] *Supra* p. 46. And see 34 CAL. S.B.J. 623 (1960) for summary of other 1959 legislation relevant to superior and municipal court jurisdiction and procedures. See also Karlen, *Judicial Administration,* ANNUAL SURVEY OF AMERICAN LAW 672 *et seq.* (1959), containing discussion of 1959 California court reform legislation.

[16] CAL. CONST. art. VI, §1a (as amended Nov. 8, 1960).

[17] Tolman, *supra* note 6.

both too limited in jurisdictional power and restricted in range to fulfill the function we are seeking here.

The state of Washington, which has a state court administrator, also has a court administrator for the most populous county, who operates within the framework of the state court system.

We have not been able to learn of any other major attempts to organize the integration of all the trial courts within a metropolitan area.

Section 3. Coordinating Specific Court Activities Throughout City and Metropolitan Areas

a. Methods for Coordinating Court Records

Baltimore and Newark point out that the state court administrator provides a method for coordinating the records of all courts throughout the metropolitan district. Charleston, West Virginia, reports that one clerk handles the records of all courts.

Minneapolis states that the clerk, under court direction, keeps daily records of cases filed and disposed of, while the calendar judge also makes a daily record. The latter operation does not take place in the country districts. In the state of Washington, each county has a clerk responsible for keeping all court records. Wichita Falls states that the district clerk, county clerk, and corporation clerk cooperate to integrate their records. In Cleveland, where each court keeps its own records, there is none but voluntary coordination.

Phoenix reports "limited records." In Milwaukee, each court keeps its own records. Sioux Falls "does not have this problem."

The following answered the question "no": Baton Rouge, Binghamton, New York, Boise, Brocton, Burlington, Casper, Charleston, W. Va., Las Vegas, Miami, Philadelphia, Pueblo, St. Paul, and San Jose.

b. Records of Money

Responding to the question whether there is any means of integrating the keeping and handling of money for all courts within the metropolitan area, reports from fourteen areas indicate that there is no method for such integration.[18] Charleston, W. Va., Cheyenne, Minneapolis, Phoenix, and the state of Washington identify the clerk as the agency for integrating the handling of money in various courts. Newark and Philadelphia indicate that integration takes place but do not describe the manner. Eugene, Milwaukee, and San Jose identify the county financial officer (treasurer in the first two instances, controller in the last) as the agency for coordinating the financial records of various courts.

The chaotic confusion of financial records in the Detroit courts was briefly suggested in the Detroit study.[19]

c. Probation Officers' or Court Investigators' Work

During the Detroit survey, the writer was much impressed with the lack of effective cooperation among various probation and investigating officers attached to various courts in the Detroit area.[20] In Los Angeles, the various probation services were decentralized at the time of the Holbrook study.[21]

Questionnaires contain the following information concerning integration of probation and investigation work from court to court within the metropolitan areas from which questionnaires were returned:

[18] Baton Rouge; Boise; Brocton; Burlington; Casper; Charleston, S. C.; Chattanooga; Cleveland; Des Moines; Grand Forks; Las Vegas; Miami; Pueblo; St. Paul.

[19] Detroit Study 246 *et seq.*, 270. And see Los Angeles Study 370 *et seq.*

[20] Detroit Study 236 *et seq.*

[21] Los Angeles Study 333 *et seq.*

"No integration":
Baton Rouge, Boise, Charleston, S. C., Charleston, W. Va., Chattanooga, Grand Forks, Miami, Milwaukee, Philadelphia, Phoenix,[22] Pueblo, San Jose.

"Some integration":
Binghamton, Brocton, Burlington,[23] Casper,[24] Cheyenne,[25] Cleveland, Des Moines,[26] Eugene (state board for adults, juvenile court employees for juveniles), Las Vegas (same), Minneapolis (county budget of over $1,000,000; most counties have no such system, and parole and probation are there handled through state parole board), St. Paul (all probation and juvenile court employees under control of probation officer), Wichita Falls (three judges with several laymen comprise juvenile council).[27]

The conclusion drawn from this sporadic information, then, is that we have little evidence of any established trend towards administrative integration of the work of the various courts within the metropolitan areas in these three categories, e.g., records, funds, and probation. Integration exists in one or more of the categories in some places. More research would be needed in order to generalize usefully.

d. Other Techniques of Judicial Administration

Examples of integration from court to court within a particular metropolitan area were given by several correspondents. Most of these indicate steps being taken by the judiciary, either within or outside a structurally integrated system of judicial organization, to achieve administrative integration by their own efforts or those of their functionaries. Thus, in Idaho, it is reported by our Boise correspond-

[22] Each judge appoints his own probation officer.

[23] Probation officers serve various courts; to this extent their records are available to both courts.

[24] State employees handle work for all courts.

[25] State officers.

[26] Function in district, under district officers.

[27] Two district court judges, one juvenile court iudge.

ent that one of the Supreme Court justices acts without pay as coordinator of courts for the state, "but this official hardly does the job required." In Des Moines, a study of the metropolitan courts is being made by a statistician appointed by the Supreme Court. In Eugene, Oregon, municipal, justice, and district judges meet monthly on a voluntary basis. In Las Vegas, district judges (like other judges throughout the state of Nevada) are subject to assignment by the Chief Justice of the Supreme Court to any district where the caseload needs assistance.[28]

In Milwaukee, the observation of our correspondent squares with that of the present writer: there is no coordination. Each court is run by its own judges. This writer would add, however, that in the range of family cases, this discommunication is to some extent ameliorated by the efforts of various court and court-related employees, who have organized a voluntary council to minimize the lack of court integration.

In Minneapolis, the Chief Justice is administrative head of the court. There is a chief judge for each trial district. "Metropolitan court judges themselves have generally been alert to and have handled administrative problems." In New Jersey, as Newark points out, all courts and staffs are within the administrative control of the state supreme court and the state court administrator. Philadelphia reports that each judge is on his own, with little coordination from court to court. Phoenix has a monthly judges' conference.

e. Expression of Opinion of Correspondents Concerning Need for Administrative Coordination or Structural Integration

Only sixteen correspondents were enough interested in court-to-court integration within each metropolitan district

[28] Assigning a metropolitan judge to a nonmetropolitan area would be a "man bites dog" operation. (This example would seem to be theoretical only.)

to venture comment. Of these, eleven see the need for integration and five do not.

Binghamton: "Court administration is haphazard, inefficient. It should be efficient."
Boise: "This is a requirement (integration) deemed necessary by state committee of the bar association for reform of inferior courts."
Des Moines: "We are expecting some important legislation within the next few years."
Des Moines (another questionnaire): "This is the key: chief judge takes current data on workload in single integrated district."
Miami: "Rapid growth requires it."
Minneapolis: "I think we do almost as much as is necessary. I think controls from chief justice of supreme court are of doubtful value."
St. Paul: "There is little overlapping—no need—integrated court system (1 court having present jurisdiction of all) welcome alternative."
Philadelphia: "We must have an administrative office for all courts in the state."
Pueblo: "Present justice court system would have to be scrapped."
San Jose: "All courts in the metropolitan area are governed by substantially the same sections of the practice codes . . . differences of personal attitude and of statutory construction amongst administrative personnel of the several courts result in varied applications of procedural law. Centralized control of all courts would permit shifting of judicial and nonjudicial personnel to meet work needs."

Section 4. Separate Jury Commissions

In Detroit, the coexistence of five autonomous systems for selecting juries for courts operating within the city provided a striking example of typical metropolitan multiplicity. But Los Angeles does not have anywhere near the problem of multiplicity that Detroit has.[29] This seemed worth exploring further.

Correspondents were requested to indicate whether many separate jury commissions are in existence within par-

[29] Detroit Study 97 *et seq.*, and see index references. For description of the Los Angeles jury system, which received particularly detailed and thoughtful study by Holbrook, see the Los Angeles Study, *passim.*

ticular metropolitan districts. The findings were negligible. Baltimore reports one in the city, three in the entire district; Charleston, West Virginia, reports three in the city; Des Moines and Binghamton each report two in the city, the same two in the district. Others report no more than one, or leave the question unanswered.

Boise reports that there are no juries in police courts,[30] and that probate judge or constables select juries. Cleveland reports that the matter of jury selection is handled by judges when needed and that not many juries are demanded. (Compare Los Angeles and New York!)[31]

It is suggested that the entire question of the selection, use, and supervision of juries in metropolitan trial courts needs further comparative study. These data, sporadic as they are, indicate considerable variation in concept with regard to the role of the jury in trial courts.[32]

SECTION 5. SEPARATE PROBATION DEPARTMENTS

In the Detroit study, the coexistence of several separate probation staffs of the various trial courts in that city were described. Much of the confusion and conflict in criminal and personal problem cases appeared related to the multiplicity and autonomy of these probation departments. There was considerable empire building, and some expression of hostility towards other probation staffs operating in the same city.[33] In Los Angeles, Holbrook found more than 800 persons employed by the Los Angeles probation department, but although there were numerous specialized divisions operating on a decentralized basis, there was no structural complication or duplication, nor does that study indicate the

[30] Misdemeanors, municipal offenses.

[31] Where juries are much in use. *Supra* pp. 217-20; Institute of Judicial Administration, Current Calendar Status Reports (1953-1958) mimeographed.

[32] One such study is forthcoming at the University of Chicago.

[33] DETROIT STUDY 241 *et seq.*

degree of noncooperation present during observation in Detroit.

Seeking to learn if a proliferation of separate probation departments is characteristic of metropolitan trial court systems, because of their disproportionately large caseload of family, criminal, and personal problem cases, we included a separate question on this point.

The results are presented in Table VII.

Readers interested in this problem should consult the various studies of the National Probation and Parole Association, since the structural provision for probation officers in metropolitan courts is often linked with the statewide structural pattern for health, welfare, and correctional services in general.

Section 6. Various Courts and Noncourt Agencies Dealing with Family and Personal Problem Cases

Considerable loss of time, objective, and money results when several courts, each with jurisdiction over some aspect of a personal problem case, do not smoothly integrate their work. For example, in Detroit, a criminal nonsupport defendant was able to block the efforts of Recorder's Court to collect probation and support money from him by filing for a divorce in the Circuit Court of Wayne County and agreeing to entry of a support order for a lesser amount. Similarly, examples were noted in several cities observed of the use of petitions of dependency or neglect, filed in juvenile court, to inhibit or prevent the carrying out of a custody and support order entered by another court in a matrimonial action.

Such chaos is much confounded, as was shown in the Detroit study, where several social agencies are working with the same family, and each is attempting to develop and put into effect its own plan.

Seeking to explore the extent of this special problem and

TABLE VII

Separate Probation Departments Serving Courts in Various Metropolitan Areas, As Reported by Questionnaire

Area	Metropolis	Entire district	Do they share information?
Baltimore	1	..	yes
Baton Rouge	1	..	..
Binghamton	1	..	..
Boise	2	2	..
Boise*	1	1	..
Brocton	3 (district, juvenile, superior)	6	yes
Burlington	1	1	yes
Casper	1	same	..
Charleston, S. C.	1	1	..
Charleston, W. Va.	2	..	yes
Chattanooga	0	0	..
Cheyenne	one statewide system		
Cleveland	..	12	yes
Des Moines	2	1	..
Des Moines*	1	1	..
Eugene	..	2	yes
Grand Forks	statewide system		
Las Vegas	..	2	yes
Miami	2	2	yes
Milwaukee	2	..	..
Minneapolis	1 for city ct., 1 for dictrict ct.	same	yes
Newark	1 for city	same	yes
Philadelphia	1**	..	yes
Pueblo	2	same	..
Rutland	..	1	..
St. Paul	1***		
St. Paul (2)	1	1	same
San Jose	2 (1 juvenile, 1 adult)	2	yes
Sioux Falls	2 (state, federal)	..	..
Washington state	1 for each county	..	..
Wichita Falls	1	1	..

* another
** each judge has his own officer, one central office for files and records
*** district court probation officer serves municipal court

of awareness of its existence in other metropolitan areas, inquiry was made as follows:

What, if any, arrangement is there for coordinating the efforts of various courts engaged in dealing with personal problem cases, such as family, juvenile, mental cases, and such criminal cases as involve maladjustment rather than willful violation of law?
What, if any, arrangement is there for effecting liaison between the various courts dealing with the types of cases noted in the question above, and the various public and private social agencies which may also be involved with the same problems?

Comments were invited on both questions. Results are presented in Table VIII.

Perhaps it is best to let these data speak for themselves.[34]

SECTION 7. EFFORTS TOWARDS AN INTEGRATED COURT SYSTEM

It will be recalled that correspondents were asked what efforts were being made, or should be made, to integrate the work of various courts at the *administrative* level.[35]

It is now sought to examine efforts toward *structural* in-

[34] For readers interested in further exploration of the problem suggested hereinabove, some discussion of the same matters will be found in materials cited earlier in this study, e.g., VIRTUE, CASES IN COURT, and BASIC STRUCTURE OF CHILDREN'S SERVICE IN MICHIGAN; LOS ANGELES STUDY; LEPAWSKY, THE JUDICIAL SYSTEM OF METROPOLITAN CHICAGO; Lehmann, Findings and Recommendations on Court Services of Milwaukee Courts and Agencies (unpublished); and the following material from England: *Report of the Committee on Metropolitan Police Courts and Juvenile Courts*, 93 JUST. P. 401-02 (June 22, 1929); *Report of the Royal Committee on the Dispatch of Business at Common Law* CMD. No. 5065, 59 *et seq.* (1934-36); *Final Report of the Committee on Supreme Court Practice and Procedure*, CMD. No. 8878 at 228 *et seq.* (1953); *Report of the Care of Children Committee*, CMD. No. 6922 (1954); GREAT BRITAIN, HOME DEP'T, DEPARTMENTAL COMMITTEE ON COURTS OF SUMMARY JURISDICTION IN THE METROPOLITAN AREA REPORT (1937); MCGREGOR, DIVORCE IN ENGLAND (1957); *Report of the Royal Commission on Marriage and Divorce*, CMD. No. 9678 (1956); HARVEY, CASUALTIES OF THE WELFARE STATE (1960); and a series of articles on support problems by Neville Brown of Birmingham University: *National Assistance and the Liability to Maintain One's Family*, 18 MOD. L. REV. 110 (1955); *Separation Agreements and National Assistance*, 19 MOD. L. REV. 623 (1956); *The Offence of Wilful Neglect to Maintain a Wife*, 23 MOD. L. REV. 1 (1960). And see *Report of Departmental Committee on the Social Services in Courts of Summary Jurisdiction*, CMD. No. 5122 (1936).

[35] *Supra* p. 282 *et seq.*

TABLE VIII

Coordinating Efforts of Various Courts, and of Courts with Noncourt Agencies, Dealing with Personal Problem Cases, As Reported by Questionnaire from Various Metropolitan Areas

Area	Courts	Noncourt agencies
Baton Rouge	Effective conferences between personnel	
Binghamton	None; there should be	None; there should be
Boise	None, except voluntary cooperation	None; court handling juvenile cases subject to some control by state board of health
Brocton	Nothing formal, just general cooperation	Society for Prevention of Cruelty to Children active in both district and superior courts
Burlington	No arrangement of coordination	
Casper	Same court handles all cases, no specialization	
Charleston, W. Va.	None	Very little, if any
Chattanooga	None	None
Cheyenne	None	Judges often confer with social agencies, no problem
Cleveland	Voluntary basis by judges and court personnel	Voluntary, sporadic
Des Moines	Our district court is the juvenile court. One of our judges is in charge. He has a chief probation officer, and about ten probation officers and secretarial staff. We believe it would be difficult to find a finer setup in these United States.	

TABLE VIII (*Continued*)

Area	Courts	Noncourt agencies
Des Moines*	None	None
Eugene	None	None
Grand Forks	None	District court handles this well
Las Vegas	The probation department of state and juvenile courts handles criminal matters, no other facilities available	The state welfare department examines qualifications of adopting parents. Their recommendations are not binding.
Miami	Presently handled on personal basis by judge concerned in specific cases	None
Milwaukee	None; sometimes conflict over who has jurisdiction; mental cases are heard for some purposes in the county court, but if a guardian is to be appointed, in the district court (if detention and treatment are the main purpose). Divorces are in the circuit court, paternity cases in the civil court; termination of parental rights in the children's court, and adoptions in the county court.	There is liaison with the public and private social agencies, but more use could be made of the agencies.
Minneapolis	On district court level, all is handled by a single department. In the county, family court workers are in that department. Municipal court probation office is small, but it does coordinate with district court office.	They all cooperate with each other. No difficulties appear to be encountered.

* another questionnaire

TABLE VIII (*Continued*)

Area	Courts	Noncourt agencies
Newark	Same probation officer handles cases for all courts	
Philadelphia	There is little coordination, hence the agitation for a family court	Same as at left
Pueblo	None	None
Rutland	None	None
St. Paul	Such matters are not within juridical powers. Courts have no jurisdiction unless petition filed or action commenced.	Same as at left. Such matters belong in administrative agencies until such time as judicial forum is invoked.
St. Paul*	Single probation officer compiles data	Through joint committees on voluntary basis
San Jose	Any coordination which results is due only to professional competence and experience of the agencies involved (district attorney, adult and juvenile probation officers, welfare department). There is no *directed* effort.	
Washington state	Now under superior court	Liaison unnecessary
Wichita Falls	Juvenile council cooperates with probation department and all judges	Two district judges out of three and one county judge are members of above council.

* another questionnaire

tegration by establishing a unified or integrated court system rather than by evolving stratagems to achieve administrative integration within any system.

Accordingly, correspondents were asked to comment on the advantages, if any, of a fully integrated court system. Their answers are presented in Table IX. In reading them,

TABLE IX

Advantages, If Any, of Integrated Court System, As Reported by Questionnaire from Various Metropolitan Areas

Area	Comment
Baltimore	No, not from caseload standpoint. Superior courts are in practice integrated through central assignment, but duplication in separate clerks' offices could be eliminated.
Binghamton	No. Existing courts should be reorganized along more specialized lines: general, family, and surrogate.
Boise	Yes, without any doubt. Only the probate judge and two district judges are full-time; all other judges are part-time. Salaries of all judges are entirely inadequate.
Boise*	No.
Casper	In effect, we have this.
Charleston, W. Va.	Yes, one unified court with several judges.
Chattanooga	I don't know.
Cheyenne	Yes, should be a county court which would have civil and criminal jurisdiction and civil jurisdiction to $1000, instead of present $200.
Cleveland	Yes, similar to Los Angeles.
Des Moines	There may be a better way, but I have no ideas that I consider improvements.
Eugene	No.
Grand Forks	Yes, especially for traffic cases.
Las Vegas	Police court in metropolitan area should be increased to at least two departments and greater jurisdiction in civil matters. Maximum jurisdiction is now $300. Should be increased to $2,000, and justice of peace should be qualified attorney at law.

* another questionnaire

TABLE IX (*Continued*)

Area	Comment
Miami	Some consolidation would doubtless be helpful, but not all in one court.
Milwaukee	Yes. Since the area is the metropolitan area, traffic courts would have to be set up in various locations, because in Wisconsin villages and cities pass traffic ordinances and keep the fines. Consequently in every court there is a question whether the defendant should be charged with a state violation, in which case the major part of the fine goes to the state, or with a local ordinance violation, in which case the fine goes to the municipality. Some municipalities will not give up this source of revenue and therefore need some local court to collect it. Local taxpayers are not going to furnish law enforcement officers and let the fines go to the state. In traditional criminal cases and civil litigation, there is no income revenue to the community and metropolitan area or the state, and these effectively operate without interference from the local government.
Minneapolis	Certainly. Our municipal court in Minneapolis, for instance, has no excuse for existence, except, perhaps, to magistrate functions. It has countywide jurisdiction up to $3,000 in civil matters, but is supported financially only by the cities. At times its calendar is well caught up and its judges not too busy and able to vacation a bit. We could use them in our district courts. They are well qualified and want to be with us. We lose the advantage of their help by a two-court system.
Newark	We already have.
Philadelphia	There should be one unified integrated court for the City of Philadelphia. It would be impossible to establish such for the metropolitan area, as certain sections of the area comprise counties in the State of New Jersey.
Phoenix	We have an integrated court.
Pueblo	Yes: civil, criminal, and family courts could give more specialized individual treatment.
Rutland	No.
St. Paul	Of course that is the theoretical ideal, but it is impracticable in a state of large area, where there are spotty concentrations of heavy population.

TABLE IX (*Continued*)

Area	Comment
St. Paul*	Yes, for entire area. One county almost all urban. Civil rules of procedure now uniform for all trial courts. No reasonable basis for court multiplicity. Judges' qualifications also identical.
San Jose	Yes, the court of general jurisdiction tries many cases which wind up with verdict or judgment within the jurisdiction of the inferior court; the judges of the latter courts, if they were part of an integrated court, could share the caseload. In the inferior courts, there is generally a much lighter caseload (and backlog) than in the higher court.
Washington state	We now have an integrated superior court for the entire state. Some integration of justice of peace courts would probably be desirable.
Wichita Falls	Would put reluctant parties to trial, as is probably right. Remove judge or judges somewhat from politics.

* another questionnaire

it should be borne in mind that in some areas, e.g., Los Angeles and Phoenix, a substantially integrated system is already in operation.

Section 8. Concluding Comment

In virtually all of the large metropolitan centers, some expression is given the need for integration of court services horizontally—that is, from court to court within the metropolitan district.

The total picture, however, is one of sporadic and incoherent experiment, mostly confined to the voluntary consultations or conferences of individual members of court staffs seeking to solve their own problems.

The only trend towards administrative organization of courts at the metropolitan district level is the appointment, in New York and Chicago, of deputy state court administrators to deal with the metropolitan court problems, and in Los Angeles of an executive officer to aid the Superior Court in dealing with its problems.

The need to develop a unified court structure designed to meet the internal needs of the large metropolitan districts still exists and is not being met.

CHAPTER X

Safeguarding Due Process in Metropolitan Trial Courts

SECTION 1. INTRODUCTORY COMMENT

THROUGHOUT this report, the writer has emphasized the gravity of the problem of protecting the right of metropolitan court litigants to due process. Protection of due process for all litigants, especially those who do not go through adversary trial and those who are not represented, is the most characteristic and the most serious problem of the metropolitan trial court in the large metropolis. In this chapter, an attempt will be made to organize data assembled from correspondents and bearing on this problem.

Among factors contributing to the due process problem are the structural complexities of metropolitan court systems, confusions arising out of size and rivalry within court administrative staffs, pressures towards perfunctory routine disposition of each unit in the large caseload, tendency to reduce caseload by screening out large numbers of cases for disposition by nonjudicial personnel or by administrative rather than judicial agencies, and, in personal problem cases, the tendency for the court to assume functions not appropriate to its role either (a) by withdrawing in favor of expert nonlegal professionals or (b) by attempting to perform services other than judicial.[1]

SECTION 2. NUMBER OF LITIGANTS REACHING FINAL DISPOSITION WITHOUT BENEFIT OF COUNSEL

In the Detroit study, the number of unrepresented persons who pled guilty (some of them to serious offenses),

[1] Attention is called to the percentage of cases reaching disposition other than by trial. *Supra* p. 231 *et seq.*

who were permanently committed to state mental institutions, and whose family relationships were rearranged was a matter of grave concern to those who worked on that study.[2] Also serious was the situation of the many who were defaulted in installment purchase collection cases and family support and custody cases, often without being given any opportunity to comprehend or make any attempt to avoid the legal consequences of the default. In probate court, where large numbers of estates are probated, this writer was aghast at the extent to which court employees were performing legal services which members of the bar could and should have been performing in their clients' best interests.[3] In the latter case, self-interest as well as a sense of professional responsibility ought to motivate the legal profession to examine the extent and implications of these practices with care.

But it was in the mental and juvenile cases that the assault upon due process seemed most destructive of the basic purpose for which courts and lawyers exist, for in those cases the property and familial rights and the very personal liberties of the litigants are at stake. Yet in those cases members of court staffs actively discourage litigants from seeking counsel, the legal aid bureaus do not provide counsel, and there is no practicable and accessible method of safeguarding the litigants' rights by seeing to it that they are provided with counsel.[4]

Exploring this question further, we asked correspondents to indicate how many litigants go to final disposition in the metropolis without benefit of counsel in traffic, criminal, juvenile, small claims, domestic relations, mental, and other cases. The results are presented in Table X.

The variety of answers and attitudes suggests that some consideration should be given to the role of the attorney in-

[2] DETROIT STUDY 108-17. See also BEANEY, THE RIGHT TO COUNSEL IN AMERICAN COURTS, *passim* (1955).

[3] DETROIT STUDY 114-15,

[4] *Id.* at 102-05, 117.

TABLE X

Percentage of Litigants Reaching Final Disposition Without Counsel in Various Metropolitan Cities

Metropolis	Traffic	Criminal	Juvenile	Small Claims	Dom. Rels.	Mental	Other	"Does this bother you? Why?"
Baltimore	80%	5-10%	..	50%	..	..	..	No. Minor matters with simple issues.
Baton Rouge	85%	50%	75%	80%	10%	25%	..	On all but traffic cases, believe counsel can serve useful purpose to defendant and society in making system understandable. Yes.
Biloxi	90%	90%	..	..	..	..	..	Misdemeanor cases only are tried (in court of correspondent). Court not on fee basis. Try cases only on admissible evidence. No.
Binghamton	80%	50%	50%	..	50%	..	..	In trivial cases, introduction of counsel often makes further clogging of courts without commensurate improvement in justice. No.
Boise	95-99%	80-85%	70% (?)	100%	50%	50% (?)	..	Counsel prohibited in small claims (under $100). Judges in metropolitan area, at least, are competent and fair. No.
Brocton	50%	50%	50%	50%	50%	50%	..	Most are well checked by probation officers and receive substantial justice. No.
Burlington	75-80%	50-75%	most	most	can't tell	can't tell	..	All cases needing counsel seem to have it. Courts are careful to assign or suggest counseling if any apparent need. No.
Casper	96%	75%	95%	90%	60% (divorce defendants)	90%	..	Litigants who are without defense and therefore place themselves on mercy of court. Therefore, answer "no."

TABLE X (*Continued*)

Metropolis	Traffic	Criminal	Juvenile	Small Claims	Dom. Rels.	Mental	Other	"Does this bother you? Why?"
Charleston, W. Va.	95%	5%	75%	95%	50%	(?)	..	Yes. Small claims cases are handled unfairly by J. P.'s—same with traffic cases.
Chattanooga	75%	25%	no info	75%	0%	no info	..	No. In serious cases, judges generally see that parties are represented.
Cheyenne	90%	50%	80%	95%	negligible	none	..	Yes. In criminal and juvenile cases, I feel that unfair advantage is taken by law enforcement agencies.
Cleveland	no record		no record		no record	no record		Yes. Possible miscarriage of justice.
Des Moines	large %	small %	15%	15%	none	none	..	In domestic relations cases defendant can and often does default. No. Traffic cases which are serious are almost always cases in which there is counsel. There are few criminal cases where defendant does not have counsel and it is usually his choice. In serious cases the court appoints counsel when person charged has no funds. Juvenile cases are cases where parents and minister and friends help out. Counsel obtained or appointed in serious cases. Small claims are under $100.
Des Moines (another questionnaire)	most	many, except felonies	most	many	none positively	none	..	Yes. Should be better advised in juvenile cases and criminal cases other than nonindictable.

TABLE X (*Continued*)

Metropolis	Traffic	Criminal	Juvenile	Small Claims	Dom. Rels.	Mental	Other	"Does this bother you? Why?"
Eugene	90%	fel. 5% mis. 50%	85%	100%	0%	90%	..	Yes. Our judges are very fair, but if they weren't, we could have a bad situation in our juvenile and mental cases, where there is usually no attorney.
Grand Forks	95%	80%	95%	5%	0%	90%	..	Yes. Our judicial system is based on the adversary system; attorneys should be used more extensively.
Huron	many	few	many	many	few	many	..	....
Las Vegas	95%	20%	5%	all	..	95%	..	Yes, only in mental cases. We have no adequate protection for those accused of mental illness.
Miami	statistics not available			statistics not available		statistics not available		In various courts, public defenders (criminal) and legal aid counsel (civil) represent parties. No problem here now.
Milwaukee	approx. 90%	very few	almost all	50%	almost none	almost none	..	Yes (attorney is appointed to represent mental person in each case). It bothers me in juvenile and minor criminal cases. The children's court generally took the view a child has no constitutional rights. Courts run more as social agency than as court of justice.
Minneapolis	most	most, mun. none, dist.	none any more	most	5%	none any more	..	Now use public defender for all juvenile and mental cases. Generally we see that people brought before us are protected by counsel.

TABLE X (*Continued*)

Metropolis	Traffic	Criminal	Juvenile	Small Claims	Dom. Rels.	Mental	Other	"Does this bother you? Why?"
Phoenix	very high	most, mis. few, fel.	most	many	one side often defaults	ct. apptd. where nec.	. .	The great problem is lack of post divorce representation (lack of funds) *in re* nonpayment and *in re* child custody.
Pueblo	95%	75%	75%	50%	0%	50%	. .	No. We have congestion, but legal aid and local family service groups are available in sufficient form.
Rutland	large	none	large	most	none	large	mis., large	No, except in mental cases.
St. Paul	in district court criminal cases, none							No. Too much emphasis on "due process." Maiming and slaughter on highways will increase with lawyers and judges on minor cases.
St. Paul (another questionnaire)	90%	90%, excluding felony (P. D.)	(?)	90%	(?)	0%	. .	No. In minor matters, lawyers do not care to appear usually—substantial justice is effected; courts protect citizens' rights—attorney available in gross misdemeanors and felonies.
San Jose	98%	1.0%	95%	all but about 1% appealed	0%	94%	. .	Only as to juvenile cases; in that area matters are kept very confidential and there is a greater concept of justice in the final determination of the case. It would be very salutary for counsel to attend a greater number of these hearings.
Sioux Falls	50-75%	50-75%	50-75%	50-75%	0%	75%	. .	Our people understand they can have a lawyer and, of course, in felony cases are so advised.
Washington	no info			no info		no info	. .	....
Wichita Falls	1-5%	20-30%	10-15%	90%	5-10%	0-5%		No, because of freedom of judges in appointing counsel and excellent cooperation from bar.

dividually and of the bar as a whole to see that counsel is available to all who need it. Attention is called to the suggestion that it would be salutary for counsel to attend juvenile proceedings. This suggestion could be expanded into a recommendation that bar associations in metropolitan districts appoint committees to observe a considerable number of misdemeanor, mental, and default custody and support cases, in order to assist in determining whether there is need for more vigorous participation by the legal profession in cases now reaching disposition without counsel.

SECTION 3. THE PROBLEM OF DUE PROCESS IN MATRIMONIAL ACTIONS

a. Introductory Comment

In observing courts handling matrimonial actions in Detroit, Milwaukee, San Francisco, Toledo, Chicago, Indianapolis and elsewhere, the writer had observed the special problem of judges handling such cases in obtaining enough information on the basis of which a more than superficial decision could be made with respect to terminating the marriage, arranging the financial matters of the parties, and planning for the children. These problems were concluded to be more difficult for the judges in large metropolitan areas because of the much greater size of the caseloads and the relatively greater difficulty of obtaining background information about the parties.[5] The development of the office of the Friend of the Court in Detroit, and of the family court elsewhere, as means by which the court through its own staff supplements the information offered by the litigants, has been described elsewhere.[6]

The use of persons not involved in the litigation either as parties or as counsel, to act as an arm of the court by supply-

[5] FAMILY CASES, *passim*.
[6] DETROIT STUDY 173-80; FAMILY CASES, section beginning at 182.

ing the court with information needed to discharge the court's function in matrimonial cases, is in itself a manifestation of the desire and intention of the courts to protect the rights of the parties and to avoid perfunctory routine dispositions or those in any way lacking in due process. Yet the use of such assistants by courts has given rise to many problems, some of them relating to due process.

To explore this problem further, correspondents were asked a group of questions, as follows:

(a) Does the court handling divorce cases make any effort to obtain an objective evaluation in child custody and support matters?[7]

(b) Does the court make any attempt to obtain information, other than through the parties and their attorneys, concerning possibility of reconciliation (e.g., by reference to a marriage counselor)?

(c) Does this court make any attempt to supervise collection of child support for children and/or enforcement of child custody orders after disposition of the divorce case?

(d) Is it part of the court's function to obtain objective information from parties not identified with the position of either spouse in order to achieve an adequate disposition of the case?

(e) Does an adequate disposition of divorce cases, in your view, include continuing surveillance by the court of the welfare of the children?

(f) Do you see any significant connection between pressure on courts to avoid delay and a perfunctory routine disposition of cases involving the welfare of children in divorce and other family cases?

The results of these inquiries are presented in Tables XI-XVI.

[7] By "objective" is meant "not committed to the position of either litigant."

TABLE XI

Objective (Extra-Party) Evaluation in Child Custody and Support Cases, Various Metropolitan Cities

City	Contested cases Yes	Contested cases No	Uncontested cases Yes	Uncontested cases No	Comment
Baltimore	x		(?)		Court of appeals very strong for mother. Difficult to overcome tendency to grant custody to mother.
Baton Rouge					Seldom.
Biloxi	x		x		
Binghamton	x			x	
Boise		x		x	They may in isolated cases, but I know of none.
Boise (another)	x			x	
Brocton	x		x		Frequently investigators are appointed who are usually attorneys.
Burlington	x		x		
Casper	x		x		
Charleston, S. C.	x			x	
Charleston, W. Va.	x		x		
Chattanooga		x		x	
Cheyenne	x		x		Must generally grant custody to mother unless extremely immoral, etc.
Cleveland	x		x		Official investigation by domestic relations branch of common pleas.
Des Moines	x		x		We try to know what we are doing. We should do better, however, than we do ordinarily.
Des Moines (another)		x		x	
Eugene	x		x		
Grand Forks	x		x		District court very thorough in evaluating such cases.
Huron	x		x		
Las Vegas	x			x	

TABLE XI (*Continued*)

City	Contested cases Yes	Contested cases No	Uncontested cases Yes	Uncontested cases No	Comment
Miami	x		x		Our remarks before ABA family law section at 1959 convention explain our efforts along this line. Much remains to be done.
Milwaukee	x		x		A complete financial audit must be submitted to the court. The Department of Public Welfare makes an investigation. Sometimes this is rather cursory, but child custody and support matters are generally heard on motion by divorce counsels and reviewed by the trial judge.
Minneapolis	x		x		Required in all cases.
Newark	x		x		Through probation office investigation.
Philadelphia	x			x	
Phoenix	x		x		Contested, limited; uncontested, seldom.
Pueblo		x		x	Only by agreement of counsel can independent agency reports be received in evidence.
Rutland	x		x		
St. Paul					Every good judge tries to be objective in everything.
St. Paul (another)	x			x	Having no jurisdiction in divorce, answers are from hearsay.
San Jose		x			None, at least, which is based on something other than his own objectivity with the rare exception of the case wherein the judge obtains a report from the Juvenile Probation Officer on the domestic situation of the parties (but see *Family Cases*, 14 *et seq.*).
Sioux Falls					Our courts make their own evaluations.
Washington	x		x		
Wichita Falls	x		x		Recently a family council has begun work and judges are encouraged to attend.

b. Protecting Due Process by Seeking Objective Information upon Child Custody and Support

Most matrimonial actions are defaulted. In fact, less than 10 per cent of them, in the metropolitan districts observed by this writer, are contested.[8] Therefore, the court has before it only such information as the moving party supplies, with respect to child custody. In most states, the court has a continuing responsibility in the nature of guardianship to children after making a custody order. Therefore, it is a matter of concern to judges that they have only one parent's recommendation as to custody, particularly since the party making the recommendation is involved in the emotional conflict of divorce or separation, and thus frequently not able to separate the custody problem from animus towards the opposed spouse.

Outside metropolitan areas, there are ordinarily neither the specialized facilities nor is the need keenly felt for a court-sponsored child custody inquiry. Inside the central cities of metropolitan districts, the court inquiry on behalf of the children is widely accepted as a necessary activity in order to protect the children's right to due process.

Thus, of 35 correspondents responding to the question, 26 report that in their metropolitan cities the court seeks its own evaluation of custody. Table XI shows that the cities where such information is sought tend also to be the largest metropolitan cities.

In Detroit, Ann Arbor, and other Michigan cities, the Friend of the Court, a court employee, investigates all cases where child custody is involved, and makes recommendations to the court. In the Ohio family courts, a child welfare investigation is now required in all matrimonial actions where the custody of children under fourteen is involved. In San Francisco and Los Angeles, the domestic relations in-

[8] FAMILY CASES 228 *et seq.*

vestigators and special commissioners in the domestic relations department give special treatment to such custody matters as are assigned by the judges. Lack of independent court inquiry in Chicago and Indianapolis has received comment in other studies.[9]

c. Protecting Due Process by Court Evaluation of Possibility of Reconciliation

It is in the public interest to preserve marriages, and judges handling matrimonial actions are aware of their duty in this regard. It is felt by many that the parties' rights to due process include the right to have the court make an inquiry concerning the state of the marriage and to refrain from terminating the marriage if it can be saved. Because of the lack of adversary proceedings in almost all matrimonial actions, the court must look beyond the litigants for such information. The size of metropolitan caseloads and the existence of specialized resources in metropolitan areas have combined to encourage a trend towards the making of court inquiry into the possibility of reconcilation, before proceeding to decretal hearing in matrimonial actions.[10]

Table XII shows only eight metropolitan districts reporting that courts make their own inquiries about reconciliation. In Detroit, Toledo, Los Angeles, and Milwaukee, as well as in other Ohio family courts, such inquiries are made. In Chicago and Minneapolis, the writer is advised that recent

[9] DETROIT STUDY 101, 173-80; FAMILY CASES 14 (San Francisco, Los Angeles), 95 (Chicago), 152 (Indianapolis), 183 *et seq.* (Toledo, Milwaukee, other family courts). And see HOLBROOK, LOS ANGELES STUDY 151 *et seq.*; Burke, *Problems of Court Administration in a Metropolitan Court,* 43 J. AM. JUD. SOC'Y 190 at 199 (1960). For New York, see GELLHORN, CHILDREN AND FAMILIES IN THE COURTS OF NEW YORK CITY 304 *et seq.*; for England, see *Report of the Royal Commission on Marriage and Divorce,* CMD. No. 9678 p. 105 and references therein cited (1951-55).

[10] *Supra* p. 190; FAMILY CASES 215 *et seq.*, and see index references for specific localities; Burke, *supra* note 9, at 198, describing the Los Angeles Court of Reconciliation; *Report on Royal Commission on Marriage and Divorce, op. cit.*, at 93 *et seq.*; GELLHORN, *op. cit.*, 356 *et seq.*

TABLE XII

Attempt by Court to Evaluate Possibility of Reconciliation, by Obtaining Information Other Than from Parties

City	Yes	No	Comment
Baltimore		x	If matter has gone so far as to get to court, not much point.
Baton Rouge			Seldom.
Biloxi		x	
Binghamton		x	
Boise		x	
Boise (another)		x	
Brocton	x		By means of investigators.
Burlington		x	
Casper		x	
Charleston, S. C.		x	
Charleston, W. Va.			Very rarely.
Chattanooga		x	
Cleveland	x		By salaried employees of domestic relations bureau of common pleas court.
Des Moines		x	Ordinarily no. There are some exceptions.
Des Moines (another)		x	
Eugene		x	
Grand Forks		x	Who else would know whether reconciliation is possible? (See *Family Cases*, 215 *et seq.*).
Huron		x	
Las Vegas		x	While we are accused of running a divorce mill, our four departments handle about 1200 cases per year, most of which, at least 70%, are local. In contested cases about 80% of plaintiffs fail to prove a case, and divorce is denied.

TABLE XII (*Continued*)

City	Yes	No	Comment
Miami	x		1959 legislation passed authorization law, but no appropriation yet.
Milwaukee		x	Excepting such report as given by welfare department if the case was previously before it, if case was referred to welfare for investigation by trial judge.
Minneapolis	x		Where there are children, both parties are required to come to court, and there they are questioned on this subject. But Hennepin County is the only district in Minnesota having such a system.
Newark	x		Through probation office investigation in Essex and by means of Reconcilation Master of Superior Court in 10 counties in state. See attached description of reconciliation program (Appendix F).
Philadelphia	x		The Municipal Court of Philadelphia has a staff of social workers, but it has no jurisdiction in divorce, and any marital matters are limited to support orders.
Phoenix		x	Generally, no.
Pueblo		x	
Rutland		x	
St. Paul		x	Judges are supposed to decide upon what is produced in court. This procedure is unlawful unless consented to by the parties.
St. Paul (another)			Having no jurisdiction in divorce, answers are from hearsay.
San Jose		x	(But see Judge Burke's article, cited in text.)
Sioux Falls		x	We have a 60-day waiting period for this purpose, which is of dubious value.
Washington	x		
Wichita Falls	x		Makes effort to obtain information through Family Court.

innovations have resulted in the commencement of court-based reconciliation inquiries. The table indicates that in Miami and Newark, also, new resources are being devised for this purpose.

d. Protecting Due Process by Court-Collected Child Support

Routine or selective collection of child support by the court itself is a practice which has been growing, especially in metropolitan areas. The practice is related to due process in two ways: (1) Support in matrimonial actions is difficult to collect because of the obligor's hostility and because of the low economic status of many litigants. (2) Counsel is difficult to obtain for postdecretal collection of support, for the reasons that collections are both slow and unprofitable to the attorney and that the clients often are difficult and unappreciative. The metropolitan trial court has another motive, also, for actively pursuing collection of child support, namely, the fact that unless it does so, the number of court contacts resulting from support collection problems are likely to multiply, adding to the size, confusion, and delay of the caseload.

Table XIII shows the extent of court-supervised child support collections as reported by our correspondents. Note that in fifteen areas reporting, such collections are said to be made. The two Des Moines correspondents are attached to different courts. The Detroit and Los Angeles studies reported on collection of child support in those areas, and *Family Cases in Court* contains information on various other metropolitan courts.[11]

[11] DETROIT STUDY 156-65, 173-80; LOS ANGELES STUDY 341; FAMILY CASES 163, 186, 178-80 and see index references; GELLHORN, *op. cit. supra* note 9, at 172, 195, 344; *Report of Royal Commission on Marriage and Divorce, op cit. supra* note 9, at 152; and see the Neville Brown articles cited *supra* p. 290 n. 34.

e. Balancing Dangers to Due Process Encountered Where Court Takes Initiative

It has been made clear that this writer's view is that the conditions under which a metropolitan trial court operates are such that in matrimonial actions the only way to protect the right of the litigants and their children to due process is for the court itself to obtain information which it needs to make proper decisions, but is not getting because of the conditions under which the cases are presented. In order to meet this challenge, as has been shown, courts are themselves developing administrative arms for obtaining the necessary information. In this trend, there lurks a danger as well as a benefit to due process—the danger that courts will go beyond the proper prerogatives of the judicial process.

To obtain other opinions on the relative advantages and disadvantages of the exercise of court initiative in matrimonial actions, we asked our correspondents to express their views concerning the propriety of the court's obtaining information from persons not identified with the position of either spouse with the purpose of arriving at better solutions in matrimonial actions. The results are set forth in Table XIV. A related question, whether "adequate disposition" of divorce cases includes continuing surveillance by courts over the welfare of children, drew similarly mixed response (see Table XV).

And, finally, we invited comment on the connection between pressure on judges to avoid delay and perfunctory routine disposition of cases involving children, and learned, from Table XVI, that most correspondents feel that judges will resist pressures where children are concerned.

Perhaps the extent of exercise of court initiative in cases involving children is more indicative of the judicial philosophy of the court and/or judge than of the amount of pressure to avoid delay. The necessity for keeping up with the

TABLE XIII

Supervision of Collection of Child Support by Court

City	Yes	No	Comment
Baltimore	x		Through probation department.
Baton Rouge			Infrequently.
Biloxi	x		Upon petition for citation for contempt by parties involved.
Binghamton		x	
Boise		x	
Boise (another)		x	
Brocton	x		Through probation officer.
Burlington		x	
Casper	x		Court appoints attorneys on alphabetical basis to enforce uniform reciprocal support cases.
Charleston, S. C.	x		
Charleston, W. Va.	x		If requested.
Chattanooga		x	
Cheyenne		x	Must be initiated by parties; then only in about 50% of cases are efforts fruitful.
Cleveland	x		Under state law when brought to attention of court.
Des Moines		x	There is much room for us to improve here.
Des Moines (another)		x	Assistant county attorney works on this.
Eugene	x	x	Ordinarily not unless brought before court by a party or a county official.

TABLE XIII (*Continued*)

City	Yes	No	Comment
Grand Forks	x		Clerk of court often handles child support money; for other matters, parties or their attorneys must petition court for enforcement.
Huron		x	Upon application of counsel only.
Las Vegas		x	The usual orders for contempt have been unusually successful.
Miami	x		We hear many rules to show cause weekly.
Minneapolis	x		But not in all cases.
Newark	x		Through probation office. Payments made through that office when judge so orders, and that office initiates contempt proceedings for failure to abide.
Philadelphia	x		
Phoenix		x	We have no personnel to do so.
Pueblo		x	
Rutland		x	
St. Paul		x	Except at times, the money is ordered paid to probation office or some social agency.
St. Paul (another)		x	Usually, matter of enforcement is parties' problems.
San Jose		x	The initiative remains with litigants to enforce the court orders by resort to execution, order to show cause, or notice of motion.
Sioux Falls		x	This is law business. County attorney can prosecute for nonsupport.
Washington	x		Through juvenile division.
Wichita Falls	x		Through probation department.

TABLE XIV

Does Court's Function Include Information from Objective Sources Not Identified with Position of Either Spouse for Adequate Disposition of Matrimonial Actions?

City	Yes	No	Comment
Baltimore	x		Could get probation department investigation, if desired.
Baton Rouge	x		
Biloxi		x	
Binghamton		x	
Boise		x	A better counseling service or some screening of case should be available.
Boise (2)		x	
Brocton	x		If minor children are invloved.
Burlington		x	
Casper		x	
Charleston, W. Va.	x		
Chattanooga		x	
Cheyenne		x	
Cleveland	x		When minor children are involved.
Des Moines		x	We look down the throats of the parties and their counsel.
Des Moines (2)		x	
Eugene			Ordinarily not.
Grand Forks	x		North Dakota law requires corroborating testimony even in default divorce cases.
Las Vegas		x	

TABLE XIV (*Continued*)

City	Yes	No	Comment
Miami		x	Not under present circumstances; 1959 law when implemented with help.
Milwaukee		x	The court is to decide questions of law and order presented to it, not to run social agencies. There is no guarantee that a court seeking information will get truth or has any better means of getting it than our present system of examination and cross-examination.
Minneapolis	x		At times, especially as to custody evaluation.
Newark	x		
Philadelphia	x		But not in divorce proceedings where the jurisdiction is in the Court of Common Pleas.
Phoenix		x	
Pueblo		x	
Rutland		x	
St. Paul		x	Judges are supposed to decide on what is presented in court. Procedure unlawful unless consent.
St. Paul (2)		x	Usually not done.
San Jose	x		In a limited sense and only in the cases which appear to the judge in the light of his experience to deserve additional screening and scrutiny.
Sioux Falls		x	Court usually gets evidence of this kind—can on its own motion.
Washington	x		Through juvenile division.
Wichita Falls	x		In cases where the family has "juvenile" problems.

TABLE XV

Does "Adequate Disposition" of Divorce Cases Include Continuing Surveillance by Court of Welfare of Children?

City	Yes	No	Comment
Baltimore	x		But practically impossible unless someone raises the question.
Baton Rouge	x		
Biloxi		x	
Binghamton	x		
Boise		x	
Boise (2)		x	
Brocton		x	Children of divorced parents shouldn't be treated any differently by the courts than other children, and no surveillance should be continued unless need was clearly indicated.
Burlington	x		
Casper		x	
Charleston, S. C.		x	
Charleston, W. Va.		x	No facilities.
Chattanooga	x		
Cheyenne		x	Unless initiated by the parties—it's not practical with the volume.
Cleveland		x	Not by court—this is not a judicial problem.
Des Moines		x	
Des Moines (2)	x		But this is a tremendous undertaking.
Eugene	x		County welfare does what it can. We have the usual shortage of funds.
Grand Forks		x	Once the case has gone through judgment, the court should not be concerned except at the petition of either party.
Huron	x		

TABLE XV (*Continued*)

City	Yes	No	Comment
Las Vegas	x		By retention of jurisdiction.
Miami	x		Until 21.
Milwaukee		x	The court is always available to change the custody or the amount of a child's support in divorce cases. It is up to the parents to bring their differences before the court and not the function of the court to have continuing surveillance of the child or its parents. I believe this would be contrary to our American accepted idea of government.
Minneapolis	x		In some cases.
Philadelphia	x		But not in divorce proceedings where the jurisdiction is in the Court of Common Pleas.
Phoenix	x		No personnel to do so. We exercise jurisdiction only if complaint made and hearing had.
Pueblo	x		Support money should be collected without necessity of counsel.
Rutland		x	
St. Paul		x	A court functions judicially. The judge is not a policeman.
St. Paul (2)	x		
San Jose	x		The parties are generally vigilant in preserving their rights and the welfare of the children, even if they are in part prompted by spite.
Sioux Falls		x	This gets into the realm of the welfare worker.
Washington		x	This continued surveillance would seem to be a function of the administrative branch of government—not the judicial branch.
Wichita Falls	x		Through probation department.

TABLE XVI

Connection Between Pressure to Avoid Delay and Perfunctory Routine Disposition of Cases Involving Welfare of Children

City	Yes	No	Comment
Baltimore		x	A judge can take all the time he wants or needs to dispose properly of a case. Administrative office of courts doesn't frighten anybody.
Baton Rouge		x	
Binghamton	x		
Boise		x	
Boise (2)		x	
Brocton		x	There is no pressure in our probate courts.
Burlington		x	
Casper		x	
Charleston, S. C.		x	
Charleston, W. Va.		x	
Chattanooga		x	
Cheyenne		x	
Cleveland	x		A busy court must budget its time.
Des Moines		x	We have no such condition here.
Des Moines (2)	x		Heavy load.

TABLE XVI (*Continued*)

City	Yes	No	Comment
Eugene		x	Our judges aren't under much pressure here, and wouldn't let it hurt children anyway.
Grand Forks		x	We have no delay problems in North Dakota.
Las Vegas		x	
Miami	x		We must not use indecent haste in destroying the family relationship.
Milwaukee		x	
Minneapolis	x		Although I think we are now meeting that pretty well.
Newark		x	
Philadelphia		x	An efficient judge will do a proper job, and an inefficient one will not, irrespective of the time element.
Phoenix		x	
Pueblo		x	Not in this jurisdiction. More time is now spent in controversial argument on trivial points.
St. Paul		x	
St. Paul (2)	x		
San Jose		x	Pressure on our courts results from a backlog of jury cases (negligent tort) rather than from domestic relations cases.
Sioux Falls		x	Have we got judges or incompetents?
Washington		x	Our judges are most interested in the welfare of children.
Wichita Falls		x	

caseload is, however, a reason frequently offered for perfunctory routine attention to cases involving children.

SECTION 4. THE DUE PROCESS PROBLEM IN CRIMINAL CASES

The high percentage of criminal defendants reaching final disposition by guilty plea,[12] or who were *nolle'd* after corridor bargaining, or who pled to a lesser offense at the prosecutor's suggestion, has caused concern to this writer, as to others consulted who have recently had occasion to observe the administration of criminal justice in large metropolitan areas. Because of the tremendous power of decision in the prosecutor's office, the great work load required of prosecutors, and the large number of persons going through without counsel, one fears that due process may on occasion be more honored in the breach than in the observance. The high over-all percentage of convictions is not reassuring. Courtroom observation has not allayed, but has rather served to enhance, the suspicion that there is need to look to protection of the basic rights of defendants in criminal cases, and particularly the lower level of misdemeanor cases. There the caseload is largest, the pressures towards perfunctory routine greatest, and the opportunity for changing the direction of the individual most challenging.[13]

Accordingly, correspondents for this study were asked whether their prosecutors screen out a substantial number of cases from the judge's orbit of authority by *nolle pros,* by bargaining for plea to lesser charge, or by pressuring for guilty pleas, or otherwise.

Results are presented in Table XVII. Most correspondents indicate by their comments that they do not equate the use of these devices, all of which are of course necessary and legitimate to the exercise of the discretion of the prosecutor, as in fact operating to deprive defendants of the bene-

[12] DETROIT STUDY 108.
[13] *Supra* p. 100.

TABLE XVII

Does Prosecutor Screen Out Substantial Number of Cases by Nolle, Lesser Plea, Guilty Plea, Other?

City	Nolle	Lesser	Guilty	Other	Comment
Baltimore	no	no	no		Not substantial.
Baton Rouge	no	no	no		
Biloxi	yes	yes	no		
Binghamton	yes	yes	yes		
Boise	not av.	yes	yes		I have seen, as a j.p., several cases which I believe could have been settled by the prosecuting attorney for lesser offense rather than place the responsibility on the committing magistrate by preliminary hearing.
Boise (2)	no	yes	no		
Brocton	no	no	no		
Burlington	no	some	no		
Casper	yes	yes	no		The prosecutor bargains when the litigant is represented by counsel, and he realizes the evidence has weak spots and also the matter of expense is taken into consideration. He never bargains with the litigant.
Charleston, S. C.	yes	yes	yes		
Charleston, W. Va.	yes	yes	yes		
Chattanooga	yes	yes	yes		
Cheyenne	. .	yes	yes		
Cleveland	no judge must consent	yes			

TABLE XVII (*Continued*)

City	Nolle	Lesser	Guilty	Other	Comment
Des Moines	no	no	no		The judge in charge of our criminal division keeps an eagle eye on every move of the county attorney, and the county attorney returns the favor in kind. There is nothing improper going on that I am aware of. . . .
Des Moines (2)					The prosecutor screens not guilty plea cases but generally tries them. The grand jury washes out some doubtful cases.
Eugene					Not sure I understand question. Prosecutor dismisses cases he finds are not sound, as he should do. There is some reduction of charge for plea, and reasonable effort to get people to admit crime, but nothing that seems out of line to me. I don't see any screening out of the judge's authority.
Grand Forks	yes	yes	no		If prosecutor thinks he has no case, he can move to dismiss or reduce the charge. In every case, the court can grant or deny the motion, as it sees fit.
Las Vegas	no	no	no		
Miami	no	no	no		Only capital cases in circuit court.
Milwaukee	no	minor	no		
Minnesota					We would discourage all of this; there is very little nolle pros.
Philadelphia	yes	yes			

TABLE XVII (*Continued*)

City	Nolle	Lesser	Guilty	Other	Comment
Phoenix	not av.		no		Large number cases disposed of by pleas to lesser offenses, some included, some not and by plea to one of several counts.
Pueblo	no	no	no		
Rutland	yes	yes			
St. Paul	yes	yes	no		I know of no good prosecutor taking unfair advantage of a defendant, and every good prosecutor tries to prevent the filing of an unmeritorious complaint.
St. Paul (2)	no	no	no		Answer confined to city prosecutor and criminal branch municipal court dismissing multiple charges or counts in exchange for plea to one.
San Jose	not av.	yes	yes		I think this goes on everywhere; the Internal Revenue Service does it.
Sioux Falls	yes	yes	yes		We keep it pretty clean.
Washington	no	no	no		
Wichita Falls	no	yes	yes		Most confirmed felons cop a plea, and especially if case is very strong against them and a low fine or term is offered.

fits of judicial inquiry and decision. The consensus appears to be that such screening is necessary and "We keep it pretty clean."

Exploring further, we asked if anyone else sees a due process problem arising out of these practices through deprivation of the full use of the judge's knowledge and discretion. Four correspondents[14] express concern. Cheyenne comments: "I think many indigent prisoners plead guilty merely to avoid sitting in the county jail." Wichita Falls: "More importantly, his objectivity is not called upon."

Pressing on, we inquired if the problem looks any different where the defendant is without counsel. Ten correspondents apprehend a due process problem under these conditions.[15]

"Is the problem more or less interesting to you in misdemeanor or felony cases?" was the next question. Several correspondents point out that the protection of the defendants' rights is equally important in both misdemeanor and felony cases.[16] Minneapolis comments: "I want the full story in all cases and watch to assure our process in all." Others feel that the graver punishment in felony cases makes the problem more acute there.[17] Several see no problem in either type of case. In Miami, the public defender handles both types of cases satisfactorily. In Las Vegas, felony cases can-

[14] Casper; Cheyenne; Minneapolis; Wichita Falls; Boise thinks there may be problems in certain cases; Des Moines (1) is dubious; Milwaukee sees the problem, but declines to label it "due process"; Philadelphia believes that pre-sentence reports by qualified investigators would help; San Jose comments that the district attorney is better informed than the judge would be (this is part of what this writer is afraid of!); Sioux Falls believes the defendants should hire lawyers or that lawyers should be appointed for them at state expense.

[15] Charleston, W. Va.; Des Moines; Huron; Miami; Milwaukee; St. Paul; San Jose; Chattanooga; Cleveland ("possible miscarriage of justice"), Burlington. In Minneapolis, which has a public defender, the problem is handled by that office and the same could be said of San Francisco and Los Angeles with respect to some cases. See LOS ANGELES STUDY 87, 83-86.

[16] Cheyenne; Grand Forks; Milwaukee; Minneapolis.

[17] Des Moines; Huron; Burlington; Binghamton; Phoenix; Rutland; San Jose.

not be reduced by plea or selection of lesser count without counsel from the court.

Finally, we asked for an indication of the over-all percentage of guilty pleas in all criminal cases, and for an evaluation (too low, too high, or what?). In Biloxi, Binghamton, Cheyenne, Cleveland, Des Moines, Minneapolis, and St. Paul, the percentage was given at 90 per cent or higher. Binghamton places this as "about right; in most cases the plea is to a lesser charge and this, in itself, is a form of leniency." Des Moines agrees, on the basis that "we think we do a good job." Minneapolis: "I think we receive pleas from a number whom a jury would never convict." St. Paul (misdemeanors only) reported: "Frequently a case will be dismissed after a plea, the court being then informed of the facts. . . . From what I have seen in my courtroom no innocent defendant has pleaded or been convicted . . . but many guilty have been acquitted. This is about right; it is interesting to note that the ratio is similar in both felony and misdemeanor cases. For FY 1958-1959, there were 519 pleas of guilty out of 829 felony cases disposed of and 5,746 pleas of guilty out of 8,157 misdemeanor cases disposed of."

Placing the percentage of guilty pleas between 80 and 90 per cent was Boise.[18]

Baton Rouge, Brocton, Burlington, Casper, Charleston, S. C., Eugene, Huron, Sioux Falls, and Pueblo placed the over-all percentage of guilty pleas as between 50 and 75 per cent. Las Vegas estimated it at 20 per cent though no statistics were available; Newark reported 47 per cent.

The writer recommends that local bar associations in large metropolitan areas conduct inquires based on adequate observation to learn whether the requirements of due process are being fully observed in both misdemeanor and felony cases.

[18] "There are probably few pleas of guilty erroneously made except in traffic cases, probably fewer than convictions obtained by trial."

SECTION 5. PROTECTING DUE PROCESS IN MENTAL CASES

In a recent issue of the *Journal of the American Bar Association,* Dr. Morton Birnbaum points out that incarceration in a state mental hospital which is without the facilities to offer proper treatment is a deprivation of liberty without due process of law.[19]

Throughout the course of the metropolitan court survey, the writer has been much concerned with the large numbers of persons, particularly indigent elderly persons, being committed to mental hospitals without anything remotely resembling either an adequate legal or medical evaluation.[20]

In some states, judicial hearings in mental cases have been dispensed with entirely, and many persons from both medical and legal professions now take the position that since judicial hearings are likely to be perfunctory, they should be eliminated.[21]

Observation suggests that many elderly indigents are committed at the point where they might otherwise become public charges of local units of government, and it is not unlikely that the desire of these local units to shift financial responsibility to the state, in such cases, is related to the incidence of commitments. One state mental hospital administrator, discussing this pattern, indicates awareness that many inmates are not mentally ill, but points out that there is no other facility available for many of them, and adds: "We can take care of them cheaper."

California is one of the states which provides several methods of commitment not requiring court action.[22] Where court action is required, the hearings are conducted in the

[19] Birnbaum, *The Right to Treatment,* 46 A.B.A.J. 499 and see references therein cited (May 1960).

[20] DETROIT STUDY 141, 186-93, 216; and see Appendix C therein.

[21] See Ross, *Commitment of the Mentally Ill: Problems of Law and Policy,* symposium in 57 MICH. L. REV. 945 (1959). Various types of summary and judicial commitment statutes are described at 967 *et seq.* and Tables I to IV of Appendix I.

[22] LOS ANGELES STUDY 242.

psychopathic unit of the county hospital, and social workers and medical experts are present.

Several questions were asked of correspondents for this study concerning handling of mental cases in various metropolitan areas. Attention is called to the study now being conducted by the American Bar Association's special committee on procedures in mental cases, through the facilities of the American Bar Foundation.

Results are presented in Tables XVIII-XXIV.

Space does not permit extended comment on these tables. They are included to document the existence and seriousness of the problem. Note that existence of judicial safeguards does not necessarily indicate that they are exercised. Lack of facilities to provide diagnosis or treatment may make a mockery of such procedural devices as compulsory diagnostic commitment. Most correspondents share the writer's unwillingness to substitute affidavit after observation for judicial hearing. In the references given for the Detroit and Los Angeles surveys will be found examples of "diagnoses" arrived at after a total of less than five minutes with the patient. Observation indicated that these are not isolated examples.

The attention of the legal profession, and especially of bar and medical associations in large metropolitan centers, is especially invited to the challenge of developing better understanding and cooperation between psychiatry and law. Besides the right to personal freedom, many questions are involved concerning the patient's right to vote, sign checks, sell securities, make family decisions, and so on. Observation indicates that mental hospital personnel should be protected from assuming responsibility for decisions in the latter area. Each profession has its essential role to play.

The "role conflict" is alluded to only for constructive purposes, with the purpose of indicating the need for interprofessional cooperation. In addition to civil commitments, the

TABLE XVIII

(1) In Handling Mental Cases, Do Courts in Metropolitan Areas Require Full Hearing Before Commitment in All Cases? (2) Is There Any Difference Inside and Outside Metropolis?

City	(1) Yes	(1) No	(2) Yes	(2) No	Comment
Baltimore		x		x	Can be committed on affidavit of two doctors.
Baton Rouge	x			x	
Biloxi					All mental cases referred to chancery court, which has exclusive jurisdiction.
Binghamton		x		x	
Boise	x			x	Probate court has concurrent jurisdiction in each county with district court, although probate court almost always handles these cases.
Boise (2)	x				None outside.
Brocton		x		x	
Burlington		x		x	
Casper		x		x	Recommitment may be without hearing and in some instances where there is a waiver.
Charleston, S. C.	x				Nothing outside.
Charleston, W. Va.	x			x	
Cattanooga	x			x	
Cheyenne	x			x	Good handling of mental cases.
Cleveland		x			Outside has no felony jurisdiction.
Des Moines	x			x	Counsel appointed to represent the individual.
Des Moines (2)	x			x	Handled by commission, def't has an attorney.
Eugene	x				They have a hearing. What is a "full hearing"? (One where defendant is either present or represented, and in which factual evidence is required.—MBV)

TABLE XVIII (*Continued*)

City	(1) Yes	No	(2) Yes	No	Comment
Grand Forks	x			x	All mental cases are handled in county court located within metropolis.
Huron	x			x	
Las Vegas	x			x	There is only one court having jurisdiction.
Milwaukee	x			x	This is because courts in metropolis cover entire area.
Miami	x			x	County judges handle these cases.
Minneapolis	x			x	
Newark		x		x	
Philadelphia	x				
Phoenix	x				
Pueblo	x			x	
Rutland	x			x	
St. Paul	x			x	
St. Paul (2)	x			x	Because our probate court does outside business also.
San Jose		x		x	In the great majority of cases the judge holds a brief (5-10 min.) hearing on each mental case, basing his decision on the hospital superintendent's report of a brief observation and on the conclusion of two medical examiners ***who see and hear patient only during hearing.*** (Emphasis supplied.) Jury or court trial is available to patient if he demands it within 10 days of hearing.
Sioux Falls	x			x	All handled by county court.
Washington	x			x	All handled by superior court.
Wichita Falls	x			x	We have a temporary commitment statute; however, judges are reluctant to use it.

TABLE XIX

Total Mental Caseload; Requirement That Persons Alleged To Need Mental Hospitalization Be Represented by Counsel

City	Annual Caseload	Counsel required: Always	Usually	Never	Comment
Baltimore			x		Under defective delinquent act counsel will be appointed.
Baton Rouge				x	
Binghamton	25		x		
Boise	60	x	x		
Burlington				x	Court doesn't require counsel, though there usually is.
Casper				x	No statutory provision for allowance of same.
Charleston, W. Va.		x			
Cheyenne	20		x		
Des Moines	273	x			Includes all of Polk County. Met. area slightly smaller, perhaps 265. Figure is interesting because it represents almost exactly one person per thousand population.
Eugene			x		Now in judge's discretion, if no request made. I think counsel should be mandatory.
Grand Forks				x	Not too familiar with this, but doubt if county court ever requires counsel.

TABLE XIX (*Continued*)

City	Annual Caseload	Counsel required: Always	Counsel required: Usually	Counsel required: Never	Comment
Huron			x		Our system requires judge to make exam in addition by qualified psychiatrist or two medical men.
Milwaukee		x			If question of commitment, court appoints counsel if deft does not have one.
Minneapolis	880	x			
Philadelphia			x		
Phoenix		x			There is court appointed counsel present at all hearings.
Pueblo		x			
Rutland			x		
St. Paul	400 (approx.)	x			Statute so provides.
San Jose	979		rarely		Representation by counsel is rare, and even more rarely results from a requirement by the court.
Sioux Falls					Discretionary with the court. He isn't going to put anyone away wrongfully. There would be hell to pay.

TABLE XX

(1) Does Court Require Psychiatric Testimony by Qualified Psychiatrist in All Cases?
(2) Other Medical Testimony?

City	(1) Yes	(1) No	(2) Yes	(2) No	Comment
Baltimore		x		x	Not necessarily testimony, can proceed on affidavit.
Baton Rouge		x	x		
Biloxi		x	x		
Binghamton		x	x		
Boise		x	x		Two doctors' certificates required.
Brocton		x		x	Requires medical report.
Burlington		x	x		
Casper		x	x		There are two doctors on the lunacy commission, and both submit testimony as to their conclusions from observations and tests.
Charleston, S. C.		x	x		
Charleston, W. Va.	x		x		
Chattanooga		x	x		
Cheyenne	x				Under statute.
Cleveland		x		x	
Des Moines		x		x	Our Insanity Commission is composed of the Clerk of the Court, a lawyer, and a doctor recommended by the Medical Society.
Eugene		x	x		
Grand Forks		x		x	In some few cases only.
Huron		x			

TABLE XX (*Continued*)

City	(1) Yes	No	(2) Yes	No	Comment
Las Vegas		x			Only when one is available that we can get at the small fee allowed by law.
Miami			x		
Milwaukee	x				Court appoints its own psychiatrist. Parties can also produce their own as witnesses.
Minneapolis	x		x		Depending upon the case, such as where syphilis is claimed.
Philadelphia	x				
Phoenix		x	x		Great majority by psychiatrist.
Pueblo		x	x		
Rutland		x	x		
St. Paul	x				Many cases obvious to judge alone. Nevertheless, statute requires two M.D.'s, and here the practice is to hire psychiatrists.
San Jose	x		x		The patient is detained for several days at the State Hospital under care and observation of staff psychiatrists prior to hearing, and superintendent of hospital gives written report to court; additionally, as requirement of California law, two medical examiners, who need not be psychiatrists, assist the court at the hearing and give a written report.
Sioux Falls		x	x		Local physician on board determines sanity.
Washington		x			
Wichita Falls					Depends on definition of "qualified psychiatrist."

TABLE XXI

(1) Does Law in Your State Require Diagnostic Commitment? (2) If So, Is It Compulsory in All Cases? (3) If So, Fully Enforced?

City	(1) Yes	(1) No	(2) Yes	(2) No	(3) Yes	(3) No	Comment
Baton Rouge		x					
Boise		x					
Brocton		x		x			
Burlington		x		x			
Casper		x				x	
Charleston, S. C.		x		x			
Charleston, W. Va.	x			x			
Chattanooga	x		x		x		
Cheyenne	x		x		x		
Cleveland							
Des Moines		x					
Grand Forks		x		x			
Huron							A physician is a member of the board and must submit report after examination.
Las Vegas	x		x				
Miami	x		x		x		

TABLE XXI (*Continued*)

City	(1) Yes	No	(2) Yes	No	(3) Yes	No	Comment
Milwaukee	x		x		x		Yes, when commitment. No, if only guardian appointed.
Minneapolis	x		x		x		In Hennepin County, but not in smaller communities of state.
Philadelphia	x			x		x	Not sufficient facilities available.
Pueblo	x		x		x		
Rutland	x		x		x		
St. Paul	x		x		x		
San Jose	x		x		x		No order for commitment shall issue unless the two medical examiners state in their written report that the condition of the patient is such as to require care and treatment in an institution for the mentally ill. Section 5050.8, Welfare & Institutions Code of California.
Washington		x					Not required, but frequently used.
Wichita Falls	x		x		x		

TABLE XXII

(1) Are Juries Ever Used in Mental Cases? (2) Often? (3) Do They, in Your View, Serve Any Useful Purpose?

City	(1) Yes	(1) No	(2) Yes	(2) No	(3) Yes	(3) No	Comment
Baltimore	x		x		x		Under defective delinquent law, jury is valuable safeguard against overenthusiasm of state phychiatrists to cure antisocial personality disorders of convicted criminals by having indeterminate sentence imposed.
Baton Rouge		x					
Biloxi	x						
Binghamton						x	Seldom.
Boise	very rarely					x	Only used in criminal cases.
Brocton	x			x	x		
Casper		x					There is a question whether the same is provided for by our Constitution. The conclusions of the lunacy commission are based on medical background and therefore of more value than a conclusion of a jury.
Charleston, W. Va.		x					
Chattanooga		x					
Cheyenne	x						I think they may protect the eccentric but not the insane.
Des Moines	x		x		x		It simply means that the right to trial by jury is preserved and available if party wants it.
Des Moines (2)	x			x	(?)		Juries on appeal from commission.
Eugene							Jury decides insanity plea in criminal cases.

TABLE XXII (*Continued*)

City	(1) Yes	No	(2) Yes	No	(3) Yes	No	Comment
Grand Forks		x		x	x		In questionable and contested cases, the jury system is the best.
Las Vegas		x					
Miami		x					
Milwaukee		x				x	Presume the question refers to cases where the only question is whether a person ought to be committed only by reason of mental condition.
Minneapolis		x				x	Such a proceeding would be bad for one mentally ill, except if there be an appeal to district court.
Newark	x		x		x		
Philadelphia		x					
Phoenix		x				x	
Pueblo	x		x			x	
Rutland	x		x			x	
St. Paul		x					
San Jose	x			x	x		They are available on demand following the cursory hearings mentioned above, and provide a safeguard against arbitrary action by the court.
Sioux Falls							In criminal cases where defense is insanity—always.
Washington	x			x			
Wichita Falls	x		x		x		Bring an average intelligence to play.

TABLE XXIII

(1) Are Borderline Senile Indigent Old Persons Put in Mental Hospitals To Relieve Local Governmental Units of Financial Burden of Their Support in Your Metropolitan Area? (2) Does It Worry You?

City	(1) Yes	(1) No	(2) Yes	(2) No	Suggestions
Baltimore	x		x		Enforcement of Parent Support Laws, private charity, possibly public aged homes.
Baton Rouge		x			
Biloxi		x			
Binghamton					I doubt it.
Boise	x		x		More nursing homes.
Boise (2)		x			
Brocton		x			
Burlington	x		x		Develop greater family responsibility.
Casper	x			x	
Charleston, S. C.		x			
Charleston, W. Va.					If so, very rarely.
Chattanooga		x			
Cheyenne		x			
Des Moines		x			It used to happen, I understand, but no more. One reason is better protection before the commission, and another is our institutions are crowded.

TABLE XXIII (*Continued*)

City	(1) Yes	No	(2) Yes	No	Suggestions
Des Moines (2)	x		x		Closer screening.
Eugene		x			
Grand Forks		x			
Huron	x		x		
Las Vegas	x		x		It is a legislative problem.
Miami		x			Law provides for guardianship of property only to deal with such cases.
Milwaukee		x	x		Custodial homes as distinguished from mental hospitals; latter cost more to run than homes for aged.
Minneapolis		x			It would worry me. Other counties are different. But Hennepin County has a rigid 10-day observation period before psychiatric commitment.
Philadelphia	x		x		More beds, mental hospitals, and homes for aged and senile.
Pueblo	x			x	
Rutland		x			
St. Paul	x			x	Statute authorizes commitment for senility alone.
San Jose		x			
Sioux Falls	x			x	This is the best facility we have.
Wichita Falls		x			

TABLE XXIV

Does It Seem a Good Idea for Commitment Decision To Be Left to Phychiatrist, with No Hearing Provided For Except upon Request After Commitment on Demand of Patient?

City	Yes	No	Comment
Baltimore		x	Distrust of psychiatrists.
Baton Rouge		x	
Biloxi		x	We have had a few psychiatrists who needed to be committed themselves.
Binghamton		x	
Boise		x	Due process must always be observed and judicial process made available in juvenile and mental cases.
Boise (2)		x	
Brocton		x	
Burlington		x	In some instances it could result in serious deprivation of civil rights.
Casper	x		The matter of commitment is a mental question and therefore the immediate commitment without hearing would result in patient being treated quicker, and, furthermore, decision of specially trained psychiatrist is more reliable than nontrained individuals.
Charleston, S. C.		x	Don't trust psychiatrists' judgment.
Charleston, W. Va.		x	Patient should have counsel or guardian *ad litem* at all times.
Chattanooga		x	
Cheyenne	x		Would give less publicity, but still protection exists.
Cleveland	x		
Des Moines		x	I like our system the way it is administered. Some alleged psychiatrists are two-thirds jelly and one-third wind and know no more than those of us who do not pretend to be experts. Horse sense has a good deal to do with protecting people from being imposed upon.
Des Moines (2)	x		Similar to Iowa system.
Eugene		x	The courts should retain control, using psychiatrists for advice. This affords better protection to individual.

TABLE XXIV (*Continued*)

City	Yes	No	Comment
Grand Forks		x	This makes psychiatrist become prosecutor, judge, and jury. I have not found psychiatrists generally to be so infallible.
Huron		x	
Las Vegas		x	The protection of rights of persons are too easily violated.
Miami		x	Constitutional safeguards as to notice and opportunity to be heard should be preserved.
Milwaukee		x	No one should be deprived of his liberty without prior judicial hearing. Psychiatrists and social agencies belong in the witness chair, not on the bench. There is too much government by agencies now.
Minneapolis		x	It is terrible. It puts the burden of proof on a person to establish his right to freedom. Even the insane usually know when they are deprived of due process procedures. The evidentiary concepts of psychiatrists with whom I have talked are such that human freedom should not be determined by them. After commitment, the mentally ill would have problems of seeking aid in a court other than his home court often, or he would have trouble getting counsel of his choosing or have greater expenses for his defense. He would get into court with a strike against him, and with the stigma of being a person already committed. Mentally ill people, who can think, want the advance protection of the court.
Philadelphia		x	A judge should pass on these questions assisted by impartial and able psychiatrists.
Phoenix		x	
Pueblo		x	We get cases where spouses dispose of unwanted spouses in this manner—also other family members to escape financial responsibility.
Rutland	x		
St. Paul		x	I approve of the Minnesota practice. The probate judge sitting with two M.D.'s conducts a judicial hearing even though it usually takes place in a hospital.
San Jose		x	Such a procedure would make too easy the wrongful detention of ignorant, feeble, or sick and disoriented persons.
Sioux Falls		x	I take a dim view of a lot of this psychiatry.
Wichita falls		x	Not enough qualified psychiatrists and most M.D.'s no more qualified than a jury of average intelligence.

problem of substituting hospitalization and treatment for trial and incarceration of those accused or convicted of crime is suggested in several of the tables.

To explore the direction of thinking among our correspondents in this area, the following question was asked:

> Recently a psychiatrist remarked that the law never did a worse disservice to itself, to society, or to psychiatry than when it permitted substitution of psychiatric diagnosis and treatment for trial in such cases as those involving criminal sexual psychopaths. Please comment.

Four correspondents agreed with the quoted statement, but made no further comment. One placed agreement on the basis that final decision is the prerogative of the court, and several others made the same point. Another noted "Great deal of panic here."

Several others disagreed with the quoted statement on the general basis that psychiatric evaluation, intelligently performed, advances the law a long step forward, *provided* that the physical facilities and professional manpower to provide the treatment are available. But, as several point out, in many areas the real problem is that the lack of treatment resources is such that the patient is discharged before the condition which resulted in court contact has been brought under control. Where this happens, the safety of the community is imperiled.

One correspondent doubts whether a psychiatrist really made the quoted statement. The statement was made. Its author directs a large public mental institution in New England. Its point is that each profession has been looking blindly to the other for a panacea that neither is able to provide. Where legal safeguards such as guaranteed right to trial are relaxed in order to provide diagnosis, hospitalization, and treatment which is unavailable or of doubtful effectiveness, the result is that the community, the patient, the law, and medicine are all done a disservice. This is the point Dr. Birnbaum made in his article.[23]

SECTION 6. PROTECTING DUE PROCESS IN JUVENILE CASES

In the Detroit and other surveys, the threat to due process inherent in "unofficial" handling of juvenile court cases has been discussed.[24] Correspondents were asked if they approved of long-term handling of juvenile court cases on an "unofficial" basis—that is, without the filing of a petition, and hence without the acquisition of jurisdiction by the court. Fourteen indicated approval; seven indicated nonapproval.

The general problem of due process in juvenile court cases has received attention by several writers lately. The problem centers around the use of nonlegal professionals who are not familiar with the requirements of due process, but who exercise supervision over persons in contact with the court. Another facet of the problem is that concentration on the need for rehabilitative treatment, together with informal and confidential proceedings, may obscure or even eliminate the proof of facts essential to establish the court's authority to intervene in the circumstances. Where this occurs, the authoritative aura of the court is used to influence the behavior of litigants, although no court authority exists, thus perverting the essential role and character of both the juvenile court and of noncourt administrative agencies which may be working with the same children.

Correspondents were asked for comments concerning the

[23] Birnbaum, *supra* note 19. As is often pointed out, one can serve life for window-peeping under some psychopath statutes which substitute medical diagnosis and treatment for trial.

[24] DETROIT STUDY 103 *et seq.*, 166 *et seq.*; VIRTUE, BASIC STRUCTURE OF CHILDREN'S SERVICES IN MICHIGAN 229 *et seq.*, and in Foreword, at x, where Chief Justice Vanderbilt comments, ". . . illegal and constitutionally unwarranted procedure"; LOS ANGELES STUDY 337 *et seq.* ("probation department performs services in . . . non-court cases . . . the . . . officer may . . . postpone the filing of a petition . . . This allows him to exercise supervision over the child and attempt to adjust the situation without the necessity of filing a petition.")

juvenile court due process problem. Twelve see a due process problem, making such comments as that the existence of guilt may not be fully established, that careful administration is necessary to protect the rights of juveniles, and that the admission of possibly unreliable statements or reports may interfere with the fair and impartial hearing to which everyone is entitled. Eleven correspondents do not see a due process problem. They point out that in effect the informality of juvenile court procedures amount to counseling, which is successful only if understood and acquiesced in by the litigants. If this voluntary cooperation does not work, they point out, the more traditional procedures can be invoked.

With respect to the loss of identity problem (confusion of function as between judicial and administrative agency), ten correspondents are concerned with this problem, and ten others are not. Typical of the view of those who are concerned with due process is the comment that welfare workers tend to be empire builders, and that some of them look on courts as a necessary evil obstruction to their function. "They make inroads." Those who are not concerned with the problem say, for example, "Juvenile cases are not handled well by inflexible procedures. The best hope for rehabilitation is the case by case approach of dedicated social workers."

One comment is that the "identity" question is less important than getting the job done; another, that although the due process problem exists, the juvenile court is better left as it is than to transfer the entire operation to the judicial process, or to leave the judicial process without specialized personnel to provide personal treatment to rehabilitate juveniles.

This appears, then, to offer another opportunity for interprofessional discussions to develop a clear division of function, so that each may make its distinctive contribution without invading the prerogatives or weakening the contribution of the other.[25]

Section 7. Use of Court Marriage Counselors

One of the most interesting current developments in current family law is the use, by courts handling matrimonial actions, of court-employed marriage counselors to advise the court concerning the appropriate method of dealing with the litigation (e.g., if the parties can be reconciled, the case should be dismissed), or to counsel with an attempt to reconcile the litigants, or both. Detroit and Los Angeles have recently set up such counseling programs. Toledo has had one for some time. Certain courts in New Jersey are now experimenting.

The use of court marriage counselors raises a number of problems, including the due process problem. For example, where a court-employed marriage counselor deals largely with persons who are neither in litigation nor contemplating litigation, and where such counseling goes beyond advising the court concerning the litigation into the area of counseling or administering therapy to the parties, there is a question of misuse of a judicial agency and of deprivation of the rights of the parties.[26]

Correspondents were asked if their courts employ marriage counselors. Charleston, S. C., Newark, San Jose, Minneapolis, and Washington state answer affirmatively. At this writing, New Jersey experiments. In Boise, a voluntary counseling service is available but is reported as insignificant in impact. Twenty-eight correspondents indicate no counselor employed.

[25] For discussion of the general problem see, *inter alia*, *Employment of Social Investigation Reports in Criminal and Juvenile Proceedings*, 58 Colum. L. Rev. 702 (May 1958); Paulsen, *Fairness to the Juvenile Offender*, 41 Minn. L. Rev. 547 (1957).

[26] Family Cases 215; Burke, *Problems of Court Administration in a Metropolitan Court*, 43 J. Am. Jud. Soc'y 190, 198; and see *supra* p. 222 *et seq.*

In Charleston, S. C., San Jose, Minneapolis, and Washington, the counselor's services are reported available for those who wish them, rather than on a compulsory basis. Charleston also reports that the judge does not refer at his discretion on a case by case basis, and similar answers were received from San Jose[27] and Minneapolis. Washington state reports that such references are made by the judge.

With respect to whether compulsory reference of all litigants by the court to a marriage counselor is proper, thirteen find it improper and three regard it as proper.

With respect to whether it is proper for a court marriage counselor to spend all or most working time with persons not in litigation, ten correspondents answered "no," commenting that no judicial function is involved until litigation is started, and that other available agencies should be used instead. Five correspondents regard the practice as proper, since it will reduce the potential caseload, and will enrich the experience and usefulness of the counselor. The Toledo and Detroit marriage counselors operate on this basis.

"Does the propriety of the practice of permitting a court counselor to work largely with nonlitigants look different if the court is the only agency offering marriage counseling?" Five of those who regard the practice as generally improper find it looks different when the court is the only agency offering the service. Four others still find it improper, as beyond the court's function.

We asked correspondents to define the proper function of a court marriage counselor. The following definitions were received: "to screen cases,"[28] "to encourage wide use of noncourt marriage counselors,"[29] "people differ on the court's function,"[30] "to help avoid divorce if possible and to try to

[27] But see Burke, *supra* note 26, at 198.
[28] Des Moines.
[29] Miami.
[30] Milwaukee.

bring willing parties together if they can do so happily,"[31] "to effect reconciliation if possible; if not, to advise the parties on their personal actions towards each other and the children on separation, and to develop the best possible solution to problems of child custody and support."[32]

The field of court marriage counseling appears to be new, to be growing, and to involve interesting problems of due process. Its development will probably be restricted to metropolitan areas, since only there can the necessary specially trained personnel be assembled or supported as part of a court staff.

SECTION 8. PROTECTING DUE PROCESS IN DEFAULTED CASES

In the cities observed for these studies, almost all traffic and small claims cases were defaulted by defendants not represented by counsel. Certain other types of cases often defaulted have already been mentioned. In the Detroit study, attention was called to the general problem of safeguarding due process in cases where judicial safeguards theoretically available are not in use.[33] Specifically, note the large numbers of traffic and small claims cases in which final disposition is reached without any challenge to the moving party's statement of the case.[34] For example, the present writer, observing traffic cases in company with Professor Holbrook and some of his staff, was present when a traffic judge administered a brutal tongue-lashing to a woman who had had the temerity to request a hearing on a traffic violation instead of pleading guilty and paying her fine. This was described as a common occurrence. When combined with present statewide police campaigns for reducing traffic hazards by con-

[31] Minneapolis.

[32] San Jose.

[33] DETROIT STUDY 133, 214-15 *et seq.*; LOS ANGELES STUDY 277-78, 171, and index references. For a good analysis of the general problem of due process in traffic courts see Netherton, *Fair Trial in Traffic Courts*, 41 MINN. L. REV. 577 (1957); Small Claims, *supra* pp. 75-76, 179 *et seq.*

[34] For percentage of defaulted cases see Table V, *supra* p. 233.

ducting intensive drives against violators, this attitude towards the traffic defendant who does not default suggests a due process problem.

Correspondents were asked to indicate their reactions to the existence and significance of such a problem.[35] Eleven express concern; nineteen indicate they are not concerned.[36] One of the Des Moines correspondents comments: "The party charged may challenge if he wishes and frequently does in our court." Minneapolis: "The small claims court here is a 'conciliation' court. The judge looks to general fairness and is not bound by the law. If anybody is unhappy, he can appeal easily to regular municipal court. Traffic offenders are not ordinary criminals. The real purpose of the court is to help reduce violations and call violator's attention to the rules. Most pay fines rather than have to have a trial."

Next was asked: "Do you think the public trusts the integrity of traffic police? of Justices of the Peace? Of small claims court judges?"

Twenty-two correspondents replied that the public trusts traffic police; six think they do not; one reports that he believes there is partial trust; another answers: "yes and no."

Sixteen correspondents express the opinion that the public does trust the integrity of justices of the peace; fourteen are of the belief that they do not; one answers "yes and no."

Twenty-three correspondents express the opinion that the public trusts the integrity of small claims judges; one of these qualifies by indicating that there are "areas of doubt." Six express the opinion that the public does not trust the integrity of judges handling small claims cases; one answers

[35] Boise; Charleston, W. Va.; Cheyenne; Des Moines; Grand Forks; Huron; Miami; Milwaukee; Philadelphia; Pueblo (qualified); St. Paul (qualified).

[36] Baltimore; Baton Rouge; Binghamton; Boise (2); Brocton; Burlington; Casper; Charleston, S. C.; Chattanooga; Cleveland; Des Moines (1); Eugene; Minneapolis; Phoenix; Rutland; St. Paul (2); San Jose; Sioux Falls; Washington; Wichita Falls. Sioux Falls reports that this is a municipal court function here, with the municipal judge paid as much as a circuit judge.

"yes and no." One cautions against the possible negative public relations effect of discussing the question.

Correspondents were invited to answer this question:

Do you see a problem of loss of the traditional function of courts by present 'slot machine' handling of traffic and installment credit cases in large metropolitan cities?

Ten correspondents do not see a problem, their typical comment being that these are trivial minor cases which must be handled routinely as a practical matter, and that the due process requirement is satisfied by the theoretical right to hearing upon demand and right to appeal.[37] The Boise correspondent sees the problem, but prefers efficient summary administration under a trained judge to scattered justice courts operated by untrained persons. Minneapolis reports that anyone who makes an issue of being rushed gets a pretty good trial, even with summary procedures.

San Jose reports that in California the court is always part of the machinery and ready to render redress whenever a litigant feels aggrieved.[38] This correspondent makes the interesting suggestion that part of the problem can be solved by refusing recourse to "small claims courts" by the assignee of an obligation, thus eliminating collection agency cases. Las Vegas makes the same suggestion and recommends legislation to this effect.

Casper remarks that a large number of the *defendants* see "push-button" justice, and, as a result, public opinion of the judicial process is based on the experiences and evaluations of this group of people. Cheyenne comments that many people do not realize they have the right to oppose the claim, and feels that judges have the obligation to make this right clear; public education is needed. Several comment that

[37] Baltimore; Baton Rouge; Burlington; Charleston, S. C.; Chattanooga; Des Moines; Grand Forks; Minneapolis; Sioux Falls. The State of Washington also expresses this view.

[38] See *supra* p. 349.

outlying justices of the peace have the reputation of setting excessive fines and costs.

Miami points with pride at its new "metropolitan" traffic court, which was designed especially to solve the problem under discussion, with the help of the American Bar Association's special committee on traffic courts.

Milwaukee expresses concern with the problem, and Pueblo believes it is steadily increasing. Philadelphia designates the loss of traditional court function through "push-button" justice as obvious. Wichita Falls bases concern for loss of court function upon the fact that "police and justices of the peace in a high percentage of cases can be and are wrong."

In New Jersey, State Court Administrator Edward B. McConnell recently called attention to the lack of professional legal interest in traffic courts. "In view of their widely recognized importance it is rather disturbing," he said, "that in most states the traffic courts have been treated rather poorly and . . . have seldom been considered an integral part of the judicial system." Their importance in the judicial hierarchy, he points out, is "not so much because of the nature of the cases they handle as the tremendous number of persons with whom they come in contact each year."[39]

What is a "trivial" case?[40]

Correspondents were, finally, asked to say whether the legal profession has a responsibility to see that traffic and small claims courts are handled fully in accordance with the theory of due process.

Twenty-two answer "yes." Among these, Des Moines makes the point that large numbers of people are involved in these cases, and if "not treated properly here, they mis-

[39] The Place of the Traffic Court in a State Judicial System, address of Honorable Edward B. McConnell before the Law and Laymen Conference, Section of Judicial Administration (Aug. 25, 1959).

[40] *Supra* p. 351.

trust the whole judicial system." Miami, Casper, and San Jose took the same position; Grand Forks adds that kangaroo courts must be avoided; Las Vegas recommends that the legal profession should take the initiative by lobbying for laws with proper standards and safeguards.

One correspondent believes that lawyers have no more interest in this "political" problem than any other citizen; another cautions that we may not make any friends by insisting that those accused of traffic violation have their constitutional rights.

On the other hand, St. Paul notes that to most defendants such courts are not only their first contact with the judiciary, but are "the government itself." And Milwaukee: "If the legal profession does not have this responsibility, who has?" Who, indeed?

"What do you see as a workable solution?" correspondents were asked. Among the suggestions were fuller participation by attorneys, continuing observation and appraisal by the press, and safeguarding rights of appeal. Most correspondents, however, recommend full-time courts with qualified personnel, supervised by well-paid and highly trained judges. The recommendation is best summed up in the language of New Jersey State Court Administrator McConnell:

> . . . the requirements of a good traffic court . . . include a full-time and legally trained judge, a competent clerical staff, a prosecuting attorney, a respectable courtroom and other facilities, modern rules of procedure and administration, including the uniform non-fix traffic ticket, and complete independence from other branches of government, especially the police, and complete separation from politics and other extraneous influences. The problem is to get all the traffic courts in a state to measure up to these standards. . . . First, the number of courts must be reduced to manageable limits which generally will mean that their jurisdiction cannot be limited solely to traffic matters. Second, they must be completely integrated into the state's judicial

system and subject to the superintending eye of its Supreme Court and Chief Justice, aided by an Administrative Office of the Courts. . . .[41]

Section 9. Concluding Comment

The pre-eminence of the due process problem in this discussion of metropolitan trial courts arises from the fact that the types of cases which seem to predominate in metropolitan areas tend to be cases brought before inferior courts with less highly trained judges and cases in which the adversary process, the aggressive counsel, and the full-dress trial are least likely to be found. Yet they are also the types of cases in which the vast majority of litigants are involved, and from which most of the lay public derives its opinion of the honesty, conscientiousness, and dedication of the legal profession (and perhaps of government itself, as a correspondent suggests). Furthermore, some of these cases (e.g., juvenile, mental, matrimonial) involve intricate problems of personal adjustment.[42]

To solve the problems encountered in handling such cases amid the rush, the crowds, and the anonymity of Metropolis, courts have recruited quasi-judicial personnel to screen out some of these cases, have developed administrative staffs of nonlegal experts to evaluate and supervise the litigants in personal problem cases, and have departmentalized courts and staffs to reach special types of cases with specially trained personnel. They have done so in order to give litigants better service, but in doing so have created a due process problem at the other end of the spectrum, for highly specialized courts multiply and create problems of jurisdictional conflict and confusion, while highly specialized non-

[41] McConnell, *supra* note 39; Netherton, *supra* note 33, at 577: ". . . legal reforms must not go so far in seeking efficiency that they sacrifice the ideal of fair trial as a living symbol of the role that courts play. History teaches that whenever efficiency has become the dominant concern in handling a certain type of legal problem, ways have been devised to relieve the courts of primary responsibility for handling such problems."

[42] *Supra* pp. 53-75.

judicial and nonlegal professionals tend to confuse the judicial function with that of administrative agencies operating outside the court, so that the very identity of the court may be threatened.

This is the special dilemma of Metropolitan Trial Court: to meet the due process problem without losing its judicial identity.

CHAPTER XI

Remedies

SECTION 1. STRUCTURAL

a. Introductory Comment

IN *The States and The Metropolitan Problem*[1] are listed five remedies available to solve general governmental problems caused by the rapid growth and increasing internal complexity within metropolitan areas: (1) annexation, (2) county consolidation, (3) city-county separation, (4) federation, and (5) functional transfers and joint efforts.

Some of the solutions proposed for the special problems of metropolitan courts parallel those recommended for other metropolitan units: (1) extension of geographic jurisdiction outwards geographically and upwards financially; (2) unifying all courts within a countywide or statewide system or both; (3) developing specialized courts with separate jurisdictional control; (4) federating existing courts through state and district court administrators and rule-making power; and (5) regrouping functional areas within courts to evolve more efficient methods for utilizing available judgepower to handle congested dockets, and joint efforts between courts to integrate handling of records, finances, duplicate caseload, and multiple investigative and supervisory problems.

Of these efforts towards court reform, structural reorganization has fared least well, though it has received much attention. In any work on court reform, it is obligatory to refer to the late Chief Justice Vanderbilt's observation that

[1] COUNCIL OF STATE GOVERNMENTS, THE STATES AND THE METROPOLITAN PROBLEM, 15 *et seq.* (1956).

it is "no sport for the short-winded." Structural reorganization of courts is even more difficult than governmental reorganization generally, because to general public inertia and vested interest in preserving the *status quo* is added the problem of widely conflicting views within the legal profession concerning the need for and proper direction of reform. Upon encountering determined and highly organized professional resistance to structural reform of courts, general public support often becomes uncertain and crumbles. This was the late Edson Sunderland's experience with a county court to replace the justice of the peace system in Michigan; it has been the fate of the Detroit metropolitan court plan to date. Recent experience with sweeping court unification plans in New York and Illinois provide other examples. This is the rock upon which most court reform plans observed by this writer within the last fifteen years have splintered.

There seem to be two aspects to this intraprofessional conflict. First, there is conflict within the legal profession as to the proper role of the trial court. Is he to be a mere moderator, or is he to be master of his courtroom and to see that equal justice under law is dispensed to each and every litigant? Second, there is conflict among various specialized court reform groups with respect to the desirability of any plan to join together to support one over-all plan for court reform. There is a peculiar difficulty in obtaining strategic consensus among various legal groups working with court reform, perhaps because our legal training conditions us against surrender or compromise once a thoughtful position has been taken.

The American Bar Association's recommendation for unified state court systems is contained in *Minimum Standards*,[2] where will be found an analysis of the various court

[2] VANDERBILT, MINIMUM STANDARDS 32.

systems.[3] The exemplary achievement is that of New Jersey, described by many writers.[4] California, with a more unified trial court system than most states, unified its municipal and justice courts in 1950 to the extent described by Holbrook,[5] and now has proposed further reforms along those lines.[6] Puerto Rico, Hawaii, and Alaska have unified court systems.[7] The *Annual Survey of American Law* reports major court integration achieved in 1959 in Connecticut and Wisconsin. Other ambitious court reform programs have not been successful, are stalled, or have been diminished so as not to constitute unification.[8]

No metropolitan district, however, has been found in which anything like a unified court structure has been achieved to systematize and coordinate *all* courts serving the metropolitan district. The closest thing to it is the Superior Court of Los Angeles, as described in the Holbrook study, which, however, shows structural disorganization in branches of both superior and municipal court as well as in autonomous outlying courts.[9]

"Miami Metro," a recent notable achievement, is a

[3] See also TRIAL COURTS OF GENERAL JURISDICTION IN THE FORTY-EIGHT STATES, listing at p. 15 only four states with a single statewide trial court (Connecticut, Maine, New Hampshire, Rhode Island) (1951 & 1953 supplement thereto).

[4] E.g., A.B.A. SECTION OF JUDICIAL ADMINISTRATION, IMPROVEMENT OF THE ADMINISTRATION OF JUSTICE (handbook) 22 (3rd ed. 1952).

[5] LOS ANGELES STUDY 8.

[6] See, e.g., (Walters) A Proposal for the Consolidation of the Superior and the Municipal Courts and an Analysis of the Workability of the Proposal within Los Angeles County, Court Committee, Municipal Judges' Association, Los Angeles County (1958); Joint Judiciary Committee on the Administration of Justice, Partial Report on the California Judiciary, Second Partial Report on the Operation of the Courts, Third and Final Report on Crime and Criminal Courts in California (1959); Karlen, *Judicial Administration,* ANNUAL SURVEY OF AMERICAN LAW 672 (1959).

[7] Karlen, *op. cit. supra*; 42 J. AM. JUD. SOC'Y 52 (1958); THE BOOK OF THE STATES, 1958-1959, at 95.

[8] See, for current list of projects: Karlen, *supra* note 6; current BOOK OF THE STATES; current report of JUSTICE CALLING, the annual report of the Section of Judicial Administration; and current issues of the JOURNAL OF THE AMERICAN JUDICATURE SOCIETY.

[9] *Supra* notes 1-3 and authorities cited therein.

Metropolitan Court established under the Home Rule Amendment of the Florida Constitution, which gives the electors of Dade County power to create by charter a court with jurisdiction to try all offenses against county ordinances,[10] and which further provides that no other court shall have concurrent jurisdiction. But this is not a general trial court, rather a consolidation and unification of inferior courts within the central county of the metropolitan district.

The proposed metropolitan court plan for Detroit, which has been presented unsuccessfully to the Michigan legislature for several years and which is still alive, is a partial attempt to unify all trial courts within the central county (Wayne) of the Detroit metropolitan district, but falls short of unification in that it does not include all the trial courts, nor does it include the two other counties in the metropolitan district. This plan, nevertheless, is the closest current attempt to square up the court system with the geographic area served.[11]

Only by some such structural unification, the boundaries of which reach the boundaries of the special problems, can the special structural problems of metropolitan courts be solved. Reference is had to the original recommendations of the American Judicature Society,[12] and the attention of the profession is invited to it. As some of our correspondents have pointed out, a few metropolitan areas span states, and some span international boundary lines. Where this is the case, a unified court system for the metropolitan area could be achieved by preserving the original court system in each portion of the area and erecting a supercourt to cover the entire district, by compact. A similar method of preserving

[10] FLA. CONST. art. 8, § 11 (adopted Nov. 6, 1956); HOME RULE CHARTER, DADE COUNTY, OFFICIAL RECORDS Bk. 182, 9. 667; PUBLIC RECORDS OF DADE COUNTY art. VI (adopted May 21, 1957) (see Appendix D *infra*); Ord. 57-13 (see Appendix D *infra*).

[11] Appendix C *infra*.

[12] Appendix B *infra*.

the original county or city structure while achieving over-all unification could be used to obtain full geographic jurisdiction for a single unified court system in metropolitan districts involving more than one county or more than one city (e.g., Minneapolis–St. Paul).

A frequent obstacle to the attempt to reach the boundary of the metropolitan district with the unified court system is the fact of the rapid growth and spread of the metropolitan districts. It is suggested that the basic constitutional amendment or enabling act could contain language automatically increasing the geographic jurisdiction of Metropolitan Court whenever the population of any contiguous district reached a certain level.[13] By this means, the unification of courts within any metropolitan district could be achieved and maintained.

Such unification should not compete with, but should be within and a part of, the statewide unified court system already recommended by the American Bar Association.

Section 2. Special Types of Cases

Much interest exists, and progress has been made, towards eliminating lay fee'd justices of the peace.[14] Recent notable developments include establishment of a circuit court in Connecticut to handle minor civil and criminal matters. This court has been brought within the state hierarchy of trial courts and is under judicial supervision of the chief justice.[15] Minnesota and Ohio are among the states which have recently abolished their justice of the peace systems. Partial consolidation and modernization of minor courts in

[13] As in California, where it is provided that there shall be a municipal court "in each district containing a population of more than 40,000 inhabitants and in each consolidated city and county." Holbrook, Los Angeles Study 31. See also *id.* ch. I, §4 and p. 9 n.26 citing Cal. Const. art. VI, §§ 1, 11, and 23 (as amended 1950). And see statutes cited in Los Angeles Study at 9 n.27.

[14] *Supra* p. 175 *et seq.* and references cited.

[15] Karlen, *supra* note 6, at 681; Conn. Pub. Acts Reg. Sess. 1959, No. 28; and see 43 J. Am. Jud. Soc'y 25 (1959).

the New York metropolitan area are reported.[16] Many states, such as Michigan, are enacting legislation to substitute municipal courts for justice courts in cities. The use of rule-making power to bring justice courts within the judicial supervision of the highest court on a statewide basis is a recent constructive effort, as reported from Texas and Michigan. Some of the improvement, as previously noted, may be in name only.[17] The new Metropolitan Court at Miami, established by county ordinance, is a laudable achievement, but it is not integrated with the rest of the trial court system serving the Miami metropolitan district.

In the field of family cases, the National Probation and Parole Association and the National Association of Juvenile Court Judges now recommend that family courts be established with jurisdiction over all major types of family litigation, including divorce-custody and juvenile cases.[18] Experience has indicated that where the court handling matrimonial actions is separate from that dealing with juvenile cases, a good deal of conflict and confusion is likely to develop. Recommendation for a new family court is reported from New York. It will not have jurisdiction over divorce, and will not become an operating court until further action by the legislature and the electorate.[19] Other developments and trends in the family court field have been discussed.[20] It is in this field that the pressure towards spe-

[16] Karlen, *supra* note 6, at 681.

[17] *Supra* p. 177.

[18] NATIONAL PROBATION AND PAROLE ASS'N, STANDARD FAMILY COURT ACT (1959).

[19] Karlen, *supra* note 6, at 673.

[20] *Supra* Chapter VI, especially at 188-89, 195. For recent materials discussing suggested remedial measures, the following have been found helpful: Report of the Joint Legislative Committee on Matrimonial and Family Laws (New York 1957); Manual for Guidance of Juvenile Conference Committees appointed by the Juvenile and Domestic Relations Court, Administrative Office of the Courts (N. J. 1958); Report of the New Jersey Supreme Court's Commitee on Juvenile and Domestic Relations Courts (April 19, 1956); The Citizen and the Courts, A Report by The Special Committee on the Administration of Justice on a Proposed Simplified State-

cialization is greatest in metropolitan districts, and the danger of creating more confusion through overspecialization most likely to be encountered.

The solution preferred by this writer is a specialized judge working in a fully staffed separate division, but selected by and responsible to the presiding judge of the metropolitan court, and subject to such adjustment in caseload and administrative facilities as the judicial supervisors may find advisable from time to time.

The special needs of courts handling mental cases seem to constitute one of the largest unsolved problem areas. The device used in Los Angeles, where mental hearings occur in a hospital with benefit of diagnostic reports made by hospital personnel, is interesting, but it was not felt that the due process problem has been solved there, nor in any metropolitan area under survey. The extension of the idea of the impartial medical panel to mental cases, together with required judicial hearing for all cases, might result in obtaining proper medical care for those who need it without sacrificing their rights or distorting the role of the court.

Section 3. Personnel

Careful consideration of the problems presented in the previous chapters leads to the conclusion that in the last analysis there is an overriding necessity for a strong, independent, and dedicated trial bench. Given this, most of the mechanical, staff, and procedural problems cease to arouse much anxiety.

The problem of recruiting able judges for metropolitan trial courts, including courts trying so-called "trivial" cases, is receiving attention. The Missouri Plan, long recommended by the American Bar Association, was recently dis-

wide Court System, Assoc. of Bar of the City of New York; Judge Theodore Knudsen, Report on Family Court Observations, Minneapolis District Ct. (unpublished) (Jan. 6, 1959); and Report of the Interim Commission on Domestic Relations Problems, (Minn. 1951).

cussed at the National Conference on Judicial Selection, sponsored jointly by the American Bar Association and the American Judicature Society.[21] Consensus was unanimous for a strong and independent judiciary, but not unanimous with respect to the best method for obtaining such a judiciary. The special problems of obtaining qualified judges in populous metropolitan areas, where the electorate cannot hope to know the abilities and records of candidates, was brought out during this conference. Recent constitutional and legislative enactments are reported in the current *Survey of American Law.*[22]

Attention is called to extensive efforts in various metropolitan cities to augment judicial manpower by bringing in quasi-judicial personnel, or by referring screened-out cases to them: examples are use of masters in divorce, referees, *pro tem* judges, compulsory arbitration, impartial medical panel, and so on.[23] The preceding pages teem with examples. A very recent, and startling, suggestion along the same line is that masters be used to handle pretrial conferences instead of judges![24]

As Harry Kalven points out:

> . . . it is disturbing to find so much enthusiasm for proposals for delegating the core work of the court, adjudication, to substitute judges, and . . . for taking tort suits . . . out of the courts altogether. If one adds to this the pervasive enthusiasm for having cases settled rather than adjudicated, one is left to wonder whether we any longer think there is *any* case that is proper for adjudication.[25]

It is ironic that all these plans for augmenting judicial manpower by bringing in persons who are not judges are developing right along with a trend towards compulsory re-

[21] See 43 J. AM. JUD. SOC'Y 40 (1959).
[22] [1959] ANNUAL SURVEY OF AMERICAN LAW 674 *et seq.*
[23] *Lagging Justice,* 328 ANNALS 53, 75, 116 (March 1960).
[24] [1959] ANNUAL SURVEY OF AMERICAN LAW 685.
[25] 43 J. AM. JUD. SOC'Y 211 (Apr. 1960) (review of *Lagging Justice,* which is cited *supra* note 23).

tirement for judges.[26] Very recently, a countertrend towards utilizing the services of retired judges as continuing members of judicial conferences and councils, subject to assignment as needed, is noted. The bar might well consider whether, if qualified judges are so needed in metropolitan areas (and elsewhere), it is altogether wise to insist on compulsory retirement on a calendar age basis.

The marshaling of judicial manpower on a statewide basis through judicial organizations such as conferences and councils, and through the rule-making power, continues to develop. The movement to extend the reach of judicial power through use of rule-making power and through procedural reform is enhanced by the recent Report of the Joint Committee on Michigan Procedural Revision, which was accepted by the 1961 legislature of Michigan.[27]

Extensive utilization of nonlegal professional personnel by courts handling personal problem cases is typical of large metropolitan cities, no doubt because the caseload pressures motivate such use there, and also because the large population makes such specialized personnel available. The presence of psychologists, psychiatrists, social workers, marriage counselors, probation officers, and similar professionals, whether employed as part of the court staff or otherwise brought in, raises questions of due process and of adherence to the proper role of the court. Thus, here, again, the requirement for a strong judiciary is experienced.

Employment of adequate clerical and administrative personnel to establish and maintain control over records, finances, personnel, and other nonjudicial operations of the court is currently much stressed. The possibility of unifying

26 [1959] ANNUAL SURVEY OF AMERICAN LAW 677.

27 *Report of the Joint Committee on Michigan Procedural Revision* (result of a three year study under chairmanship of Professor Charles Joiner of the University of Michigan Law School), 38 MICH. STATE BAR J. (1959) (the entire issue is devoted to the text of the report). MICH. PUB. ACTS 1961, Act No. 236.

all housekeeping functions of the entire trial court system of a metropolitan area is suggested by recent appointment in Chicago of deputy state court administrators to unify the operations of courts on a metropolitan-wide basis, and in Los Angeles of an executive officer to assist the Superior Court in dealing with its problems.

Section 4. Machinery for Handling Dockets and Caseload

This subject has been discussed hereinbefore.[28] Much current writing emphasizes mechanical efficiency, to the potential peril of the existence of the trial court as a purveyor of even-handed justice to all litigants. It is a day in *court* litigants want, not an efficient prompt trip through a slot machine. Many expedients now proposed to decrease delay (e.g., screening out minor or defaulted cases, use of printed jury instructions identified by number, use of compulsory arbitrators, systematic discouragement or disuse of juries, rubber-stamping by judges of decisions made by administrative aides) strike this writer as more likely to destroy the judicial process than to uphold it.

Adequate mechanical systems of course there must be, for the size and complexity of the metropolitan caseload demands special facilities to prevent clogging of dockets. The central assignment system, administered by a long-term presiding judge with authority to shift any part of the caseload, preserves the essential judicial control without which the mechanical system is meaningless.

Section 5. Integration and Cooperation Among Various Courts Within the Metropolitan Area

No structural unification of courts within a metropolitan district has been found, though in such areas as Los Angeles and Phoenix a considerable degree of structural unification

[28] *Supra* at 231-71.

occurs by reason of the structure of the statewide court system. Horizontal marshaling of the judicial manpower within the metropolitan district, as by establishing a judges' meeting or conference of all trial judges within the district, has not been found or reported, though this technique was recommended long ago by the American Judicature Society. Integration of housekeeping functions on a metropolitan basis may follow the use of a deputy court administrator working on a metropolitan basis, as in Chicago. Economies of money, manpower, and effort might well be so achieved, as well as improved total performance of the entire court system in each metropolitan area.

Horizontal integration of both judicial and nonjudicial court personnel on a metropolitan-wide basis seems to this writer the only expedient likely to bring under control the typical metropolitan court problem of sprawl, confusion, chaos, and cross-purpose, which has been observed to obtain even where the over-all court structure is relatively simple.

Section 6. Due Process

Protection of due process for all litigants seems to this writer to be the most serious problem of metropolitan courts, viewed either from the point of view of the litigants or that of the profession. The overriding question about courts in metropolitan areas is whatever happened to due process. The reader who considers this overstated is invited to spend one day in the largest metropolitan city near him, observing the following cases: traffic, mental, domestic relations, and petty criminal.

If due process is a luxury to be afforded only by the litigant able to retain counsel to try a contested negligence case, then the judicial process is not serving the purpose the public thinks it is serving, and the profession is not discharging the obligation to the public it holds itself out to be ready, willing, and able to fulfill. The problem is intensified by the fact that the general impression of courts, of government, and even of democracy is largely drawn, by the public, from its experience with traffic, small claims, domestic relations, mental, and petty criminal cases. This is where the great bulk of the caseload is.

The problem is again intensified by the fact that able, qualified judges and the services of counsel for all parties are least likely to be brought to bear upon the types of cases just mentioned.

The problem is again intensified by the fact that even in tried cases the mechanical problems of delay and professional preoccupation with mechanical methods of solving this problem have resulted in pressure to *prevent* cases from being dealt with by able, qualified judges, by screening out cases and diverting them to commissions, arbitrators, administrative agencies, or nonlegal professionals. The previous chapters have shown that kangaroo courts for traffic, juvenile, and some domestic cases are maintained outside the court system by some metropolitan police or social agencies, and that in juvenile and domestic relations courts kangaroo courts are conducted by nonlegal professionals on the payroll of the court but with professional loyalty and orientation strongly opposed to the concepts of due process.

It seems appropriate to suggest that the profession reexamine the basic functions and responsibilities of the bar, the judge, and the trial court system, and to devote at least as much attention to the obligation of the profession to see that litigants are accorded due process as to the purely mechanical problems of bookkeeping and case progress. Unless we are on the right road to justice, it matters not whether the carburetor is working at peak efficiency.

Chapter XII

Conclusion

Introductory Note

THESE conclusions are the considered conclusions of this writer, drawn from all material known to her, including but not restricted to the fact studies conducted for the Section of Judicial Administration. The conclusions drawn herein are presented for the further study, consideration, and action of various national and local groups concerned with the proper functioning of the judicial process.

Conclusion and Recommendations

The special problem of the metropolitan trial court is the same as the special problem of any metropolitan function: adjustment of the zone of services to the area being served. Just as Metropolis requires a system of superhighways and supermarkets, so it requires a supercourt, with jurisdiction, administrative facilities, and personnel available to reach throughout the metropolitan district.

The following minimum requirements are suggested for a metropolitan court system:

I. Jurisdiction

1. A single unified tribunal, having jurisdiction over all types of cases, should serve each metropolitan district, or at least the central county of the area.

Unification with extensions of the metropolitan district, as it develops and grows, can be brought about by statutory provision attaching to the Metropolitan Court such areas as achieve a required population basis. Preservation of existing courts as divisions within the Metropolitan Court system can be achieved and will probably be the most practical method. A judicial conference would be established to comprise all judges from the area being unified, with power to transfer cases and administer procedural matters throughout the area. A presiding judge should be established for the Metropolitan Court. For example, a child custody matter arising in one court, if found to involve a family problem already before another court, should be disposed of *in toto* by whichever court was found, upon authority of the judicial administrator responsible, to be the proper court. The same technique could transfer to the small claims division or court cases originally filed in a higher level court.

2. Certain fundamental levels of jurisdiction, such as appellate, general trial, and limited jurisdiction, should be permanently established as separate operating tribunals by constitution or statute, as courts with separate identity but as integral parts of the Metropolitan Court.

3. Special types of cases requiring specialized handling, such as misdemeanor, felony, small claims, traffic, family, and mental cases, should be established by and under the authority of the Metropolitan Judicial Conference, and subject to its continuing discretion with respect to types of cases assigned, extent of judicial and other professional personnel employed, relationship with other parts of Metropolitan Court, and relationship with noncourt agencies. These should be special divisions, or parts, of Metropolitan Court, but need not be cemented into permanent shape by constitution or statute.

4. Metropolitan Court should be an integral working part of a statewide unified court, but should have firm structural and administrative control horizontally throughout the metropolitan area.

5. The courts exercising jurisdiction over cases originally

handled by justices of the peace, however named or organized, should be an integral part of Metropolitan Court, and subject to the supervisory control of its bench.

II. Special Types of Cases

6. The special divisions, or parts, for such cases as family and mental cases, should be manned by long-term specialized judges, preferably selected and assigned by the Metropolitan Judicial Conference, with provision for additional judicial manpower and for training judges to specialize through assignment from other divisions as the weight of the caseload indicates.

(Note: There is irreconcilable controversy among lawyers and judges as to the necessity for specialized judges in specialized courts, particularly family, mental, and traffic courts. It is the writer's personal conclusion that a nonspecialized judge with a highly specialized staff can do the job, and that some participation by nonspecialized judges is necessary in order to preserve the relationship of the specialized division to the rest of the court system. Nevertheless, it has been concluded that as between a nonspecialized judge and a specialized judge, the latter is preferable, for two reasons: (1) a specialized judge will be better able to exercise control over his specialized nonlegal professional staff, because he will understand the necessities both of the specialty and of the judicial process; (2) a specialized judge can, in the long run, develop a better quality of disposition of such cases as family cases, which demand certain qualities of temperament and which should include carefully developed and maintained liaison with many noncourt agencies throughout the metropolitan community. This is not to say that only a long-term specialized judge is acceptable, since the fact is that in some areas no suitable judge will be found who will accept certain specialized assignments on a long-term basis.)

7. The specialized divisions should be staffed with non-legal professionals to act as court aides, as necessary, and should be subject to the authority of the specialized judge or presiding judge in charge of the specialized division, subject to the ultimate authority of the bench of the Metropolitan Court.

8. In family courts, or parts, or divisions, jurisdiction should include all matrimonial actions, family-based criminal matters, juvenile delinquency and neglect, adoption, and personal guardianships of minors, if possible. The irreducible minimum is matrimonial actions, juvenile cases, and adoption. Divorce and other matters involving the marital relationship should be segregated in a separate division or docket within the family court from matters involving the children primarily.

III. Personnel

9. All judges functioning at any level within the Metropolitan Court, including family and justice courts, should be required by constitution or statute to be fully qualified lawyers.

10. Retirement systems for judges should not arbitrarily require descent from the bench on the basis of calendar age; retirement systems should make provision for using the experience of judges, even after retirement, as commissioners, referees, and for relieving congestion or for *causes célèbres*.

11. Use of quasi-judicial personnel, such as referees, should be carefully restricted and supervised, to provide assurance that the judicial function is exercised only by qualified judges.

12. Provision should be made, by whatever means are feasible, to provide for counsel available to all classes of litigants at all phases of litigation, with emphasis on such

availability in petty criminal, mental, juvenile, and family cases.

13. In addition to the nonlegal professionals employed by special courts (7, *supra*), provision should be made for supplying the court with the services of psychologists, social workers, and psychiatrists, either as witnesses or as court aides on a per diem basis or by reference to noncourt clinics, in such cases as those involving the diagnosis of psychopaths, emotionally disturbed children, retarded or mentally ill persons. No such case should go to final disposition without a professional diagnosis being made available to the court.

14. A single jury commission should serve Metropolitan Court, under statutory provision establishing a nonpartisan and objective method of recruiting qualified jurymen (such as the key number system). No juries should be required by statute in mental cases or those involving psychopaths.

15. All nonjudicial employees should be responsible to the judge immediately in contact with their work; ultimate responsibility for employment, promotion, and dismissal should rest with the bench of Metropolitan Court, with administration delegated to the Metropolitan Court Administrator or to a civil service commission of the court.

16. Judges should be selected on a nonpartisan basis for terms of not less than six years, preferably longer.

IV. Machinery for Handling Dockets and Disposing of Caseload

17. Judicial responsibility for case progress in each part of Metropolitan Court should be upon the presiding judge of such part, who should have adequate authority to handle the problem. Metropolitan Court should have a central assignment system, with an Assignment Clerk responsible to the Presiding Judge of the Metropolitan Court.

18. Pretrial should be employed at least in the major

felony and civil trial parts of Metropolitan Court, under a system established by court rule and subject to the supervisory authority of the Presiding Judge of Metropolitan Court.

19. Judicial personnel should be assigned by authority of the bench of Metropolitan Court, with general assignment being made by the Presiding Judge of Metropolitan Court to the individual courts or parts, for specific assignment by the presiding judge of each such court or part, but with all assignments subject to the overriding authority of the Presiding Judge of Metropolitan Court, as authorized by the bench, to control assignments as the condition of the caseload from time to time makes appropriate.

20. A detailed record of case progress should be kept by the Assignment Clerk for the Presiding Judge, and docket practices controlled in light of this data.

21. Legal safeguards should not be discarded in order to achieve a better statistical showing in terms of "delay."

22. Delay should be measured from the date at which the case is at issue to the date of final disposition. Court rule should provide for automatic dismissal of cases not placed at issue through procrastination of counsel. The judge responsible for each case should have authority to control its progress by evaluating the need for extensive pretrial, requests for continuances, and so on.

23. In designing systems for controlling delay, recourse should not be had to penalizing or disadvantaging certain types of cases in order to make a better statistical showing on delay in other types of cases. Awareness of the delay problem should deprive no litigant of his full day in court.

V. Effective Integration and Cooperation Among Courts and Related Agencies Within the Metropolitan Area

24. There should be a court administrator for Metropolitan Court, subject to the supervision of the Presiding Judge

of Metropolitan Court, and working closely with the state court administrator. There should be, in each separate court or division within Metropolitan Court, an administrative officer responsible to the Metropolitan Court Administrator for work related to Metropolitan Court as such.

25. The Metropolitan Court Administrator should establish and administer a unified system of court records, money and financial records, probation work, and other aspects of judicial administration as determined by the Metropolitan Judicial Conference.

26. If probation is a function of the courts in a given metropolitan area, then all probation work in all parts of Metropolitan Court should be handled through a single probation department, with a probation supervisor responsible to the Presiding Judge of Metropolitan Court. Each specialized court or division within Metropolitan Court having a probation staff should have a department supervisor responsible to the judge for performance on each case and responsible to the probation administrator for professional standards and supervision.

27. Each public and private social and medical agency in the metropolitan area should have a full-time liaison worker assigned to Metropolitan Court, or to each separate part or court thereof if necessary, for the purpose of achieving maximum integration of purpose and performance between social agencies and courts. Representatives of the staffs of various courts and agencies should establish a court advisory council, meeting regularly, with the responsibility of reporting regularly to the Presiding Judge of Metropolitan Court concerning problems of procedure or integration.

28. All social workers employed by any part of Metropolitan Court should be organized into a Social Service Department, with professional supervision provided through the head of that department, who should be responsible to the Presiding Judge of Metropolitan Court.

29. Representatives of hospitals, psychiatric and mental institutions, and medical associations working with Metropolitan Court should comprise an advisory council, meeting with a representative of the metropolitan bench and such court staff members as he designates, at such times as the council finds useful, to develop more effective liaison between judicial and medical personnel.

VI. Safeguarding Due Process

30. Provision should be made by Metropolitan Court for use of counsel in all cases where desired or advisable, and especially traffic, criminal, juvenile, small claims, domestic relations, and mental cases, the majority of which now go to final disposition without counsel.

31. Courts handling divorce and juvenile cases should have access, through court aides, to objective information concerning the possibility of reconciliation, the welfare of the children, and other personal problems affecting the decision, but misuse of such personnel should be safeguarded by court rule and by supervision of the family court judge to prevent loss of due process.

32. The presiding judge of the criminal division, or court, or part, of Metropolitan Court, should control loss of due process by bargaining of prosecutor, police, or both, for guilty pleas.

33. Full hearings should be required in all mental cases, such hearings to include psychiatric evaluation as well as legal inquiry. If diagnostic commitment has been established in a particular metropolitan area, provision should be made by court rule for the transfer of cases between court of initiation and court of location of diagnostic clinic. Within the metropolitan area, provision should be made for the conduct of mental hearings in the hospital, clinic, or institution where the patient is confined. Particular caution should be exercised in dealing with mental petitions involving in-

digent elderly persons to guard against the "dumping" of such persons in order to relieve local government units of the financial responsibility for their care.

34. Use of "unofficial category" in juvenile cases should be severely restricted, under supervision of the Presiding Judge of Metropolitan Court, to prevent exercise by that division or part of judicial authority over cases not properly before the court by persons not qualified as judges.

35. The use of marriage counselors as court employees should be restricted to those having litigation before the court or those actually "on the threshold" of litigation.

36. Care should be taken, by judges of individual courts or parts subject to the supervision of the Presiding Judge of Metropolitan Court, to preserve due process and decorum in traffic, small claims, and other courts now presenting a problem of loss of public confidence.

37. Representatives of the bench of Metropolitan Court should meet, from time to time, with representatives of community groups at all levels, including the press, to explore the extent to which the judiciary is performing the function desired by the community, as selected and qualified representatives of various community groups can interpret public opinion. The goal of such meetings should be, and should clearly be seen to be, not yielding of judicial authority to public pressure, but an interpretation by the judiciary to the public of the problems of the judiciary and the function of the judicial process.

Concluding Note

In his article on justice in the modern city, written in 1913,[1] Dean Pound recommends: freedom from domination by forces unfamiliar with the special problems of metropolitan courts; availability of first-rate men as judges of

[1] Pound, *Administration of Justice in the Modern City*, 26 Harv. L. Rev. 302 (1913).

so-called "petty" courts in metropolitan areas; and organization of judicial department of the whole metropolitan area as a unit under an administrative head to prevent waste, to direct the application of all parts of the metropolitan court system in the most efficacious manner, to direct strong judges exercising full power, and to have adequate control of all its clerical and executive force.

He cautioned that we must not be in too much of a hurry.

We haven't been.

Much earlier, an even more basic and appropriate recommendation was made by Lambarde with respect to the special problems of metropolitan courts: that heed and care ought to be taken in the deciding of controversies, and, specifically, that courts pronounce their judgments in the gates of every city "that both all men might behold the indifference of their proceedings, and that no man should need to goe out of his way to seeke justice."

With respect, confidence, and appreciation, the writer commends these recommendations to her brothers in law.

APPENDICES

Appendix A

Bulletin I.[1] American Judicature Society, 1, January 6, 1914
Causes for Dissatisfaction With the Administration of Justice in Metropolitan Districts

INTRODUCTORY

I. The causes for dissatisfaction with the administration of justice are more numerous and more emphatically apparent in a metropolitan district than anywhere else.

II. The causes group themselves about the following six subjects:
- A. Selection, retirement and discipline of judges.
- B. Organization of the judges after they are selected.
- C. Selection of jurors as judges of the facts, the guidance of the jury and discrimination in its use.
- D. Rules of practice and procedure.
- E. Efficiency in the offices of clerks of courts.
- F. Selection, retirement, discipline and organization of the bar.

I.

Selection, Retirement and Discipline of Judges

I. It has been suggested that in the metropolitan district where the elective system prevails the following is a fair description of the actual mode of selecting and retiring judges and the weaknesses of that system.
- A. Judges are usually not really elected, but are designated by the leaders of the party political machine dominant in the district. These leaders appoint the nomination. The electorate only decides which of two or three sets of nominees it prefers. The compulsory primary has but little altered the situation.
- B. These leaders have too little responsibility for the due administration of justice. They have the strongest motives

[1] Bulls. Am. Jud. Soc'y 3-30 (Jan. 1914).

for rewarding purely political service to an organization. The occasional instances when the political leaders exercise power to good purpose do not alter the fact that the system is lacking in adequate efficient responsibility.

C. The judges are subject not merely to a recall, but to a progressive series of recalls—first, by the leaders of the party organization refusing nomination; second, by a wing of the party knifing the candidate at the polls; third, by an upheaval in a national election, and fourth, and most rarely, by actual public dissatisfaction with the judge himself. These recalls for the most part retire the judge from office regardless of the character of his services. The recall at any time by petition will operate to place the judges even more in the power of the political party machine organization than they are now.

D. There is at present no means of disciplining judges at all.[2] There is no chief justice or presiding justices of different divisions of the court to whom the rank and file of judges are responsible for the performance of their duties.

E. There are no service test requirements which permit judges to be selected from among those practitioners only who have obtained some success in actual practice before courts.

F. The mode of selecting and retiring judges is so unsatisfactory and the character of the duties of judges is such as to stifle competition for places on the bench by men who have succeeded in practice.

II. It has been suggested that the selection of judges in the sense of the picking out by the electorate of those among the lawyers who it desires above all others is impossible for a metropolitan district having over one hundred thousand population; that such an apparent method of selection results in appointment by the political party leaders; that therefore if by a nonpartisan ballot the political party machine influence could be eliminated or so greatly reduced as not to be controlling, nothing but chaos would result; that as a matter of fact the great influence of the political party machine would continue to be the predominant principal force in the election of judges even with the non-partisan ballot.

[2] Except in the Municipal Court of Chicago and a few others similarly organized.

III. It has been suggested that the bar association should be given power to place upon the official ballot a bar association ticket which could have upon it candidates who had been nominated by any of the other political parties. The question, however, has arisen whether this would result in a greater power in an unbiased bar association to select good judges, or in the lining up of lawyers in political camps controlled by the leaders of the political party machines.

IV. It has been suggested that nothing of great value can be accomplished until the fact is faced that judges in a metropolitan district are practically certain to be appointed and that the only proper appointing power is one which is legal, conspicuous, subject directly to the electorate and interested in and responsible for the due administration of justice; that this principle may be worked out in various ways:

A. Suggested that judges may be appointed by the state executive; that this is better than the present mode, but objectionable because of the governor's interest in promoting a legislative program, the building up of a political machine, and his remote responsibility for the administration of justice; also that he is frequently a stranger to the metropolitan district.

B. Suggested that appointment be by the highest appellate tribunal of the State, the members of which are subject to the electorate; that this is better than the present method and better than appointment by the governor because such a court is more responsible than the executive for the due administration of justice and the members of it have a stronger motive for appointing fit men, as well as an excellent opportunity for determining the character and ability of lawyers. On the other hand, most of them may be strangers to the metropolitan district. Also there is danger that the most important tribunal of the State may become involved in politics. Furthermore, responsibility for selection is not concentrated.

C. It has been suggested that the appointment be by a chief justice who is a resident of the metropolitan district and who is subject to the electorate at fairly frequent intervals and in whom should be vested large powers to oversee and direct the work of the courts. It has been suggested that such a chief justice would be conspicuous and in a high degree responsible for the due administration of justice and therefore most interested in the selection of fit men for judges.

1. If such a plan be adopted the following questions arise concerning the selection of the chief justice:
   - (a) Shall he be elected at a general November election, or a general city election in the spring, or at a special judicial election in June, when no other offices are filled?
   - (b) Shall there be a separate judicial ballot?
   - (c) Shall the ballot be partisan or non-partisan?
   - (d) If partisan—
     - (1) Shall nominations be by primary?
     - (2) May candidates run on as many party tickets as choose to include them?
     - (3) Shall there be a special bar association ticket which may include upon it candidates running on other tickets?
   - (e) If non-partisan—
     - (1) Shall nominations be by petition? or
     - (2) Shall anyone eligible be free to run upon making a deposit in money which will be returned to him if he receives at least half as many votes as any person elected to office?
   - (f) It has been suggested that the eligibility test for the chief justice should be—
     - (1) That he has been a lawyer in active practice in the handling of litigation in courts of the State for fifteen years; that he should have been also a resident of the metropolitan district and a practitioner at the bar of that district for not less than ten years.
     - (2) If any organization of the bar is effected which gives special recognition to practitioners who specialize in the handling of litigation in the courts, the chief justice should be selected from this class only.
     - (3) That judges already sitting be eligible to run for chief justice only upon resigning at least thirty days prior to the election.
2. Under the plan of selection by the chief justice of the other judges of the court several questions arise:

(a) Shall some of the judges be appointed by the chief justice with the consent of the governor or any other body while other judges are appointed by the chief justice alone?

(b) Shall the eligibility test permit any citizen of the United States who has been admitted to the bar for a given number of years and practiced in any state to become a judge?

(c) Should an eligible list be created consisting of twice as many members as there are judges of the court, to be selected by the chief justice of the court and the heads of the different divisions of the court, to the end that the chief justice may be required to select at least every other judge appointed from the eligible list?

3. The question also arises as to the proper mode of selecting masters or assistant judges:

(a) Shall they be appointed by the chief justice alone, or

(b) By the chief justice and the presiding justice of any division of the court to which the master is to be attached, and in case of disagreement, the presiding justice of the Appellate division to make a third member of the selecting committee, or

(c) Shall appointment be by the chief justice and the presiding justice of the division to which the master is attached in rotation, or

(d) Shall the appointment be by the presiding justice of the division to which the master is attached?

(e) Shall there be a civil service examination providing an eligible list and testing candidates' knowledge with respect to the duties of the office and their experience?

(f) Shall any citizen of the United States admitted to the bar in any state be eligible?

V. It has been suggested that the retirement of judges is an entirely different problem from that of their selection; that the problem of retirement also differs, according as the judge is a chief justice with power to appoint judges, or is merely one of a number of judges who have been appointed or otherwise selected.

A. Retirement of the chief justice.

1. What shall be the limit of his term?

2. Shall he be subject to impeachment, or
3. Recall by joint resolution of the legislature, or
4. Recall by popular vote which at the same time operates to elect another?
5. In case of retirement by failure to be re-elected shall the chief justice continue to remain one of the judges of the court, subject to assignment to duty by his successor?

B. Retirement of judges other than the chief justice.
1. Shall they be retired by impeachment, or
2. Recalled by joint resolution of the legislature, or
3. Recalled at any time by popular vote which merely vacates the office, leaving it to the chief justice to fill the place by appointment, or
4. Shall the name of the judge be submitted to the electorate at specified periods, such as three, six and nine years; the question being whether the judge's place shall be vacated, leaving it to be filled by the appointment of the chief justice, or
5. Shall the judge be removable by a vote of the judicial council consisting of the chief justice and the presiding justices of the different divisions of the court after a hearing and after cause shown, the cause to be as general as under civil service acts, namely, inefficiency, incompetency, neglect of duty, lack of judicial temperament and conduct unbecoming a judge?

C. Retirement of masters.
1. They may hold at the will and pleasure of the appointing power; or
2. The will and pleasure of the judicial council; or be
3. Dischargeable only for cause which must be stated in writing but need not be proved, said discharge to be by the head of the division to which the master is regularly attached, with the consent of the chief justice; or
4. Discharge only for cause and upon a hearing before the judicial council.

VI. Suggested that the discipline of judges is a different matter from their retirement.

A. That an elective chief justice with power to appoint judges to the court should not be subject to any disciplinary authority on the part of the court.

B. As to the judges other than the chief justice who are appointed to places by the chief justice, it has been suggested:

1. That the council of judges composed of the chief justice and the presiding justices of the several divisions of the court should have power to reprove any judge privately or publicly, to transfer any judge to some other division of the court upon a hearing and for cause shown, such as inefficiency, incompetency, neglect of duty, lack of judicial temperament and conduct unbecoming a judge.
2. That judges, especially in the trial courts, would be held in check and to a proper line of judicial conduct if there were present in the court a specialized and expert bar and by the constant reportings of selected rulings by members of the bar.

C. No special provision for disciplining masters is needed because of the manner in which they may be removed.

VII. It has been suggested that competition for places on the bench by successful practitioners would not be promoted by raising salaries so much as by

A. An improved mode of selection and retirement of judges which tends to give security of tenure to those who do satisfactory work;

B. The improvement in the personnel of the bench and its better organization for the purposes of efficiency, as hereinafter suggested, so as to furnish proper fields of specialization for judges.

C. The creation of important administrative positions, such as the presiding justices of the divisions, who should be *ex-officio* judges of the appellate division. This would also attract men of special ability at the bar who might be disinclined to take an ordinary judicial position.

D. These features need only be added to the present salary arrangement in many places to make the positions on the bench sufficiently attractive to draw able and successful members of the bar.

II.

THE ORGANIZATION OF JUDGES AFTER THEY ARE SELECTED

I. It has been suggested that the problem presented by the court of general jurisdiction in a metropolitan district where many judges are working at the same time over extensive dockets of cases of all sorts, is this: How can each judge in the time spent upon the bench be brought most effectively into contact with litigation? How can his energies be applied so that he wastes the least time and does the most accurate thinking, which leads to a determination of the cause? This is an ordinary problem for an efficiency expert.

II. It has been suggested that an efficiency expert would first classify and arrange the work.

A. That he would find that all of it fell into at least four classes:

1. Non-contested matters—defaults, motions of course, amendments, etc.—
2. Contested motions, demurrers, etc.
3. The trial on the merits.
4. Appeals.

III. It has been suggested that the efficiency expert would then stop the spending of time by the judge on the more trivial work which others could do as well; that he would utilize the services of less highly paid masters or asssitant judges to handle motions of course, ordinary defaults and uncontested matters.

IV. It has been suggested that the efficiency expert would then take care that individual judges did not have to cover too wide a field in the handling of causes.

A. That he would find that no man could become expert when he must cover all kinds of practice and substantive law, such as criminal pleading, practice, trials and substantive law; common law pleading, practice, trials and substantive law; chancery pleading, practice, hearings and substantive law; appellate practice and substantive law and practice in all sorts of cases appealed.

B. That the efficiency expert would find that there are several extensive fields of substantive law and of practice in which judges could specialize profitably to themselves, to the public and without unduly restricting the scope of their work, such as

1. Civil and criminal jury trials.
2. Commercial cases tried with and without a jury.
3. Cases tried without a jury, covering the field now largely covered by what is known as chancery practice.

4. Probate, Divorce, Juvenile Court, and Family Relations in general.

C. That the obvious step is for each judge to be assigned to final hearings in one of these classes of cases—a sufficient number of judges being assigned to each class to dispose of it.

V. It has been suggested that it is obviously unwise to let six or fifteen or thirty judges go to work as they please on a long unspecialized docket of several thousand cases; that to obtain the best results there must be divisional heads who will have large administrative powers and responsibility for the docket of each division. Hence, each division should have a presiding justice.

VI. It has been suggested that all these arrangements should be merely tentative; that actual experience may show that it will be advisable to transfer some classes of cases from the docket of one division to that of another and some judge from one division to another, and to make new rules for the conduct of judicial business and the function of masters. Hence there must be some managing authority at the head of the whole organization. The chief justice of the entire court is therefore necessary. He should be the head of an executive committee composed of the heads of the several divisions, with full powers of management. The same powers should reside in the court as a whole, if it chooses to exercise them.

VII. That an important cause for dissatisfaction is the attitude of appellate tribunals toward the trial courts, the former frequently administering corrections to the trial judge through reversals. It attempts to discipline and educate by the same means. The result is the trial judge and the appellate tribunal become estranged and in their bickerings the litigant and the public suffer. The remedy for this is obtained by the organization above suggested, where the appellate tribunal and the trial courts are subject to the same central authority, namely, the chief justice and council of judges. By this means trial judges may be corrected and disciplined in a suitable way and by proper authority if they be at fault, without the litigant suffering. The appellate division on the other hand, may be compelled by the same authority to attend solely to the administration of justice and to refrain from exercising the function of educating and disciplining trial judges.

III.

SELECTION OF THE JURY AS JUDGES OF THE FACTS, AND ITS GUIDANCE

DISCRIMINATION IN THE USE OF THE JURY

I. Jurors, when used, are the judges of the facts in controversy. The public service of administering justice consists in part of their mental operations in determining facts. Property and personal rights are subject to the determination of jurors. The subject of the method of their selection, the choice of causes in which their services are used and the guidance of the jury by the court is of great imporance. Defects in any of the three respects mentioned may give rise to serious dissatisfaction with the administration of justice.

II. Methods of selecting jurors. This has several stages.

A. The drawing of panels by jury commissioners.

B. The preliminary examination by the judge and excusing men or finding them disqualified. Where this is performed by the judge for every panel, it is a waste of time and energy and he should be relieved of it and the duties placed upon some less important official acting under the direction of the judge or the presiding justice of division.

C. The examination of jurors when called into the box and sworn to answer questions touching their qualifications. Here is presented the problem of shortening up the examination, preventing abuses in the extent of examination, which may result in great waste of judicial energy. *Quaere:* Whether the extensive examinations permitted do not in part find their justification in the fact that in many states under the present system the jurors obtain no guidance from the court in the performance of their function as judges of the facts.

III. It has been suggested that to meet the case of the absence of a member of the panel in long cases there should be additional jurors, or the taking of a verdict of less than the total number.

IV. It has been suggested that the verdict of less than the entire number of jurors hearing the case be sufficient.

V. Discriminating in the use of jurors:

A. It has been suggested that in some classes of cases jurors are of no value at all, *viz.*, in suits depending upon the construction of documents or the legal rights arising from documents. Their use in this class of cases is now eliminated in chancery causes.

B. It has been suggested that juries are of value where the result depends upon the evidence of witnesses regarding human actions and conduct. In these cases juries are a protection against a one-man view of the evidence. A chance is provided for debate among several minds looking at the evidence and observing the witnesses. A chance is given for an appeal from the experienced judge to the judgment of twelve less specially trained minds.

C. At present the cases where juries are not used and where they are used is to some extent illogical, depending upon historical considerations of whether the cause was originally in chancery or at law. It has been suggested that the matter should be reduced by rules of court or by legislation to a more rational line of distinction between the cases where juries are of special service and where they are of no service. In cases lying between the two extremes juries might be permitted upon application and upon terms.

D. It has been suggested that less than twelve jurors be used, especially in cases involving small amounts.

VI. Expert guidance of the jury by the courts: It has been suggested that as the jury with its numbers is a safeguard against the judge, so the judge with his experience should be a safeguard against the jury; that the two should be responsible together for securing a correct view of the facts. The judge, therefore, should have freedom to give to the jury not only his views of the law, but also in his discretion his analysis of the evidence.

IV.

THE RULES OF PRACTICE AND PROCEDURE

I. It is suggested that there can be no solution of the problem of efficient rules of practice and procedure so long as the rules which are promulgated are made by the legislature and put out in the rigid and unchangeable form of statutes, which can only be altered or amended or repealed by further act of the legislature; that the subject-matter of rules of procedure and practice has to do with the details incident to the rendering of a public service. The matters dealt with are too minute and technical to secure adequate attention from the legislature. Legislative enactments on such details, however satisfactory to start with, are certain in the course of time and with changing conditions, to fail.

II. It is suggested therefore that the first and most important step in the improvement of practice and procedure is for the legislature to place the rule-making power in the hands of the courts, with authority to make readjustments from time to time.

V.

THE METHOD OF SELECTING, RETIRING AND DISCIPLINING OFFICERS OF THE COURTS, THE CLERKS AND THEIR ORGANIZATION AND DUTIES

I. Here the chief causes of inefficiency are to be found in the multiplication of clerks for different courts instead of a central clerk's office; the complete isolation and independence of the separate clerks by reason of the fact that they are elected and subject only to statutory duties and beyond the power of control by the judges.

II. It is suggested also that the fact that they are elected simply hands the filling of these offices over to the political party leaders who for the time being are successful; that this is in fact an appointment and not an election; that an election in the sense of the electorate choosing is out of the question in a metropolitan district because of the inconspicuousness of the office and that, therefore, some method of appointment is inevitable.

III. It is suggested that a much better method of appointment would exist if the chief justice or a judicial council of the court were authorized to appoint one clerk for one central clerk's office, to hold at the pleasure of the appointing power.

VI.

METHODS OF SELECTING, RETIRING AND DISCIPLINING MEMBERS OF THE BAR AND THEIR ORGANIZATION

I. As to the selection, retirement and discipline of members of the bar.

A. As to the methods of selecting lawyers much has been done to raise standards, moral and educational, for admission to the bar. It has been suggested, however, that further steps may be taken, viz.:

1. That two years of general collegiate education be required.
2. That a law school education be required, the period to be the usual one of three years.
3. That admission upon examination at the end of three years law school study permit practice, excluding, however, any right of being heard in the courts in contested matters; that to acquire the right of being heard in such contested matters in each division of a metropolitan court, a period of apprenticeship in practice be required and a further and special examination, oral and written, which would relate to the practice and rules of substantive law handled in the particular division to which admission is desired.
4. It is suggested also that the whole matter of enforcing compliance with rules for admission to the bar be placed in the control of the governing board of a legally incorporated society of all the lawyers (as indicated hereafter under II) which governing board should act under the supervision of the highest appellate tribunal of the State.

B. It has been suggested that our present method of retiring lawyers by disbarment is so cumbersome as to be quite inadequate in a metropolitan district having from five hundred to five thousand lawyers.

1. It has been pointed out that disbarment proceedings are brought in the highest appellate court of the State, where the matter is referred to a referee for the taking of testimony in support of the charges, the referee reporting his conclusions upon the issues. Thereafter there is a trial *de novo* before the full bench of the Supreme Court on the entire evidence as reduced to writing. Such disbarment proceedings are in fact a great burden upon the highest appellate tribunal and take up the valuable time of the most important judicial body of the State over what can be as well done by the governing board of a properly organized bar.
2. As a practical matter the grounds of disbarment are the commission of crimes or very serious offenses involving

the breach of fiduciary obligations and in rare cases, gross fraud and deception of the court. Some courts have even doubted their power to impose lesser penalties, such as suspension from practice for a limited length of time.

3. It has been suggested that to remedy the above conditions the grounds for disbarment should be codified as completely as possible by the Supreme Court, or under its direction, and that the enforcement of the code be conferred upon the governing body of a legally incorporated society of all the lawyers in the metropolitan district, subject only to a review by the courts upon terms fixed by rules promulgated by the highest appellate tribunal.

C. It has been pointed out that for the lesser and more prevalent sorts of unprofessional conduct no authoritative code of conduct for lawyers exists except that contained in the grounds for disbarment. The highest tribunal of the State might issue such a code and provide for its enforcement, but it has not done so. Hence no means now exists for requiring a high standard of conduct from lawyers.

1. It has been suggested, therefore, that the Supreme Court prepare, or have prepared under its direction, an authoritative code of conduct for lawyers.
2. That the enforcement of such a code should be placed in the governing board of an incorporated society of lawyers with possibly a review within limits by the courts, as provided by the rules of the Supreme Court.
3. That for the infraction of the rules of the code of conduct the governing board of the legally incorporated society of lawyers be permitted to punish by the giving of private warnings, public warnings, public resolutions of condemnation and suspension from practice for a limited period.

II. As to the organization of the bar.

A. It has been pointed out that the present organization of lawyers is purely social and voluntary, including in many instances only a small part of the total number of lawyers. It has no such organization or powers as enable it to take charge of admissions to the bar or the matter of disbarment or the discipline of members of the bar and enforcement of an authoritative code of legal ethics.

B. It has been suggested that what is needed is a legally incorported society which shall include all lawyers by the simple process of fixing the fees to be paid and the requiring of every lawyer, as a condition to continuation in practice, to keep up his membership in the society; that the governing board of such society should be composed of representatives elected for a considerable term and that the governing board should have power conferred upon it to enforce the rules of the highest court of the State as to admissions to the bar; also to enforce any authoritative code of legal ethics and disbar members. The governing board might be given power to promulgate a code of legal ethics and to enforce it by suspension from practice for a limited term.

C. It has been suggested that the present bar associations are properly organized and well adapted for the functions which they now perform, namely:

1. Discussion of public questions such as selection of judges, the changes in procedure and substantive law.
2. Social activities.

III. As to the specialization of lawyers with respect to their professional activity.

A. It has been suggested that the same reasons which demand specialization among the judges in the interest of efficiency, require it even more among lawyers. It has been urged that to permit lawyers in a metropolitan district to be heard in any court at will at the same time that they are carrying on all the possible lines of activity which the lawyer touches in the business of the commercial world or in the personal affairs of clients, is to introduce the same sort of disorder and inefficiency as would occur in any large department store if all the employees were allowed to serve the public in any way they saw fit.

B. It has been suggested that the fundamental line of cleavage in the activities of lawyers is between the counselor and the advocate.

1. The position of the Counselor has been thus described: The counselor is the lawyer who has clients. Their affairs, business and personal, so far as they touch the

law, are his principal care. His success is founded in his ability to keep his clients out of trouble; to adjust their differences; to see that the instruments they execute have no pitfalls for them and that their sales and purchases, their creation of trusteeships and organization of corporations, are accomplished within the law. It is the counselor's duty to play safe for his client at all times and to keep him out of difficulty. In a metropolitan district where great business interests center and the wealth of individuals and corporations is very great, the counselor's entire time and energy is frequently given to his special branch of the profession.

The counselor may be an individual lawyer with a small office and a very quiet line of counseling. Frequently several organize in a firm and specialize their counseling somewhat in different directions. Some firms are so large and have such an enormous business that a long list of partners is necessary, many of whose names do not appear in the name of the firm. Many clerks and assistants are employed and different branches of legal business are handled in different departments of the office. Some counselors devote themselves as individuals to special lines of counseling. They are counselors to trust departments of a bank. They are counselors for corporation management and the issuance of corporations' securities or for particular kinds of corporations. Often their offices are with the executive offices of the corporation, or adjacent to the business office of the individual. Sometimes they are independent and serve several corporations or individuals requiring the same sort of counsel.

The counselor with any extensive practice in metropolitan district has no time for work in the courts in important contested matters. The simpler and uncontested work in the courts is performed by clerks, assistants and junior partners under the counselor's direction. The counselor discovers that he loses money whenever he goes into court in a contested case. His clients cannot reach him and he cannot serve them satisfactorily. When the counselor's client becomes involved in important litigation it is economically to the advantage of the counselor to prepare the case fully in view of his complete knowledge of all the affairs of the client, and then to secure the services of a trained advocate who can fully absorb the case and does so under the guidance of the counselor, and then conducts the case through the courts, with or without the co-operation of the counselor, as the counselor prefers.

2. The advocate's line of activity has been thus described: The advocate answers the inevitable demand of the counselor for a well-trained and effective trial lawyer. The advocate makes a business of practicing in the courts in contested cases, especially those of more than usual importance to the parties engaged. His success depends upon the development of individual talent in the handling of litigation in the courts on the civil and criminal side, or both. He must satisfy, not the layman who is a client, but the trained counselor who is able to distinguish ability from bluff. The advocate, therefore, has no time for or interest in the miscellaneous affairs of clients. His energy is concentrated upon the handling of particular cases in the courts. Whatever counseling he may do is merely such as he may contribute at the request of counselors in particular matters where his advice, in view of his experience in the courts, may have particular value. The advocate's days are spent in the preparation of cases for hearing or in actual trials. His earnings accrue as the result of conducting litigation which the counselor decides is necessary or inevitable. Specialization among advocates is probably inevitable. Some will devote themselves to jury trials, civil and criminal, and appeals; others to commercial causes tried with and without a jury, and appeals; others to chancery causes and appeals.

3. It has been suggested that in view of the special development of the counselor in the United States his position must be the more prominent and important branch of the profession. Socially, financially and from the point of view of influence in the community, his is the more desirable position. The advocate is clearly dependent upon the counselor for business and consequently must seek the favor of the counselor. The advo-

cate always stands in the community as an individual with individual talents. He gets nowhere professionally as the member of an organization. He renders always individual and personal service. The financial rewards on the average are comparatively small. He tends toward an interest in the academic side of the law rather than toward a development of commercial and financial astuteness. The advocate, however, chooses his profession because he prefers the work which he selects to that which the counselor does and his own special reward is the attainment of success as an advocate and after a mature experience, a place upon the bench.

C. It has been suggested that a *sine que non* to the development of the distinction between the counselor and the advocate is that the advocate shall not invade the sphere of activity of the counselor by dealing with clients and that the counselor in return shall not undertake the handling of contested matters in the courts except as he does so in cooperation with the advocate. The latter rule is a fair exchange for the former. The keeping of the advocate away from handling clients is absolutely necessary as a guarantee that a popular advocate who has a public following shall not steal the clients of a counselor.

D. The advantages of such specialization among lawyers have been put forward as follows:

1. These advantages are very great from the point of view of the individual. He has a chance for more agreeable work by reason of the specialization, and also in case of success, an opportunity for greater profits.

2. From the point of view of the public the advantages are:

(a) The specialization furnishes a service test for candidates for judgeships, since judges would for the most part be selected from those who specialize in the handling of contentious business in the courts.

(b) The motives for expediting the work of the courts by the lawyers are vastly increased.

(1) The lawyer handling contentious business in the courts wishes to go ahead with trials as rapidly as possible, since his income depends upon doing this work.

(2) The client wishes work in the courts done

expeditiously because he is paying an expert for special services.

(c) Greater assistance is rendered the court. Court and advocate can drive at the main point of controversy with the greatest speed. The advocate can eliminate much that he knows by experience to be not worth presenting without fear of injuring the client's cause.

(d) False and fraudulent claims and ill-founded suits are more easily than now to be discouraged because the advocate must protect his standing with the court.

(e) Greater knowledge of the rules of the courts by the bar is developed and the criticism and scrutiny of the judge's work is much closer and holds the judge much more in check than the present system.

(f) There is better service to the client.

(1) Legal business better attended to.

(2) Litigation more quickly reached and disposed of.

(3) Better representation on the firing line in litigation.

(4) Better preparation for trial.

(g) Overcontentiousness would be reduced because the advocate must protect his standing with the court.

(h) The objection that a separation of the advocate from the counselor is a bad thing is founded largely in the sentiment and pride of present members of the profession, all of whom call themselves members of the bar, and have freedom to range the courts when and where they please. It is said also that a man who is in touch with the client's entire affairs prepares a case better for trial. But even when an advocate is employed the client's regular counselor has the chief burden of the case's preparation and there is no reason why the advocate should not have the greatest freedom of intercourse with the client and the witnesses in preparing cases for trial. No canons of professional etiquette should ever be allowed to keep the advocate from direct contact with the client and his witnesses, or separate the counselor from easy conference with the advocate while in court. As for the counselor's pride in having free audience in the court, that should not stand in the way of efficiency in the work of the courts and the service rendered clients.

E. It is suggested that such specialization among lawyers may be promoted in the following ways:

1. The competitive method: Under this the advocate makes it clear that the counselor cannot compete with him in the handling of litigation in the courts. This results in the following developments:

(a) Large firms of counselors, with large and varied clients, employ one or more advocates to give all their time to the litigated work of the firm.

It has been suggested, however, that this is a transition stage only, because

(1) It does not provide any way for the smaller firms of counselors and single counselors to secure expert advocacy without running the risk of losing their clients to the big firms of counselors.

(2) It has the disadvantage of cutting off the large firm of counselors from securing the best advocate for the particular case. It requires the employment of the same advocates for all sorts of cases.

(3) This arrangement is unsatisfactory to the advocate in the long run, for he finds it continually more difficult to become expert when he must deal with the difficult cases arising in a metropolitan district handling many thousands of important cases in all branches of the substantive law and practice.

(b) The moment the system whereby an advocate gives all his time to a firm of counselors begins to break down the individual advocate appears. He first answers the demand of smaller firms and individual counselors who wish to secure expert advocacy in particular cases, and by restricting the field of his advocacy he is able to compete successfully in his line with the advocates employed by the big firms who must cover a very much wider field.

2. The slightly coercive method: This involves the imposition of special requirements for admission to practice in the courts in the handling of contested matters and trials, *viz.*:
   (a) First, a general admission to practice as counselor.
   (b) Practicing as a counselor for a limited term.
   (c) Then a special examination for admission to practice as an advocate in each trial division of the metropolitan court.
   (d) This might result in many persons staying out of practice in contentious matters, especially in courts where they never expected to practice. It would tend to cause one who had taken the trouble to secure admission to practice in particular divisions, to practice there and to receive a share of contested causes heard in those divisions.
   (e) This plan leaves every lawyer free to practice both as a counselor and as an advocate, but imposes special requirements on practicing as an advocate which would tend to cause anyone so practicing and succeeding to devote himself largely to advocacy.
   (f) It should be a rigid rule, even under this system, that any lawyer practicing as an advocate should be barred from ever or for a considerable time dealing as a counselor with any client whom he represented as an advocate for any counselor.
3. Compulsory division:
   (a) The counselor might be ruled out of all audiences in the courts in contested causes except as he appeared associated with an advocate and the advocate might be ruled entirely out of the sphere of the counselor, and the requirements for admission to each branch of the profession might be fixed independently, with the right of any member of either branch of the profession to transfer to the other branch.

APPENDIX B

Model Metropolitan Court Act, American Judicature Society

HOW TO UNIFY THE COURTS OF A LARGE CITY[1]

CONSOLIDATE all existing courts into a single Metropolitan Court with a chief justice as executive head.

FIXED DIVISIONS: Create from three to six divisions, depending upon the number of judges, and distribute the judges among them. The divisions are to represent the principal classes of proceedings, as criminal, civil jury, equity, probate and civil non-jury.

PRESIDING JUSTICES: Give to each such division a presiding justice who shall control the calendars by classifying causes, and shall assign the judges of his division to special calendars.

JUDICIAL COUNCIL: Organize responsibility for the proper business management of the court by establishing an executive board composed of the chief justice and presiding justices.

RULE-MAKING AND ADMINISTRATIVE POWERS: Confirm in the judicial council the power to make and modify rules of procedure subject to legislative correction; repeal existing procedural acts as statutes but continue them as rules of court; confer the power to assign and transfer judges and to control the clerk and other officers of the court.

CLASSES OF JUDGES: Confer upon every judge of the unified court complete trial jurisdiction at law, in chancery and as to crimes; if expedient provide that certain of the judges blanketed into the new court shall be junior judges, having complete trial jurisdiction, but ineligible to appointment as presiding justices, and entitled to less salary than senior judges. The junior judges should be eligible to promotion whenever a vacancy occurs among the senior judges.

MASTERS: Permit the judicial council to employ masters for such divisions as may require them, to serve subject to the rules made and under the direction of presiding justices.

MEETINGS: Require judges of divisions to meet monthly and the judges of the entire court to meet at least once a year; special meetings to be subject to call.

[1] 1 J. AM. JUD. SOC'Y 178 (April 1918).

ORGANIZATION PLAN FOR A METROPOLITAN DISTRICT COURT
Chart taken from 1 J. AM. JUD. SOC'Y 164 (April 1918)

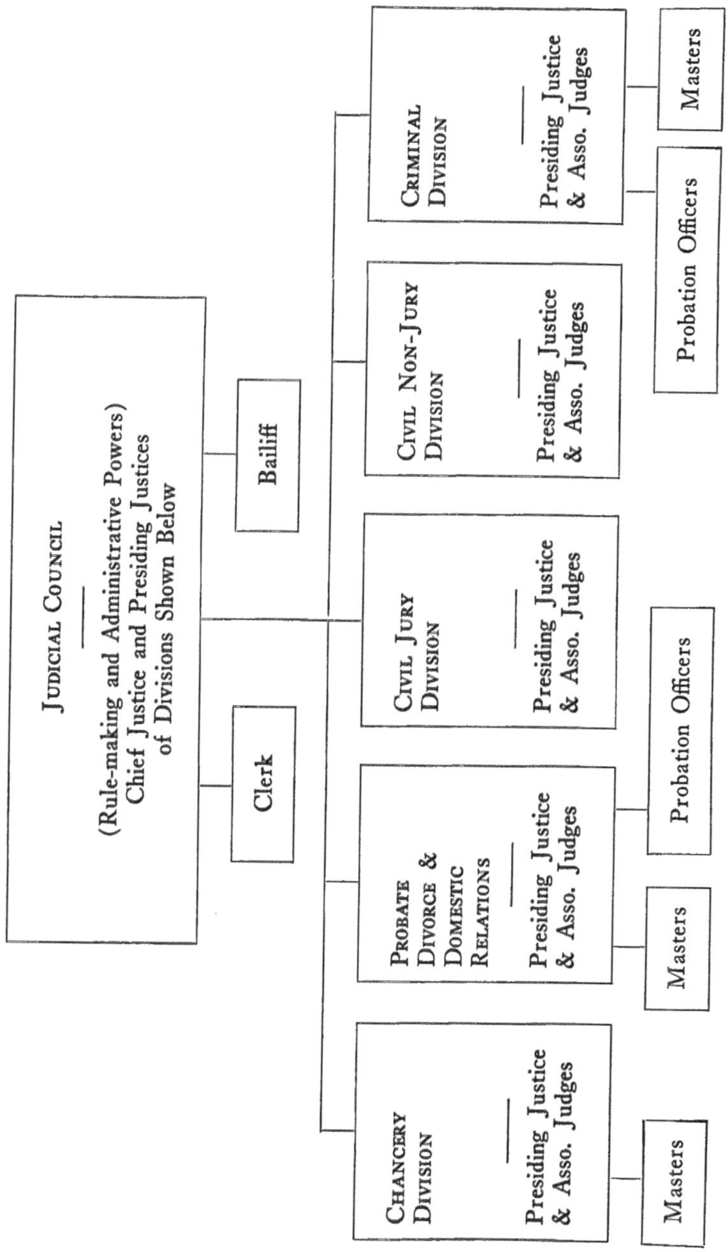

Reports: Require the chief justice to submit a report annually showing the business of every division and of the entire court in detailed classification; require monthly reports of presiding justices of division.

Clerk: Consolidate all existing clerks' offices into one, provide for the selection of a clerk and his deputies by the judicial council.

Officers: Make the police of the city deputy bailiffs for the service of all process; confer in the judicial council power to employ such other officers as are needed for the court's purposes.

BULLETIN IV-B

AMERICAN JUDICATURE SOCIETY
to Promote the Efficient Administration of Justice

SECOND DRAFT of a Model Act to ESTABLISH A COURT for a METROPOLITAN DISTRICT

PROPOSED CONSTITUTIONAL AMENDMENT[1]

Be it **RESOLVED** by the Senate [or House of Representatives] of the General Assembly of the state of ______________, that the following amendment to Article _____ of the constitution of this State be proposed and that the same be submitted to the electors of the State pursuant to Article _____, Section _____, of said constitution.

There shall be added to Article _____ [naming the judicial article of the constitution] of the constitution the following sections, which shall be known as Sections _____ of said Article.

SECTION _____ **Removal of Limitation upon the Power of the Legislature.**]

The provisions of this article, which limit the power of the legislature with respect to

The creation and organization of any court or courts in the [here name the metropolitan district], or

The methods of selecting and retiring the judges of such court or courts, or

The rules of practice and procedure therein,

Shall remain in force

Subject to the power of the legislature to alter, amend and repeal the same; and

Subject to any alteration, amendment and repeal which may occur by reason of the adoption of Schedule A as herein provided.[2]

* * *

SECTION _____ **Submission of Schedule A.**] At the time of the submission of this amendment to the constitution for adoption, there

[1] See original text for "Note on the Necessity of a Constitutional Amendment to Support the Model Act Presented," 1 BULLS. AM. JUD. SOC'Y, Bull. IV-B at 5 (Jan. 1916).

[2] See p. 8, original text, for note on importance of framing constitutional amendment not as grant of power, but as release of restrictions upon power of legislature.

shall also be submitted, in accordance with the provisions thereof, Schedule A hereto attached.[3]

* * *

SECTION ——— **Schedule A, if adopted, to be in force.]** If upon the adoption of this amendment to the constitution there shall also be adopted Schedule A hereto attached, then until otherwise provided by any Act of the legislature, the provisions of said schedule shall be in full force and effect.

SECTION ——— **Powers conferred upon the legislature.]** The legislature shall be deemed under this constitution to have power sufficient at least to have enacted into law all and each and every part of the Act contained in said Schedule A.

SECTION ——— **Effect of this amendment if it amends more than one article.]** If this amendment shall be deemed or held to amend more than one article of the constitution contrary to any provision of the constitution, such part of it as amends Article ——— [naming the article relating to the judicial department] of this constitution and no more shall stand as an amendment to this constitution.[4]

* * *

SCHEDULE A

An Act to Create the Metropolitan Court of [here name the Metropolitan District] **and to Provide for the Practice and Procedure Therein.**

Be it enacted by the People of the State of ———, Represented in the General Assembly as follows:

PART I

Constitution and Judges of the Metropolitan Court

SECTION 1. **Consolidation of courts.]** The following courts: [here name the courts (except any intermediate appellate court) which

[3] See p. 9, original text, for note.
[4] See p. 10, original text, for note.

operate in the district] shall be united and shall constitute under and subject to the provisions of this act one Metropolitan Court for [here name the metropolitan district].[5]

* * *

SECTION 2. **Present judgeships not abolished but continued in the office of judge of the Metropolitan Court.]** Upon the expiration of the terms of office respectively of the judges of [here name all the courts united by this Act], said offices shall not be filled in the manner hitherto provided by law, but the same shall be deemed filled by such one or more of the judges of the Metropolitan Court of ______ as may be entitled to exercise all or any part of the jurisdiction or power heretofore exercised by the judges of the courts united by this Act.[6]

* * *

SECTION 3. **Abolition of Justices of the Peace.]** From and after the expiration of the terms of office of the present justices of the peace respectively, the office of justice of the peace so far as it is judicial in its nature shall be abolished and all jurisdiction of justices of the peace to exercise any part of the judicial power of the State in the [here name the metropolitan district] shall thereupon cease.[7]

SECTION 4. **First Judges of the Metropolitan Court—Selection and Tenure.]** The first judges of the Metropolitan Court shall be

The Chief Justice;

[5] In original text, p. 11, there follows an explanatory note, reading in part as follows: "The first step in the reorganization of the courts of a metropolitan district by wiping out all hard and fast lines of jurisdiction is accomplished by this first section. The fact that all the courts are united into one court does not mean that all judicial business will be transacted by any judge of the court. The court, as appears hereafter, will be separated into divisions for the dispatch of different specialized sorts of judicial business. It is only the arbitrary jurisdictional lines which require a case brought in the wrong court to be entirely dismissed out of court and commenced over again that are to be obliterated *in limine*. By this means waste in judicial power is avoided and the foundation is laid for the fullest exercise of judicial power by freeing from jurisdictional difficulties and prohibitions the transfer of all judges from one division to another and the assignment of judicial business as may be most expedient for its disposal. It should be remembered that the notion of a fixed jurisdiction within a single state is nothing but a relic from the days when Kings Bench, Exchequer, Common Pleas and Chancery competed with each other for power.

If the jurisdiction of justice of the peace courts is not included in the jurisdiction of other courts, then the justice of the peace courts should also be united with the others."

[6] See p. 13, original text, for explanatory note.

[7] See p. 14, original text, for explanatory note.

All the judges of the [here name all the courts united by this Act], and

_______ additional judges.

The Chief Justice and the additional judges respectively shall be selected in the manner and for the term hereinafter provided.

The term of the judicial office of each of the other judges respectively shall be the same as it was before the taking effect of this Act.[8]

* * *

SECTION 5. **All judges to have in general equal power, authority and jurisdiction—senior and junior associate judges.]** All the judges of the Metropolitan Court shall have in all respects save as in this Act otherwise expressly provided, equal power, authority and jurisdiction.

The judges of the Metropolitan Court, other than the Chief Justice, shall be associate justices.

Those associate justices who were at the commencement of this Act judges of the [here name the courts of appellate and general and superior jurisdiction united by this Act, the judges of which received a salary higher than other judges sitting in courts of inferior and limited jurisdiction] shall be senior associate justices.

All the other judges of the Metropolitan Court shall be junior associate justices.

The number of senior and junior associate justices shall remain respectively the same as upon the taking effect of this Act.[9]

[8] See p. 15, original text, for explanatory note.

[9] See p. 16, original text, for explanatory note, quoted in part hereinafter:

"This section makes clear the general principle that all the judges of the Metropolitan Court are to have in general equal judicial power, authority and jurisdiction. There is not to be one set of judges held aloof for the more important work and guarded against doing judicial business usually allotted to inferior courts in handling the simple civil and criminal cases. Nor is another set of judges to be committed irrevocably to the hearing of what are sometimes called petty cases, civil and criminal, and those alone. The true view is that every man's cause may be as important to him and to the state as any other man's. There are no petty causes.

* * *

". . . There must be an abandonment of the idea that the simpler civil and criminal cases shall always be handled by a judge who is marked from every point of view as inferior. If the handling of these cases is the weakest spot in the administration of justice by the court, there should be the power to send into this work the strongest men the court possesses.

"There are several grounds for making a difference between junior and senior judges.

"One is to avoid friction in uniting a Municipal Court having inferior

SECTION 6. **Masters of the Metropolitan Court.]** There shall be attached to the Metropolitan Court such number of masters, not exceeding ——, as the judicial council hereinafter mentioned shall determine.

They shall exercise all or such part of the judicial power of the Metropolitan Court and perform such duties in respect to the business

Of said court, or

Of any branch thereof, or

Of the office of the clerk of the Metropolitan Court,

as may be provided for by this Act or by any rules or orders of the judicial council hereinafter mentioned.

They shall be selected as hereinafter provided.[10]

SECTION 7. **Abolition of the present Masters in Chancery.]** The present masters in chancery of the [here name the courts united by this act of which masters are officers] shall continue to hold office until the expiration of their respective terms of office and until that time they shall be additional masters under this Act, with the same powers and duties and the same mode of compensation as before the commencement of this Act. When and as the terms respectively of each of said masters in chancery shall expire, their said office shall cease to exist.[11]

---

jurisdiction with a Superior Court of general jurisdiction, making the judges of both courts the first judges of the consolidated court. . . .

"The grounds for making this distinction permanent are as follows:

"Where there is a large volume of judicial business of all sorts to be handled by a large corps of judges and the judicial business differs widely in character, a great deal of it may be satisfactorily done by younger men of less judicial experience who start at a less salary and commence with the handling of the less difficult, the less responsible and often less agreeable work, with a view to developing a capacity for handling the more difficult, more responsible and often more agreeable business of the court. The situation is not different from that in any executive office or in a firm with a large number of partners. . . .

"The saving of money spent in salaries is not the only reason for having junior judges. Human nature is such that it needs the stimulus of possible promotion. To give a man a position in which he is to stay for the rest of his life with no promotional steps ahead which he may compete for is to discourage endeavor and stifle ambition. This is recognized in every business enterprise. . . ."

[10] See p. 20, original text, for explanatory note.

[11] See p. 22, original text, for explanatory note.

PART II

Selection and Retirement of Judges and Masters

[Here insert the sections appropriate to one of the plans for the selection and retirement of judges appearing in Bulletin IV-A.[12]

The plans there suggested may for convenience be here summarized as follows:

First Plan: Appointment by the governor and retirement by impeachment, or removal by the governor upon the address of both houses of the legislature—the Massachusetts plan. (6 Sections.)

Second Plan: Selection of the Chief Justice and associate judges by popular vote, to hold for an indefinite tenure and until retired in any one of the following ways: (1) By impeachment; (2) By removal by the legislature; (3) By retirement by popular vote at a special retirement election held periodically at the end of four, twelve and twenty years from the date of selection, at which retirement election the only question presented to the voter would be "Shall the judge be continued in office?" (23 Sections.)

Third Plan: Election of the Chief Justice for a short term of years; the appointment of associate judges by him to hold until retired in any one of the following ways: (1) By impeachment; (2) By removal by the legislature; (3) By removal by the judicial council for cause shown and after a hearing; (4) By retirement by popular vote at a special retirement election held periodically at the end of three, nine and eighteen years from the date of selection, at which retirement election the only question presented to the voter would be "Shall the judge be continued in office?" (29 Sections)

Fourth Plan: The same as the third plan except that retirement by popular vote at a special retirement election is omitted. (23 Sections.)

SECTION 38. **Qualifications for the office of master.]** Only citizens of the United States who have

1. Been admitted to the bar in any court of record of the United States or of any State, and
2. Practiced law for not less than five years, and
3. Resided for not less than one year in the State,

shall be eligible to become a master of the Metropolitan Court.

SECTION 39. **Appointment of Masters.]** The Judicial Council hereinafter mentioned shall from time to time determine what number from among all the masters shall be attached regularly to each division of the court.

[12] Bulletin IV-A, American Judicature Society, is found in the bound volume 1-6 BULL. AM. JUD. SOC'Y., under date of April 1915.

Masters shall be appointed by the Chief Justice and the Presiding Justice of the division to which each respectively is to be regularly attached.

In case of disagreement the Presiding Justice of one of the other divisions, to be determined by lot, shall be the third member of the selecting committee and shall vote only for the nominee of the Chief Justice or the nominee of the Presiding Justice of the division.[13]

SECTION 40. **Removal of masters from office.]** Masters may be removed from office for reasons assigned in the order of removal by the Chief Justice, with the approval of the presiding judge of the division to which the master is regularly attached.

PART III

Jurisdiction

SECTION 41. **Jurisdiction conferred upon the Metropolitan Court.]** The Metropolitan Court established by this Act shall be a court of record.

There shall be conferred upon and vested in such court,

1. All original jurisdiction;
2. All the jurisdiction and powers

   Of [here name the courts united by this Act] as constituted before the taking effect of this Act,

   Or capable of being exercised by all or any one or more of the judges of said courts respectively, sitting in court or chambers or elsewhere, when acting as a judge or judges in pursuance of any statute, law or custom;
3. All powers given to any such court or to any such judge or judges by any statute, and
4. Ministerial powers, duties and authorities incidental to any and every part of the jurisdiction so transferred.

It is proper to confer upon the court all original jurisdiction, civil and criminal, and in law or equity, so that the chances of the jurisdiction in any case turning upon the historical question of what jurisdiction the courts consolidated had may be as far as possible eliminated.

On the other hand, it is wise to confer jurisdiction by reference to the jurisdiction administered by the courts consolidated by the act, so that any peculiar or special jurisdiction which they may have exercised shall not be inadvertently lost.

[13] Explanatory note of p. 24, original text.

SECTION 42. **Transfer to the Metropolitan Court of duties and powers other than judicial.]** If in any case not expressly provided for by this Act, a liability to any duty or any authority or power not incident to the administration of justice in any court whose jurisdiction is transferred by this Act to the Metropolitan Court, shall have been imposed or conferred by any statute, law or custom, upon the judges, or any judge of any such courts, every judge of the said Metropolitan Court shall be capable of performing and exercising, and shall be liable to perform and empowered to exercise every such duty, authority and power in the same manner as if this Act had not been passed and as if he had been duly appointed the successor of a judge liable to such duty or possessing such authority or power before the taking effect of this Act.

Provided, however, that the Chief Justice,

1. May perform wholly or in part said duties, or exercise such authority and powers on behalf of the Metropolitan Court; or
2. May assign, either wholly or in part, the performance of such duties and the exercise of such authority and powers to such judge or judges respectively as he may in his discretion determine.[14]

PART IV

Sittings and Distribution of Business

SECTION 43. **Terms retained for special purposes—Court may sit at any time and in any place within the district.]** In all cases in which under the law as now existing, the terms into which the legal year is divided are used as a measure for determining the time at or within which any process is required to be returned, or any act is required to be done, the same may continue to be referred to for the same or like purposes, unless and until provision is otherwise made by any lawful authority or by the Judicial Council.

Subject to rules of the said Judicial Council the Metropolitan Court shall have power to sit and act at any time and in any place within the district for the transaction of any part of the business of such court, or of such judges, or for the discharge of any duty which by act of the legislature or otherwise, is required to be discharged during or after term.

SECTION 44. **Time and place of sittings of the Court.]** Sittings of the different divisions of the Metropolitan Court shall be held at such time and at such places as may be provided by the Judicial Council,

[14] Explanatory note, p. 29, original text.

and the different branches of the different divisions shall be held as may be determined by the said Judicial Council, and subject thereto all branches of the Metropolitan Court shall be held as the courts united by this Act were held, as nearly as may be.

SECTION 45. **Power of Judicial Council to make rules relating to vacations.]** The Judicial Council of the Metropolitan Court hereinafter mentioned, with the consent of the Chief Justice, shall have power to make, revoke or modify orders regulating the vacations to be observed by the Metropolitan Court and in the respective offices of said court; and any order of the said Council made pursuant to this section, shall, so long as it continues in force, be of the same effect as if it were contained in this Act.

NOTE ON DISTRIBUTION OF JUDICIAL BUSINESS

INTRODUCTORY

This section deals only with the number of divisions, their names and the number of judges holding the regularly constituted places in each.

No determination, however, can be made upon these features until we decide in general how the judicial business of the court is to be distributed. This leads necessarily to a classification of the entire judicial business of the Metropolitan Court. All of it falls into the following groups of related matters:

(1) Civil causes in which a jury cannot be demanded or in which the jury's verdict, if permitted in some cases, is purely advisory. The basis for this class of judicial business is the historical jurisdiction of the court of chancery. It involves not merely the absence of jury trial but also the administration of the extraordinary remedy of injunction, decrees for specific performance, receivers, etc.

(2) Civil causes in which a jury may be demanded as of right but where the service rendered by the jury is of comparatively little importance and where the parties are easily induced to waive trial by jury, viz., many contract cases, ejectment, mandamus, etc.

(3) Civil causes in which a jury may be demanded and is as a matter of practice regularly called for. For instance, actions for damages for torts.

(4) Probate business. There is great deal of administrative work connected with this. Many of the questions which arise are settled by the rules worked out in the chancery courts of England.

(5) Domestic relations, divorces and the administration of the Juvenile Court Act and Acts for non-support, etc. There is much administrative work connected with the exercise of jurisdiction in these cases, especially in the Juvenile Court cases where the court is assisted by an extensive corps of juvenile officers who are really, like masters in chancery, assistants to the judge.

(6) Taxes, special assessments, elections. There is much administrative work connected with the exercise of jurisdiction in these cases.

(7) Criminal causes where the verdict of a jury is required.

(8) Criminal causes where a jury may be waived and is waived.

(9) Examinations in criminal causes where no jury need be used.

THE CHANCERY AND PROBATE AND DOMESTIC RELATIONS DIVISIONS

Out of these classes of judicial business it is not difficult to find occupation for two substantial divisions, each composed of several judges and each dealing with a wide but related field of work.

First: There are two radically different sorts of relief given by courts in civil cases. One is the judgment for damages. The other is specific performance or specific prevention by injunction and the administration of property by receivers. The principles upon which these different sorts of relief are given are so different and the subject involved in the administration of each sort of remedy are so extensive and so such an extent practically (though not necessarily) exclusive of each other, that any specialization in the work of courts ought to be fundamentally along this line.

The question of what names should be given to the two divisions—the one handling the remedy by damages and the other the remedy by specific performance, injunction and receiverships—is immaterial. It is just as well, however, if the name suggests the fact that each division for the most part handles the remedy with which its name is associated.

To divide causes into those tried by a jury and those not so tried, and to place each in a separate division, would, it is believed, not produce as good results. It is true that judges trying cases in which juries are not used and specific performance or prevention is decreed, must determine questions of fact and therefore become adept in so doing. This gives them a certain qualification for handling cases tried without a jury in which only damages are asked. Nevertheless the judge who handles the rules applied in suits involving specific performance, injunction and receiverships must master a field of substantive law which is quite wide enough to keep him busy without his being forced as a novice from time to time into the trial of causes without a jury involving subjects of substantive law with which he does not ordinarily deal. If any judges are required for the trial of causes in which only damages are sought and in which trial by jury is waived, let them be taken from the corps of judges regularly assigned to the administration of the remedy involving the assessment of damages.

These remarks apply, of course, to a metropolitan district where there is a substantial volume of business involving decrees for specific performance, injunctions, receivers, construction of instruments in writing, and decrees *in personam* generally, to keep judges and a corps of masters busy all the time.

Second: It would be natural to place probate business, divorce and juvenile court cases, in a single division. The judicial work here is not so much in hearing individual contested cases as in handling an enormous amount of uncontested business. There is more administration here than contested business. The same is true of causes involving general taxation, special assessments and elections. It might be wise to place all this judicial business in one division. Where the total number of judges exceeded sixty this division would probably not require more than three or four judges. The branches held by each one could subdivide the business, viz., probate to one judge and his assistants; juvenile court to another and his assistants; taxation, special assessments and elections to a third, with his assistants; divorce, and other matters to a fourth, with his assistants. Arrangements of business among the several judges of the division should, however, be left to the Presiding Justice of the Division. It is impossible to formulate any plans for such a division in advance, either by rules of court or by the Act.

This division would naturally be called the probate and domestic relations division.

PLANS FOR HANDLING RESIDUE OF JUDICIAL BUSINESS

The difficult question then remains: what shall we do with the judicial business included in (1) civil cases, (a) in which a jury may be demanded but is usually waived, (b) and those in which it is regularly insisted upon; and (2) criminal cases, (a) where a jury is required, (b) where the jury may be waived and usually is, and (c) examinations where no jury at all is used.

The situation admits of a considerable variety of plans. The residue of judicial business in question may be divided among three divisions, two divisions, or all given to a single division. . . .[15]

SECTION 46. **Separation of the court into five divisions.]** For more convenient dispatch of business (but not so as to prevent any judge from sitting when required in any court or division other than his own) there shall be in the Metropolitan Court five divisions consisting of the number of judges hereinafter mentioned, that is to say:

(1) The Equity [or Chancery] division, consisting regularly of ______ judges.[16]

(2) The Probate and Domestic Relations Division, consisting regularly of ______ judges.

(3) The Civil Jury division, consisting regularly of ______ judges.

[15] The balance of this long note is omitted. See pp. 36 *et seq.*, original text.
[16] P. 41, original text, contains note commenting on this division of labor.

(4) The Civil Non-Jury division, consisting regularly of ____ judges.[17]

(5) The Criminal division, consisting regularly of ____ judges.

It should be observed that this section does not arbitrarily fix the number of judges in each division. The increase or decrease of the number of judges is provided for in the powers of the Judicial Council, *post*, sec. 70.

The number of divisions is, however, fixed by the Act and cannot be changed without legislative action. The power of the judicial council, however, to make rules regarding the assignment of business to one division or another, *post*, sec. 70, introduces a considerable flexibility in the arrangement of classes of causes to be heard by the different divisions.

The reason for making the number of divisions permanent and determining their general character is to indicate a legislative policy that there shall be specialization of effort and that the fundamental outlines of the plan are not to be too lightly abrogated by the judges themselves. At the same time full power is lodged in the Judicial Council to make considerable readjustments as to the practical working out of the division of business.

SECTION 47. **Assignment of judges to each of said divisions.]** The regularly constituted places in the divisions of the said Metropolitan Court shall, upon the organization of the said Metropolitan Court under this Act, be filled by the assignment of the Chief Justice from among all the judges of the Metropolitan Court.

SECTION 48. **Presiding Justices of divisions.]** Each of said divisions of the Metropolitan Court shall have a Presiding Justice, who shall be appointed by the Chief Justice from among the senior judges of the division over which he presides.

No provision is made for the Chief Justice becoming a Presiding Justice of any division. He will assign himself to judicial work as his opportunities permit.

In order that he shall be the Chief of the Presiding Justices, it is provided, *post*, sec. 52, that he may exercise in his discretion the powers conferred upon the Presiding Justices of divisions.

SECTION 49. **Powers of Presiding Justices of divisions.]** Such Presiding Justice shall, subject to the rules and regulations of the Judicial Council hereinafter mentioned,

(1) Have the control and management of the calling by the judges sitting in his division of the docket of cases assigned to his division;

[17] P. 42, original text, contains note.

(2) Superintend the preparation of the calendar of cases for trial in his division; and

(3) Make such classifications and distribution of the same upon different calendars, to be called by different judges, as he shall deem proper and expedient.

These are ample powers to enable a Presiding Justice of a division to see that each case assigned to his division shall go to one judge for all purposes, thereby avoiding the confusion and waste of time caused by different judges hearing the same case at different stages.

SECTION 50. **Tenure of Presiding Justices of divisions.]** Each Presiding Justice shall hold his office during the period of his judicial tenure.

SECTION 51. **Acting Presiding Justices.]** Upon the occurrence of a vacancy in the office of Presiding Justice of any division the judge of the division who shall have been longest a judge of the Metropolitan Court shall become the acting Presiding Justice and shall hold said office till the vacancy shall be filled by the Chief Justice.

In case two or more judges shall have served the same length of time, the acting Presiding Justice shall be selected from them by lot.

SECTION 52. **Powers of Presiding Justices to be exercised by Chief Justice.]** In addition to the powers by this Act conferred upon him, the Chief Justice shall have and exercise in his discretion any and all powers conferred upon the Presiding Justice of any division of the Metropolitan Court.

This insures the position of the Chief Justice as the administrative head of the court and the proper subordination to him of the Presiding Justices of divisions.

SECTION 53. **Tenure of places in divisions.]** The appointees to the regularly constituted places in the several divisions of the Metropolitan Court shall hold such places during the period of their judicial tenure or until they shall have been transferred to a regularly constituted place in another division in the manner herein provided.

In a municipal court of limited jurisdiction in civil and criminal causes having fifteen to thirty judges, it is no doubt advisable that a single Chief Justice should have full power in his discretion to assign judges to different sorts of work and to classify the business of the court. This principle is carried into the present Act by giving the Presiding Justice of each division of the court full power to classify the work of his division and to assign the judges of the division to different sorts of work in the division. In short, intradivisional assignment is entirely in the hands of the Presiding Justice of each division.

If the court for the Metropolitan District has fifteen judges or less the feature of fixed divisions may very properly be eliminated. The Chief Justice would exercise all the powers conferred upon Presiding Justices of divisions and would have power to assign judges to their work in any way that he deemed expedient. The same power might be given to the Chief Justice where there were thirty judges and two divisions each with a Presiding Justice.

When, however, we come to the metropolitan district with a million inhabitants and over and from thirty-five to seventy judges, and with the enormous mass of judicial business of a more fixed and permanent specialization by the judges is demanded in the interests of efficiency. The consequence is a higher degree of expertness in each field and a consequent inability to undertake effectively judicial work of a widely different sort. For instance, the judge who has been for five or six years working to become an expert chancery judge in a metropolitan district which can keep four or six such judges and eight or twelve masters busy all the time with difficult litigation, will find himself utterly out of his element if suddenly placed in charge of an important jury trial, civil or criminal, in the common law division. . . . These considerations require that in the court for the larger metropolitan districts the judge's place in one of the four main divisions of the court be protected to some extent from the power of free transfer by the Chief Justice. Section 53 as it appears in the Act presented is drawn with a view to fair compromise between too much power of transfer in the Chief Justice and too little.

SECTION 54. **Filling vacancies in divisions.]** When a vacancy shall occur in one of the regularly constituted places in any division of the Metropolitan Court the same may be filled,

1. By the assignment by the Chief Justice of any judge newly appointed a judge of the Metropolitan Court and not already assigned to any regularly constituted place in any division of the court; or

2. By the assignment by the Chief Justice from among any judges of the Metropolitan Court already occupying regularly constituted places in other divisions;

a. Provided, always, that the Presiding Justice of the division in which the judge assigned shall have held a regularly constituted place shall consent to said assignment and transfer.

SECTION 55. **Transfer of Judges.]** The Chief Justice shall in his discretion have power to interchange judges, other than Presiding Justices of divisions from one division to another, so that each will occupy the regularly constituted place in the division formerly occupied by the other; provided always, that the Presiding Justice of at least one of the divisions affected shall consent thereto.

SECTION 56. **Power of Chief Justice to make temporary assignments and to assign judges not occupied.]** The Chief Justice shall, in his discretion, have power

1. To make temporary assignments for a period not to exceed six months of any judge of any division, except Presiding Justices, to any other division, and
2. To require any judge of the Metropolitan Court who shall not for the time being be occupied in the transaction of any business assigned to the division to which he may regularly be attached, to take part in the sittings of any branch or of any division of the Metropolitan Court.

SECTION 57. **Masters—their functions and assignment.]** Masters shall be eligible to sit in any court or to discharge any judicial function, provided, that a lawful authority expressed in writing shall be conferred upon them by the Judicial Council hereinafter mentioned.

Until then the duties of the masters shall be those now required and permitted by law to masters in chancery.

After the appointment of masters as hereinbefore provided and their attachment regularly to a particular division of the Metropolitan Court, they shall be subject to assignment to any other division of the Metropolitan Court by the Chief Justice in his discretion, with the consent of the Presiding Justice in the division to which said master is regularly attached.

SECTION 58. **Assignment of causes by rules of court.]** All causes and matters which may be commenced in or which shall be transferred by this Act to the Metropolitan Court, shall be distributed among the several divisions and judges in such manner as may from time to time be determined by any rules of court or orders of transfer to be made under the authority of this Act.

In the meantime and subject thereto, all such causes and matters shall be assigned to said divisions respectively in the manner hereinafter provided.[18]

SECTION 59. **Assignment of causes to the Equity division.]** There shall be assigned (subject to rules of court as aforesaid) to the Equity [or Chancery] division:

(1) All causes and matters pending on the chancery side of the

[18] Note at p. 49, original text.

[here name the court of general jurisdiction, the jurisdiction of which has been transferred to the Metropolitan Court] upon the taking effect of this Act.

(2) All causes and matters to be commenced after the taking effect of this Act, which before the taking effect of this Act might have been heard upon the chancery side of the [here name the same last mentioned court] except divorce cases and all cases brought under the Juvenile Court Act.[19]

SECTION 60. **Causes assigned to the Probate and Domestic Relations division.]** There shall be assigned (subject to rules of court as aforesaid) to the Probate and Domestic Relations division:

(1) All causes and matters pending in the [here name the court having probate jurisdiction and any other court having special and limited jurisdiction other than the Municipal Court or justices of the peace, the jurisdiction whereof has been transferred to the Metropolitan Court] at the time of the taking effect of this Act.

(2) All causes and matters commenced after the taking effect of this Act which might before the taking effect of this Act have been commenced in the [here name the last mentioned court or courts]; also all divorce cases and suits for separate maintenance and support and also all matters and causes arising under the Juvenile Court Act [here mention other special Acts under which causes originate which would be appropriate to a domestic relations division, such as the Widows' Pension Act or the Wife Desertion Act]; provided, however [here insert provision which will cause a review of the probate division causes to be made directly by the appropriate Appellate Court on the record made in the probate division, without any trial *de novo*.][20]

SECTION 61. **Assignment of causes to the Civil Jury division.]** There shall be assigned (subject as aforesaid) to the civil jury division:

(1) All civil causes pending at the taking effect of this Act in any Court, the jurisdiction whereof is transferred by this Act to the Metropolitan Court, which require, in the absence of any waiver thereof by the parties, a trial by jury, and in which a trial by jury has not been waived, and which have not by this Act been assigned to any other division of the Metropolitan Court.

(2) All civil causes commenced after the taking effect of this Act

[19] Note at p. 50, original text.
[20] Note at p. 52, original text.

which require a trial by jury and which are not assigned by this Act to any other division of the Metropolitan Court.

SECTION 62. **Assignment of causes to the Civil Non-Jury division.]** There shall be assigned (subject as aforesaid) to the Civil Non-jury division:

(1) All civil causes pending at the commencement of this Act in any court, the jurisdiction whereof is transferred by this Act to the Metropolitan Court, and which have not been assigned to any other division of the Metropolitan Court by this Act and in which a trial by jury is not permitted or has been waived.

(2) All civil causes commenced after the taking effect of this Act and not assigned to any other division of the Metropolitan Court by this Act, in which trial by jury is not permitted or has been waived. Provided, however, [here insert some suitable provision to the effect that jury trial shall be deemed waived unless a special demand is made for it, and in certain classes of cases in which a jury is of the least value, such as suits on judgments, negotiable instruments, contracts in writing and suits for possession of land or between landlord and tenant, requiring the demand for a jury to be accompanied by an advance payment of the actual cost to the district of a jury for one day to be taxed as costs against the unsuccessful litigant.]

SECTION 63. **Assignment of causes to the Criminal division.]** There shall be assigned (subject as aforesaid) to the Criminal division:

(1) All criminal and quasi criminal causes pending at the commencement of this Act in any court the jurisdiction whereof is transferred by this Act to the Metropolitan Court.

(2) All criminal and quasi criminal causes commenced after the taking effect of this Act and not assigned by this Act to any other division of the Metropolitan Court.

> [The sections appropriate for the plan of two divisions or of one division in place of the civil jury, civil non-jury, and criminal cases, as adopted, are given in Appendix A.]

SECTION 64. **Method of assigning causes to the proper division.]** Subject to any rules of court and to the provisions of this Act and to the power of transfer, every person by whom any cause or matter may be commenced in the said Metropolitan Court, shall assign such cause or matter to one of the divisions of the said court, as is required by this Act or by any rules of Court, by marking the document by which the same is commenced, with the name of such division and giving notice thereof to the proper officer of the court.

Provided that:

(1) All interlocutory or other steps or proceedings in or before the said Metropolitan Court, in any cause or matter subsequent to the commencement thereof, shall be taken (subject to any rules of court and to the power of transfer) in the division of said court to which such cause or matter is for the time being attached.

(2) If any plaintiff or petitioner shall at any time assign his cause or matter to any division of the said Metropolitan Court to which, according to the rules of court or to the provisions of this Act, the same ought not to be assigned, the court or any judge of such division, upon being informed thereof, may, on a summary application at any stage of the cause or matter,

a. Direct the same to be transferred to the division of said court to which, according to such rules or provisions, the same ought to have been assigned, or

b. If he think it expedient so to do, retain the same in the division in which the same was commenced; and

c. All steps and proceedings whatsoever taken by the plaintiff or petitioner, or by any other party, in any such cause or matter, and all orders made therein by the court, or any judge thereof, before any such transfer, shall be valid and effectual to all intents and purposes in the same manner as if the same respectively had been taken and made in the proper division of the said court to which such cause or matter ought to have been assigned.

SECTION 65. **Transfer of causes from one division or judge to any other division or judge by rules of court.]** Any cause or matter at any time and at any stage thereof, and either with or without application therein of the parties thereto,

1. May be transferred by such authority and in such manner as the Judicial Council, by rules of court, may direct, from one division or judge of the Metropolitan Court to any other division or judge thereof, or

2. May, by the like authority, be retained in the division in which the same was commenced, although such may not be the proper division to which the same cause or matter might in the first instance have been assigned.

SECTION 66. **Transfer of causes to a judge of another division by the Chief Justice.]** Any cause or matter assigned to any division of the Metropolitan Court may be heard at the request of the Presiding Justice of such division, with the concurrence of the Chief Justice, by any judge of any other division of the Metropolitan Court.

SECTION 67. **Hearing of causes by a judge of one division for another judge of the same division.]** Any proceeding in any cause or matter assigned to any judge of the Metropolitan Court may, at any time, upon the request and on behalf of such judge, be heard and disposed of by any other judge of the same division, who may be willing to hear and dispose of the same, without any transfer:

Provided that, if any party to such proceeding shall object to the same being so heard and disposed of, the same shall not be so heard and disposed of without the concurrence of the Chief Justice, to be signified by an order in writing under his hand.

SECTION 68. **Judges of other courts of record in the State eligible to sit in the Metropolitan Court.]** Every judge of [here name the courts of record of general jurisdiction in the state] and no others, shall be eligible to sit as a member of the Metropolitan Court of [here name the district] with his consent and pursuant to assignment by the Chief Justice.

[The above section is inserted on the supposition that the Act presented will apply to a single metropolitan district in the State; and that outside, the usual arrangements now existing will continue. Of course, if the judiciary of the entire State be reorganized so that the judges in other districts are arranged under proper administrative heads, the above section should be so altered that while any judge may be eligible to sit anywhere in the State, his actual transfer from the duties in one court to the duties in another would depend upon not only his consent, but the consent of the Chief Justice of the court in which he was regularly serving.]

PART V

Practice and Procedure—Judicial Council

SECTION 69. **Constitution of the Judicial Council.]** The Judicial Council hereinbefore and hereinafter referred to, shall consist of

1. The Chief Justice;

2. The Presiding Justices of each of the several divisions of the Metropolitan Court; and

3. One other senior judge of the Metropolitan Court, to be appointed by the Chief Justice from time to time in writing, under the hand of the Chief Justice, such appointment to continue for such

time as shall be specified therein, but not longer than the term of office of the Chief Justice.

> If the number of judges in the district does not exceed fifteen and the divisional features of the court are eliminated, a majority of the judges of the court, with the concurrence of the Chief Justice, should be given authority to exercise all the powers here conferred upon the Judicial Council. The Judicial Council as such may then be omitted.

SECTION 70. **Powers of the Judicial Council.]** The Judicial Council, in addition to the powers hereinbefore and hereinafter conferred upon it, shall have power:

1. To reduce or add to the present number of judges of any division of the Metropolitan Court;

Provided that the total number of judges by this Act determined shall not be increased or diminished, and also

Provided that the reduction of the regularly constituted places in one division and the increasing of those of another shall be effected only when a vacancy occurs in the one in which the number is reduced.

2. To prescribe generally by rules of court the duties and jurisdiction of Masters.

3. To make, alter, and amend all rules:

(a) For regulating
The sittings
Of the Metropolitan Court;
Of any branch thereof, and
Of the judges sitting in chambers; and
All vacations of judges.

(b) For regulating the pleadings, practice and procedure in the Metropolitan Court;

(c) Generally for regulating any matters relating to
Practice and procedure
In the Metropolitan Court, or
Any permament or other division or branch thereof;
Or the duties of the officers thereof,
Or the costs of proceeding therein.

4. To make all rules and regulations

(a) Respecting the mode of conducting the business of
The Clerk of the Metropolitan Court, and
The jury commissioners hereinafter mentioned;

(b) Prescribing the duties
Of said Clerk and his subordinates, and
The said jury commissioners and their subordinates.

SECTION 71. **Jurisdiction to be exercised in the same manner as heretofore unless changed by this Act or by rules of court.]** The jurisdiction by this Act transferred to the Metropolitan Court shall be exercised (so far as regards procedure and practice) in the manner provided by this Act or by such rules or orders of court as may be made pursuant to this Act.

When no special provision is contained in this Act, or in any such orders of court, with reference thereto, it shall be exercised as nearly as may be in the same manner as the same might have been exercised in the respective courts from which such jurisdiction shall have been transferred.

SECTION 72. **Methods of procedure to remain the same except as otherwise provided in this Act or by rules of court.]** Save as by this Act or any rules of court may be otherwise provided, all forms and methods of procedure and all rules and orders of court which at the commencement of this Act were in force in any of the courts whose jurisdiction is by this Act transferred to the said Metropolitan Court, and which are not inconsistent with this Act, or with any rules of the said Metropolitan Court, may continue to be used and practiced in the said Metropolitan Court in such and the like cases, and for such and the like purposes, as those to which they would have been applicable in the respective courts of which the jurisdiction is so transferred, if this Act had not been passed.

SECTION 73. **Power of judges to exercise the powers vested in the Judicial Council.]** The Metropolitan Court may at any time, with the concurrence of a majority of the senior judges thereof, present at any meeting for that purpose held (of which majority the Chief Justice shall be one), alter and annul any rules of court for the time being in force, and have and exercise the same powers as is by this section vested in said Judicial Council.

SECTION 74. **Rules of practice and procedure established by the legislature to be subject to rule-making power.]** The present rules regulating the pleading, practice and procedure in the court united by this Act, which are not inconsistent with or repealed by this act or any rules included in the schedule attached to this Act, whether the same be effective by reason of any Act or Acts of the legislature or otherwise, are hereby repealed as statutes and are by this Act constituted and declared to be operative as rules of court for the Metropolitan Court, but subject to the power of said court and the Judicial Council thereof, conferred by this Act, to make, alter and amend the rules regulating pleadings, practice and procedure in the said court.

SECTION 75. **Publication of rules.]** At least forty days before the making by the Judicial Council of any rules or orders pursuant to this Act, or under its authority, notice of the proposal to make the rules and of the place where copies of the draft rules may be obtained shall be published in some newspaper of general circulation throughout the [here name the Metropolitan District].

During those forty days any person may obtain copies of such draft rules on the payment of not exceeding _____ cents per folio, and any representations or suggestions may be made in writing by any person to the authority proposing to make the rules.

On the expiration of those forty days the rules may be made by the rule-making authority, either as originally drawn or as amended by such authority, and shall, unless an emergency exists, take effect only on August 1 next after they are adopted.

SECTION 76. **Meetings of judges of divisions.]** It shall be the duty of the Presiding Justice of each division of the Metropolitan Court and of the associate judges of each division

1. To meet together
   a. At least once in each month, except the month of August, in each year, at such time and place as may be designated by the President Justice of the division, and
   b. At such other times as may be required by the Presiding Justice.
2. For the consideration of such matters pertaining to the administration of justice in the division to which the judges so meetting belong, as may be brought before them.

At such meetings the judges of division shall receive and investigate, or cause to be investigated, all complaints presented to them pertaining to said division and to the officers thereof and shall take such steps provided by law as they may deem necessary or proper with respect thereto.

The said divisional judges so meeting shall have power and it shall be their duty to recommend to the Judicial Council all such rules and regulations for the proper administration of justice in their divisions respectively as to them may seem expedient.

The Chief Justice shall be notified of all such meetings of the judges of any division and shall, in his discretion, attend, take part in, and preside at the same.

SECTION 77. **Meetings of judges.]** It shall be the duty of the Chief Justice and of all the judges of the Metropolitan Court

1. To meet together
   (a) Once at least in every year, at such time and place as may be designated by the Chief Justice, and
   (b) At such other times as may be required by the Chief Justice;
2. For the purpose of
   (a) Considering the operation of this Act and the rules of court for the time being in force; and also
   (b) The working of the several offices; and
   (c) The arrangements relative to the duties and officers of said court; and
   (d) Inquiring and examining into any defects which may appear to exist in
       The system of procedure, and
       The administration of law by said Metropolitan Court.

It shall be the duty of the Chief Justice at such meeting

1. To present his annual report relating to the work of the court. This report shall include
   (a) Full judicial statistics regarding the business done by the court and by each permanent division thereof for the year ending January first next preceding; and
   (b) The state, on said last mentioned date, of the dockets of the permanent divisions of the said Metropolitan Court and of the several subdivisions and branches of the permanent divisions respectively.
   (c) Such statistics shall be collected under at least the five following heads or others as detailed and comprehensive:
       Litigation
       Efficiency
       Social
       Criminal
       Financial
2. To submit to the meeting,
   (a) Any amendments or alterations which it would in his judgment be expedient to make
       In this Act, or
       Otherwise relating to the administration of justice; and

(b) Any other provisions which cannot be carried into effect without the authority of the legislature, which in his opinion are expedient for the better administration of justice.

The Chief Justice shall report to the governor of the state what, if any, action was taken by the Metropolitan Court with reference to any recommendations or proposals submitted by him.

PART VI

Jury Commissioners

SECTION 78. **Commission of three—powers and duties.]** A commission of three jury commissioners shall have such powers and duties relating to the selection of jurors and grand jurors (if any) for service as shall be from time to time prescribed by the orders and rules of the Judicial Council hereinbefore created, and in the meantime and until the same are repealed, altered or amended, their powers and duties shall be such as are prescribed by an Act [here insert the title of any jury commissioners' Act which may be in force in the Metropolitan District.]

SECTION 79. **Present jury commissioners continued—Successors appointed by Chief Justice.]** The jury commissioners holding office under an Act [here insert the title of the last mentioned Act] shall be the first jury commissioners under this Act and shall hold office for such period as is prescribed by the said Act. Upon the expiration of the term of office of each commissioner respectively, as determined by the said last mentioned Act, his place as a jury commissioner under this Act shall be filled by the appointment of the Chief Justice of the Metropolitan Court for the time being, and each jury commissioner so appointed by the said Chief Justice shall hold office as jury commissioner for the period of three years.

SECTION 80. **Removal of jury commissioners.]** Any jury commissioner may be removed from office by the Judicial Council for cause stated in writing by the Chief Justice of the Metropolitan Court and proved upon a hearing before said Judicial Council.

PART VII

Clerk and Clerk's Office

SECTION 81. **Consolidation of clerks' offices and creation of office of clerk of the Metropolitan Court.]** The several clerks' offices hereinafter mentioned, that is to say, the offices of the clerks of the [here name all the courts consolidated by this Act which have clerks], shall be united and consolidated together and shall constitute under and subject to the provisions of this Act, the office of the Clerk of the Metropolitan Court of [here name the district]. There shall be one Clerk of said Court, and he shall be appointed by a majority of the Judicial Council hereinbefore referred to, and shall hold office at the pleasure of a majority of said Judicial Council.

SECTION 82. **Powers and duties of such Clerk.]** Save as by this Act, or by any rules of court may be otherwise provided, all powers and duties which at the commencement of this Act were conferred or imposed upon the clerks of any of the courts whose jurisdiction is by this Act transferred to the said Metropolitan Court under and by virtue of any law, or rule whatsoever, and which are not inconsistent with this Act, or any rules of court, shall continue and be transferred to the clerk of the Metropolitan Court.

SECTION 83. **Present clerks to be continued in office—No new clerks to succeed present clerks in office.]** The persons holding at the commencement of this Act the offices respectively of the [here name all the clerks whose powers and duties have been transferred to the Clerk of the Metropolitan Court] shall continue to hold said offices for their unexpired terms respectively, and during the continuance of said offices shall be entitled to the same compensation and salary as at the commencement of this Act.

But they shall during their unexpired terms respectively be subject to assignment to duty by the Clerk of the Metropolitan Court as his principal deputies, and shall be required to perform, as nearly as may be, the duties now required of them by law under the direction of said Clerk of the Metropolitan Court.

Upon the expiration of the terms of office respectively of the said clerks of the courts, the jurisdiction of which is hereby by this Act transferred to the said Metropolitan Court, said offices shall not be filled as in the manner heretofore provided by law, but the same shall be deemed to be occupied by the Clerk of the Metropolitan Court.

SECTION 84. **Central and branch clerks' offices.]** A central clerk's office and branch offices throughout the [here name the metropolitan district] shall be established at such place or places respectively as the Judicial Council may by rule determine.

Until such determination the central office shall be at [here name the place].

SECTION 85. **Appointment, removal and duties of persons to keep**

order in the courts.] The Chief Justice may, from time to time, make regulations with respect to the appointment, removal and duties of persons to keep order in the various branches of the respective divisions of the Metropolitan Court, and in any other matters necessary or incidental to the use or management of the said Metropolitan Court or any branch thereof. Any remuneration paid under this section shall be paid out of money voted by the [here name the local authority for making appropriations].

SECTION 85-A. **Supplies to be furnished the Court.]** All blanks, books, papers, furniture and supplies necessary to the keeping of the records of the Metropolitan Court and the transactions of the business thereof shall be furnished the officers of said Court upon the requisition of the Chief Justice by the [here name the local municipal corporation which raises the funds for the operation of the Court by taxation.]

PART VIII

Fees and Salaries

SECTION 86. **Salary of Chief Justice.]** The Chief Justice shall receive a salary of fifteen thousand dollars ($15,000) per annum.[21]

SECTION 87. **Salary of first judges under this Act.]** All the judges under this Act who shall have been at the commencement of this Act judges of the courts united by this Act, shall receive for the remainder of their terms of office, respectively, the salary provided by law before the commencement of this Act. This shall apply to such of the first judges under this Act as shall be appointed Presiding Justices of divisions.[22]

SECTION 88. **Salary of judges subsequently selected.]** All other judges who shall hold office under the terms of this act shall receive salaries as follows:

(1) The Presiding Justices of the several divisions of the Metropolitan Court shall receive twelve thousand five hundred dollars ($12,500) per annum.

(2) The senior Associate Justices of the Metropolitan Court shall receive eight thousand dollars ($8,000) per annum at the commencement of their service, and this sum shall be increased after each three years of service the sum of five hundred dollars ($500) per

[21] See comment in note, p. 79, original text.

[22] Note, p. 79, original text.

annum until a maximum of ten thousand dollars ($10,000) per annum is reached.

(3) The junior associate justice of the Metropolitan Court shall receive five thousand dollars ($5,000) per annum at the commencement of their service, and this sum shall be increased five hundred dollars ($500) per annum for each three years of service until a maximum of eight thousand dollars ($8,000) is reached.

(4) Provided, however, that "each three years of service" as used in this section, shall be determined for each of the first judges of the Metropolitan Court who may be appointed an associate justice under this Act by including the time that each of such judges shall have served continuously as a judge in any of the courts united by this Act prior to the taking effect of this Act.

SECTION 89. **Salary of Masters.]** Masters shall receive such salary as the judicial council may determine, but not to exceed five thousand dollars ($5,000) per annum upon the commencement of their service.

Their salary shall for every three years of service be increased the sum of five hundred dollars ($500) per annum, but never to exceed six thousand five hundred dollars ($6,500) per annum.

SECTION 90. **Salary of jury commissioners.]** The first jury commissioners under this Act shall be entitled to receive the same salary or compensation that they received at the commencement of this Act and shall receive such salary or compensation during the remainder of their term of office. Thereafter all jury commissioners appointed and holding office under this Act shall receive such salary as the Judicial Council shall determine, but not to exceed three thousand dollars ($3,000) per annum.

SECTION 91. **Salary of Clerk of Metropolitan Court.]** The Clerk of the Metropolitan Court shall receive the sum of seven thousand five hundred dollars ($7,500) per annum.

SECTION 92. **Pensions for judges.]** Each judge of the Metropolitan Court upon having served at least ten years and having reached the age of sixty-five years, shall be entitled to retire upon half pay during the remainder of his life. Each judge of the Metropolitan Court upon having served twenty years and reached the age of seventy years, shall be entitled to retire upon full pay for the remainder of his life; provided, however, that any judge who shall be entitled to retire upon half pay or upon full pay may be so retired by the Judicial Council upon the request of the Chief Justice, for the good of the service.

SECTION 93. **Salaries to be paid monthly.]** All salaries provided by this Act shall be paid by the [here name the fiscal authority of the Metropolitan District] in monthly installments upon warrants issued by the auditor of [here name the same fiscal authority].

SECTION 94. **No person to solicit political contributions from judges, officers of the court, Clerk or employes.]** No person shall solicit orally or by letter or be in any manner concerned in soliciting any assessment, contribution or payment for any political party or any political purpose whatever

1. From the Chief Justice or any judge, or Master of the Metropolitan Court, or
2. From the Clerk of said court, or from any deputy or employe of the said Clerk, or
3. From any person employed to keep order in the several branches of the Metropolitan Court, or any of them, or to render services to the Chief Justice or any judge or master of the said court, or
4. From any one who has been nominated for or is seeking the nomination for Chief Justice, or who is a candidate for appointment or seeking appointment to any office of judge or master of the Metropolitan Court.

SECTION 95. **No judge, officer of the court, Clerk or employe to make any contribution for political purposes.]** No Chief Justice or any person nominated or seeking the nomination of Chief Justice, and

No judge or master of the Metropolitan Court, and

No person seeking appointment as judge or master of said court, and

No Clerk of the said Court or any deputy or employe of the said Clerk, and

No person employed to keep order in any branch of the said Court or to render services to the Chief Justice or any judge or master of the said Court

Shall make any contribution or payment or any promise of contribution or payment to any political party or to any person or persons whatever for any political purpose whatever,

Except for his own election or any retirement election to which he is subjected.

SECTION 96. **Penalty.]** Any person who shall wilfully or through culpable negligence violate the provisions of the foregoing sections 94 and 95 shall be guilty of a misdemeanor and shall, on conviction thereof, be punished by a fine of not less than Fifty Dollars and not to exceed One Thousand Dollars, or by imprisonment in the county jail for a term not to exceed six months, or by both such fine and imprisonment, in the discretion of the court.

SECTION 97. **Cause for removal.]** If any person shall be convicted under the last preceding section, any public office or place of public employment which such person may hold shall by force of such conviction be rendered vacant. Provided, however, that any violation of said sections 94 and 95 shall also be a cause for removal within the meaning of Section — of this Act. [See Bulletin IV-A, Sec. 10, p. 31.]

SECTION 98. **What officers to prosecute.]** Prosecutions for violation of Sections 94 and 95 of this Act may be instituted either by the attorney-general, the state's attorney for the county in which the offense is alleged to have been committed, or by the Council of Judges hereinafter mentioned, acting through its special counsel.

Such suits shall be conducted and controlled by the prosecuting officers who instituted them unless they request the aid of other prosecuting officers.

SECTION 99. **Fees.]** Subject to rules of court as hereinbefore provided, the fees taxed shall be such as were at the time of the commencement of this Act provided by law, and where there have been differences in the fees taxed, depending upon the court in which the cause was brought in at the time this Act took effect, the same differences shall continue to exist, depending, as nearly as may be, upon the division or branch of any division to which the cause may be assigned. All masters' fees shall be taxed and paid to the Chief Clerk of the Metropolitan Court, together with all other fees legally taxed. All fees and costs paid to said Chief Clerk shall be accounted for and paid to the [here name the appropriate fiscal authority of the district].

PART IX

Miscellaneous Provisions

SECTION 100. **Effect of invalidity of portions of the Act.]** The invalidity of any part of this Act shall not affect the validity of any other part thereof which can be given effect without such invalid part.

SECTION 101. **Referendum.]** This Act shall be submitted to the legal voters of the [here name the metropolitan district] at the general election to be held on the ____ day of ______, A. D. 19____.

The ballots to be used at said election in voting upon this act shall be in substantially the following form:

For consenting to the Act entitled "An Act to create the Metropolitan Court of [here name the metropolitan district] and to provide for the practice and procedure therein."	
Against consenting to the Act entitled "An Act to create the Metropolitan Court of [here name the metropolitan district] and to provide for the practice and procedure therein."	

If a majority of the legal voters of the said district voting on the question at such election shall vote in favor of consenting to this Act, then an election for Chief Justice shall be held in accordance with the provisions of this Act at the next general election occurring on the ____ day of ________. Thereupon on said last mentioned day this Act shall be operative and in full force and effect.[23]

[23] Appendix A, consisting of sections for enactment if the plan be adopted of having two divisions, one to handle important civil cases tried by a jury and jury waived and important criminal cases tried by a jury, and the other to deal with less important civil and criminal cases tried for the most part without a jury, found at pp. 89 *et seq.* of original text, are omitted. The appendix also contains sections for adoption if the plan be adopted of sending all civil cases to a common pleas division, and all criminal cases to a criminal causes division (pp. 91 *et seq.*, original text), and sections for adoption if the plan be adopted of sending all jury cases to one division, and all nonjury cases, both civil and criminal, to another (pp. 92 *et seq.*, original text). See also p. 94, section in substitution of sections 61, 62, and 63, if all cases are to be handled by a single division.

Appendix C

Proposed Metropolitan Court Act for Detroit

A bill to coordinate and consolidate the courts of large metropolitan areas having a population of 750,000 or more to more effectively dispense justice; to create a metropolitan circuit court of record for such metropolitan areas; to prescribe the jurisdiction and powers of the metropolitan circuit courts; to provide a referendum thereon; and to supersede certain acts and parts of acts.

THE PEOPLE OF THE STATE OF MICHIGAN ENACT:

Sec. 1. Each county in the state having over 750,000 population according to the latest or any succeeding federal decennial census shall be a separate judicial circuit by itself and there shall be established therein a metropolitan circuit court, which shall be a circuit court of record and shall have all the powers, duties and jurisdiction of any court existing within the county at the effective date of this act in any such county, whether state, county or municipal, except justices of the peace in organized townships and municipal courts, under whatever name existing, in municipalities of less than 250,000 population and the probate court, and no municipality of more than 250,000 population, after the effective date of this act, shall establish any court which will have jurisdiction over any matter cognizable by the metropolitan circuit court. During the period of transition as provided in section 2 hereof, the metropolitan circuit court shall exercise concurrent jurisdiction with the courts to be consolidated therein, to the extent of the jurisdiction of the last mentioned courts as heretofore existing.

Sec. 2. The courts to be consolidated and superseded by the metropolitan circuit court shall continue to exist after the effective date of this act in the county until the end of the current term of the judge thereof having the longest term with reduction in the number of judges from time to time as herein provided, and the judges so continuing shall continue to function during the period with the same powers, duties and jurisdiction as heretofore. At the expiration of the current term of any judge or the occurrence of a vacancy in any court by death, resignation or otherwise, there is hereby created an additional circuit court judge to serve in the metropolitan circuit court for each judge of the courts consolidated herein whose terms shall have expired or whose position shall have become vacant through death, resignation or otherwise. When a vacancy occurs in any court to be consolidated into or superseded by the metropolitan circuit court, the governor shall not fill the vacancy created in the court, but shall appoint a new circuit judge in the manner provided by law for the judicial district to serve the metropolitan circuit court. The additional circuit court judges provided by this act shall be nominated at the primary election and elected at the general election next prior to the expiration of the term of the respective judges of the several courts superseded by the metropolitan circuit court, and they shall hold office until the next general election of circuit court judges or until their successors are elected or appointed as provided by law. Any judge of a court superseded by the metropolitan circuit court and who is a judge of any court so superseded on the date of the primary election and general election next prior to the establishment of the court or the creation of any additional judgeships therein, and who desires to run for the office of metropolitan circuit judge as provided in this act shall fulfill all other requirements for the nomination and election of circuit court judges as otherwise provided by law and shall have the right to have his name printed upon the ballots used for the primary election and general election, with a designation under his name as judge of the court in which he serves at the time of the election.

Sec. 3. Within 30 days after the establishment of the metropolitan circuit court, the judges of the court, including the judges of the courts to be consolidated into or superseded by the metropolitan circuit court, shall meet and by a ⅔ majority vote of all the judges of the court elect a chief presiding judge to hold office for the duration of his term as a judge of the metropolitan circuit court, and 4 members to act with the chief presiding judge as a judicial council to organize the court and to establish such divisions as they deem necessary and 1 administrative division and assign such judges to the divisions as created as the judicial council believes proper, providing the judges have jurisdiction over such matters. The chief presiding judge shall have full authority and control over all matters of administration, reports and the administrative division. The chief presiding judge may move the judges of the several divisions from one division to another division when he believes it necessary on a temporary basis for not more than 3 months, if the judges have jurisdiction over the matters of that division. The chief presiding judge shall designate the presiding judges of the several divisions, with the approval of the judicial council, and they shall hold office for 1 year, or at the pleasure of the judicial council. The presiding judge of each division must have jurisdiction to consider all matters assigned to the division. The entire judiciary of the court shall meet at least 4 times during each year to discuss problems pertinent to the operations of the court, and at such other times as the judicial council shall determine, or on call of the chief presiding judge. The chief presiding judge may be relieved of his duties by a ⅔ majority vote of all of the judges of the court at any time and a new chief presiding judge shall be elected by a ⅔ majority vote of all of the judges of the court at any time a vacancy occurs. The chief presiding judge shall hold office for the duration of his term as a judge of the court, unless relieved of his duties as above provided.

Sec. 4. Following the organization of the court, the first judicial council shall cease to function and thereafter the judicial council for the court shall consist of the chief presiding judge and the presiding judge from each division created by the judicial council and 1 judge from each of the divisions appointed by the chief presiding judge. The judicial council shall adopt such rules of procedure as it deems proper for the administration of justice in the court, but only after notice and hearing with the members of the local bar and after approval by the supreme court of the state. The judicial council shall provide for the assignment of judges among the several divisions, and enact rules for the assignment of such cases to the respective judges. Assignment of cases shall be made to judges of the several divisions from a calendar established for each division by an assignment clerk of the metropolitan circuit court as a part of the administrative division. All matters pending before any court or judge superseded by the metropolitan circuit court shall be automatically transferred to such division of the court as the judicial council shall designate, and all functions of the several courts or judges superseded by the metropolitan circuit court shall be performed by the divisions of the metropolitan circuit court as the judicial council shall determine.

Sec. 5. In any action or proceeding, civil or criminal, pending before any justice court or municipal court continuing in the county after the creation of the metropolitan circuit court, which might have been brought in the metropolitan circuit court, the defendant, within 10 days of the date when the case is at issue, may request that the case be transferred to the metropolitan circuit court for further proceedings, and the clerk of the court, within 5 days after the request, shall transmit the case to the clerk of the metropolitan circuit court where the case shall be docketed as a case at issue to be heard by the metropolitan circuit court in its regular course of business.

Sec. 6. The judicial council shall establish within the metropolitan circuit court an appellate review court consisting of 3 judges of the court appointed by the judicial council, which shall review such final judgments, decrees or orders of the metropolitan circuit court as the supreme court of the state shall prescribe by rule, including the manner and method of review. Alternate judges shall also be appointed from the court to sit in the appellate review court in case of the disqualifications of any of the judges appointed to regularly so sit, which alternates shall serve in the order in which appointed. Review in all cases where no appeal is taken to the appellate review court and of all other final judgments, decrees or orders of the metropolitan circuit court shall be in the manner prescribed for review of final judgments, decrees or orders of the circuit courts of this state. The judge rendering the decision appealed from shall not sit on the appellate review court. Appeals to the supreme court of the state from a decision of the appellate review court shall be in the same manner as from circuit courts. Appeals from probate, justice and municipal courts within the county and divisions of the metropolitan circuit court performing the functions of such courts shall be made to the metropolitan circuit court in the same manner as now provided for appeals from these courts to circuit courts and shall be heard by the appellate review courts as above provided, except where a trial de novo is required by law.

Sec. 7. The judges of the metropolitan circuit courts shall be circuit judges and shall be elected or appointed at the same time and in the same manner as now or hereafter provided for the election or appointment of circuit judges, except that the additional judges created by this act shall be elected in the first instance as provided in section 2 of this act. No person shall be elected or appointed to the office unless he shall have the legal qualifications for circuit judge.

Sec. 8. The administrative division shall perform all functions heretofore performed for the courts superseded by the metropolitan circuit court, by the probation departments, the psychopathic clinic, the friend of the court, the sheriff, constables, bailiffs or other process servers, and the county clerk to the extent permitted by the constitution of this state and as provided in this act. To the extent permitted by the constitution of this state, all such departments, bureaus and commissions, including the clerks and employees of the probation departments, psychopathic clinics, friend of the court, the sheriff, constables, bailiffs, process servers and all other clerks and employees are hereby transferred to the administrative division of the metropolitan circuit court, except the employees of other departments, bureaus or commissions not a part of the metropolitan circuit court administrative division who are working in or are loaned to perform work for any part of the administrative division of the metropolitan circuit court, such as, but not by way of limitation, police officers of a municipality working in or loaned to or for the benefit of any court superseded by the metropolitan circuit court. For the purpose of this act, all employees of the departments so transferred to the administrative division of the metropolitan circuit court shall become employees of the administrative division of the metropolitan circuit court on the date the metropolitan circuit court is created under this act, and to the extent that they are classified under civil service, municipal or otherwise, they shall be classified under county civil service in the classification they held under civil service prior to this transfer. All employees of the administrative division of the metropolitan circuit court are hereby declared eligible to participate in the county civil service program and they shall be classified in accordance with the law and regulations applicable thereto, protecting and preserving, however, the seniority status of such employees, if any, at the time of transfer and thereafter. Any contributions made by any employee to the pension fund, such as, but not by way of limitation, the annuity savings fund, to the extent such exists on the effective date of this act for the benefit of any of the employees so transferred, shall be transferred to the county, unless otherwise requested by the employee or employees, to be administered by the board of county auditors or such other commission having jurisdiction over the county pension program in the same manner as the pension plan for county employees. The judges of the metropolitan circuit court shall be entitled to receive the same pension benefits as those provided for circuit judges. The appointment of new employees to and the separation of employees from the administrative division of the metropolitan circuit court shall be made by the head of the administrative division to the extent permitted by law and, to the extent the constitution does not permit such action by the head of the administrative division, then the appointments and separations shall be made in the same manner as provided by law in the county on the effective date of this act. The board of supervisors shall classify and fix the salaries of all employees of the administrative division and establish a budget for all expenditures of the court.

Sec. 9. All salaries of clerks and other employees of the metropolitan circuit court, costs of housing and maintaining the court, and pensions for its clerks and employees eligible for pensions shall be paid by the county from county funds in such amounts as the board of supervisors shall determine. The judges of the metropolitan circuit court shall receive such salaries from the state as the legislature shall provide and may also be paid such additional salaries by the county as the board of supervisors shall provide. The municipalities whose courts are consolidated into or superseded by the metropolitan circuit court shall reimburse the county treasury not less often than every 3 months for that part of the salaries of judges, clerks and other employees of the administrative division of the court and costs of operating and maintaining said court including pensions paid for the benefit of such municipalities. Costs for past service credits for pensions to be paid under the county pension plan to employees transferred from the municipality payroll to the county shall be paid by the municipality as a reimbursement to the county treasury, limited by the number of years the employees were on the payroll of the municipality and under the municipal pension plan, bears to the total years of service in computing said pension or pensions in the ratio that such costs heretofore paid by the municipality for the courts consolidated into the metropolitan circuit court bears to the total of such costs for the metropolitan circuit court at the time of its establishment.

Sec. 10. In the event that any judge of a municipal court superseded by the metropolitan circuit court is authorized, empowered or required to serve on or supervise any commission, department, bureau or other body politic, the function shall be performed by a judge of the metropolitan circuit court selected by the legislative branch of the body politic. The judge serving in any such capacity as provided in this section shall not receive any additional compensation therefor.

Sec. 11. The jurors to serve in the metropolitan circuit court shall be drawn by the officers now authorized to draw jurors by the law in effect in relation to the circuit court of any such county on the effective date of this act in such county. If a jury commission shall be so acting in relation to the circuit court, the commission in acting for the metropolitan circuit court shall function in accordance with Act No. 83 of the Public Acts of 1923, as amended, being sections 725.101 to 725.162 of the Compiled Laws of 1948; the words "city officers" wherever appearing therein being deemed to read "public officers" who shall function accordingly, and the words "municipal court of record" wherever so appearing being deemed to read "metropolitan circuit court".

Sec. 12. All fines collected by the metropolitan circuit court for the violation of any municipal ordinance cognizable by any municipal court merged into the metropolitan circuit court shall be remitted for the benefit of any special fund provided by law and to the extent that the fines are remitted to the general fund of the municipality, they shall be so remitted.

Sec. 13. This act shall supersede and revoke any acts or parts of acts in conflict herewith, but only to the extent of such conflicts, including, but not by way of limitation, Act No. 369 of the Public Acts of 1919, as amended, being sections 725.1 to 725.25 of the Compiled Laws of 1948, and Act No. 260 of the Public Acts of 1929, as amended, being sections 728.1 to 728.30 of the Compiled Laws of 1948, and Act. No. 279 of the Public Acts of 1909, as amended, being sections 117.1 to 117.38 of the Compiled Laws of 1948, except that condemnation proceedings instituted by a municipality, whose courts have been consolidated into or superseded by a metropolitan circuit court, shall be conducted under the charter provisions of the municipality before a jury or jurors selected pursuant to section 11 from residents of the municipality.

Sec. 14. The provisions of this act shall not be in force or take effect in any county until a majority of the voters voting thereon at an election as hereinafter provided shall have voted in favor of the same. The question of the adoption of the provisions of this act may be submitted to the voters of any county to which it may apply at any general election, after the passage of this act, by a resolution of the board of supervisors; and like notice of the submission of the same shall be given as required by law in the case of elections to elect county officers, and shall be submitted in substantially the following form:

"Shall the provisions of Act No. ______ of the Public Acts of 1958, providing for the coordination and consolidation of the courts of large metropolitan areas having a population of 750,000 or more to more effectively dispense justice; to create a metropolitan circuit court of record for such metropolitan areas; to prescribe the jurisdiction and powers of the metropolitan circuit courts; to provide a referendum thereon; and to supersede certain acts and parts of acts, take effect in this county?

Yes ( )
No ( )".

After a majority of the electors voting on such proposition in any county, as determined by the canvass of the votes cast, shall vote in favor thereof, from and after January 1 next succeeding, the provisions of this act shall be in force therein.

Whenever petitions for the submission of such proposition signed by 5% of the qualified electors of said county as shown by the last preceding general election shall be filed with the county clerk of said county, the board of supervisors of such county shall submit such proposition to the electors at the next general election.

Reasons and purposes for enactment of the Metropolitan Circuit Court Bill:

The Detroit Bar Association is again presenting to the Michigan Legislature a proposed Bill to consolidate the Courts of Wayne County. We ask the support of all civic minded citizens who seek to improve our judicial system.

The Metropolitan Circuit Court Bill was drafted for the following reasons:

1. The large metropolitan areas of the Country have found over a period of years that problems result in not coordinating the efforts of all of the courts serving these large populated areas.
2. In developing new courts to care for the needs of a growing community, the several courts have become so specialized that a litigant is unable to obtain relief except in different courts with respect to matters growing out of the same problem. In fact, a litigant can be charged or tried in two or three courts with respect to the same matter.
3. Duplicating agencies for the several courts have grown up (2 probation departments, 2 jury commissions, 2 domestic relations divisions, etc.) increasing the cost of judicial administration.
4. Some of the judges at times do not work full time and there is no way to compel assignment of those judges who do not have a full day of work, to the work of other courts where work is available or do additional work in their own courts.
5. Some judges are better able to handle certain types of cases than others. It should be possible to assign judges where they can do their best work.

The Bill will accomplish the following:

1. Create one court with 39 judges who can be assigned by the judges, where more man power is needed and to the type of work that each judge can do best, thereby eliminating the slack which presently exists in one court while another court is in arrears in its work.
2. Make it possible for a litigant to receive all relief in one court (except Probate Court).
3. Eliminate overlapping and duplicating agencies and courts, such as:
   a) There is a probation department for the Recorder's Court and also one for the Circuit Court.
   b) There is a Jury Commission for the Recorder's Court and one for the Circuit Court.
   c) There is a Friend of the Court handling domestic problems for the Circuit Court and a domestic relations department taking care of such matters for the Recorder's Court.
   d) There is a psychiatric clinic for the Recorder's Court and a separate division thereof for the Traffic Court.
   e) There is an assignment clerk for each court.
   f) There are clerks for each court.
   g) In non-support cases growing out of domestic relation matters a party can be charged in the Recorder's Court and the Circuit Court.
   h) There is an overlapping jurisdiction between the Circuit Court and the Court of Common Pleas of the City of Detroit.
4. It would combine the administrative agencies under one division eliminating duplication and make all of the services available to all judges. Over a period of time the savings would amount to a minimum of $100,000.00 per year. This estimate is not unreasonable when we consider that these courts are presently staffed by approximately 450 persons. A reduction over a period of time of 25 persons would accomplish this savings.
5. It has been suggested that the present Circuit Court should be increased by six (6) judges. With the adoption of this Bill, this would not be necessary. In fact, the Metropolitan Circuit Court would be able, for many years to come, to take care of the needs of metropolitan Detroit. Detroit is a growing community and with the coming of the seaway it will grow even

faster. We must be prepared for this growth now and not wait like other metropolitan centers until the judicial system has become chaotic.

6. There would be no increase in cost to the City of Detroit, Wayne County, or the State of Michigan, at this time. Over a period of years any increase in judicial salaries which would be provided by the State, County of Municipal Governments would be offset by the savings in operation of the court.
7. It would provide speedier administration of justice through greater flexibility in the use of judicial man power.
8. It would provide an appellate procedure to permit reviews with a minimum of cost and delay.
9. It has been suggested very strongly that because of the heavy domestic relations case load that a new domestic relations court be established which would require additional judges. The Metropolitan Circuit Court Bill would eliminate the necessity of increasing the judicial man power, providing additional clerks and other expenses for the reason that a domestic relations division can be established within the framework of the Metropolitan Circuit Court without any additional expense by making proper use of our present judicial man power and administrative division.
10. It will permit control of the activities of judges so as to bring about the best possible relations between the judiciary, the lawyers and the public.

John F. Langs, Chairman
Co-Ordination of Courts Committee
Detroit Bar Association

Appendix D

"Miami Metro": Metropolitan Court

FLORIDA CONSTITUTION
HOME RULE AMENDMENT, A. 8, S. 11
ADOPTED NOVEMBER 6, 1956

Section 11. *Dade County, home rule charter.*

(1) The electors of Dade County, Florida, are granted power to adopt, revise, and amend from time to time a home rule charter of government for Dade County, Florida, under which the Board of County Commissioners of Dade County shall be the governing body. This charter: . . . . *such charter may create new courts and judges and clerks thereof with jurisdiction to try all offenses against ordinances passed by the Board of County Commissioners of Dade County and none of the other courts provided for by this Constitution or by general law shall have original jurisdiction to try such offenses,* although the charter may confer appellate jurisdiction on such courts, and provided further that if said home rule charter shall abolish any county office or offices as authorized herein, that said charter shall contain adequate provision for the carrying on of all functions of said office or offices as are now or may hereafter be prescribed by general law. . . .

HOME RULE CHARTER

Recorded Official Records Book 182, page 667, Public Records of Dade County.
Adopted May 21, 1957

PREAMBLE

We, the people of this County, in order to secure for ourselves the benefits and responsibilities of home rule, to create a metropolitan government to serve our present and future needs, and to endow our municipalities with the rights of self determination in their local affairs, do under God adopt this home rule Charter.

ARTICLE 6

METROPOLITAN COURT

Section 6.01. Metropolitan Court Established.

A. A Court is hereby established, the name of which shall be the Metropolitan Court. There shall be as many judges of this Court as the Board shall deem necessary to administer promptly and expeditiously the business of the Court.

B. The judges shall be appointed by the Board by vote of two-thirds of the members of the Board to serve for six years. Terms of office of judges may be staggered. The senior judge shall be the administrative officer of the Court. All judges shall be attorneys who have been qualified for five years to practice law in the State of Florida. The compensation of the judges and all Court employees shall be fixed by ordinance.

C. Any judge may be removed for malfeasance, misfeasance, or nonfeasance by vote of two-thirds of the members of the Board after public hearing.

Section 6.02. Jurisdiction and Procedure.

A. The Court shall have jurisdiction to try all cases arising under ordinances adopted by the Board.

B. The clerk of the Metropolitan Court shall be appointed by the Board. The clerk may appoint deputy clerks upon approval of the Manager. The Court may hold sessions in such places as the Board may designate.

C. Arrests, complaints, prosecutions, and convictions shall be instituted and processed in the manner provided by the rules of the Court. When the complaint is made in the name of the county, a formal complaint shall not be necessary to give the Court jurisdiction of offenses triable in such Court, but the accused may be tried for the offense for which he is docketed, provided such docket entry is sufficient to put the accused upon notice of the offense with which he is charged.

D. No person shall upon conviction for the violation of any county ordinance be punished by a fine exceeding $1,000 or imprisonment in the county jail for more than one year or by both such fine and imprisonment. If the offense is punishable by a fine exceeding $500 or imprisonment in the county jail for more than 60 days, the accused shall be entitled to a trial by jury upon demand.

E. All prosecutions for violations of any ordinance punishable by fine or imprisonment shall be conducted by the State Attorney of this county, if he be willing, and, if not, by the department of law. The Board may by ordinance provide for a public defender.

F. Appeals will lie to the Circuit Court of this county from any final judgment. All such appeals shall be taken within 20 days from the entry of the judgment in the manner provided by the rules of the Circuit Court. The decision of the Circuit Court shall be subject to review in the same manner and within the same time as any other decision of the Circuit Court.

G. The Judges of the Metropolitan Court are hereby empowered to adopt rules of procedure governing the Court, to punish for contempt of court including imprisonment not in excess of 48 hours, to issue search warrants, and to fix the amount of bail and appeal bonds. The judges and the clerks or their deputies may administer oaths, issue witness subpoenas, and warrants for arrest.

METROPOLITAN COURT

ORDINANCE 57-13

Section 3.01 Number of Judges. The metropolitan court established by the charter shall consist of judges appointed by the commission by two-thirds vote.

Section 3.02 Jurisdiction. The court shall have exclusive original jurisdiction to try all cases arising under ordinances adopted by the commission. No person shall be punished by a fine exceeding one thousand dollars or imprisonment in the county jail for more than one year or by both such fine and imprisonment. The court may punish contempt by fine or by imprisonment not more than 48 hours, may issue search warrants and fix the amount of bail and appeal bonds. When the complaint is made in the name of the county, a formal complaint shall not be necessary to give the court jurisdiction of offenses triable in the court, but the accused may be tried for the offense for which he is docketed, if the docket entry is sufficient to put the accused on notice of the offense with which he is charged. Each judge, sitting alone, may exercise all the power and jurisdiction of the court, except that the judges shall adopt uniform rules of procedure by a majority vote.

Section 3.03 Appeals. Appeal will lie to the circuit court of the county from any final judgment. All appeals shall be taken within 20 days from the entry of the judgment by the clerk. All appeals shall be taken in the manner provided by the rules of the circuit court.

Section 3.04 Fines. All fines, forfeitures and costs received from violations occurring within the boundaries of any municipality, shall be held in a separate account by the finance director who shall pay monthly to each municipality a sum equal to two-thirds of the monies received from violations occurring within that municipality. After the close of each fiscal year, the finance director shall remit to each municipality the balance of the monies received from violations occurring within that municipality, less the proportionate expense of operating the court, including all salaries and other expenses incurred in the operation of the court and less the proportionate expense of apprehending such violators, including all salaries and other expenses incurred in the patrolling of arterial highways within municipal boundaries. Provided, however, no municipality shall receive any monies under the provisions of this section unless it permits such use by the metropolitan court of its court room facilities and jails as is requested by the senior judge of the metropolitan court.

Section 3.05 Judges—qualification. Each judge shall be a county resident who has been qualified for not less than five years to practice law in the state. He shall devote his full time to his judicial duties and he shall not engage in the practice of law during his term.

Section 3.06 Judges—term. The judges initially appointed shall serve for terms of six years, who shall serve as senior judge for a term of one year; thereafter the senior judge shall be selected by the judges of said court for a term of two years. The commission shall appoint one of the judges as the senior judge. He shall be the administrative officer of the court. All judges appointed to fill any vacancy shall serve for the unexpired term of the replaced judge. Every additional judge appointed shall serve for six years from the date of his qualification.

Section 3.07 Judges—salary. Each judge shall receive a salary of thirteen thousand five hundred dollars per annum, payable in equal monthly installments.

Section 3.08 Judges—disqualification. The disqualification of judges shall be as prescribed in Chapter 38 F.S.

Section 3.09 Judges—removal. Any judge may be removed for malfeasance, misfeasance, or nonfeasance by two-thirds vote of the commission after public hearing.

Section 3.10 Clerk—appointment, salary. There shall be a clerk of the court who shall be appointed by the commission for a term of six years and who shall receive a salary of ten thousand dollars per annum in equal monthly installments.

Section 3.11 Clerk—duties. The clerk is the custodian of the dockets, books and papers of the court and shall maintain such records and render such reports as may be required by the senior judge. The clerk may administer oaths, and shall issue such warrants, subpoenas and other process as may be directed by rule of the court. The clerk shall approve or disapprove bonds as prescribed by rule of court. The clerk shall accept all fines and forfeitures and shall account to the finance director in such manner and at such intervals as he may require. The clerk shall perform any other duties directed by the senior judge.

Section 3.12 Clerk—deputies. The clerk may appoint deputy clerks upon approval of the manager. The salaries of all court employees shall be fixed by ordinance. The clerk shall be liable for the acts of his deputies. The deputy clerks shall have and exercise every power the clerk himself may exercise, except the power to appoint a deputy.

Section 3.13 Clerk—Bond. Before being commissioned, the clerk shall file with the clerk of the circuit court a bond in a penalty not less than twenty-five thousand dollars payable to the commissioners and their successors in office, conditioned upon the faithful discharge of the duties of his office. The senior judge shall determine the amount and form of the bond and the sufficiency of the surety.

Section 3.14 Court reporters. The senior judge shall designate sufficient court reporters, at compensation fixed by the commission, so that a court reporter shall be present at each session of the court. The court reporter shall furnish any person a transcript of any portion of the proceedings upon payment of the cost as fixed by the rules of the court. One person may serve as court reporter and deputy clerk.

Section 3.15 Location. The court may hold sessions in such places in the county as the commision may designate and at such times as the senior judge directs.

Section 3.16 Term. The first term of court shall commence on October 1, 1957, and end on September 30, 1958. Each succeeding term shall commence on October 1st and end on September 30th.

Section 3.17 Seal. The senior judge may adopt a seal for the court. The clerk shall keep the seal and shall seal any paper or instrument as directed by a judge or rule of the court.

Section 3.18 Service. Service of every summons, subpoena, writ or other process of the court shall be made in the manner provided for the process of the circuit court, except that service may be made by any county or municipal police officer under the direction of the public safety director and the return of service shall be made to the clerk upon a form prescribed by the senior judge.

Section 3.19 Demand for jury trial. If the offense is punishable by a fine exceeding $500 or by imprisonment in the county jail for more than 60 days, the accused is entitled to a trial by jury upon demand made at any time before the commencement of his trial.

Section 3.20 Venire. All jury trials shall be conducted by the senior judge and such other judges as he may designate. Under the procedure provided by general law, the senior judge shall get from the clerk of the circuit court a list of not less than twelve persons residing in the county neither disqualified nor exempt as defined in sections 40.07 and 40.08 F.S. from jury duty. At least ten days before the commencement of any jury trial, the clerk of the metropolitan court shall deliver summonses for such persons to the public safety director who shall cause them to be served as are other process of the court. Jurors shall be paid as provided by general law. The penalty for failure of a person duly summoned to attend as a juror who neglects to attend without any sufficient excuse is a fine not exceeding twenty dollars imposed by the senior judge. Jurors shall serve for one week unless the senior judge requires them to serve for a longer time.

Section 3.21 Selection of jury. Six persons constitute a jury. The county and the defendant are each allowed three peremptory challenges. The examination, challenging and impanelling of jurors shall be as provided in chapter 913 F.S.

Section 3.22 Costs. The judges by majority vote shall adopt a schedule of court costs reflecting as accurately as may be the expense incurred by the county. Costs may be assessed against a person convicted.

Section 3.23 Administration. As administrative officer of the court, the senior judge shall direct the division of cases among the judges, fix the hours of court sessions, rotate the judges from time to time, conduct judicial conferences regularly so that the procedure and sentences of the judges shall be uniform, and he may require such reports from each judge as he may deem necessary.

Section 3.24 Definitions. In construing the foregoing provisions and each and every word, phrase or part thereof, where the context will permit, the definitions provided in Section 1.01 F.S. shall apply.

Section 3.25 Severability. It is intended that if any section, subsection, sentence, clause or provision contained herein is held invalid, the remainder shall not be affected.

Section 3.26 Repeal. All county and municipal ordinances, county and municipal resolutions, municipal charters, special laws applying to this county and general laws applying only to this county or any general law which this commission is specifically authorized by the Constitution to supersede, nullify or amend, or any part of any such ordinance, resolution, charter or law in conflict with any provision contained herein is hereby repealed.

Section 3.27 Effective date. This ordinance shall become effective 10 days after its enactment. (Effective October 5, 1957)

METROPOLITAN DADE COUNTY · FLORIDA
OFFICE OF COUNTY ATTORNEY
July 13, 1959

Mrs. Maxine Boord Virtue
Secretary, Metropolitan Trial
Courts Committee
1035 Legal Research Building
Ann Arbor, Michigan

Dear Mrs. Virtue:

Re: Dade County Metropolitan Court

Your letter of July 7 requests "the history of the achievement together with a copy of the legislation establishing the (Metropolitan) Court."

The Metropolitan Court of Dade County was implemented by Dade County Ordinance 57-13 (10-5-57), a copy of which is enclosed. This ordinance has recently been amended in one minor particular by Ordinance 59-21 (6-30-59), a copy of which is also enclosed.

The court was created by the Home Rule Charter adopted in a referendum by the people of Dade County on May 21, 1957. Section 6 of this Charter pertains to the Metropolitan Court. A copy is enclosed.

The Home Rule Charter was, in turn, authorized by an amendment to the Florida Constitution, A. 8, S. 11, adopted in a statewide referendum on November 6, 1956. Section 11 (1) (f) specifically authorizes the establishment of the Metropolitan Court. A copy of this particular amendment is enclosed.

The validity of this particular amendment was upheld in *Gray v. Golden,* Fla., 89 So. 2nd 785, which I assume is available in your library. This opinion includes a concise but clear outline of the ills which the constitutional amendment was designed to cure.

There have been five decisions of our Supreme Court pertaining to the constitutional amendment and the charter which I believe you would find well worth studying in connection with your problem. *Dade County v. Kelly,* Fla., 99 So. 2nd 856, *Chase v. Cowart,* Fla., 102 So. 2nd 147, *Dade County v. Dade County League of Municipalities,* Fla., 104 So. 2nd 512, *Dade County v. Young Democratic Club of Dade County,* Fla., 104 So. 2nd 636, *Miami Shores Village v. Dade County,* Fla., 108 So. 2nd 468.

Specifically, the concept of a Metropolitan Court and the general popular support of the concept are due, in my opinion, to a general public feeling of impatience with and a lack of confidence in the 26 municipal courts, presided over by part-time judges applying conflicting laws in a conflicting manner within Dade County. In most instances the municipal courts were openly and frankly operated as a revenue measure. Because of the extremely rapid growth of this area, municipal boundaries bore virtually no relationship to either physical or economic boundaries within the county.

Since the final establishment of the Metropolitan Court, its history has been largely a strugggle between the Metropolitan County Government on one hand and the several municipalities on the other as to whether the County has exclusive jurisdiction under a Metropolitan Traffic Code which was adopted with the intention of repealing all the various municipal traffic ordinances and making all traffic violations triable in the Metropolitan Court. As of this date, two of the 27 municipalities still operate their own municipal courts, and the matter may ultimately have to be resolved in litigation.

For the past several months, the County has employed Mr. James P. Economos, Director of Traffic Court Program, American Bar Association, 1155 East 60th Street, Chicago 37, Illinois, to survey our entire Metropolitan Court Program, make recommendations and supervise the implementation of the recommendations. The Board of County Commissioners has consistently followed all of the recommendations, the great majority of which have already been put into effect. Mr. Economos can give you considerable information regarding the procedures of the Court.

While I believe I have furnished the sort of information you had in mind, I realize that I have not completely answered, if indeed I could, the very general and broad inquiry you have made.

With kindest regards,

Sincerely,
Darrey A. Davis
County Attorney

DAD:TCB:bjj
Prepared by:
Thomas C. Britton
Assistant County Attorney

Appendix E

Questionnaires for This Study

AMERICAN BAR ASSOCIATION
ORGANIZED 1878
SECTION OF JUDICIAL ADMINISTRATION
1958-1959

Dear

As you will see from Mr. MacKinnon's covering memorandum, we are not asking you to take responsibility for assembling data for a new study, but rather are hoping you will help us to check the depth and soundness of a ten-year study, a written summary of which is being finished and prepared for publication in the form of a brief volume next year. Your expert help at this stage will immeasurably enhance the study, and will make it a far more effective tool for the Section to present to the bench and bar.

The response to our preliminary inquiries has been so cooperative, and indicates such interest in the bench and bar, that we venture to hope you will enjoy reading and answering the questionnaire, and will be stimulated by it to evolve your own analysis of metropolitan court problems as you see them in your own community.

If you find any part of the questionnaire impossible to answer, please fill in what you can answer, and return it anyway. At this point, we want whatever assistance we can obtain by this questionnaire. If you want to refer us to other people for answers to any part of the questionnaire, we shall be grateful for their names and addresses, and, within the time limits imposed for this study, shall follow up such references.

We know there is no way of measuring the time, energy and good will that goes into answering such a questionnaire. We can never thank you enough. You will have the deep and permanent gratitude of the personnel of the Section, and my special thanks.

Yours sincerely,
Maxine Boord Virtue
Director
Metropolitan Court Survey

AMERICAN BAR ASSOCIATION

SECTION OF JUDICIAL ADMINISTRATION

Memorandum on Questionnaire for Metropolitan Trial Court Survey
From: F. B. MacKinnon, Director of State Activities
To: Recipients of Questionnaire

In 1947, the Section established a Committee on Metropolitan Trial Courts to inquire into the existence and nature of the special problems, both structural and administrative, of metropolitan courts, exclusive of federal courts. The Committee's objective was to test the theory that the system of courts serving any metropolitan area has problems similar to those in other metropolitan areas but different from those of trial courts in the state outside metropolitan areas. These special problems were thought to result from the geographic location of metropolitan trial courts, from the size and complexity of their workload, from the cultural dominance of metropolitan areas, and from special behavioral patterns of metropolitan populations.

If this theory is sound, trial court systems in metropolitan areas should be subject to separate observation and analysis, and recommendations should be developed to deal with their special problems.

The first major project to test the theory was undertaken in 1957 when, at the request of the Committee, the University of Michigan Law School employed Mrs. Maxine Boord Virtue as research associate to conduct a two-year study. The faculty sponsor of this study was the late Professor Edson R. Sunderland, who supervised the study and the preparation of the published report (Virtue, *Survey of Metropolitan Courts: Detroit Area,* Michigan Legal Series. University of Michigan Press, 1950). Although this study included the entire range of library materials dealing with metropolitan courts, other than federal courts, its special feature was an exhaustive first-hand report on the organization and operation of trial courts in the Detroit area. Mrs. Virtue spent more than a year in direct observation, interviews, and other field research in the Detroit courts.

The results of the Detroit study demonstrated the value of examining trial courts in metropolitan areas in the context of their relationship to the metropolitan community rather than as a part of the general state and county organization of judicial systems. Therefore, the Committee undertook to continue its series of studies, and appointed Mrs. Virtue as Director of the Metropolitan Court Survey.

The Committee developed detailed plans for large-scale studies (similar in scope and therefore comparable to the Detroit study) in

London, New York, Philadelphia, Los Angeles and several other areas. It was decided that the Section would not itself conduct them, but would encourage local bar associations to sponsor and finance their own studies. Of the several plans submitted which had met with the approval of the Committee, only Los Angeles has completed a full scale study, broad enough and exhaustive enough to furnish data comparable to the Detroit study. (Holbrook, *Survey of Metropolitan Courts: Los Angeles Area.* University of Southern California Press, 1956.)

In recent years other organizations have been making studies in the subject area in which the Metropolitan Trial Court Committee is primarily interested.* Also, several general articles have been published by Mrs. Virtue and considerable data was accumulated over the years by the Committee in the form of notes on preliminary and reconnaissance studies in London, New York, Chicago, Indianapolis, San Francisco, Los Angeles, Philadelphia and other areas.

Further, the participation of Mrs. Virtue in court research undertaken for other organizations has resulted in an accumulation of valuable material now available to the Section. For example, her book, *Family Cases in Court,* published by Duke University Press in 1956, represents a series of intensive fact and library studies of that phase of trial court operation in various large metropolitan areas.

In view of the considerable current interest and the amount of factual information now available from other surveys to provide a context for the Committee's work, it was decided to round out the Section's Metropolitan Court Survey by the publication of a volume which would summarize and analyze the Committee's experience. In this book the Committee, for the first time, would attempt to reach some general conclusions about the identity of the metropolitan court's special problems, and would indicate generally such remedial measures as appear to offer the best method of dealing with such problems.

At the request of Honorable Ira W. Jayne, Chairman of the Committee, the University of Michigan Law School agreed to sponsor and publish this study.

Mrs. Virtue has been working for over a year on the manuscript, having been given leave, part time, from her duties as Assistant At-

* See, for example, Studies by the Institute of Judicial Administration; The Temporary Commission on the Courts in New York; Council of State Governments; Delay in the Court: A Study in Judicial Administration, University of Chicago; Administration Project, Institute of Legal Research, University of Pennsylvania.

torney General of Michigan to accept appointment by the University of Michigan Law School as research fellow.

In order to provide a final check upon the completeness and soundness of both factual and analytical material contained in this study, it is desired to test and verify some of the data and hypotheses against the information and opinions of knowledgeable people in each of the standard metropolitan areas as identified by the U. S. Bureau of the Census. It is for this purpose that the enclosed questionnaire is being distributed to a list of individuals selected for their familiarity with judicial administration in these metropolitan areas.

Please fill in the questionnaire, with any additional comments you may have, and return it to me at the American Bar Center, 1155 E. 60th Street, Chicago 37, Illinois by

Sincerely yours,
F. B. MacKinnon

Committee on Trial Courts

Honorable Ira W. Jayne, Chairman
Paul W. Alexander
Joseph Ford
John B. Johnston
Philbrick McCoy
Maynard E. Pirsig
E. Wayne Thode

Maxine Boord Virtue, Secretary
Charles E. Clark
Ralph M. Holman
Abraham L. Marovitz
Harold R. Medina
Paul C. Reardon
James C. Toomey

Lewis Simes, Advisor

AMERICAN BAR ASSOCIATION

SECTION OF JUDICIAL ADMINISTRATION

Please return to
F. B. MacKinnon
Director of State Activities
American Bar Center
Chicago 37, Illinois

City____________________
Metropolitan Area____________________
____
____
____

METROPOLITAN COURT SURVEY QUESTIONNAIRE

Group One. Jurisdictional and Structural Problems

Existing studies of state metropolitan court systems share the conclusion that a multiplicity of separate courts, with great overlap, duplication, and confusion of jurisdiction, is typical of the condition in any large metropolis. In the following questions, we are trying to confirm or challenge this hypothesis, and also to learn what we can about the extent, seriousness, and implications of these characteristics as they look to you.

1. How many different trial courts are there, including justice and other "inferior" courts, in your area? (excluding federal courts)
   a. Total *number* of courts in the metropolis itself__________ (number)
   b. Total *number* of courts in the metropolitan area including its satellite territory outside the city limits of the metropolis __________(number)

Please list courts by name:

(Please use back of this page for additional comments)

2. How much duplicating, overlapping or concurring jurisdiction is there among these courts? Please include partly as well as wholly duplicating jurisdiction, and state the major areas of overlap, or concurrence.

	Title of courts having jurisdiction	
a. Small Claims	__________	__________
b. Misdemeanors	__________	__________
c. Family Cases	__________	__________
d. Others	__________	__________
e. __________	__________	__________

3. Does this overlap, in your view, *interfere with* or *assist* the prompt and efficient function of your metropolitan court system viewed as a service area for the community?
   Interferes with__________ Assists__________

Comments____________________

(example: a "small claims court" usually shares with the general court of original trial jurisdiction a certain monetary bracket of jurisdiction in the higher reaches of small claims. There is controversy among attorneys and judges about the implications. Some regard it as a healthy choice of tribunals; others as a shocking waste of judicial resources and an invitation of smalltimers to pretend they're in the bigtime.)

(Please use back of this page for additional comments)

4. Does the justice of the peace system still obtain in your *state?*
   Yes__________ No__________

Has it been replaced in the *metropolis* by municipal courts, mayors' courts, small claims courts, or other modern substitutes for the township justice?

Yes_________ No_________

a. How many justices of the peace operate one-man courts within the metropolis? _________(number)
In the satellite areas within the metropolitan area outside the city limits of metropolis _________(number)
Are these justices required by law to be qualified attorneys?
Yes_________ No_________
Are they paid in whole or part on a fee basis?
Yes_________ No_________

b. What modern replacements for the old justice system have been established (a) in metropolis, (b) outside metropolis in metropolitan area? (Please include municipal courts, city courts, small claims courts, and any other so-called "inferior courts") Please list by title of court.
(a) In metropolis (b) Outside metropolis in metropolitan area
In which courts are the judges *Not*-required by law to be qualified attorneys? Please list.
In which courts are judges paid in whole or part on a fee basis?
(Please use back of this page for additional comments)

Group Two Special Types of Cases

One of the most complex problems of metropolitan court systems is that of finding the best way to handle special types of cases, such as criminal, small claims, domestic relations, mental and borderline mental cases. There seems to be a tendency to progress through successive stages: first, a specialized docket or calendar; second, a specialist judge; third, development from a separate docket to separate division, or part, with a specialized staff under a specialized judge; fourth, change from specialized separate division to separate specialized court. Here we encounter the problem of multiplicity of courts.

There are conflicting opinions concerning the advisability of specialization, and its proper extent.

Having in mind that we are concerned with a hypothetical court system designed and operated in such a way as to give the best service to a metropolitan community, please consider the "specialist" problem in terms of the following questions, and any others that may occur to you.

5. Please list the courts of specialized subject matter jurisdiction which now exist:
   a. in metropolis
   b. in *satellite area* within metropolitan district but outside city limits of metropolis
6. Please list any specialized *divisions* or *parts*, technically within a general court, but actually operating separately:
   a. in metropolis
   b. in satellite area
7. Please identify specialized or separate dockets or calendars in general courts.
   a. in metropolis
   b. in satellite area

(Please use back of this page for additional comments)

8. Please indicate fields and numbers of individual specialist judges who handle special subject matter caseloads:
   a. in metropolis
   b. in satellite area
9. Are these judges
   a. elected to a specialized judgeship Yes____No____
   b. assigned by other judges on a long-term basis Yes____No____
   c. assigned on a rotating basis Yes____No____
   d. other methods
10. Is there a "family court"
   a. in metropolis Yes____No____Title__________
   b. in satellite area Yes____No____Title__________

   If so, does it have complete jurisdiction over all of the following: out of wedlock, adoption, and juvenile cases? Yes____No____

   If its jurisdiction is not that inclusive, please indicate the extent of its jurisdiction

	Check
divorce and custody	________
separate maintenance	________
misdemeanor and felony matters	________
juvenile dependence, neglect, delinquency	________
paternity out of wedlock	________

adoption ________
guardianships of minors ________
other

________________ ________

________________ ________

If these areas of subject matter are scattered around among different courts, is there in your opinion a resulting conflict or confusion of jurisdiction? Yes____No____Please Comment

____

(Please use back of this page for additional comments)

Group Three Personnel

The problem of obtaining qualified judicial and other personnel emerges from this and other studies as a major problem of metropolitan courts. These questions seek to explore the professional competence of court personnel.

11. How many judges (other than justices of the peace) are there
 a. in metropolis____(number) b. in satellite area____(number)
12. Other than j.p.'s how many judges are compensated wholly or in part on a fee basis?
 a. in metropolis____(number) b. in satellite area____(number)
13. What qualifications are required of judges other than j.p.'s?
 a. in metropolis______________________________
 b. in satellite area______________________________
14. How many judges are not lawyers?
 a. in metropolis____(number) b. in satellite area____(number)
15. Is there a judicial retirement system now in effect?
 a. In metropolis Yes__No__ b. In satellite area Yes__No__
 compulsory Yes__No__ compulsory Yes__No__
 voluntary Yes__No__ voluntary Yes__No__
16. What is the average age of judges?
 a. in metropolis____ b. in satellite area____

(Please use back of this page for additional comments)

17. How many quasi-judicial officers such as referees or commissioners, function in a decision-making capacity in courts?

	Titles	Total Number
a. in metropolis	________	________
b. in satellite area	________	________

18. How many of these quasi-judicial officers are not lawyers?
 ____________(number)

19. Is there provision for obtaining counsel for indigent litigants?

Please check

	Yes	No
a. in metropolis		
(1) in criminal cases	____	____
(2) in small claims cases	____	____
(3) in civil cases	____	____
(4) in juvenile cases	____	____
b. in satellite areas	Yes	No
(1) in criminal cases	____	____
(2) in small claims cases	____	____
(3) in civil cases	____	____
(4) in juvenile cases	____	____

c. Please describe procedure where counsel is obtainable ____

____

20. *In what courts* are nonlegal professions, such as marraige counselors, social workers, psychologists, psychiatrists or others, used

a. in metropolis

1. as *full time* members of the staff of a
   - A. criminal court ________
   - B. juvenile court ________
   - C. other

   (Please use back of this page for additional comments)

2. on a *case by case* basis by a
   - A. criminal court ________
   - B. juvenile court ________
   - C. other
3. on a *referral basis* by a
   - A. criminal court ________
   - B. juvenile court ________
   - C. other

Please describe the size and function of any specialized court departments in this category________________

21. By what methods are juries chosen in various courts?

a. in metropolis________________________

____

b. in satellite areas________________________

____

22. What are major qualifications for jurors?________________

a. in metropolis________________________

b. in satellite areas________________________

23. Have studies been made concerning occupational or other bias on the part of the juries?__________If so, please give title and author of study__________

(Please use back of this page for additional comments)

24. What is the total number of people employed by courts on a full time basis?

a. in metropolis — Number
1. in judicial capacity __________
2. in quasi-judicial capacity __________
3. in professional capacity, other than legal __________
4. in executive or administrative capacity __________
5. Stenographic and clerical __________
6. other

b. in satellite area — Number
1. in judicial capacity __________
2. in quasi-judicial capacity __________
3. in professional capacity, other than legal __________
4. in executive or administrative capacity __________
5. Stenographic and clerical __________
6. other

25. Are all or any of these employees selected on a civil service basis?

Yes______ No______

Please give us the courts and categories of employees now served by a civil service system.__________

(Please use back of this page for additional comments)

26. Are judges appointed or elected?

a. in metropolis appointed________ elected________
b. in satellite areas appointed________ elected________

27. If elected, are they nominated on a basis that is

a. partisan______ b. nonpartisan______

Please comment__________

Comments on questions regarding qualifications of judges and personnel

(Please use back of this page for additional comments)

Group Four

Machinery for Handling Dockets and Disposing of Caseload

28. In the court of general trial jurisdiction in metropolis
   a. is there a presiding or chief or executive judge? Yes__ No__
   b. if so, what is his term____________________
   c. if so, how is he selected____________________
   d. If there is no presiding judge, how is judicial responsibility for case progress handled____________________
29. How are cases assigned for trial or other disposition?

	Please check
a. by assignment clerk	________
b. by "Cleveland system" (centralized written assignment system)	________
c. by presiding judge calling the docket each day	________
d. other (describe)	
____________________	________
e. ____________________	________

30. Is pre-trial used?	Please check
a. in all civil cases	________
b. in selected civil cases	________
c. in all criminal cases	________
d. in selected criminal cases	________
e. by court rule	________
f. by agreement of counsel	________
g. otherwise	________

   h. What percentage of the case load is disposed of at pretrial hearings?

____________________(percentage)

(Please use back of this page for additional comments)

   i How do you feel about the function, extent of use, and implications of judicially required pretrial conference?________
31. a) What is the total caseload in the trial court of general jurisdiction in the metropolis? (last year for which data complete)
   Total caseload ____________ Year ______
   b) What is the caseload per judge for that year in that court?______
32. In that court, what is the *average* length of time between date case at issue and date of final disposition for

(Years or months)

a. all cases ____________
b. chancery (equity) cases ____________
c. criminal cases
  1. jury ____________
  2. nonjury ____________
  3. total ____________
d. law cases
  1. jury ____________
  2. nonjury ____________
  3. total ____________
e. negligence cases as such (if available)
  1. jury ____________
  2. nonjury ____________
  3. total ____________
f. others

____________________________ ____________

34. In that court what percentage of total caseload is disposed of other than by trial

Percentage

a. total ____________
b. chancery ____________
c. criminal ____________
d. law ____________
e. negligence as such (if available) ____________
f. others________________ ____________

(Please use back of this page for additional comments)

35. In that court what percentage of total cases tried are tried to a jury?

Percentage

a. total ____________
b. chancery ____________
c. criminal ____________
d. law ____________
e. negligence cases as such (if available) ____________

36. In that court are litigants encouraged to waive jury trials by assignment system giving priority in time to nonjury cases? Yes___ No___ if so, by what means?______________________________

37. a) Is there a problem of case delay or logjam in the metropolis?
Yes______ No______

b) If so, is it in your opinion serious or minor?
Serious______ Minor______

38. What in your opinion is or are the major cause or causes of delay: (Please rank in order of importance: 1, 2, 3, etc.)

a. Insufficient judges ______
b. Incompetent or undiligent judges ______
c. defects in structure of court system ______
d. Inadequate administrative system for handling docket, calendar, and assignment problems ______
e. deliberate maneuvering by counsel ______
f. other______ ______

39. What measures are being taken to cope with delay problem?
(Please use back of this page for additional comments)

40. What in your opinion is or are the most promising remedy or remedies for the problem of logjam?______

41. Do you see a problem of "quick justice," or perfunctory routine disposition of cases, resulting from pressure upon judges to maintain prompt disposition of caseload? Yes______ No______ Please comment______

42. a) Is it, in your opinion, the prerogative of the judge to require that a case be disposed of at a certain time? Yes______ No______

b) Is there any danger that exercise of such prerogative will interfere with the prerogative of the attorney? Yes______ No______

43. What, in your opinion, is the basic function of a trial judge?
(Please use back of this page for additional comments)

Group Five — Effective Cooperation among Various Courts and Related Agencies within a Metropolitan Area

Studies already complete indicate that the effective operation of the trial court system in a metropolis is hampered by the existence of many independent courts with confused and overlapping jurisdiction, and competing or duplicating functions without integration from court to court throughout the metropolis. The following questions are designed to throw light on this problem.

44. a) Is there a state court administrator in your state? Yes___ No___
b) Is there a state court administrator for the metropolitan area?
Yes_____ No_____

45. Is there any method within the metropolis, or within the entire metropolitan area, for coordinating
a. the keeping of court records Yes_____ No_____
if so, please describe_____________________________
b. the handling of money Yes_____ No_____
if so, please describe_____________________________
c. the work of probation officers or court investigators Yes_____
No_____ if so, please describe_____________________________
d. other aspects of judicial administration (please describe)_____
if not, should there be, in your opinion? Yes_____ No_____
(Please comment)_____________________________

46. How many separate jury commissions are there
a. in metropolis _______(Number)
b. in the entire metropolitan area
including the satellite area _______(Number)

(Please use back of this page for additional comments)

47. How many separate probation departments are there
a. in metropolis _______(number)
b. in the entire metropolitan area _______(number)
(including the satellite territory)
c. Is there any sharing of information
between them Yes_______ No_______

48. What, if any, arrangement is there for coordinating the efforts of various courts engaged in dealing with personal problem cases, such as family, juvenile, mental cases, and such criminal cases as involve maladjustment rather than wilful violation of law. Please comment _____________________________

49. What, if any, arrangement is there for effecting liaison between the various courts dealing with the types of cases noted in the question above, and the various public and private social agencies which may also be involved with the same problems? Please comment _____________________________

50. Would there be any advantage to the establishment of one integrated court for the metropolis or for the entire metropolitan area, in terms of achieving more efficient disposition of all or any part of the caseload. Please comment_____________________________

(Please use back of this page for additional comments)

Group Six — Safeguarding Due Process

It is our conclusion that safeguarding due process is one of the most serious of metropolitan court problems. Among the factors contributing to this problem are the complexity of the court system, the confusions arising out of the size and complexity of the administrative staff, the pressures toward perfunctory routine disposition of each unit in the large caseload, the tendency to reduce caseload by screening out large numbers of cases for disposition other than by judicial process, and, in personal problem cases, the tendency for the court to assume functions not appropriate to its role either (a) by withdrawing in favor of expert nonlegal professionals who may or may not be available; or (b) by attempting to perform services other than judicial.

We realize this problem is not susceptible of scientific demonstration by means of questionnaire, but offer the following questions in order to provoke your comments about the extent, seriousness, and implications of this problem.

51. How many litigants go to final disposition in the metropolis without benefit of counsel?

	Percentage
a. traffic cases	________
b. criminal cases	________
c. juvenile cases	________
d. small claims cases	________
e. domestic relations cases	________
f. mental cases	________
g. other________	________
h. ____________	

Does this bother you? Yes_____ No_____ Why? (please comment) ________________________________

52. a) Does the court which handles divorce cases in the metropolis make any effort to obtain an objective evaluation in child custody and support matters
(1) in contested cases? Yes_____No_____ (2) in uncontested cases Yes_____No_____ Comment________________________

b) Does this court make any attempt to obtain information, other than through the parties and their attorneys, concerning the possibility of reconciliation in divorce cases? Yes_____No_____
Comments________________________________
(Please use back of this page for additional comments)

c) Does this court make any attempt to supervise collection of child support for children and/or enforcement of child custody orders, after disposition of the divorce case? Yes_____ No_____Comment____________________

d) Is it part of the court's function for a court to obtain objective information from parties not identified with the position of either spouse, in order to achieve an adequate disposition of the case? Yes_____No_____Please comment__________

e) Does an adequate disposition of divorce cases, in your view, include continuing surveillance by the court of the welfare of the children? Yes_____No_____Please comment__________

f) Do you see any significant connection between pressure on courts to avoid delay, and a perfunctory routine disposition of cases involving the welfare of children in divorce and other family cases? Yes_____No_____Please comment__________

53. a) In handling criminal cases in the metropolis, does the prosecutor screen out of the judge's orbit of authority any substantial number of cases, as by

1) Nolle pros Yes_____No_____
2) Bargaining for plea to lesser charge Yes_____No_____
3) Pressuring for a guilty plea Yes_____No_____
4) Other ____________________

Please comment____________________

(Please use back of this page for additional comments)

b) Do you believe there is due process problem arising out of these practices, through deprivation of the full use of the judge's knowledge and discretion? Yes_____No_____Please comment ____________________

c) Does the problem look any different to you where the defendant is without counsel? Yes_____No_____Please comment ____________________

d) Is the problem, if any, more or less interesting to you in misdemeanor or felony cases? Please comment__________

e) What is the overall percentage of guilty pleas in all criminal cases in the metropolis? _______(percentage) Is this too low, too high, or where it ought to be? Too low_______ Too high_______ Please comment__________

54. a) In handling mental cases, do the courts in the metropolitan area both inside and outside metropolis require a full hearing before commitment in all cases? Yes_____No_____ Is

there any difference inside metropolis, and outside? Yes_____ No_____ Please comment____________________

b) What is the total caseload of mental cases inside metropolis? ____________(number) ____________(year)

c) Does the court require that persons alleged to be in need of mental hospitalization be represented by counsel: Always_____ Usually_____ Occasionally_____ Never_____ Please comment ____________________

(Please use back of this page for additional comments)

d) Does the court require psychiatric testimony by a qualified psychiatrist in all cases? Yes_____No_____ Other medical testimony? Yes_____No_____ Please comment__________

e) Does the law in your state require diagnostic commitment? Yes_____No_____ If so, is it compulsory in all cases? Yes _____No_____ If so, is it fully enforced? Yes_____No_____ Please comment____________________

f) Are juries ever used in mental cases? Yes_____No_____ Often? Yes_____No_____ Do they, in your view, serve any useful purpose? Yes_____No_____ Please comment__________

g) It is sometimes said that large numbers of elderly indigents, slightly senile and in need of custodial care, are committed to mental hospitals for want of a better facility, and in order to relieve local public authorities of financial and other responsibility for their care.
Does this happen in your metropolitan area? Yes_____ No_____ if so, does it worry you? Yes_____No_____ If so, what remedy do you suggest?

h) It has been suggested that mental commitments should routinely be handled other than by a judicial hearing, with decision upon commitment to be made by psychiatrists, and with no provision for judicial hearing except after commitment and upon demand by patient.
Does this seem to you to be a good idea? Yes_____No_____ Please comment ____________________

(Please use back of this page for additional comments)

55. Recently a psychiatrist remarked that the law never did a worse disservice to itself, to society, or to psychiatry than when it permitted substitution of psychiatric diagnosis and treatment for trial in such cases as those involving criminal sexual psychopaths. Please comment____________________

56. In handling juvenile cases, some courts routinely set up an "unofficial category," into which some cases are channeled and maintained, sometimes for several years. In these cases, the court accepts no petition, but court-employed caseworkers make a file, and provide direction and supervision. This technique saves the judge's time and prevents overwhelming him with a large caseload, avoids the making of a record against the juvenile, and enables the social workers to establish and maintain a better rapport with the juveniles and their families.

a. In terms of providing the metropolitan community with the best possible court services, do you approve of this? Yes_____ No_____ Please comment_____

b. Do you see a due process problem? Yes_____ No_____ Please comment _____

c. Do you see a loss-of-identity problem through a confusion of the function of the judicial process with that of a non-judicial administrative agency? Yes_____ No_____ Please comment _____

d. Do you encounter the problem, if any, more extensively inside than outside metropolis? Yes_____ No_____ If so, how do you recommend solving it?_____

(Please use back of this page for additional comments)

57. a) Does any court in your area employ a marriage counselor? Yes_____ No_____ Title of court_____

b) If so, does the counselor see all cases

	Please check Yes	No
1) Coming before the court on a compulsory basis	_____	_____
2) Are Counselor's services available to those who wish them	_____	_____
3) Does the judge refer at his discretion	_____	_____
4) Other_____	_____	_____
_____	_____	_____

c) Does the counselor see any persons who are not involved in litigation in his court? Yes_____ No_____ If so, how much of the counselor's total caseload is not in litigation?

_____ (percentage)

d) Do you regard it as proper for a court employed marriage counselor to see all court cases on a compulsory basis? Yes_____ No_____ Please comment_____

e) Do you regard it as proper for a court employee to spend a substantial part of his working time in counseling persons not involved in litigation before the employing court? Yes_____ No_____ Please comment_____

f) Does it look any different to you if the court is the only agency in the community which does offer marriage counseling?

_____

g) What is the function of court marriage counseling in terms of assisting the court to achieve better performance of the court's function? Please comment_____

(Please use back of this page for additional comments)

58. Almost all traffic and small claims cases in the metropolitan courts so far studied go to final disposition without any challenge of the moving party's statement of the case.

a. Does this bother you? Yes_____ No_____

b. Do you think the public trusts the integrity

(1) of traffic police Yes_____ No_____

(2) of justices of the peace Yes_____ No_____

(3) small claims court judges Yes_____ No_____

c. Do you see a problem of loss of the traditional function of courts by the present "slot machine" handling of traffic and installment credit cases? Please comment_____

d. Do you think the legal profession has a responsibility to see that traffic and small claims cases are handled fully in accordance with the theory of due process? Please comment_____

e. What do you see as a workable solution?_____

(Please use back of this page for additional comments)

59. a) Does *the public* look to a judge in your view, primarily to: (please rank 1, 2, 3, etc.)

(1) see that justice is done to each individual _____

(2) see that traditional legal procedures are carried out no matter what happens to the people _____

(3) provide a fair opportunity for trial lawyers to represent their clients' interests _____

(4) see that cases are disposed of promptly and in an orderly manner _____

(5) join and enjoy the privileges of a gentlemen's club _____

(6) grandstand for the reporters, with an eye on the next election ______

b) Whichever public image of the judge you have marked as dominant, do you think the judges in your community are living up to that image? Yes______No______Please comment

____

____

c) Whatever your view of public opinion concerning the performance of your judges, does this view leave us with a problem? If so, what is it? Please comment______________

(Please use back of this page for additional comments)

60. Can you assist us by listing what you consider to be three major problems of metropolitan trial courts, together with your recommendations for solving these problems?

(1)____

(2)____

(3)____

THANK YOU. PLEASE FEEL FREE TO ADD ANY FURTHER COMMENTS THAT OCCUR TO YOU. IF YOU PERCEIVE ANY SERIOUS OMISSIONS, BIAS, OR LOOSE THINKING, PLEASE COMMENT ON THIS ALSO.

____

Name of person answering questionnaire*

____

Date of answering questionnaire

* If you prefer not to sign, please omit signature and return questionnaire. In no event will an adviser be identified by name in the published version of the study.

Bibliography

Alexander, Paul William. "The Family Court of the Future," 36 Journal of the American Judicature Society 39, 1952.

American Bar Association, Section of Judicial Administration. Committee on Metropolitan Trial Courts: Progress Report. (Mimeographed.) 1953.

———. Improvement of the Administration of Justice; A Handbook. 3rd edition, 1952.

———. "Justice Calling, 1958." 4th edition, 1958.

American Bar Foundation. Court Calendar Studies. Chicago, 1960.

"An Analysis of the Illinois Court System," 46 Illinois Bar Journal 571, 1958.

Association of the Bar of the City of New York. Bad Housekeeping: The Administration of the New York Courts. 1955.

———. Proceedings, Preliminary Report of Special Committee on Congested Calendars 397, 1926.

———. Special Committee on the Administration of Justice. The Citizens and the Courts, A Report on a Proposed Simplified State-Wide Court System. 1956.

Atkinson, T. E. "Organization of Probate Courts and Qualifications of Probate Judges," 23 Journal of the American Judicature Society 93, 1939.

Aumann, Francis Robert. The Instrumentalities of Justice: Their Forms, Functions and Limitations. Columbus: Ohio State University Press, 1956.

———. "Ohio Tackles Justice Court Problem," 13 Journal of the American Judicature Society 25, 1929.

Baldwin, Simeon E. The American Judiciary. New York: The Century Company, 1905.

Beaney, William M. The Right to Counsel in American Courts. Ann Arbor: University of Michigan Press, 1955.

Beard, Charles Austin. The Office of Justice of the Peace in England, in Its Origin and Development. New York: Columbia University Press, 1904.

Birnbaum, Morton. "The Right to Treatment," 46 American Bar Association Journal 499, 1960.

Blackburn, William J., Jr. The Administration of Criminal Justice in Franklin County, Ohio. Baltimore: The Johns Hopkins Press, 1935.

Bolster, W. "The Municipal Court—Its Origin, Development, and Practice Before It," 23 Massachusetts Law Quarterly, No. 2, p. 1, 1938.

Brand, George. "Pretrial in Detroit," 16 Journal of the American Judicature Society, August 1942.

Bridge, Franklin M. "Metropolitan Areas: A Developing Field of Public Policy," 19 Ohio State Law Journal 80, 1958.

Brown, L. Neville. "National Assistance and the Liability to Maintain One's Family," 18 Modern Law Review 110, 1955.

———. "The Offence of Willful Neglect to Maintain a Wife," 23 Modern Law Review 1, 1960.

———. "Separation Agreements and National Assistance," 19 Modern Law Review 623, 1956.

Brownell, Emery E. Legal Aid in the United States; A Study of the Availability of Lawyers' Services for Persons Unable to Pay Fees. Rochester, New York: Lawyers' Co-operative Publishing Co., 1951.

Bruce, Andrew Alexander. The American Judge. New York: Macmillan, 1924.

Bryce, James. The American Commonwealth. London & New York: Macmillan, 1888.

Buell, Bradley, & Associates. Community Planning for Human Services. New York: Columbia University Press, 1952.

Burke, Louis. "Problems of Court Administration in a Metropolitan Court," 43 Journal of the American Judicature Society 190, 1960.

Cain, W. M. "Law's Delays and Proposed Remedies," 90 Central Law Journal 333-42, 1920.

Calamandrei, Piero. Eulogy of Judges. (transl. John Clarke Adams and C. Abbott Phillips, Jr.) Princeton, New Jersey: Princeton University Press, 1942.

California, Judicial Council Reports. Annual beginning in 1956.

"California Judicial Council Unifies California Courts," 12 Journal of the American Judicature Society 18, 1928.

California. "Summary of 1959 Legislation," 34 California State Bar Journal, 1960.

California, Joint Judiciary Committee on the Administration of Justice. Third and Final Report on Crime and Criminal Courts in California, 1959.

California. Partial Report on the California Judiciary, 1959.

California. Second Partial Report on the Operation of the Courts, 1959.

California Courts Committee, Municipal Judges' Association, Los Angeles Judicial District. A Proposal for the Consolidation of the Superior and Municipal Courts, and an Analysis of the Workability of the Proposal within Los Angeles County. (Mimeographed, Report dated September 10, 1957.) 1958.

Callender, Clarence Newell. American Courts: Their Organization and Procedure. New York: McGraw-Hill, 1927.

Callison, Israel Putnam. Courts of Injustice. New York: Twayne Publishers, 1956.

Cardozo, Benjamin N. The Nature of the Judicial Process. New Haven: Yale University Press, 9th printing, 1937.

Cedarquist, Wayne B. "The Continuing Need for Judicial Reform in Illinois," 4 De Paul Law Review 153, 1955.

Chandler, Henry P. "The Problem of Congestion and Delay in the Federal Courts," 328 American Academy of Political and Social Science 144, 1960.

Clark, Charles E. "An Experiment in Studying the Business of Courts of a State," 14 American Bar Association Journal 318, 1928.

———. "Yale Study of Connecticut Courts," 15 American Bar Association Journal 326, 1929.

Clark, Charles E., and Richard D. O'Connell. "The Working of the Hartford Small Claims Court," 3 Connecticut Bar Journal 123, 1929.

Clark, Charles E., and Harry Shulman. A Study of Law Administration in Connecticut. New Haven: Yale University Press, 1937.

Cleveland Bar Association, Committee on Court Congestion and Delay in Litigation. Report and Recommendations on Trial Delay in the Common Pleas Court of Cuyahoga County, Ohio. May 1958.

Cleveland Foundation. Criminal Justice in Cleveland. (Roscoe Pound and Felix Frankfurter, editors.) Cleveland, Ohio: The Cleveland Foundation, 1922. (See contributors listed in index: Herman M. Adler, Raymond B. Fosdick, Alfred Bettman, Howard F. Burns, Reginald Heber Smith, E. K. Wickman, and M. K. Wisehart.)

Community Services Society of New York, Bureau of Public Affairs. A New Pattern for Family Justice (Pamphlet.) 1954.

Council of State Governments. State Court Systems. (Mimeographed, Revised Edition.) 1953.

———. The States and the Metropolitan Problem. 1956.

———. Trial Courts of General Jurisdiction in the Forty-Eight States. (Mimeographed.) 1951, and 1953 supplement by Frederick and Spector.

The Daily Mirror Spotlight on Justice. London: Daily Mirror (Cave ed.), November 1954.

Dawson, John P. Judges: Oracles of the Law. (To be published) Cooley Lecture Series, University of Michigan Law School.

"Detroit's Unified Criminal Court," 14 Journal of the American Judicature Society 180, 1931.

"Detroit Circuit Court Integrated," 14 Journal of the American Judicature Society 175, 1931.

Dodd, W. F., editor. "Notes on Judicial Organization and Procedure," American Political Science Review vol. 23, p. 930; vol. 24, pp. 117 and 416; vol. 25, p. 357; vol. 25, p. 80; vol. 26, p. 470; vol. 27, p. 957.

Douglass, Paul. The Justice of the Peace Courts in Hamilton County, Ohio. Baltimore: The Johns Hopkins Press, 1932.

———. The Mayors' Courts of Hamilton County, Ohio. Baltimore: The Johns Hopkins Press, 1933.

Duncan, Otis Dudley, and A. J. Reiss. Social Characteristics of Urban and Rural Communities, 1950. Census Monograph Series, 1956.

Economos, James P. "The Traffic Problem, Traffic Laws, and Traffic Courts," 287 The Annals of the American Academy of Political and Social Science 13, 1953.

Edwards, G. "Toward a Family Court for Wayne County," 16 University of Detroit Law Journal 169, 1953.

Elliott, Mabel A. Crime in Modern Society. New York: Harper & Brothers, 1952.

Elliott, Shelden. "Judicial Administration," New York University Law Review, annually, 1952——.

Ellis, Ronald. "The Criticism of Courts," 10 American Lawyer 111, 1902.

"Employment of Social Investigation Reports in Criminal and Juvenile Proceedings," 58 California Law Review 702 (comment), 1958.

Faris, E. L., and H. Warren Dunham. Mental Disorders in Urban Areas. Chicago: University of Chicago Press, 1939.

Foote, Caleb. "Vagrancy-type Law and Its Administration," 104 University of Pennsylvania Law Review 603, 1956.

Fortune Magazine, editors of. The Exploding Metropolis: A Study of the Assault on Urbanism and How Our Cities Can Resist It. Garden City, Long Island: Doubleday Anchor, 1957.

Fussell, Paul. The Holbrook Report—Eight Months Later. (Mimeographed.) 1957.

Gehlke, Charles Elmer. Criminal Actions in the Common Pleas Courts of Ohio. Baltimore: The Johns Hopkins Press, 1936.

Gellhorn, Walter, with Jacob D. Hyman and Sidney H. Asch. Children and Family Cases in the Courts of New York City: A Report by a Special Committee of the Association of the Bar of the City of New York on the Study of the Administration of Laws Relating to the Family. New York: Dodd, Mead, 1954.

Giles, Francis T. The Magistrates' Courts. Harmondsworth, Middlesex: Penguin Books, 1955.

Gist, Noel P., and L. A. Halbert. Urban Society. New York: Thomas Y. Crowell Co., 1937.

Goodrich, Herbert F. "Judicial Council for Michigan," 6 Michigan State Bar Journal 201, 1927.

Great Britain. Home Department. Departmental Committee on Courts of Summary Jurisdiction in the Metropolitan Area (London). 1947.

Great Britain. Parliament. Command Papers. Care of Children Committee Report. Cmd. 6922, reprint, 1954.

———. Command Papers. Committee on Supreme Court Practice and Procedure, Final Report. Cmd. 8878, 1953. (Cited as Evershed Report.)

———. Command Papers. Royal Commission on the Dispatch of Business at Common Law. Report, 1934-36. Cmd. 5065, 1936.

———. Command Papers. Royal Commission on Marriage and Divorce. Report, 1951-55. Cmd. 9678, 1956.

Harley, Herbert. "Court Organization for a Metropolitan District," 9 American Political Science Review 507, 1915.

Hartshorne, Charles H. "How Can We Improve Our Judicial System," New Jersey Law Journal vol. 27, p. 260, 1904; vol. 28, p. 132, 173, 1905.

Harvey, Audrey. Casualties of the Welfare State. Fabian Society, 1960.

Hawley, Amos H. The Changing Shape of Metropolitan America: Deconcentration Since 1920. Glencoe, Illinois: The Free Press, 1956.

———. Human Ecology: A Theory of Community Structure. New York: Ronald Press Co., 1950.

Hentig, Hans von. Crime: Causes and Conditions. New York: McGraw Hill, 1947.

Holbrook, James. A Survey of Metropolitan Trial Courts, Los Angeles Area. Los Angeles: University of Southern California, 1956. (Cited as Los Angeles Study.)

Illinois Association for Criminal Justice. The Illinois Crime Survey. (John H. Wigmore, editor. A. V. Lashly, Director's Introduction.) Los Angeles, 1929. See contributors listed in index: Andrew A. Bruce, E. W. Burgess, Gustave F. Fischer, Charles Elmer Gehlke, Albert J. Harno, John J. Healy, William D. Knight, John Landesco, Arthur V. Lashly, Raymond Moley, Earl D. Myers, Clifford Shaw, H. Douglas Singer, Bruce Smith, and August Vollmer.

Institute of Judicial Administration. Appellate Courts. Internal Operating Procedures; Preliminary Report. (Mimeographed.) July 5, 1957.

———. Assignment Systems in Civil Cases, Continuances and Civil Vacations. (Mimeographed.) August 1956.

———. Check-List Summary of 1958 Developments in Judicial Administration. (Mimeographed.) (Annual from 1953.)

———. Compulsory Arbitration and Court Congestion: The Pennsylvania Arbitration Statute. Delay and Congestion—Suggested Remedies Series No. 11, 4-U46. (Mimeographed.) July 1, 1956.

———. Compulsory Automobile Insurance. Delay and Congestion—Suggested Remedies Series No. 10, 2-U60. (Mimeographed.) August 10, 1956.

———. Court Administration. No. 3-U8. (Mimeographed.) August 1, 1955.

———. Court Administration—1959. No. 7-U3. (Mimeographed.) August 1, 1959.

———. Court Commission Systems and References. No. 3-U5. (Mimeographed.) July 18, 1955.
———. Criminal Records, New Jersey. No. 2-U41. (Mimeographed.) July 1, 1955.
———. Delay and Congestion in the Superior Court of Maricopa County, Arizona. Reprinted from Arizona Weekly Gazette, 1955. (Cited as Phoenix Study.)
———. Judicial Retirement Statutory Provisions and Comment. No. 4-U51. (Mimeographed.) May 8, 1956.
———. Jury Costs. No. 3-U2. August 15, 1955. Supplement, No. 8-U12. (Mimeographed.) August 15, 1960.
———. Juvenile, Family and Domestic Relations Courts, Separately Constituted. No. 3-U28. (Mimeographed.) September 1, 1955.
———. Juvenile Courts—Jurisdiction. No. 2-U21. (Mimeographed.) March 18, 1954.
———. Law Enforcement Criminal Statistics Study, New Jersey. No. 2-U41. (Mimeographed.) June 20, 1955.
———. Pensions and Benefits for Judicial Dependents. No. 4-U68. (Mimeographed.) August 17, 1956.
———. Pre-trial Rules. No. 2-U22. (Mimeographed.) December 11, 1953.
———. Public Defenders. No. 3-U48. (Mimeographed.) May 18, 1956.
———. Rule-making Power of the Courts. No. 3-U15, 16, 17. June 1, 1955. 1958 Supplement, No. 6-U79. (Mimeographed.) August 15, 1958.
———. Selected Methods of Assignment of Criminal Cases in Criminal Courts. No. 3-U25. (Mimeographed.) July 15, 1955.
———. Selection, Tenure and Removal of Judges in the 48 States, Alaska, Hawaii and Puerto Rico. (Mimeographed.) August 10, 1956.
———. Small Claims Courts in the United States. No. 3-U6. (Mimeographed.) August 10, 1955.
———. State Trial Courts of General Jurisdiction. Calendar Status Study. (Mimeographed.) 1953 and annually.
———. Statutory Right of the Jury to Fix Punishment in Criminal Cases. No. 3-U1. (Mimeographed.) July 7, 1955.
———. Waiver of Jury Trial in Felony Cases: An Analysis of the Applicable Constitutional and Statutory Provisions in the 48 States. No. 3-U53. (Mimeographed.) July 25, 1955.
"Interstate Compacts: A Survey," 27 Temple Law Journal 320, 1954.

"Is Stupid Waste of Time Essential," 4 Journal of the American Judicature Society 155, 1921.

Jackson, R. M. The Machinery of Justice in England. Cambridge, 1940.

Janowitz, Morris, Deil Wright, and William Delany. Public Administration and the Public—Perspectives Toward Government in a Metropolitan Community. Michigan Governmental Studies No. 36. Ann Arbor: Bureau of Government, Institute of Public Administration, 1958.

Jayne, Ira W. "Foreword" (Pre-trial Procedure), 17 Ohio State Law Journal 160, 1956.

———. with Maxine B. Virtue. "Survey of Metropolitan Courts: Detroit Area," 37 American Bar Association Journal 444, 1951.

———. "Organizing the Business of the Court," 25 American Bar Association Journal 875, 1939.

Johns Hopkins University, Institute of Law, with the Judicial Council of Ohio, Ohio State Bar Association. A Study of the Administration of Justice in Ohio. (Series of 12 bulletins), 1929-1933.

Johns Hopkins University, Institute of Law. Analysis of Ohio Municiple Court Acts. A Report to the Judicial Council of Ohio. Baltimore: The Johns Hopkins Press, 1932.

Kahn, Alfred J. A Court for Children. A Study of the New York Children's Court under the Auspices of the Citizens' Committee on Children of New York City. New York: Columbia University Press, 1953.

Kales, Albert M. "The English Judicature Acts: Concise Description of Statutes which Unified Numerous Courts," 4 Journal of the American Judicature Society 133, 1921.

———. "Reorganization of the Circuit and Superior Courts of Cook County," 7 Illinois Law Review 218, 1912.

Kalodner, Howard I. and Staff. "Metropolitan Criminal Courts of First Instance," 70 Harvard Law Review 320, 1956.

Karlen, Delmar. "Judicial Administration." 1959 Annual Survey of American Law 672.

Kefauver Committee Report on Organized Crime. Special Committee to Investigate Organized Crime in Interstate Commerce. New York: Didier, 1951.

Kincaid, Clarence. A Judges' Handbook of Pretrial Procedure. Prepared under the auspices of the American Bar Association, Section of Judicial Administration. (Reprinted from 17 Federal Rules Decisions.) 1955.

Knudsen, Theodore. Report on Family Court Observations, Minneapolis District Court. January 6, 1959. (Unpublished.)

Lacey, Forrest. "Vagrancy and Other Crimes of Personal Condition," 66 Harvard Law Review 1203, 1953.

"Lagging Justice," (Glenn R. Winters, ed.) 328 Annals of the American Academy of Political and Social Science. Symposium. See contributors listed in index: Walter Alessandroni, Bernard Botein, John R. Dethmers, Samuel H. Hofstadter, Roger A. Johnsen, Harry Kalven, Jr., Irving R. Kaufman, Alfred P. Murrah, Orin Thiel, Leland L. Tolman, William M. Trumbull, Maxine Boord Virtue, and Hans Zeisel.

Lambarde, William. Archeion, or the High Courts of Justice in England. (Charles H. McIlwain and Paul L. Ward, editors) Cambridge, Massachusetts: Harvard University, 1957 (reprint of 1635 British edition).

Lane-Reticker, Edward. Connecticut Local Courts, Connecticut Public Expenditure Council, 1956. (Mimeographed.)

Langbein, Geo. F. "Municipal Court Rotation as Affecting Jurisdiction and Practice," 6 Bench and Bar 16, 1906.

Lehmann, Virginia North. Findings and Recommendations on Court Services. Division Report of Milwaukee County Survey of Social Welfare and Health Services. July, 1950. (Unpublished.)

Lepawsky, Albert. Home Rule for Metropolitan Chicago. Chicago: University of Chicago Press, 1935.

———. The Judicial System of Metropolitan Chicago. Chicago: University of Chicago Press, 1932.

Levin, A. Leo, and Edward A. Wooley. Dispatch and Delay: A Field Study of Judicial Administration in Pennsylvania. Philadelphia: University of Pennsylvania, Institute of Legal Research, 1961.

Los Angeles County, Municipal Court Judges' Association, Courts Committee. Proposal for consolidation of Superior and Municipal Courts and an Analysis of the Workability of the Proposal within Los Angeles County. Prepared by Byron J. Walters and Morton L. Barker. (Mimeographed.) 1958.

Los Angeles Superior Court. Statement to the Joint Judiciary Committee on Administration of Justice . . . in Opposition to the Proposed Single Trial Court for Los Angeles County. (Mimeographed. Dated April 28, 1958. Philbrick McCoy, Chairman. Opposition to Walters-Barker report proposing a single trial court by consolidating municipal with superior court.) Los Angeles, 1958.

Lou, Herbert H. Juvenile Courts in the United States. Chapel Hill, North Carolina: University of North Carolina Press, 1927.

Long, Huey P. "Reform of the Judiciary," 28 Louisiana Bar Association 79, 1928.

Lummus, Henry T. The Trial Judge. Chicago: Foundation Press, 1937.

McConnell, Edward B. "The Place of the Traffic Court in a State Judicial System," (address) Law and Laymen Conference, Section of Judicial Administration. August 25, 1959.

McGregor, O. R. Divorce in England. London: Heinemann, 1957.

McKenzie, Roderick Duncan. The Metropolitan Community. New York: McGraw Hill (Recent Social Trends Monograph), 1933.

Maguire, James M. "Poverty and Civil Litigation," 36 Harvard Law Review 361, 1923.

Mannheim, Hermann. Group Problems in Crime and Punishment. London: Routledge and Paul, 1955.

Mars, David. "Court Reorganization in Connecticut," 41 Journal of the American Judicature Society 6, 1957.

Marshall Leon C., and Geoffrey May. The Divorce Court. Baltimore: The Johns Hopkins Press, 1932.

Marshall, Leon C., with statistical assistance of Elva L. Marquard. Unlocking the Treasuries of the Trial Courts. Baltimore: The Johns Hopkins Press, 1933.

Martin, Kenneth J. Waiver of Jury Trial in Criminal Cases in Ohio. Baltimore: The Johns Hopkins Press, 1933.

"Metropolitan Criminal Courts of First Instance," 70 Harvard Law Review 320, 1956.

Michigan Department of Health. Michigan Health Statistics, 1954.

Michigan Department of Social Welfare. Adoptions in Michigan in 1957. (Mimeographed.) 1957.

Michigan Supreme Court. Office of the Court Administrator. Annual Report and Judicial Statistics for 1956-1959.

Milwaukee County Survey of Social Welfare and Health Services. Findings and Recommendations on Court Services. Division Report. July, 1950. (Unpublished.)

Miller, Jesse A. "Would Improve Iowa Courts," 7 Journal of the American Judicature Society 17, 1923.

Missouri Association for Criminal Justice. The Missouri Crime Survey (Raymond Moley, ed.). New York: Macmillan, 1926. See contributors listed in index: Jesse W. Barrett, M. A. Bliss, James E. Boggs, Charles E. Gehlke, J. Hugo Grimm, and Herbert S. Hadley.

Moore, J. D. "Avoidable Delay in the Trial Courts," 18 Yale Law Journal 112, 1908.

Morgan, E. M. "Judicial Regulation of Court Procedure," 2 Minnesota Law Review 81, 1918.

Morse, Wayne L., and Ronald Beattie. Survey of the Administration of Criminal Justice in Oregon. Oregon Law Review, Supplement, Vol. 11, No. 4, June 1932.

Mumford, Lewis. The Culture of Cities. New York: Harcourt, Brace, 1938.

National Association of Attorneys General. Proceedings. "Roundtable on Administration of Criminal Justice." 1956.

National Probation and Parole Association. Standard Family Court Act. 1959.

Naujoks, H. H. "Compacts and Agreements between States and Between States and a Foreign Power," 36 Marquette Law Review 219, 1952-1953.

Netherton, Ross D. "Fair Trial in Traffic Court," 41 Minnesota Law Review 577, 1957.

New Jersey. Administrative Office of the Courts. Annual Report. 1955; 1956.

New Jersey. Supreme Court's Committee on Juvenile and Domestic Relations Courts. Report. (Mimeographed.) April 19, 1956.

New York State Commission on the Administration of Justice. The Organization and Operation of the Supreme Court and Appellate Courts, 1934. (Legislative Document No. 50 (c).) 1934.

New York Temporary Commission on the Courts. 1957 Report.

Nims, Harry Dwight. Pre-Trial. New York: Voorhis, 1950.

North Carolina Bar Association, Committee on Improving and Expediting the Administration of Justice in North Carolina. Subcommittee on Court Structure and Jurisdiction, Tentative Report. March 1958.

Northrop, E. H. "Small Claims Courts and Conciliation Tribunals, a Bibliography," 33 Law Library Journal 394, 1940.

Olson, Harry. "The Municipal Court of Chicago," 40 American Lawyer 111, 1902.

———. "The Municipal Court of Chicago," 40 Chicago Legal News 26; 32, 1907.

Owen, Wilfred. The Metropolitan Transportation Problem. Washington, D.C.: The Brookings Institution, 1956.

Paulsen, Monrad G. "Fairness to the Juvenile Offender," 41 Minnesota Law Review 547, 1957.

Peck, David W. "Court Organization and Procedures to Meet the Needs of Modern Society," 33 Indiana Law Journal 182, 1958.

Perkins, Nellie L. "The Need for Socializing Court Procedure in Commitments to the State Training Schools for the Feeble-Minded," 16 Journal of Criminal Law and Criminology 589, 1926.

Philadelphia. 43 Annual Report of the Municipal Court of Philadelphia (Frank S. Drown and Thomas P. Monahan, editors). 1956.

Pickard, Jerome P. Metropolitanization of the United States. Washington: Urban Land Institute (Research Monograph No. 2), 1959.

Porter, Charles O. "Defects in the Administration of Justice in Hamilton County (Cincinnati), Ohio," 32 Journal of the American Judicature Society 14, 1948.

Potter, William L. "Judicial Power in the United States," 27 Michigan Law Review 1; 67; 285, November and December 1928; January 1929.

Pound, Roscoe. "Administration of Justice in the Modern City," 26 Harvard Law Review 302, 1913.

———. "A Bibliography of Procedural Reform, Including Organization," 5 Massachusetts Law Quarterly 332, 1920.

———. "The Causes of Popular Dissatisfaction with the Administration of Justice," 29 American Bar Association Report 395, part 1, 1906; Reprinted in Vanderbilt. Cases and Materials in Modern Procedure and Judicial Administration 32, 1952.

———. Criminal Justice in America. New York: Henry Holt and Co., 1930.

———. "Judicial Power," 35 Harvard Law Review 787, 1922.

———. Organization of Courts. Boston: Little, Brown & Co., 1940.

Powell, Homer G. "Justice Without Denial or Delay," 10 American Bar Association Journal 188, 1924.

Powell, Thomas Reed. "Home Rule for Whom?" 2 Public Administration Review 171, 1942.

Public Administration Service. The Administration of Court and Legal Services in the Government of Milwaukee County. (Mimeographed.) 1955.

———. The Government of Metropolitan Miami. 1954.

———. The Government of Metropolitan Sacramento. 1957.

———. Judicial Administration in Puerto Rico. Survey Report. (Mimeographed.) 1952.

———. The Organization and Methods of the Office of the Clerk of Superior Court, Maricopa County, Arizona. (Mimeographed.) 1953.

Ragland, George, Jr. Discovery Before Trial. Ann Arbor: University of Michigan Law School, 1932.

Randall, J. J. "American Plan of Revision of Our Courts," 31 New Jersey Law Journal 130, 1908.

"Report of Committee on Metropolitan Police Courts and Juvenile Courts," 93 Justice of the Peace 401, 1929.

Ross, Hugh Allan. "Commitment of the Mentally Ill: Problems of Law & Policy" (Symposium), 57 Michigan Law Review 945, 1959.

Rutherford, Geddes W. Administrative Problems in a Metropolitan Area: The National Capital Region. Public Administration Service, Special Publication No. 61, 1952.

Ryan, Thomas H. "Shall Municipal Courts Which Have Limited Concurrent Jurisdiction with the Circuit Courts Be Abolished?" 9 Marquette Law Review 33, 1924.

Salisbury, Harrison E. "The Shook Up Generation," New York Times, March 24-30, 1958.

Schramm, Gustav L. Piedpoudre Courts, A Study of the Small Claims Litigant in the Pittsburgh District. Pittsburgh: The Legal Aid Society, 1928.

Shumaker, Ross. "An Appraisal of Pretrial in Ohio," 17 Ohio State Law Journal, 1956.

Simes, Lewis M., and Paul Basye. Model Probate Code. Ann Arbor: University of Michigan Law School, 1946.

Skillman, W. "Youth Court Proposed: Special Treatment Urged for Offenders in 17-21 Age Bracket," 23 Detroit Law 102, 1955.

Smith, Reginald Heber. Justice and the Poor. Carnegie Foundation for the Advancement of Teaching, Bulletin 13, 1919.

Steffens, Robert Lincoln. The Shame of the Cities. New York: American Century Series, 1948.

"Suggestions for Improving Court Procedure in Texas," 1 Texas Law Review 67, 1922.

Sunderland, Edson R. "An Appraisal of the English Procedure," 24 Michigan Law Review 109, 1925.

———. Cases and Materials on Judicial Administration, 2d ed. Chicago: Callaghan and Co., 1948.

———. "Defects of English and American Statistics," 16 American Bar Association Journal 773, 1930.

———. "The Efficiency of Justices' Courts in Michigan," 4 Michigan Judicial Council Report 169, 1934.

———. "A Study of Justices of the Peace and Other Minor Courts: Requisites for an Adequate State-Wide Minor Court System," 15 Michigan Judicial Council Report 53, 1945.

———. "Subject Matter Jurisdiction of Minor Courts," 29 Journal of the American Judicature Society 175, 1946.

———. "Tentative Draft of an Act to Establish County Courts of Record, 16 Michigan Judicial Council Report, 1945.

———. "Territorial Jurisdiction of Minor Courts," 29 Journal of the American Judicature Society 147, 1946.

———. "The Theory and Practice of Pre-Trial Procedure," 36 Michigan Law Review 215; 21 Journal of the American Judicature Society 125, 1937.

Sunderland, Edson R., with Morse D. Campbell. "Michigan Probate Procedure for the Commitment of Insane, Feeble-minded and Epileptic Persons to Institutions for Their Care and the Release of Such Persons," 13 Michigan Judicial Council Report 57, 1943.

Sutherland, Edwin H. White Collar Crime. New York: Dryden Press, 1949.

Taft, Donald R. Criminology. New York: McMillan, 3d. ed., 1956.

Taft, W. H. "The Delays of the Law," 70 Albany Law Journal 300, 1908.

Talbott, Forrest. Intergovernmental Relations and the Courts. Minneapolis: University of Minnesota, 1950.

Tappan, Paul W. Delinquent Governments in Court, A Study of the Wayward Minor Court of New York. New York: Columbia University Press, 1947.

"Texas Unifies Trial Courts," 11 Journal of the American Judicature Society 38, 1927.

Tocqueville, Alexis de. Democracy in America. (Phillips Bradley, editor) 2 volumes, New York: Vintage Books, 1954.

Traynor, Roger J. "The Work of State Appellate Courts," 24 University of Chicago Law Review 211, 213, 1957.

"Trial by Jury," University of Cincinnati Law Review 120, 1937.

Tunnard, Christopher. "America's Super-Cities," Harper's Magazine 59, August, 1958.

United States Bureau of the Budget, Standard Metropolitan Statistical Areas. (pamphlet prepared by the Office of Statistical Standards), 1959.

United States. Bureau of the Census. 1957 Census of Governments.

———. Statistical Abstract of the United States. (Annual) 1957-1960.

———. County and City Data Book: 1956 (A Statistical Abstract Supplement). 1957.

United States. Bureau of Prisons. Prisoners in State and Federal Prisons and Reformatories. 1929-1930.

United States. Federal Bureau of Investigation. Uniform Crime Reports for the United States and Its Possessions, vol. 27, no. 2 Annual Bulletin, 1956.

United States. National Commission on Law Observance and Enforcement. Report on the Causes of Crime. 1931.

Vanderbilt, Arthur T. Cases and Materials on Modern Procedure and Judicial Administration. New York: Washington Square Publishing Corp., 1952. (Cited as Cases and Materials.)

———. "The Essentials of a Sound Judicial System," 38 Northwestern Law Review 1, 5, 1953.

———. Minimum Standards of Judicial Administration. (Judicial Administration Series. National Conference of Judicial Councils) New York: New York University Law Center, 1949. (Cited as Minimum Standards.)

Virtue, Maxine Boord. "The Court Problem in Detroit," 20 The Detroit Lawyer 15, 1952.

———. "The Detroit Court Survey," 90 Michigan State Bar Journal 40, 1951.

———. Family Cases in Court. Durham, North Carolina: Duke University Press, 1956.

———. "Improving the Structure of Courts," 287 American Academy of Political and Social Science 141, 1953.
———. Interim Report. Director of State Committees. Section of Judicial Administration. American Bar Association. March 25, 1955. (Unpublished typescript.)
———. Study of the Basic Structure for Children's Services in Michigan. Ann Arbor: American Judicature Society for the James Foster Foundation. 1953.
———. Survey of Metropolitan Courts: Detroit Area. Ann Arbor: University of Michigan Law School, 1950.
———. "What is the Logjam Problem?" 15 Federal Rules Decisions 207, 1954.
Voorhees, Theodore. "Lawyer Referral Service and the British Aid and Advice Act," 44 American Bar Association Journal 418, 1958.

Waite, Edward F. "Courts of Domestic Relations," 5 Minnesota Law Review 161, 1921.
———. "Domestic Relations Court of Cincinnati," 3 University of Cincinnati Law Review 444, 1929.
———. "How Far Can Court Procedure Be Socialized Without Impairing Individual Rights?" 12 Journal of Criminal Law & Criminology 339, 1921.
Walton, Eloise. Let's Work Together in Community Service. (Summary of Results of Milwaukee Study of Bradley Buell & Associates.) Public Affairs Pamphlet No. 194. New York: Columbia University Press, 1953.
Warren, George. Traffic Courts. (Judicial Administration Series, National Conference of Judicial Councils.) Boston: Little, Brown and Co., 1942.
Weber, Max. The City. (Martindale and Neuwirth, translators.) Glencoe, Illinois: The Free Press, 1958.
Webster, Arthur. "The Courts and Procedural Reform," 6 Michigan State Bar Journal 191, 1927.
Wigmore, J. H. "Does Chicago Have the Best Municipal Justice in the United States?" 3 Illinois Law Review 290, 1908.
Wilcox, Roy P. "Simplifying the Organization of the Courts of the State," 9 Marquette Law Review 25, 1924.
Willoughby, William F. Principles of Judicial Administration. Washington, D.C.: The Brookings Institution, 1929.

Wisconsin, Judicial Council. Court Organization Studies. (7 mimeographed pamphlets) 1954.

Woodle, Edwin F. "Discovery Practice in Ohio—Pathway to Progress," 8 Western Reserve Law Review 117, 1957; 456, 1957.

Woolston, Howard. Metropolis: A Study of Urban Communities. New York: Appleton-Century, 1938.

Worthington, George E., and Ruth Topping. Specialized Courts Dealing with Sex Delinquency. New York: D. H. Hitchcock, 1925.

Yankwich, Leon R. "Crystallization of Issues by Pretrial: A Judge's View," 58 Columbia Law Review 470, 1958.

Zeisel, Hans, Harry Kalven, Jr., and Bernard Buchholz. Delay in the Court. Boston: Little, Brown & Co., 1959.

Index

Printed and bound by CPI Group (UK) Ltd, Croydon, CR0 4YY
16/09/2026
14963492-0006